LAW AND GOVERNANCE: THE OLD MEETS THE NEW

Cavendish
Publishing
Limited

London • Sydney

I0894902

LAW AND GOVERNANCE: THE OLD MEETS THE NEW

N Douglas Lewis
LLB, FRSA, Barrister
Director of Centre for Socio-Legal Studies
University of Sheffield

Cavendish
Publishing
Limited

London • Sydney

First published in Great Britain 2001 by Cavendish Publishing Limited,
The Glass House, Wharton Street, London WC1X 9PX, United Kingdom
Telephone: +44 (0)20 7278 8000 Facsimile: +44 (0)20 7278 8080
Email: info@cavendishpublishing.com
Website: www.cavendishpublishing.com

First edition 2001

Douglas Lewis, N
Law and governance
1 Law
I Title
340

ISBN: 978-1-85941-547-4

PREFACE

This is an essay, not a textbook. It is an essay from a constitutional lawyer who is trying to take stock of the macro-political new world from which at least a part of constitutional law must now ply its trade. Certain kinds of constitutional changes announce themselves to us prominently; membership of the European Union and the concomitant (formal) loss of omnicompetence, the appearance of the Scottish Parliament and the Welsh Assembly, the incorporation of the European Convention on Human Rights and the like. Others are more insidious, but no less absorbing.

The move from government to governance (see the essay at large) has been largely dialectic or organic, and by no means a necessary historical conjuncture. Certain themes or strains may have been more or less accurately foreshadowed by the insightful (now professionally organised as futurologists), but even 20 years ago it would have been a shot in the dark to describe the meld of socio-economic and politico-managerial material which now characterises the world we inhabit.

Increasing numbers of acute social scientists have been more or less accurately telling us where we have been and what has been changed. A few have even told us what the immediate future is likely to hold for us. The maelstrom of inputs into this process have converged in a wholly surprising fashion. In particular, business and management experts have been having intellectual sex with public administrators, political scientists and civil service practitioners to produce new ways of looking at how public services are delivered and through what agencies. The essay seeks to describe some of these developments, but the note to strike at the outset is that the old State (see, especially, Chapter 1) has given way to something barely recognisable for whatever it is now that has at its mandate the requirement to ensure the delivery of public services against a background of settled cultural expectations. Given the slow, stately and relatively undisturbed historical path that the UK has travelled, the changes over the period in question have been startling in both their pace and their nature.

It is scarcely surprising that constitutional and administrative law have struggled to keep up. There needs to be a concerted effort to ensure that constitutional theory matches the new management theories that characterise the new systems of governance. For governance is the language we must now speak. Government speaks of older ways, whereby parliaments, the Executive and the Civil Service deliver in a more or less direct fashion what was promised in election manifestos. Furthermore, there was a clear-ish break between the public and the private spheres with government expected to leave the latter substantially untouched. All this has changed. Not only has government at the centre given up trying to deliver many 'public goods', but it sees as its task in a competitive and globalised world the need to act as the strategic fulcrum for the nation as a whole, including much of the private sector.

Government remains the strategic hub around which the nation turns, but what it is engaged in is 'governance' whereby it orchestrates a wide range of actors (to mix a metaphor) not only to provide public goods but to achieve 'added value' for the nation. Government was always a tricky business, but governance is worryingly complex. It engages in partnerships, it encourages and stimulates them, it prods and suggests, it awards and monitors contracts, it regulates for competitive markets and social purposes. In short, it seeks to pursue the nation's interests by whatever means and methodologies available and is inevitably engaged in experimentation to determine which delivery system best fits which public goods. This is a far cry from traditional political science and yet, to a large extent, our public law is still living with that past.

The essay speaks both to public lawyers and to other social scientists. The latter will, hopefully, recognise most of what follows. For them, any novelty will lie in suggestions for new forms of accountability, the traditional and central concern of the public lawyer, even if many of them are sketched in very pale colours at this time. For the public lawyer schooled in the old ways, or dependent perhaps too greatly on the analyses offered by the textbooks, much of what follows will be less familiar. Of course, the modern public lawyer will be aware of New Public Management, contracting out and much else besides, but they may not have had the luxury or time to reflect at length on the developments which surround their craft on all sides. They will hopefully take something of value from what follows.

Even public lawyers have largely been moulded in a positivistic and pragmatic mould so that juridical responses to the New World Order, where they exist, have exhibited similar tendencies. That is bound to change with the advent of the Human Rights Act 1998, and with luck it will encourage them to look outwards to think about institutional as well as substantive ways of dealing with the shaming poverty both at home and, much more graphically, in the developing world. We must not forget, however, that there are three generations of human rights: civil and political, social and economic, and environmental. All three require attention, and the law has a part to play in all of them. Furthermore, if a debate about a constitutional theory fit for the modern age of governance can be generated, then we can all begin to look at newer public law ways of helping governance to operate more smoothly.

As this essay progressed, it became more and more clear that the issue of globalisation was intruding unexpectedly frequently. Not only does governance predicate that governments cannot govern unaided, it suggests a degree of helplessness in the global New World Order. In fact, governments can still do a great deal even in the contemporary context, but they need encouragement from many quarters, not least from the public lawyer. It is at this point that the interests of the public lawyer and the public international lawyer come closer than at any time in our history. We must learn increasingly to talk each other's language and to learn from each other. What was a gleam in the eye when pen first touched paper became a heavy pregnancy by the time it was put down. Hence, what at first sight seems like a disproportionately large concluding chapter. In terms of symmetry it is disproportionate, but in terms of its relative newness about new ways of doing law, and in particular public law, it can be defended.

The chapters are written as follows:

Chapter 1 is an essay within an essay. It seeks to describe the nature of the modern State and, in particular, where the UK fits in. The UK polity has never been happy with the nature of statehood and, consequently, rarely speaks the language of purpose and values. Such are the changes occurring in the modern world that we are in danger of being swept away by them and losing our collective identity unless stock is taken of where we as a nation wish to be. This requires institutional responses to the machinery of government.

Chapter 2 provides an overview of governance. It seeks to describe the components of governance and the challenges it poses.

Chapter 3 deals specifically with New Public Management. It explains its centrality to the concept of governance and how it needs to relate to the other components of the phenomenon.

In Chapter 4 another central feature of governance is described: viz, networks and civil society. Given the customer/provider split, government is increasingly dependent on networks of partners, including civil society, for delivering public services and purposes. But who is accountable to whom for what?

The issue of the relationships between policy making and evaluation and implementation is considered in Chapter 5. There has been great change in methods of service delivery, but are the mechanisms for policy making adequate and sufficiently accountable?

Chapter 6 deals with privatisation and contracting out, not in a technical or exhaustive fashion, but again in terms of arrangements for accountability.

Chapter 7 pays a very brief visit to markets and regulation. There is little new here, and it is included mainly for the sake of completeness.

Competition policy and corporate governance are addressed in Chapter 8. If the world is being marketised, then accountability demands an effective competition policy and insists that corporate governance takes on board the interests of other stakeholders. Again, this is not a textual approach to these issues, but rather calls for greater concentration by public lawyers on these issues than has previously been the case.

Chapter 9 is about reinventing public law and the constitution to confront the problems raised by governance. No blueprint is offered; merely a set of problematics and general directions to which we need to turn.

The somewhat lengthier Chapter 10 is titled 'Governance and Globalisation'. It argues that there is something like a global constitution out there which we have yet to chart and to infuse with respect for human rights.

It is a big project which will take a long time, but we need urgently to address the task.

I would like to take this opportunity to thank the British Academy for the small grant which assisted me with the fieldwork for this book.

N Douglas Lewis
July 2001

CONTENTS

CHAPTER 1

THE MODERN STATE

INTRODUCTION

The concept of the State has been subjected to less analysis in the UK than in most European democracies. There has been an absence of a 'State tradition', whereby the sum of public purposes and institutions takes on something of a personality of its own; where it gives identity to the nation and speaks to something larger and more permanent than current habits and personalities.[1] Instead, in the UK, the mystery of the Crown has largely concealed the reality of the sometimes ruthless control of affairs by a Parliament dominated by the ascendant political party. This is nowhere better illustrated than in the so called 'omnicompetence' of Parliament, whereby the direction of the nation may be as dramatically altered as the contingencies of pragmatic accommodation permit. Conventions, of course, exist, as do notions of auto-limitation, while there are cultural expectations born out of experience and moments of forced and intense compromise. Even so, if concepts of the State lie on a spectrum, with institutions at one end and purposes at the other, then the UK is very much on the institutions end. The reasons for this state of affairs have been well charted and no purpose would be served in repeating them. The summary is merely background to the here and now, since the 'now' is altering shape before our eyes.

At the moment of writing, significant constitutional changes are taking place in the UK, which, taken together, are probably motivated by principle and belief more than expediency. They will not be reversed, so that hundreds of years of history will be recast if not sundered. The domestic alterations are marching hand in hand with the rapid evolution of the European Union, and all these have to be viewed against sea changes in the way a nation can be expected to conduct its business because the world is shrinking and re-shaping. These latter developments will be discussed shortly. However, is the absence of a State tradition and of a coherent written constitution an impediment or an advantage in these rapidly changing times? Does the fact that the UK has been very much a government of 'men' rather than 'laws' constitute an advantage over its partners and rivals? There is the possibility that a tradition of pragmatism and flexibility represents a flying start in a world in flux. On the other hand, it may be that in times of rapid change and uncertainty, the eternal verities and the capacity to hold on to them is what

1 The classic exposition is Dyson, K, *The State Tradition in Western Europe*, 1980, Martin Robertson.

really matters. One thing is clear: the place of law (both at the grand constitutional level and more mundanely) needs to be reviewed in the light of the changing nature of the modern State; and, in particular, as government gives way to 'governance'.[2] What follows seeks to describe the challenges and to point up possible directions in which we might move.

LOOKING FOR THE PILOT

The UK governmental tradition is aberrant. Although it has often spoken the language of tolerance, culture and pluralism it has never been a 'Rechstaat', never a 'human rights' State – or, indeed, according to many, a State at all. Its unruptured, relatively seamless, progress has been characterised by pragmatism and concession without the primary institutions appearing to undergo any structural change. And the notion of omnicompetence really has been very much at the heart of the polity, in spite of the cultural overlay of despotic denial. This representation of governing reality which was, of course, unsustainable did not survive the end of Empire and the sterile discourse surrounding the potential for repeal of the Statute of Westminster 1931, *inter alia*.[3] Post-Suez reality and the need to hitch the UK's star to Continental Europe were merely the next stage in the process of adaptation. Mrs Thatcher, the removal of exchange controls, the free and uninterrupted flows of capital and the technological revolution continued the story. Far from claiming parliamentary omnicompetence, except at a relatively trivial ritual level, the question becomes whether the British government can any longer deliver on its promises. Indeed, the world is such a cauldron of complexity that prime movers are hard to identify. Can we really find the pilot?

We have been used to hearing about the end of politics in recent years, and we know that, for good reasons as well as bad, there has been a decline in the confidence of government to deliver its promises. Indeed, some scholars, tracing the interdependence of the strands of governance, have expressed doubts about what roles even central government can play when locked into a range of policy networks. This is a world where 'centralization coexists with fragmentation and independence; where policy intentions drown under their unintended consequences'.[4]

Let us begin by saying a little about the emergence of 'governance' and its significance in altering traditional understandings about representative government. Take a mix of the following: there is a growing belief that

2 For a useful summary of these changes, see Rhodes, RAW, *Understanding Governance, Policy Networks etc*, 1997, OUP.

3 See, eg, Bradley, AW and Ewing, KD, *Constitutional and Administrative Law*, 12th edn, 1997, Addison Wesley Longman, p 31 and at various points.

4 *Op cit*, Rhodes, fn 2, p 4.

international, national and local systems of government are increasingly out of step with emerging challenges. The debate reflects the belief, too, that although markets and private production are what are generally needed, capitalism and transnational corporations in particular are, in some senses, beyond control. Now, the problems of governance are much more than problems of traditional government faced with the demands and the potential of the private sector. Even so, some of the flavour of the task of governance is afforded by examining those relationships. Thus, issues of accountability, responsibility and influence lie at the core of the debate on the relationship between the public and the private sector, and the linkages between national governance and corporate governance. Government's duty is not to 'second guess' individual commercial decisions, but to ensure as best it can that the structure it creates for companies contains checks and balances that are effective in resolving the tensions between different legitimate claims. The improvements of living standards must co-exist with the enhancement of social cohesion.[5]

Many of the opportunities and dilemmas have been summarised by a ministerial symposium on the future of public services and much of what immediately follows seeks to summarise the main body of its findings.[6] It seems, now, to be widely accepted that a polity needs more than efficient and public management. It also relies on the ability of democratic institutions to function well in the modern environment of rapid change, global communications and the like. In the past, public management was seen as a matter of designing administrative structures to carry out public programmes efficiently, executing laws and regulations and responding to political leaders. Although some of this command-and-control bureaucracy will remain, OECD ministers were, instead, asked to concentrate on new relationships between democratically elected bodies, ministries and government agencies, private profit making and not-for-profit enterprises, interest groups, the media and citizens.

The Chair of the Symposium noted seven ways in which OECD countries were responding to the pressures for change in the role and structure of government:

- decentralisation of authority within governmental units and devolution of responsibilities to lower levels of government;
- re-examination of what government should pay for and do, what it should pay for but not do, and what it should neither pay for nor do;
- downsizing the public service and the privatisation or corporatisation of activities;

5 WBCSD, *Corporate Leadership and Governance: Securing the Social License to Operate (The Challenge Brief)*, 1997, WBCSD, Chapter 21, pp 1–2.

6 PUMA, March 1996, OECD.

- consideration of more cost-effective ways of delivering services, such as contracting-out, market-type mechanisms, and user charges;
- customer orientation, including explicit quality standards for public services;
- benchmarking and measuring performance; and
- reforms designed to simplify regulation and reduce its costs.

The issues surrounding globalisation will be addressed at regular intervals, but it is worth pointing out that whatever opportunities the phenomenon presents, governments are often forced to react quickly, hampering traditional consent procedures.[7] How, in short, are decisions made about the proper scope for government activity and how, in the context of fiscal authority, do they find new answers to the question of what constitutes proper public expenditures? There was widespread agreement that public administration is not a scientific force unto itself, but is merely one delivery mechanism for complex democratic ideals. The Commission on Global Governance has also provided a useful definition:

> ... the sum of the many ways individuals and institutions, public and private, manage their common affairs. It is a continuing process through which conflicting or diverse interests may be accommodated and co-operative action may be taken. It includes formal institutions and regimes empowered to enforce compliance, as well as informal arrangements, that people and institutions have agreed to or perceive to be in their interest.[8]

The World Bank adds that governance consists of:

- the form of political regime;
- the process by which authority is exercised and the management of a country's economic and social resources for development;
- the capacity of government to design, formulate and implement policies and discharge functions.[9]

Public management now encompasses the broad range of techniques and strategies that are used to carry out the responsibilities assigned to governments. It includes, but goes beyond, the structure and administration of the public service. In contrast, 'public administration' refers to the techniques by which government policies are carried out.

A number of the issues outlined here will be picked up in later chapters, but it is important to flag up a number of challenges. First, a concern with productivity and innovation have become prominent concerns for public management. Alongside this goes a concern with rational regulatory

---

7 We shall see that, in this respect, new opportunities for consultation can turn out to be very much a two edged sword.

8 Commission on Global Governance, *Our Global Neighbourhood*, 1995, UN.

9 OECD Symposium, Ministerial Symposium on the Future of Public Services, 1996, p 11.

processes, with privatisation, contracting out and their linkages with competition policy. The challenge to vertical decision making here is obvious. Strategic oversight by politicians and public servants over the business of government is a prerequisite, which makes the traditional governmental 'empires' – or departments – less relevant than formerly. One of the central problems was clearly stated at the OECD Symposium:

> First, there are efforts to improve the strategic oversight by politicians over the business of government. The focus here has been primarily on financial management and on budget cycles, on utilising some of the information now becoming available to critically review existing programmes, on prioritising, on approval processes that place clear limits on expenditure and set clear expectations and outcomes, and yet that allow medium-term planning.[10]

Governance involves, then, not only New Public Management (NPM, of which more later), but involves horizontal decision making which affects not just the traditional public sector, which for the most part is diminished, but taking into account the environment, national and global, in which the private sector operates as well as the range of partnerships between government at all levels and a wide range of others. It represents a 'new way of governing'.[11] Partnerships are very much the current flavour and represent an opportunity and a challenge to exhort the private sector to grow and expand, but also to accept the need to incorporate social concerns: what is sometimes called the 'triple bottom line'.[12]

All of these developments pose fresh dilemmas about where accountability lies, and what yardsticks for it are applied to whom.[13] One problem which constitutionalists in the UK have largely backed away from is how a version of the public interest is vindicated when power is so fragmented. There is much talk of the client/customer these days, but there may be a single person or group whose needs are to be satisfied, but which by no means represents the public at large. Pressure groups have become more active and demanding, and political and administrative mechanisms have not yet developed the protections or defences needed, whatever they might be. However, before proceeding, a word about NPM in the UK.

For many readers, the reforms of the UK public service will be well known, so that only an outline sketch will be attempted. The Citizen's Charter, in particular, is well known, but it is worth repeating that it forms an integral part of the 'marketisation' of State services. Reform of those services probably began with the Financial Management Initiative in 1982, followed by

10 *Op cit*, OECD, fn 9, p 16.

11 See Lewis, ND, 'The Citizen's Charter and Next Steps: a new way of governing?' (1993) 64 Political Quarterly 316, pp 316–26.

12 Lewis, ND, 'Governance, corporate governance and the public interest' (1998) 2 Corporate Governance International 13, pp 13–21.

13 And see *op cit*, Rhodes, fn 2.

the 'Next Steps' Agency programme, the Charter, the Code on Access to Government Information, the 'prior options' exercise, market-testing and much else besides.[14] These crucial developments have not always been accompanied by the most advanced methods of accountability in a constitutional sense, although Whitehall is a much more open place than it was 15 or so years ago.

It will be useful to concentrate, for present purposes, on what was, until recently, called the 'prior options' exercise and which has now been retitled 'appraising options'.[15] Under current arrangements, all governmental activities are considered and reviewed in a green-field fashion every five years. The options are: discontinuing the activity, privatising it, contracting it out to the private sector, market testing the activity or internal restructuring. The various processes cannot be considered here, but there is strong evidence of a democratic deficit in the way in which the procedures are conducted. A 'Contracts Ombudsman' to oversee the whole process would be one way of responding to this perceived deficit, although an effective Freedom of Information (FOI) Act would go some way to repairing the situation.

Some of the linkages between NPM and governance are beginning to emerge. Pushing decision making down to consumers, to community organisations and to other manifestations of civil society necessitates opening up the workings of government, to decentralising it in important respects. Almost all the developments accompanying governance require greater levels of transparency than government has afforded in the past. Yet, the need for government at various levels to keep control of the agenda remains. At this point, dilemmas arise about the definition of the public interest and the accompanying ethical basis for action as broadly distributed. A few of these issues can be spelled out a little, although potential solutions to the dilemmas will be left open for later chapters.

First, government needs to pursue more active communication policies if they are not just to react passively to the pressure of events and emergency situations. Secondly, there needs to be a balance between the representation of pressure groups and the transparency of their action. As the OECD Report makes clear:

> Government must play the role of arbitrator, seeking balanced responses to multiple and often conflicting demands from vocal and often well organised interest groups. Capture by particular powerful interests has to be avoided. It is also the responsibility of government to define and protect the overall public

14 See, generally, Cabinet Office, *Finding Your Way Round Whitehall and Beyond*, March 1997, Cabinet Office website and *Next Steps Report*, Cm 3889, March 1997, Cabinet Office.

15 As at the time of writing, the Government is encouraging departments to make clear-cut choices between internal restructuring and contracting out whenever possible, rather than adopting the half way house of market testing. Greater consultation is also being urged. See Press Release, Office of Public Service CAB, 161/98.

> interest, including the interests of the silent majority. This [is] fundamental to democracy.[16]

Thirdly, there needs to be a solid ethical framework for public officials and public services, so as to protect them against possible risk and conflict of interest pressures, and thus to protect the public at large.[17] Fourthly, there is a need for broad, open and fair public discussion, to enable the political authorities to ensure that the general interest ultimately prevails over sectoral demands. Modern States, not least the UK, are complex, open and fast moving. They are experiencing contradictory pressures which can only be overcome through dialogue with society itself. The political authorities still retain, while answering to their constitutions, the legitimacy and the authority to remain the driving and decision making force. However, in so doing, they must reform, repair and experiment while retaining the responsibility for openness, fairness and administrative propriety in rapidly changing circumstances.

It is commonplace to remark that decisions are becoming increasingly difficult to take. Another view is that they will be become more so with the passing of time, so that not only must government rethink traditional procedures, but must vastly improve its sources of information. Integrated action between public authorities following broader and deeper consultation practices with a range of publics will also be required. It is now generally accepted that public finances will not be adequate to perform all perceived public needs in the future and that a range of instruments from regulation, market forces, partnerships with the voluntary sector, dialogue and improved information all need to be brought to bear in seeking solutions to problems identified by government. New institutions, new patterns of administration and new systems of public law all have their part to play. To some extent, this will be a process of experimentation; on the other hand, the changing times require a re-statement and a repatriation of the more enduring truths which all free societies hold self-evident.

This returns us to an earlier problem about the flexible nature of State institutions. There is no easy answer to the question posed, but it would be a mistake to believe that rampant pragmatism will provide the answer. A number of participants to the OECD Colloquium were clear on this point:

> Some countries with very strong consultative systems – an open budget formation process, systems of open and transparent government that promote open discussion of policy, or ones where the development of laws is subject to ratification processes – may have advantages here ... It is clear, in any event, that there are no short cuts to the important tasks of building public support.[18]

16 *Op cit*, OECD Symposium, fn 9, p 25.

17 And see Lewis, ND, 'A Civil Service Act for the United Kingdom' [1998] PL 463, pp 463–88.

18 *Op cit*, OECD Symposium, fn 9, p 19.

The logic of human rights underpinned by collective guarantees in the new environment is also pursued by others. Civil society appears more important than ever, and yet its underpinning is as ancient as Greece and as modern as the 18th century enlightenment. Its roots are found in the separation of powers and equality before the law. The guarantee of freedom of association and from administrative discretion has been seen by many as crucial for opening up the space between the State as political and administrative power, the economy as the mode of production, consumption and distribution, and the individual. In this space, we find civil society, which comprises all of those activities not governed by the State or the economy, based upon the free association of individuals who pursue their own interests, in line with the civic virtues and morality.[19] Civil society can, therefore, take many forms, not least grass roots NGOs acting as paradigms of social participation and democratic development. In any event, its pluralistic nature is not only the flipside of the free market economy, but is a fruitful source of information for governments seeking to build co-operation and a knowledge base for action.[20] The inability of the free market to operate effectively in the absence of an entrenched civil society has perhaps never been more graphically displayed than in the recent history of the Russian Federation. This theme will be pursued in Chapter 4.

Governments are now seeking to do more with less; this is the challenge of governance – the new way of governing. It is remarkable just how governments have copied the more successful private firms which have withdrawn from activities in which they are less competent and focus instead on the core capabilities. They collaborate with others on product development, purchasing and marketing and purchase a growing range of business services from outside suppliers. To ensure the smooth flow of crucial information within the firm as well as with outside partners and subcontractors, firms increasingly rely on information networks. It is easy to see the similarities of the problems facing both the public and the private sectors. However, the public sector must use all the optimum techniques while pursuing broad strategies which reflect public choice and the public interest.[21] Whether, as the OECD claims, 'uncertainty is the price of freedom', one thing is clear: broad social and economic interaction with the rest of the world must take place against a background of respect not only for market economies, but for democratic political systems, and respect for human rights and social values. Which leads naturally to our first skirmish with globalisation.

---

19 See, eg, Green, DG, *Reinventing Civil Society*, 1993, Institute of Economic Affairs and Lewis, ND, *Choice and the Legal Order: Rising Above Ethics*, 1996, Butterworths, esp Chapter 5.

20 See, eg, 'Civil society and civil society organisations: a review', in *Governance and Law*, 1998, British Council.

21 See, eg, OECD, 'New directions in public policy', Policy Brief No 3, 1997.

GOVERNANCE AND GLOBALISATION

One of the greatest challenges facing governments stems from the interpenetration of domestic and international issues, brought about by several concurrent trends: some toward globalisation and the reinforcement of multilateral trade arrangements and regional groupings of countries; others towards fragmentation brought about by decentralisation, and by the rising importance, in many countries, of subnational levels of government. These developments challenge governments to find better ways of managing multiple layers of policy making without losing sight of their own national agendas. We shall return to the challenges of decentralisation shortly, but international global capital, and the speed with which much of it can be moved, represents one of the clearest and most pressing challenges to the autonomy of governments. How to work with the potential which open capital markets and global technology offer is one challenge. How to combine with like minded democracies to ensure the continuation of public goods and values in the face of footloose indifference to those goods and values is another.

There is a generally accepted decline in confidence in government which is partly about globalisation and partly not. The move towards modern results-based, market or market-mimicking public management has been noted in passing. As will be seen, this has been a necessary, but not sufficient response to fiscal crises and expectations, and to providing a more consumer-oriented and efficient use of resources. However, there is little doubt that the growing mismatch between traditional values and the roles public officials play in a modern NPM environment has been responsible for some *causes célèbres* of a somewhat unethical nature. If the feeling grows that government is neither to be trusted when in control, nor generally believed to have real influence in a global environment, then the problems of effective governance are considerable. The responses of public actors to these pressures must result in changed policies, procedures, attitudes and alliances both at the municipal and the international level. There is no doubting the scale of the problem; neither is there any escaping the obligations it imposes.

Another way of stating this is that globalisation has implications for the internal balance of power in OECD countries – including between levels of government, between parliaments and the executive and between groups of countries. These changes are affecting more than governments; they are changing civil society – interest groups, citizens and the media. So far, there has been little concentration on how these changes are affecting the democratic process. The internal balance of power is, perhaps surprisingly, also being affected by globalisation. So, for example, sub-national governments are beginning to seek direct representation in international decision making arenas. This is a two way process. Thus, sub-national governments' powers are directly affected by international agreements entered into by national governments; the environment and pollution are obvious examples. On the other hand, national unity is impleaded by a government which is entering a process of international negotiations in circumstances where a degree of blackmail of regional and local governments can occur. Governments are, for instance, used to taking policy issues to the international level as a strategy to escape domestic opposition and to limit the number of players involved in policy making. One way and another, there is a clear need both to devolve, if the logic of markets and experiment and innovation is to be followed, and to seek ways of locking various layers of politics together. This requires improved co-operation through new communication techniques and more effective processes of consultation. One suggestion comes from the OECD:

> As more decisions are taken at the international level, there are also likely to be demands for more transparency and greater accountability in international fora. Citizens at the local level will demand to know who is driving the debate at the international level, and under what authority. These demands apply to both governmental and non-governmental policy actors. If international interest groups are influencing the policy debate, then citizens will be keen to know who is in charge, what their mandate is, and how they are funded.[22]

The promise afforded by unfettered markets has led the leading nations into an affair with deregulation. But its dangers are also readily apparent. The leading and most controversial case in point was the ultimately ill-fated OECD Multilateral Agreement on Investment (MAI). It was aimed at creating common legally binding rules to reduce government regulations and control of foreign investors, promoting greater legal security and protection for investments, and establishing a dispute settlement mechanism. Although, as originally conceived, it was restricted to OECD nations, it was widely assumed that its adoption would have meant that it would have been fairly quickly taken up by the World Trade Organisation. The assumption lying behind it was that it would have built up investor confidence and would have reduced discriminatory regulations on foreign investors. By providing a more secure environment for investments and by reducing costly government regulation, the MAI was expected to encourage greater levels of investment and thereby promote growth and employment. Oxfam, however, as one of the major NGO opponents to the scheme, argued, ultimately successfully, that some of the social, political and environmental repercussions could have proved extremely damaging. Perhaps most significantly, there would have been a strong possibility that, under such a treaty, multinational corporations would have been able to call into question local health, environmental and

22 OECD, 'Globalisation – what implications for democratic decision making?', in PUMA, *Strategic Management and Policy-Making*, 1996, PUMA, Pt 3, p 3.

employment protection laws if they regarded them as discriminatory.[23] Moreover, contrary to the spirit of much that is being argued here, the discussions leading up to the drafting of the proposals had been relatively secluded from the public gaze. Little attempt was made to build alliances of all interested parties through an exercise in transparency. This contempt for public opinion reaped its own rewards as opposition, especially in the form of the most active NGOs, gathered a considerable head of steam. It culminated in the failure of the Seattle WTO trade round in 1999, which was accompanied by a huge blast of critical publicity.

Globalisation is putting pressure on governments to adjust the machinery of government, in order to improve their capacity to operate in the new international environment. It, along with other transformations, is also posing challenges for civil society. One of the changes, to which it will be necessary to return, is that well organised aspects of civil society, industrial interests and even sub-national governments are seeking to become players in international decision making fora. This has important implications for the role of central governments vis à vis the 'governed' in all their many manifestations. But, let us conclude this brief section with another set of globalised problematics which will need to be addressed from time to time. Again, it comes from the OECD:

> Globalisation also has implications for the relationships between groups of countries. The development of regional groupings – such as the European Union, NAFTA and APEC – and international or multilateral agreements, particularly in the area of trade policy, such as the World Trade Organisation, demands some thought on its implications for the international balance of power ... Dependency theorists argue that globalisation strengthens strong States at the expense of small peripheral players in the global economy. Apart from their stated internal goals, regional groupings may be one way for countries – particularly small economies – to maximise their influence in global fora. So are regionalism and multilateralism contradictory or complementary trends? In practice, regionalism may be a step on the way to multilateralism, and a means to equalise the power relationships in international decision-making between heterogeneous players. During the Uruguay Round, the European Union showed the extent to which the bargaining power of individual Member States could be enhanced by collective action.[24]

In other words, both 'constitutional' structures and constitutional action are richer and more complex than is sometimes appreciated. They clearly need to be charted and analysed.

In particular, initiatives such as the MAI should be occupying serious attention since they, and their ilk, may seriously limit the ability of

23 See Briefing Paper to the OECD, *The OECD Multilateral Agreement on Investment* (MAI), 1997.

24 *Op cit*, OECD, fn 22, p 1.

governments to regulate investment in the public interest and may have the effect of transferring control over investment decisions from government to relatively unaccountable[25] companies. This issue is taken up more extensively in Chapter 10. The problems of the developed countries are, however, nothing as to those faced by the developing world. Although this essay, being essentially a contemporary reflection on aspects of the state of public and constitutional law, underplays the grinding poverty of the Least Developed Countries (LDCs), it is that very poverty which is the major humanitarian challenge to the New World Order which globalisation announces.

FRAGMENTED VERSUS CO-OPERATIVE GOVERNMENT

It should already now be becoming clear that governance requires the orchestration of public and private interests into an acceptable national (*sed quaere*) outcome or series of outcomes. Government has always been, in one sense, a partnership between government and people and, in many cases, between federal governments and their peoples. But, government has been reinvented so that it is no longer, if it ever was, capable of rowing the ship of State, so to speak, to clear destinations via defined channels. In its steering capacity, it is now obliged to work with a range of actors whose co-operation, at one time, would have seemed unnecessary. The developments which have been outlined already are compelling governments to find better ways to manage multiple layers of policy making without losing sight of their own national policy agendas. Fragmented/dissipated government must become co-operative government where more can indeed be done with less (in terms of purely public resources), provided that there are more involved. The art of government, always demanding, has become as intricate as spinning silk. A new meaning is being given to the term 'statecraft'.

Just one item in the catalogue will help to explain the predicament:

> The information explosion has multiplied the number of actors involved in public policy making. The emergence of the information society has changed the context of governance. It has increased the influence of the mass media, nurtured the development of a more educated and better informed population, and multiplied the number of interest groups and other non-governmental actors asserting the right to play a greater role in the governance process. This complex of factors has added to the external pressures bearing on governments, and has fostered a sense of fragmentation of the policy context.[26]

25 See *op cit*, Lewis, fn 12.

26 'Building policy coherence', in *op cit*, OECD, fn 22, p 2.

As well as offering learning opportunities and offering the possibilities for growing effective coalitions, these developments also pose questions relating to constructive consultation with stakeholders, the balanced participation of concerned parties, more effective and active relationships with the media, ethical dilemmas, including the avoidance of conflicts of interest, and general transparency in dealing with those interests. Many of the concerns raised can be seen in the increased influence of national governments in the business of corporate governance, both because of the economic significance of global corporations and because private industry is increasingly used by governments as a delivery mechanism for public policies.[27] Recent years have seen, for example, a swing away from prescriptive legal controls on industry towards voluntary agreements between governments and industry. Public authorities are beginning to set up the framework and targets jointly with the other stakeholders, including industry, and industry is free to choose how to attain those targets. At the larger level, various key needs can be identified; viz, the need for a strong strategic capacity at the centre of government, the need for organisational flexibility and the need for effective information gathering systems. Indeed it can be argued that the paramount need is for informed decision making, so that a high premium should be placed on developing information systems and analytical capacities.

Governance is about off-loading, about partnerships, about strategic vision which allows the more knowledgeable to act within a generally agreed framework. Whether speaking the language of 'subsidiarity', or underlining the failings of command economies, it is now widely accepted that a marketisation of government structures has much to commend it. Public management, these days, encompasses the broad range of techniques and strategies that are used to carry out the responsibilities of government. It needs to be stressed that new relationships are occurring between democratically elected bodies, as well as private profit making and not-for-profit enterprises, quite apart from the multifaceted forms of civil society. The voluntary sector, which will be addressed more fully in Chapter 4, has its own agendas and its own problems in preserving its autonomy, but sees salvation in being part of networks, alliances and coalitions.[28]

Public/private partnerships will be left over for the moment;[29] instead, a little more will be said about NGOs and other interest groups. To some extent, the present absence of FOI in the UK is being offset by the global information explosion. This increased access may be thought to have a democratising

27 See generally, *op cit*, WBCSD, fn 5.

28 See, eg, Zimmeck, M, 'To boldly go – the voluntary sector and voluntary action in the new world of work' (1998) 3(4) RSA Journal 19.

29 But see Goh, J and Lewis, ND, *The Private World of Government*, 1998, Centre for Socio-Legal Studies, University of Sheffield and OECD, *Corporate Governance: Improving Competitiveness and Access to Capital in Global Markets*, Report to the OECD by its Business Sector Advisory Group on Corporate Governance, 1998.

effect by politicising groups of citizens and mobilising them into action. For example, citizens can use information about what neighbouring governments are doing in order to challenge or pressurise their own governments. Globalisation allows people to organise themselves more quickly and effectively across national borders. They are increasingly organised internationally and capable of influencing the policy debate in several countries at the same time. Greenpeace is an obvious example. Brent Spar is a case in point where the eventual outcome was not universally agreed to be in the public interest. These developments undoubtedly make the policy process more complex, have the potential for liberating democratic sentiments, but also provide thorny problems for central government about undue influence. The information society has changed the context of governance; quite apart from the growing influence of the mass media (whose power may or may not be mediated in the future by alternatively available technology), there has been a multiplication of the number of interest groups and NGOs asserting their right to play a greater role. At its best, as will be seen in Chapter 5, this can produce creative tension and enhance the contestability of policy advice.

LAYERS OF GOVERNMENT: THE MOVE TOWARDS DECENTRALISATION

Part of the toolkit of governance is decentralisation, devolution and, in political terms, eventually something more than lip service to regionalisation. Central government and the public service will guide, steer, cajole and act as partner to a whole tranche of agencies, both public, private and hybrid. It is, however, becoming increasingly clear that the centre needs support from the periphery or hinterland; it needs information, novelty, and experimentation and best practice from lower tiers of government. It is also increasingly important that cross-cutting issues are addressed by bringing together all the agencies involved in particular policy initiatives; this includes horizontal co-ordination both at central and lower levels.

The OECD has indicated how nearly all its members are committed to both 'responsibility centres' and a decentralisation process which requires a new organic adaptation of the central government.[30] The UK response is now beginning to look extremely interesting after the establishment of the Scottish Parliament and Welsh Assembly in 1999,[31] as well as the appearance of the Regional Development Agencies, which are further discussed in Chapter 9. Although Northern Ireland is a special case, it is nevertheless an important

30 See *In Search of Results, Performance Management Practices*, 1997, PUMA, eg, p 67 and OECD, *Issues and Developments in Public Management*, Survey 1996–97 (Sweden and Spain).

31 See Scotland Act 1998 and Government of Wales Act 1998.

exercise in devolution which should, over time, enrich the UK polity. It is not possible to do justice to these changes in the space available, but two things need to be underlined. The first is that the unitary nature of the British State has been broken; a continuing UK can never be the same again with power centres being established in Cardiff, Edinburgh and London. Democratic centralism will never be the same again; experiments, partnerships and new ways of working between the different layers of government will be watched with interest. Secondly, both in Scotland and Wales, responsibility for local government, quangos (or Non-Departmental Public Bodies – NDPBs[32]) and the Training and Enterprise Councils (TECs) is being transferred with the expectation that all of them will be re-infused with a democratic spirit. Each has the chance to experiment and Westminster and the world will watch with considerable interest.

There is another angle to this. Rather than sharing and co-operating in resolving policy complexity, devolution can take another form: viz, devolving delivery functions to other levels of government in the interests of allowing the national government to focus on setting the strategic policy directions. Indeed, this is part of the justification for the purchaser/provider debate, which will be examined further in Chapter 5. Part of the *raison d'être* of NPM, unfortunately the more neglected part, is that devolving delivery functions frees up the centre to concentrate on policy. In reality, the devolution of functions will usually service both purposes; that is, contesting sources of policy advice – providing co-operation and experiment in policy initiatives – and also separating management and policy functions. Both these functions (seeing them as separate at least for ideal-typical purposes) require fragmentation and devolution. The ends of both democracy and budgetary discipline seem to be moving in the same direction.

In some countries, experiments have taken place whereby the centre makes (often diminished) block grants to localities who are then free to determine their own priorities and the consequent use to which central funds are put.[33] In France, historically notoriously centralist, important experiments in decentralisation have been taking place. One of the most important innovations has been the creation of 'responsibility centres'. The goals of the reforms were to grant managerial autonomy to responsibility centres in exchange for increased accountability. Considerable efforts have been made to devolve responsibilities to the State apparatus at the local levels through initiatives such as the Deconcentration Charter (*Charte de la déconcentration*, 1992).[34]

32 The Westminster Government has already sought to democratise the latter to some extent; see, esp, Cabinet Office, *Quangos: Opening Up Appointments*, 1998, HMSO.

33 As, eg, has recently happened in Sweden; see *op cit*, OECD, fn 30, Survey on Sweden.

34 *Op cit*, OECD, fn 30, pp 67 *et seq*.

Where, however, does this leave the State and State functions? In all the rapid changes of the last decade or so, there has been remarkable pragmatism and, in the UK at least, far too little discussion about the content and meaning of the 'core'.

CORE GOVERNMENT: CORE STATE

Ever since the functions of government have been increasingly off-loaded – in the UK, especially through privatisation, contracting out and market-testing – there has been some concern aired about just which parts of the polity are 'constitutional'; what are the 'remains of the State' or can everything apart, say, from Parliament be contracted out? There has been no really satisfactory analysis of this in the UK.[35] Here, the pragmatic view has so far prevailed: the State is whatever the government of the day says it is. The OECD Symposium, on the other hand, was clear that there needs to be a fundamental analysis of the role and scope of government, including analyses of what should be provided by other sectors and what should remain in the public sector. Furthermore, in the Netherlands, a quantitative reduction target of government activities has been accompanied by a discussion on content; that is, core tasks. On the basis of an analysis of core tasks – aimed at identifying the core business of government departments – the tasks of government have been reviewed and, where necessary, reallocated or reduced. However, in addition to reducing responsibilities and size, the government recently announced an intention to restore 'the primacy of politics'.[36] Further details are discussed in Chapter 9. Sweden, too, has abolished, amalgamated and corporatised government agencies in an exercise which has been directed at finding the optimum forms for State activity.[37] It is not acceptable for the shape of the constitution and the polity to be forged in a process of drift and reaction to events occurring, which may already be outside government's control. It seems clear that a machinery of government commission is called for with a remit to keep the shape and functions of government under constant review and supervision.[38]

35 See the author's evidence to the Treasury and Civil Service Committee on *The Role of the Civil Service*, Session 1993–94, HMSO, Vol 11, esp pp 75–76.

36 *Op cit*, OECD, fn 30, Survey on The Netherlands, p 1.

37 See fn 33, p 4.

38 See, for such an idea, Lewis, ND, 'A standing administrative conference' (1989) 60 Political Quarterly 421, pp 421–32.

PUBLIC MANAGEMENT AND THE RESTORATION OF POLITICS

The challenges of governance have been outlined. The tasks of public management have never been more demanding and the necessity to be inventive and resourceful in reasserting the primacy of politics never more obvious. Managing the continuing relationships among key parties, including the flow of information and dispute resolution procedures – not least between the various arms of government – must occur in a way which is consistent with national goals and policies and legal and constitutional compatibility. So, also, increasing the number of actors involved in the governing process often means creating new mechanisms, or adapting existing ones, in order to give new actors a voice, while maintaining the government's capacity to guide the process towards coherent results.

Governments must confront the issue of clarifying accountability in and between a network of fragmented actors. It is vital to build bases for achieving coherence that depend less on central co-ordination and more on continuous, flexible interactions between institutions and people. These include policy capacities across the government outside the centre, a sustained focus on public service values and people working together across traditional boundaries. This returns us to an earlier theme. Since governance includes not only formal institutions and regimes empowered to enforce compliance, but also informal arrangements which people and institutions have agreed to or perceive to be in their interest, the anatomy of the State and State responsibilities becomes very difficult to identify.

The problems adverted to here are very real in all modern democracies, but the UK poses particular problems on account of its lack of obvious and announced constitutionality; its lack of 'Stateness'. A more publicly visible complexity is one way of describing it. Contracting out is one example; at the level of central government, there is too little visibility and too little opportunity for any public monitoring of the public/private partnerships which are beginning to characterise the face of public services.[39] At the local level we had, until recently, the only compulsory, statutory, competitive tendering requirement in the world. As will be seen later, this has been replaced by the Best Value initiative which, although fairer and less dogmatic, does nothing to reduce the complexity which is being addressed here. The Citizen's Charter initiatives, also reinvented by the Blair Government as Service First and extremely important in themselves, have been largely informally introduced while the Government's larger thinking on its macro-constitutional obligations was announced in the form of a White Paper on *Modernising Government*. This is taken up in Chapter 9. Accompanying this,

39 See *op cit*, Goh and Lewis, fn 29.

however, has been important constitutional change introduced by statute: the devolution process, human rights legislation and other proposals in the pipeline. For all the closed nature of the deliberations of many international fora – the EU, WTO, MAI, etc – intergovernmental initiatives eventually emerge largely as formal decisions publicly adopted.

The privacy, secrecy, the cabalistic culture of British government for the most part still obtains, and much of it will only be exposed by radical FOI legislation. However, the very fact that co-operation and partnership is so much at the heart of the new governance means that there has to be a greater degree of transparency than formerly. This is inevitable if coalitions, trust and consent are to be built; if 'agents' of broad government values increase in number. It would be surprising, therefore, if the problems facing the modern State did not result in a more publicly visible complexity. Constitutional lawyers will need to familiarise themselves with the problems of government and seek to give a helping hand to accountability and effectiveness in the new setting. The constitutional landscape is becoming increasingly intricate and we can expect a patchwork quilt of legislation and much 'softer' forms of law in the shape of covenants, contracts, white papers, codes of practice, best practice comparators and so on.

CONCLUSIONS

The British State has always been something of a wraith; ghosting in and out of changed circumstances without much in the way of flesh being added to the body constitutional. But the times are changing and there is evidence that the British polity is changing with them. The outlines of the new challenges – summarised as the problems and the opportunities of governance – have been briefly addressed. The nature of the changes requires greater artifice than formerly; greater co-operation. There is a widespread sense of interdependence; neither central government nor the nation it represents are islands. In a real sense, we are all in this together. This is not to say that we are being beckoned unequivocally to the constitutional sunlit uplands. Indeed, it is clear that the new world is full of both opportunities and pitfalls. Greater co-operation, yes; but also the real danger of being hijacked by powerful interests outside the control of either politicians or community. Yet, the forces that confront government simply cannot be managed without greater transparency in partnerships, without more integrated consultation procedures and without a much wider tranche of interests having a place in the new order. This is one reality, and it is one the significance of which must be recognised and turned to advantage so that executive dominance is placed under effective challenge.

It is not clear how far the wide ranging constitutional changes taking place in the UK have been fired by the kind of analysis spoken to here. But, in most senses, this matters little. Devolution, and even the somewhat disappointing Freedom of Information Act introduced in 2000, will inevitably weaken government at the centre and make political co-operation much more fruitful than in the past. The new instrumentalities, intentionally so or not, suddenly look like extremely modern institutional adjustments to the challenge of governance. And they are extremely unlikely to be undone, as are the outward-facing institutional commitments to the EU, WTO, OECD and the like. Thus, the British State is changing dramatically; and at the most opportune time.

Where does this leave Parliament? Will it continue its impotent drift or reinvent itself? The scenario described here would appear to make it seem even more irrelevant than it has been in the recent past, but the logic of the analysis is that the Executive cannot any longer govern in the absolute sense. The logic is also that new institutions and new machinery are needed to help to produce a coherent pattern of politics. In the very recent past, Parliamentary Select Committees have been much more influential than formerly and the time now seems opportune for Parliament to abandon its medieval pretences and to use its undoubted legitimacy to monitor the progress of politics and to make informed, well resourced observations on the challenges of the new order. Indeed, given the challenges which the executive faces in changed circumstances, it may well begin to believe that it needs Parliament again. A reinvented Assembly, philosophically honed and technologically equipped – with the remit to oversee the big picture, to scan the forest while the executive prunes the trees – could be just the partner which a challenged government needs. We shall see. The dilemma has already been graphically expressed:

> ... 'lean' governments need to maintain their capacities to develop and co-ordinate important policies, as well as to implement public services. But central capacities are not sufficient on their own ...
>
> Strategically, offices at the centre of government can encourage these approaches. They should also seek to focus attention on major issues through 'big levers', such as budgets and statements of government-wide priorities. These levers can help bring together political and governmental considerations, since administrative co-ordination cannot be a substitute for a broadly coherent framework of politically determined priorities.

In spite of everything that has been said, only strong governments (though they may be much more consensual and less ideological than in the past) will be able to cope with the tide of events, so that everything possible must be done to strengthen the position of government, providing, of course, that it is a government whose primary purpose is to advance human dignity. The success of the venture depends, in no small part, on the capacity to construct new forms of public service within the framework of a democratic consensus.

Arguing for a strong centre is not as self-evident as it might appear, since there are centres and centres. Leaving it as uncomplicated as possible by restricting the critique to the EU countries, what subsidiarity actually means or can mean is still contested. There are things which only Brussels should do, and things which should only be done at a sub-Westminster level, but this by no means writes Whitehall and Westminster out of the picture. First, it has to be the ring-master of national alliances and partnerships; it presently remains the only actor with the legitimacy to guide community values into harbour. Secondly, it has to represent national sentiments and values accurately outwards to the EU (etc). In doing so, it needs something resembling all-weather, all-purpose constitutional architecture, with which it is currently still experimenting. The best prediction is that it will do so by refusing to compromise on the enduring nature of human needs while experimenting with procedures, practices and institutions that can bend and shift through co-operative learning experiences. What is needed is what the OED has called 'the tools of coherence'. Granted, these can only be currently stated at a relatively high level of generality, but it is somewhere to start.

The main tools are described as follows:

- establishing a strategic policy framework to ensure that individual policies are consistent with the government's goals and priorities;
- the existence of a central overview and co-ordination capacity to ensure horizontal consistency among policies;
- mechanisms to anticipate, detect and resolve policy conflicts early in the process to help identify inconsistencies and reduce incoherence;
- the decision making process must be organised to achieve an effective reconciliation between policy priorities and budgetary imperatives;
- implementation procedures and monitoring mechanisms to ensure that policies can be adjusted in the light of progress, new information, and changed circumstances;
- an administrative culture that promotes cross-sectoral co-operation and a systematic dialogue between different policy communities to strengthen policy coherence.

There are no short cuts to these processes, nor indeed to the crucial task of building public support. But, in the UK, the task is under way. It needs more research and analysis, more experiment and more assertion of basic values. But, as the old State withers away, the new is rising out of the ashes.

CHAPTER 2

LAW AND GOVERNANCE: AN OVERVIEW

The State is being constantly reinvented.[1] It is being 'flattened', hollowed out, asked to steer rather than row; it is an empowering State which is engaged in the business of New Public Management (NPM). It is the fashion to talk of 'governance' rather than government, a state of affairs which reflects the changes referred to here – and others, which will become apparent during the course of this essay. The theme of the essay is, however, that NPM is unworkable – in its own terms, as well as others – without reinstating old, some would say 'ancient' values. These values are those which are celebrated by public law and public lawyers. The time is overdue to put the new concerns and techniques in touch with the older ones of openness, fairness, public involvement and accountability to ensure both constitutional propriety and managerial/economic efficiency and effectiveness. Close examination of the most successful examples of modern public administration reinforce this belief again and again. Take Australia, for example.

> Governments and various authorities within the Public Service have, over time, set our values or organising principles defining the Service's dominant characteristics and the nature of employment in it.
>
> These values or principles have traditionally stressed the centrality of merit based staffing, probity and integrity, efficiency, and loyalty to governments while providing frank and fearless advice. More recently, additional emphasis has been placed on the need for responsiveness to governments, managing for results and improving accountability. These changes do not imply any retreat from traditional values. Rather, the new and the old should reinforce each other. A re-statement of public service values should better focus attention on their purpose of ensuring a Public Service which is fully effective in meeting the objectives of governments and in accordance with the law.[2]

Elsewhere, it has been remarked that 'New forms of governance may come to rest on very old ideas',[3] ideas which, in Canada, have been used to reinvent government 'one department at a time'.[4] Government's essential competence remains substantially the same throughout time, even if administrative

1 The now classic text is, of course, Osborne, D and Gaebler, T, *Reinventing Government*, 1992, Addison Wesley Longman.

2 Management Advisory Board and its Management Advisory Committee, *Building a Better Public Service*, June 1993, Canberra, paras 1.3.1 and 1.3.2.

3 Davis, G, 'The great wheel: public sector futures in Canberra and Brisbane', 84 Canberra Bulletin of Public Administration 61.

4 Ernst and Young, *Program Review: Lessons Learned and Challenges Ahead (A Report for the Canadian Centre for Management Development)*, 1997, Government of Canada.

fashions and patterns alter; even if, as at the present, strategic government is the flavour of the time. That essential competence has been described as the ability to:

- make quality long term decisions;
- create and distribute knowledge;
- implement decisions effectively; and
- mediate amongst competing interests.

Strategic government also means good government, since the quality of government will increasingly determine international competitive advantage.[5] The sentiments come from the same stable as the following:

> While efficiency is a necessary condition of wider prosperity and influence, it is not sufficient. Enduring prosperity requires societies that are safe, ordered and honest.[6]

This theme will be returned to from time to time, and especially in Chapter 4.

Under newer models of governance (New Zealand is an outstanding example), the role of leadership is about framing a vision, setting broad directions and then creating the conditions in which society as a whole can steer in the desired direction. To maintain legitimacy, democratic government must allow the wider society to share in leadership:

> The constitutional separation of power, pluralistic politics, a flourishing civil society, a free and competent media, demanding and informed customers for government services, academic freedom and an open economy all help keep government under control.[7]

This can be seen to be a paean both for the processural virtues of the common law, and its more embedded principles which are now more usually articulated in the language of human rights, even, recently, in the UK.

The more NPM is examined, the more constitutional issues come to the fore. Increasing accountability has been at the forefront of public administration reforms and one of its leading chroniclers has remarked that increased authority for managers ought to be accompanied by increased accountability; both constitutional principles and good administration demand it.[8] It has not always received it; hence the emphasis being adopted here, but the OECD has pointed the way in a state of the art report on best

5 Aberbach, J and Rockman, BA, 'Does governance matter – and if so, how? Process, performance and outcomes' (1992) 5(2) Governance: An International Journal of Policy and Administration, April.

6 McRae, H, *The World in 2000: Power, Culture and Prosperity: A Vision of the Future*, 1994, HarperCollins.

7 *Strategic Management in Government: Extending the Reform Model in New Zealand*, 1996, Wellington State Services Commission, p 14.

8 Aucoin, P, 'Comment: assessing managerial reforms' (1990) 3(2) Governance 202.

practice in public administration. When reforms have been completed involving further devolution of managerial discretion, deregulation of central controls and the privatisation of public authority, 'the box marked "public interest" always needs close attention'.[9]

CORPORATE GOVERNANCE

Governance concerns not merely the traditional institutions of government, but forms of public intervention which involve a mix of traditional bureaucracy, quasi-markets, 'self-referential' government and market mechanisms as forms of public intervention to deliver public goods. It has been described as a system by which organisations are directed and controlled, less concerned with running affairs, but giving overall direction to the enterprise. The impetus began in the private sector and has spread rapidly, and controversially, to the public. In recent years, there has been considerable unease at the lack of accountable corporate governance in the private sector,[10] but:

> The fact that public services are currently undergoing significant change enhances that need for extra vigilance and care to ensure that sound systems of corporate governance are both set in place and work in practice.[11]

Even so, the report went on to insist that certain essential principles are needed to inform both sectors. These include transparency, integrity and holding individuals responsible for their actions by the allocation of clearly definable roles and tasks.

There is no doubt that much NPM has been driven by inputs rather than outputs; that is, by cost considerations, rather than measurable targets. NPM, to that extent, is sometimes seen to be management-speak for public expenditure cuts. Nonetheless, programme review is necessary in the public services field since, regardless of political philosophy, public resources are finite. NPM, therefore, chimes with seeking out and identifying appropriate levels of government action (for example, centre versus periphery), the reduction of overlap in government programmes, the elimination of unnecessary programmes, outsourcing and contracting and targeted reductions rather than across the board reductions.[12] This has all necessitated considerable changes in styles of public administration, bringing private

9 PUMA Report for OECD Paris, Ministerial Symposium on the Future of Public Services, 1996, pp 9, 19.

10 See, generally, Campbell, ID and Lewis, ND (eds), *Promoting Participation in Government: Law or Politics*, 1999, Cavendish Publishing.

11 CIPFA, *Corporate Governance in the Public Services*, 1994, London, p 6.

12 The Canadian experience with Program *(sic)* Review, already referred to, is particularly relevant here.

management techniques and concerns into the heart of government proper. Policy roles remain vital, of course, but even these have not been untouched by the thrust of NPM.

All this represents both a response to modernity and a way of seeking to direct it. In such times, the direction of the polity needs close re-examination. There is, as will be argued, considerable potential for democratic deficits in the new forms of governance. Furthermore, government/governance both defeats effective co-ordination by the centre and grows undirected and by accretion. At such times, 'the new tribes' and the democratic deficit calls for a redefinition of the old in terms of the new.[13] However, it has to be doubted whether managerialism means a sharp break with the past, since there are substantial continuities. Undoubtedly, managerialism poses new problems; for example, contractual agreements within the public sector hold out new promises for accountability and for assuming responsibility, but a contract State needs strict laws to prevent a revolving door between industry and government, given that, in a hollow State, government spends much of its time handing out public moneys for private provision.

Similar problems surface in relation to privatisation proper for, until free competition provides effective customer choice, regulatory theory will need to keep pace with older constitutional expectations, whether through open and competitive regulatory procedures[14] or more prosaic forms of adaptive administrative law.[15] At the heart of the New Zealand reform process is the concentration on outputs and outcomes in place of inputs. As to outputs, considerable success is reported, but the latter still seem to elude not only effective evaluation, but also accountability mechanisms. How to report on outcomes when no one is entirely accountable is not only a problem for traditional ministerial accountability/responsibility, but also when NPM meets traditional government head on.[16] This is exacerbated by the life cycle of parliaments, and in particular ministers, who are not encouraged to develop strategic vision, although New Zealand again points us in a desirable direction through its 2,010 documents on strategic objectives for such areas as the environment, science and technology and education.[17] We shall return to this problem when dealing with institutional governmental reforms. Even so, broadening the decision making process is clearly part of the answer.

---

13 And see Hirst, P, *Representative Democracy and its Limits*, 1990, Polity, esp pp 31–32 and Rhodes, RAW, *Understanding Governance: Policy Networks etc*, 1997, OUP, p 197.

14 See Prosser, T, *Law and the Regulators*, 1997, Clarendon, and also, Cook, P, *Privatization and Regulation, British Council Briefing on Law and Governance*, 1996, British Council Briefing on Law and Governance.

15 See the splendid example set by OFTEL, eg, *Consultation Procedures and Transparency*, 1995.

16 Office of the Auditor General of Canada, *Toward Better Governance: Public Service Reform in New Zealand and its Relevance to Canada*, 1995, Government of Canada, p 59.

17 State Services Commission, *Strategic Management in Government: Extending the Reform Model in New Zealand*, 1996, Wellington State Services Commission, p 4.

There are problems, too, which are probably unique to the public sector and which simply do not translate from the private. It is now abundantly clear that the setting of targets and parameters will not, of itself, necessarily add to the effectiveness of programmes, even though, at one level, 'efficiency' might be enhanced.[18] Indeed, the concepts of success and failure are less clear cut in the public than the private sector, with 'accountability' in the former occupying several dimensions. Accountability without rewards and sanctions is scarcely possible, yet the question remains as to precisely what rewards and sanctions will guarantee accountability in the public domain. Although independent judgment in Canada, for example, was that performance review had been 'indisputably successful' in targeting expenditure reductions, it was less clear that this had been accomplished in tandem with a redesign of government on the basis of clear criteria. The same failure to grasp the nettle of basic constitutional form and purpose can be seen in the UK in its operation of the 'prior options' exercise.[19] In New Zealand, too, the adoption of Management By Objectives (MBO) from the private sector has proved more difficult than envisaged; it works well in conditions of predictability and quantifiability, but less so in circumstances of complexity and uncertainty. 'Institutional economics' turned out not to be 'the philosopher's stone of public administration'.[20]

This is not to say that modern public administration techniques have failed; rather that they have to be constantly evaluated against larger public concerns. In Australia, for example, it has been claimed that the corporate planning, programme management and budgeting reforms have given public service agencies a clearer understanding of their objectives, while the improvement of the working environment – devolution of authority, more participative approaches to work, etc – have produced market benefits in the way services are run.[21] One of the most comprehensive examinations of NPM has pointed up both strengths and weaknesses of the new ways of doing things to which we will do well to pay continuous heed.[22]

Problems, then, present themselves in a world where politics and the people for whose values it stands need to reassert themselves. But where does the UK stand in all this?

---

18 See, eg, Holmes, JW and Wileman, TA, *Reform in the Australian Public Service 1983–86*, 1997, Office of the Auditor General of Canada, p 77.

19 See Kroeger, A, *The Central Agencies and Program Review*, 1997, internal document, Ottawa.

20 Matheson, A, *The Impact of Contracts on Public Service Management in New Zealand*, 1995, Wellington State Services Commission, p 11.

21 *Op cit*, MAB-MIAC, fn 2, p 10.

22 Management Advisory Board, *The Australian Public Service Reformed*, 1992, Task Force on Management Improvement, pp 489–90.

THE RESPONSE OF THE UK

The UK deals with problems affecting public administration as and when they arise, and largely without recourse to legislation. However, although Prime Minister Blair is almost as reluctant to affect the machinery of government through legislation as his predecessors, there are clear signs that he understands the need for modernising government to meet the challenges being described here. The *Modernising Government* White Paper,[23] for all its limitations, is clear evidence of this insight. However, it remains the case that there is no UK Administrative Procedure Act as there is, not only famously in the US, but also in many European counties, including The Netherlands and Sweden. The UK is almost alone, too, in not possessing a Civil Service Act, although one has been half-heartedly promised. The significance of this is that some legislation elsewhere entrenches public service values and also gives statutory force to public service commissioners whose function is to uphold and promote those values and other aspects of the public service. The maintenance of traditional values and the independence and integrity of the Civil Service in times of change has already been stressed.

The government has recently conducted a review of the regulation of the utilities to ensure they deliver value for money, quality and choice to consumers. Transparency is also to be a leading principle in line with recent reports of the Public Accounts Committee. As will be discussed in Chapter 7, the Government has backed away from taking a bold constitutional approach to regulatory reform although, at least in the gas and electricity industries, traditional priorities have been ceremoniously overturned. Only the future will tell whether more holistic and principled reform will emerge and whether ancient constitutional principles will figure as being central to the regulated industries. However, since regulation is likely to assume greater significance with the growth of governance, the issue will need to be constantly re-addressed.

Difficulties attendant upon the centrality of the principle of ministerial responsibility will be addressed later, but that very centrality has often been impleaded as making public law intervention unnecessary in Westminster systems of government. The argument has not always persuaded other Westminster systems of government. In Australia, it has been remarked that

> A new body of administrative law relating to administrative appeals and freedom of information was enacted which fundamentally affected the Westminster system of ministerial responsibility and brought judicial power into administration in order to redress the balance of bureaucratic power.[24]

---

23 Cabinet Office, *Modernising Government*, Cm 4310, 1999, HMSO.

24 Wilenski, P, 'Administrative reform – general principles and the Australian experience' (1986) Public Administration 268.

A leading scholar has observed that the reforms have, *inter alia*, improved the quality and responsiveness of administration.[25] The reforms preceded many of the NPM changes, but have stood the test of time and include the establishment of the Administrative Review Council, which is empowered to investigate and report on contemporary problems of public administration.

There is no doubt that relying upon ministerial responsibility (MR) as the primary method of calling the executive to account is seriously flawed, which is why it has been subject to such intense criticism in recent years.[26] Auxiliary precautions, including a reform of constitutional and administrative law, are undoubtedly part of the necessary corrective.

There is a more modern, NPM-speak way of examining the same issue. In New Zealand, at the cutting edge of managerial reform, a number of factors which government needed to confront have been clearly identified. Including:

> An approach to accountability that had become increasingly blurred and confused: multiple and overlapping authorities and responsibilities had to be clarified. It was acknowledged that little change would be forthcoming until a serious effort was made to distinguish more precisely and visibly between the respective responsibilities and accountabilities of ministers and public servants. But it also required changes bearing on the relations of ministers and their officials, and improved methods of reporting to ministers and parliament on the performance of government, its policies and operations.[27]

Regardless of the traditional weaknesses of MR, the hollowing out of the State has necessitated new lines of control and responsibilities and new criteria and mechanisms for holding individuals and groups to account. As the Canadian Centre for Management Development has said:

> If government is going to operate with a greater focus on results rather than rules and with a higher degree of innovation in all functions (especially service delivery), there may be a need to revisit the concept of risk-taking in the public service and to develop a new understanding of acceptable risk parameters. This examination of risk parameters should extend to a discussion of the implications of public service risk-taking for ministerial accountability. One other dimension that could be explored is the appropriate risk management approach for public-private partnership arrangements which are emerging as an effective approach to many policy and service delivery issues.[28]

25 Saunders, C, unpublished paper, 1993, quoted in *op cit*, Holmes and Wileman, fn 18.

26 See, eg, Lewis, ND and Longley, D, 'Ministerial responsibility: the next steps' [1996] PL 490, pp 490–507.

27 *Op cit*, Office of the Auditor General of Canada, fn 16, p 68.

28 *Op cit*, Office of the Auditor General of Canada, fn 16, p 14.

These are issues which require constant and renewed attention, a matter which has recently been reaffirmed by the Republic of Ireland.[29]

Reform in the Australian Public Service anticipated much of this in urging not only the acceptance of the responsibilities of public officials, but also the need to respond to the increasing demands of the public to participate in government decision making, of which more later.[30] Even so, NPM has produced some improvements in both accountability and transparency already. This is a general point, but one with particular resonance in New Zealand, where changes to budget making and reportage to Parliament have been a natural reaction to new forms of governance.

> Ministerial accountability has been strengthened by virtue of the extent to which Parliament and the public are better informed ... In addition, the legislative framework governing accountability for results has reduced the discretion of the government in accounting to Parliament. The framework requires a much greater degree of disclosure of financial and non-financial information that government must provide. However, there is still considerable room for improvement in reporting on the extent to which the desired outcomes are being attained. While the parliamentary appropriations process remains a central focal point for parliamentary debate and political evaluation, the reforms in this area have improved the credibility and reliability of the information base upon which debate and evaluation occur. This serves to enhance ministerial accountability, but it also serves ministers and the government by more clearly defining the actual situation facing them.[31]

Although the UK remains reluctant to legislate for change in some of these central areas, the Chancellor of the Exchequer, Gordon Brown, has moved the pace of change fast forward in this area through his comprehensive spending reviews and the establishment of 'public service agreements',[32] of which more later.

In New Zealand, of course, accountability has also been enhanced by the more contractual basis for relations between ministers and their chief executives (CE). This encompasses both the performance expected of the CE and the policy/outputs purchased by the minister. CEs have been given the authority necessary to deliver the results expected of them because these results are clearly specified in advance. The delivery of their specified outputs (except, in part, for confidential policy advice) is subject to rigorous public reporting and audit requirements. In turn, this accountability regime gives CEs every incentive to develop well performing organisations, encompassing

29 Republic of Ireland Government, *Delivering Better Government: A Programme of Change for the Irish Civil Service*, 1996.

30 *Op cit*, MAB, fn 22, p 8.

31 *Op cit*, Office of the Auditor General of Canada, fn 16, p 78.

32 HM Treasury, *Public Services for the Future: Modernisation, Reform and Accountability, PSAs 1999–2002*, Cm 4315, 1999, HMSO.

devolved authority and accountability, precisely because the performance of the CE is intimately tied to the performance of his or her subordinates and the effectiveness of departmental management systems and operational procedures. Even so, improved parliamentary procedures for relating information about outputs to outcomes is frequently remarked upon.[33]

In New Zealand, the Public Finance Act 1989 is important in this respect. This requires the Estimates, or first appropriation Bill, to be introduced into the House of Representatives early in the fiscal year, to accommodate a three part scrutiny process; review of the government's spending intentions in the Estimates, examination of departmental performance from annual reports, and examination of the performance of State-owned enterprises (SOEs). Each of these three reviews may involve two to three months of select committee inquiry. Public sector reform in Australia has followed not dissimilar patterns, including the introduction of programme management and budgeting, corporate planning and improved reporting in performance to Parliament through annual reports and programme performance statements for senate estimates committees.

Thus, the parliamentary appropriations process provides increasingly detailed and intelligible information and the new legislative framework of government accountability has reduced the discretion of government in accounting to Parliament:

> The framework requires a much greater degree of disclosure of financial and non-financial information respecting actual performance ... However, there is still considerable room for improvement in reporting on the extent to which the desired outcomes are being attained. While the parliamentary appropriations process remains a central focal point for partisan debate and political evaluation, the reforms in this area have improved the credibility and reliability of the information base upon which debate and evaluation occur. This serves to enhance ministerial accountability, but also serves ministers and the government by more clearly defining the actual situation facing them.[34]

There is an associated point relating to audit, especially given the present fashion for contracting out of government services. It has become widely accepted that it is not sufficient to buy in or purchase performance review and audit from the marketplace. It is a long established principle that audit, checking and review procedures need to be clearly separate from procedures for performing the action or making the decision. If the review were purchased from the private sector, there is a danger that the desire for repeat business might affect the results of the exercise. As has been wisely said: 'referees should not be players and vice versa.'[35] In the UK, of course, the NAO has shown willing to undertake a fresh look at an organisation's

33 See, in Australia, eg, *op cit*, MAB-MIAC, fn 2, p 17.

34 *Op cit*, Office of the Auditor General of Canada, fn 16, p 78.

35 1997–98.

objectives and methods, and to suggest alternatives. No doubt, with further disclosure requirements, its work could be usefully extended.[36]

The UK has been active in pursuing NPM from at least as early as the Financial Management Initiative, through the Next Steps programme, the Citizen's Charter, Prior Options, privatisation and contracting out.[37] Most of this has marginalised Parliament and little of it has been accompanied by new forms of institutional accountability. Instead, some version of the market tends to be seen as the universal solvent.

The Blair Government is effecting changes; in regulatory techniques, regional agencies, FOI, human rights and the 'Better Government' initiative. It is too early to see whether there has been a break with the past. The issues will be re-addressed in Chapter 9.

NPM AND ACCOUNTABILITY

If accountability to the community is a prerequisite of democracy, then we must ask about the relationship between governance and 'good governance'. If governance is the exercise of political power to manage a nation's affairs, then good governance involves:

> ... an efficient public service, an independent judicial system and legal framework to enforce contracts; the accountable administration of public funds; an independent public auditor, responsible to a representative legislature; respect for the law and human rights at all levels of government; a pluralistic structure and a free press.[38]

There are some who argue that governance, hollowed-out government, affords citizens, or at least groups of them, an influence which they cannot or did not enjoy through traditional government channels; through networks which are created by dissipated or disaggregated government agents interacting with a wide variety of interest groups, academic, community, think tanks and the like. Leaving aside the fact that some version of pluralistic corporatism has been around for a very long time, there are problems with this scenario, but problems which point to new challenges for the legal order:

> There are important limits to the new role of citizen as user. There are significant constraints on authentic discourse within the network. Governments still restrict access to information and there are clear limits to the knowledge of citizens. There is an obvious conflict between the tenets of accountability in a representative democracy and participation in networks

36 And see Minogue, M, *Law and Governance*, 1996, British Council, pp 10–11.

37 See Goh, J and Lewis, D, *The Private World of Government (occasional papers)*, 1998, Centre for Socio-Legal Studies, University of Sheffield, p 85.

38 Leftwich, A, 'Governance, democracy and development in the Third World' (1993) 14 Third World Quarterly 610.

> which can be open without being formally accountable. These differing views of networks pose different challenges for the public manager. Is their role to regulate networks (in the sense of maintaining relationships)? Do they act as guardians of the public interest? Do they still have the authority and legitimacy to claim a privileged position in the network? Can they be privileged actors in the network without undermining the discourse?[39]

Leaving aside attempts to answer those questions for the moment, this amounts to further proof that we have moved a long way away from mere ministerial responsibility, and the relationships between elected governments, their officials, 'extended' government, contractees and whole networks need to be re-addressed, but re-addressed with secure constitutional principles in mind. This is a theme that will be returned to constantly.

Evaluation of policies will be addressed shortly, but it is obvious that improved accountability will accompany effective evaluation strategies. This will especially be the case if evaluation strategies can be refined sufficiently to focus on outcome achievement.[40] This fits into the general pattern assumed by NPM, namely, that managerial efficiency and customer satisfaction go hand in hand. A new market approach to public services must rationally see the question of serving the public as being about both consumer and citizen satisfaction, not that the latter has always been stressed. Indeed, there have been occasions when it appears to have taken a back seat:

> Efficiency is measured in the crudest possible way: by dollars and cents. Consideration of need, desert, merit, equity, equality, worth and the like are beyond the scope of the cash register.[41]

Even so, market-driven approaches often bring natural benefits to the 'consumers' of public services – for example, allocating resources to the areas of greatest demand without the need for regulation, and ensuring that the service delivered is appropriate to the demand, that is, not of a higher or lower standard than the customer needs. Where, if one likes, micro-economic approaches clearly identify unacceptable externalities, then the case for various levels of government intervention is more 'efficiently' highlighted or targeted.

At this point, a word should be said about the several meanings attached to the concept of accountability. There is, of course, internal and external accountability. The former relates to vertical or hierarchical intra-managerial accountability. This has undoubtedly been heightened and improved under NPM as responsibilities have been delegated and, correspondingly, highlighted through either contracts or performance indicators or both.

39 *Op cit*, Rhodes, fn 13, p 58.

40 See *op cit*, MAB, fn 22, Chapter 8.

41 Jackson, MW, 'The public interest, public service and democracy', 47 Aust J of Public Administration 13.

External accountability is normally thought of as to the general public and, in a constitutional sense, that remains the most crucial aspect. However, with the marketisation of many public services, the term 'client' has been used to refer to transactions among agencies and sub-units. Accountability is also increasingly developed in terms of major customers and key interest groups or stakeholders.

As to 'constitutional' accountability, this normally refers to responsiveness to citizens *qua* citizens. There is little doubt that the new governance requires us to rethink accountability responses. In doing so, there is probably value in adopting an unpacked approach to the functions of government. A useful typology is provided by separating out the services of government into three: services to government and citizens, regulatory services and the provision of direct benefits and goods.[42]

Included in the first category is policy development and advice to government, about which a great deal more needs to be said later. Regulation has already been touched upon and will also be returned to. As to the third category, some services (etc) are market-like, though those that are almost commercial tend to be privatised or contracted out these days, while others have no direct comparison in the private sector and raise questions of equity and fairness. The point to make is that in terms of accountability, each category requires separate accountability techniques. Each of these needs to be more rigorously addressed than they have been thus far. What is important, even so, is that with a results-focused approach:[43]

> ... a deliberate attempt is being made to give [the] notion of service to the public meaningful content. Each program manager is in effect required to seek ministerial endorsement for the objectives and outcomes, and is then judged by the results which might accordingly be expected from that program. Thus 'managing for results' complements and provides a realistic extension of past legitimising principles [and] provides the criteria against which ministers and administrators can be held accountable.[44]

In other words, traditional mechanisms of accountability are, hopefully, supplemented. Yet, this is no magic wand. The weight given to various aspects in making a judgment will depend on the perspective, interests and values of those involved. While both results and quality need to be defined from the perspective of the government and primary target groups for government programmes, there may be other stakeholders who need to be considered, including individual clients, families, the community, businesses, public servants and political parties and politicians. For each stakeholder,

---

42 See, eg, Government of Canada, *Public Service 2000*, Taskforce Report, 1990, Ottawa, p 9.

43 And see, esp, *op cit*, MAB, fn 22, esp pp 368 *et seq*.

44 Keating, MS, 'Managing for results in the public interest' (1990) 49 Aust J of Public Administration 9.

there will be a view on the appropriateness of a programme and often these views will be in conflict. This represents a challenge to legal concepts in the new setting. However, this probably only means shifting the focus of openness and fair dealing – ancient concepts. Thus, explaining programmes adequately and identifying objectives and their relations with larger principles should enable better management of conflict and increased governmental effectiveness.[45]

Thus, traditional mechanisms of accountability have a vital role to play in the new managerialism. Accessible information is a precondition for measuring outcomes, a condition recognised in the regulatory field as well. Thus, OFTEL has championed 'open and accountable' processes and procedures, broader consultation and 'explaining in publications reasons behind policy decisions'.[46] Openness and accountability in the new politics, however, has also meant reinventing an essentially private law doctrine in the field of public law, that is, contract.

THE CONTRACTING STATE[47]

Harden effectively calls government-by-contract the new doctrine of the separation of powers. Regardless of its weaknesses, which he is not slow to characterise, it can potentially identify responsibilities and call people to account in a way in which the traditional 'seamlessness' of politics cannot hope to do. For example, in New Zealand, there is now 'an expectation that chief executives will be able to offer ministers reliable information about their management of the Government's interests as owner, and to identify the ownership implications of Ministers' major purchasing preferences'.[48] CEs are, unlike traditional permanent secretaries, hired on contract, with performance expectations laid out in written agreements with ministers. There is, accordingly, an expectation of greater accountability by managers for results.

In similar vein, in Canada, global fiscal targets were translated into notional fiscal targets for each government department. These were set on the basis of information, knowledge and prior experience of finance officials with respect to the potential for expenditure reductions. These were not across-the-board cuts. Again, this exercise led to a focus on achieving the quality of

45 *Op cit*, MAB, fn 22, Chapter 9 generally, but esp pp 391–92. See *op cit*, Keating, fn 44, for doubts about the overall suitability of such concepts as TQM in the public sector.

46 OFTEL, *Improving Accountability*, Consultation Paper, July 1997. See, also, *op cit*, MAB-MIAC, fn 2, esp p 3.

47 The inspirational title for an influential book on the subject by Ian Harden (1992, OUP).

48 State Services Commission, *Strategic Management in Government: Extending the Reform Model in New Zealand*, 1996, Wellington State Services Commission, p 11.

central financial information through information sharing, followed by clearer responsibility for outcomes.[49] Australia has produced similar experiments backed by similar arguments.

Not unlike user charging, it was argued, contracting can promise more benefits than just achieving economic efficiencies. Opening a service to the scrutiny of competitive tendering allows managers and agencies to re-evaluate their performance, even if the service is contracted out:

> These issues have been addressed in ... *Contracting out for the Provision of Services in Commonwealth Agencies.*[50] Accountability and public interest considerations are explained as ultimately decided by the minister and delegated officials. This is reflected in the responsibility elected officials and delegates take for program performance. Statutory requirements, such as privacy considerations and administrative review mechanisms, also dictate that a decision to exercise control of a program through a third party warrants ministerial consideration. While MAB-MIAC encouraged agencies to increase evaluation of the contracting option, it does so emphasising proper assessment of the appropriateness and cost of such a shift.[51]

In a FOI regime, contracts will produce ever greater accountability. Thus, in the New Zealand public service, the range of contracts is recorded in writing, and this is given additional force by the fact that the majority of contracts are distributed to other parties or are at least accessible under the Official Information Act. The 'purchase agreement', for example, between a minister and a CE is available to Parliament and is used by it in its scrutiny of the Executive.

It has been fashionable on the new-right for some years to oppose bureaucratic discretion and to argue in favour of clearer rights and responsibilities. Traditional bureaucrats favour discretion for fairly obvious reasons, but abuse of discretionary power can be very destabilising for governments without the checks and balances of external review. Contractual obligations will normally tend to identify some detail of responsible action and thereby limit discretion. One of the other theoretical attractions of the contract culture is that it frees up the policy core to concentrate on the relationship between outputs and outcomes, a matter to which it will be necessary to return:

> Further, a contract State places great financial responsibility on the surviving policy core. Since they must handle large contracts to deliver government services, regular probity checks and transparent processes become essential. To prevent political interference or corruption, the policy core must therefore have some measure of autonomy to act impartially as major public services are contracted out. And to keep those staff, proper career paths must be re-

49 Canadian Centre for Management Development, *Programme Review: Lessons Learned and Challenges Ahead*, 1997, Ottawa, esp p 9.

50 MAB-MIAC, 1992, Canberra, p 7.

51 *Op cit*, MAB, fn 22, p 294.

> established, so public service jobs remain attractive and challenging. In short, and perhaps ironically, a contract State is likely to reinvent a permanent, autonomous, career-based and policy-focused core public service, with a commitment to impartial professional advice.[52]

There is a difficulty which contract, of itself, does not overcome. As has been observed, unlike the private sector, one cannot make the working assumption that the desire for revenue will form an adequate basis for the relationship. Contracts across the public sector/civil society divide would need to give more attention to the alignment of ultimate purposes than contracts within a domain, and the level of specification and incentives must be congruent with the motivations of the agent. This is not to say that the prevalence of more explicit contracting within the public management system cannot strengthen the operation of constitutional arrangements. This is a claim not infrequently made about New Zealand.

Management by Objectives (MBO) normally works in a quasi-contractual setting in the public sector and bears many of the hallmarks of more traditional contracting. In particular:

> The limitations to MBO for the public sector are in fact those discovered in the private sector a decade or so ago – that objective setting works well in conditions of predictability and uncertainty, but that in areas of complexity and uncertainty – especially where one wishes to reach out more than one year – hard quantifiable pre-specification is not possible and if attempted has a high potential to produce services which fail to support the desired policy goal. Contracting cannot reduce the unknowability of the future – success in dealing with complexity and uncertainty depends on taking on the characteristics of what management literature calls a learning organisation. Such organisations are characterised by devolved and responsive decision making which tends to be the antithesis of the paradigmatic contract.[53]

All of which leads inevitably to a discussion of learning within organisations – and especially within public organisations.

LEARNING AND PUBLIC ORGANISATIONS

NPM is transforming the way in which government works, according to a range of commentators. Undoubtedly, one of the strains of this new way of working is transparency in the activities of the State. This has been true even of the UK, whose Freedom of Information (FOI) Act 2000 is not only hugely complicated, but ultimately severely disappointing. With an effective FOI regime in place over the years, the phenomenon would clearly have been even

52 Uhr, J, 'Accountability without independent external review?' (1997) 84 Canberra J of Public Administration 11, p 64.

53 *Ibid*, p 11.

more marked. It has been observed, for example, that FOI in New Zealand, introduced prior to the management reforms, 'was instrumental in changing attitudes to the value of information, and in improving the volume and quality of information about government. Decisions at all levels are now based on better information, better budgeting processes and a longer time frame'.[54] As we shall see, high quality information is also exceedingly important in evaluating performance. The report by the Auditor General of Canada in 1995 on the New Zealand reforms was also clear that ministerial accountability had been strengthened by virtue of the extent to which Parliament and the public are better informed. The legislative framework demands a great deal of both financial and non-financial information which buttresses the fading utility of ministerial responsibility.[55] Even so, the sharpened NPM regime operating in New Zealand shows that MR can be made more of a reality than has been the case for some time past.

In similar vein, announcing a government review of utility regulation in the UK, the President of the Board of Trade made it clear that in promoting choice and innovation and improving efficiency, the guiding principle was to be 'transparency'. Meanwhile, back in New Zealand, the Fiscal Responsibility Act requires government to disclose 'the true state of the economy to generally accepted accounting principles on an annual basis' and in the lead-up to a general election, an innovation which the UK Chancellor, Gordon Brown, is reported to be examining seriously. New Zealand is, undoubtedly, currently well ahead of the game. Thus, under their new system of administrative law:

> ... performance information is now treated in the same way as financial information and so performance reports, be they about truancy, prison escapes, welfare services delivered or policy advisory reports proffered, are subject to internal and external audit before going to Parliament.[56]

It goes without saying that more information of itself means little if its quality is not ensured. It will be necessary to return to this theme at a later stage.[57] However, to take an obvious example: there is a need for improved qualitative performance information requiring a strong IT and training investment. There is some evidence that these ideas are being picked up in the UK; certainly as far as the Citizen's Charter programme is concerned. For example, the government recently announced a computer network aimed at sharing ideas, best practice and supporting innovation between Quality Networks, made up of public services staff around the country.[58] Agencies with substantial

54 *Op cit*, SSC, fn 48, p 3.

55 *Op cit*, Auditor General of Canada, fn 16, p 78.

56 *Op cit*, Matheson, fn 20, p 8.

57 See *op cit*, MAB, fn 22, pp 335–59.

58 See Cabinet Office, 'Regional charter networks enter the 21st century', Press Notice No 90/97.

experience agree that 'development of performance information is a long, iterative process'.[59]

It is important that policy makers receive 'competitive' advice; not undermining advice, but advice directed at securing the same objectives, but coming from different parts of the forest. Thus, in New Zealand, for example, although ministers are still responsible for the policies they adopt in turns of desired outcomes and for the outputs they decide to fund, the new arrangements have clarified responsibilities. Having both 'executive' and policy departments or sub-departments with different chief executives assigned different responsibilities, the minister will benefit from increased access to competing sources of advice on the effectiveness of current activities, their options, and the level of sources required. This process is often referred to as 'contestability', a term frequently adopted, too, in the context of competition policy. Both in terms of access to policy advice and delivery of programmes, the availability of alternative sources of advice both from within and outside the public sector is often thought to be compelling. This, in turn, opens up the need for more participative approaches to work, as well as greater consultation with informed publics.[60] All of this will be returned to.

The better information produced by the contracting model is, arguably, changing the way policy is made in New Zealand. The cabinet now adopts a 'strategic management' process based in part on the more coherent processes produced in support of the decision making process. Not long ago, this information would not have been available, but government now defines its three to five year strategic results and these inform the 'key results' of departmental action.[61] These experiments are so far ahead of the field that it will be necessary to return to them at regular intervals.

GOVERNANCE AND CONSULTATION

Consultation has traditionally been seen as a democratic desideratum. It is more than that; it is a pre-requisite for efficient and informed decision making. Too often, consultation has been seen by the powerful as a way of drawing potential opponents into the tent, without any real intention to test the mettle of their own arguments against countervailing positions. UK politics, for the most part, has been a cardinal example of this cast of mind, which is one of the reasons, no doubt, why it has refused to adopt legal obligations of a systematic nature to ensure that arguments are tested against counter-factuals.

59 *Op cit*, MAB, fn 22, p 358.

60 Failure to trawl broadly for alternatives is frequently identified in relation to Environmental Impact Assessments (EIAs); see *op cit*, Davis, fn 3, p 33.

61 *Op cit*, Matheson, fn 20, p 8.

The American Administrative Procedure Act, whatever its weaknesses, is the most robust example of a legal commitment to genuine consultation. This position has been well understood for some time. However, the imperatives of NPM are beginning to bring virtue and necessity together.

Command structures tend to produce poor decisions. Thus, the recent love affairs with markets where signals from consumers can give sound advice to producers about the reception of their products. In the world of politics, commitment to outcomes remains paramount, but the outputs necessary to produce them, to say nothing of the contingent nature of inputs in nudging outputs into place, are by no means mechanically ordained. Consultation is now beginning to be seen as a process of sharing information, of avoiding bottlenecks and of mining sources of innovation. It is increasingly clear that information gathering needs to be both internal within the decision making organisation and outward to consumers and citizens.

As to the former, it is necessary that central agencies adopt a hard position before consultation with other interested parties:[62]

> Consultation requires valid feedback from the people responsible for implementing Service-wide financial, personnel and industrial relations policies. That process should involve line agency agreement on a consultative strategy ensuring early and high quality consultation without central agencies seeking to or being seen to impose their own agenda, and avoiding a disjointed approach. Central agencies can make better use of current fora to present co-ordinated views including to elicit meaningful agency or regional perspectives on the identification of reform needs and development proposals.[63]

The Programme Review exercise in Canada was thought to be effective not least because it involved departmental employees and 'stakeholders' in the departments concerned. Indeed, before the details of the review were considered, support was sought for the programme objectives. In general, the consultation process within government was exemplary; the reservations eventually entered concerned the failure of outreach to the wider community of citizens and client groups:

> As the transformation process continues, it is likely to require even more difficult trade-offs about the role of government and the institutions of government. In this event, it will be important to identify mechanisms and means to solicit external input in order to build support for transformation and to prepare the ground for the difficult decisions that will result.[64]

The UK's shortcomings in this respect are well known, although there are signs of improvement as the imperatives of NPM begin to make their mark. The UK has been singled out for unfavourable comment over its attitude to

62 See, eg, *op cit*, MAB, fn 22, p 485.

63 *Op cit*, MAB, fn 22, p 487.

64 *Op cit*, Ernst and Young, fn 4, p 18.

consultation in environmental matters,[65] but there have been more encouraging signs of late.[66] The Citizen's Charter has always had more rhetoric than reality in its claims to involve citizens in the quality of public services, but even here there appears to have been a change of heart with its imminent relaunch seeming to take on board the need for a more bottom-up approach. The public utilities watchdogs, with OFTEL inevitably in the lead, have also begun to take American-style participation procedures more seriously.[67] On the other hand, the DTI review of utility regulation announced in mid-1997 entitled 'Putting the Consumer First' is an inter-departmental review of the usual Whitehall type, albeit that written submissions have been solicited.[68]

The more advanced practitioners of NPM have seen the future. There is a growing recognition of the need to allow community interests to take the policy initiative and to support devolved decision making with resources and information:

> We need to get closer to community interests to build our knowledge about the constraints on, and effects of, social policy choices.[69]

It is no longer possible, if indeed it ever was, to regard delivering on policy outcomes as a simple mechanical process. It is a dialectic process of checking and re-checking; of feeding new information in periodically and changing direction according to contingency. This requires the best available body of information from whatever source. Consultation must be ongoing, both within the policy machine and also with its external stakeholders.

DELIVERING POLICY OUTCOMES

It is commonly accepted that getting from inputs to outcomes is a highly complex – and very much a learning – experience. However, NPM, concentrating as it has on managerial issues, makes two crucial claims. The first is that efficiency will be improved, and the second is that while managers concentrate on managing, others can concentrate on building sound policies. They are, of course, heavily interrelated and necessitate a major revision of MR and the relationship between politicians and senior civil servants and also, in turn, the relationship of senior civil servants to lower levels of

---

65 See *op cit*, Davis, fn 3.

66 See, especially, DE Press Notice on the revised European Union EIA Directive, 310/Env, July 1997.

67 See Press Notices OFTEL 49/97 and OFWAT ONCC 5/97.

68 DTI Press Notice 97/429.

69 *Op cit*, SSC, fn 48.

management. It is widely accepted that there is a long way to go in securing these new objectives. There is considerable evidence that inputs are used more efficiently than formerly and that there is a greater concentration on agreed outputs than there used to be. This apart, the evidence is extremely mixed.

It is generally agreed that in order to evaluate programme success, rigorous evaluation procedures are required. To take Australia again as an example: from 1987, ministers and their departments were asked to prepare regular evaluation plans. This was followed by the establishment of an Evaluation Task Force to survey evaluation practices. Early experience was that internal evaluation exercises emphasised process and efficiency with too little attention paid to testing programme outcomes, effectiveness and continued relevance.

The purpose of evaluation plans was to assist organisations to anticipate future information requirements at the various stages of a programme's life cycle; to link evaluation priorities and outcomes more closely to the decision making process centrally; to make better use of scarce resources and to refocus current evaluation effort to increase the emphasis on those internal evaluations that seek to relate outcomes, impacts and effectiveness. Outcomes were required to be reported to ministers. The primary focus was upon encouraging agencies to pursue quality evaluations that would be useful for their management and priority-setting purposes and that would result in improving services to the public.[70] There has been some evidence that evaluation has been helpful in clarifying programme objectives as well as evaluating performance against existing objectives. However, the results have been undoubtedly variable.

In the Australian experience, evaluation reports are supposed to be published, though being published and being publicly available are not necessarily the same thing, an experience which is shared in the UK. However, what does seem useful is the example of the Australian International Development Assistance Bureau which produced a 'lessons learnt database' which provided a formal mechanism to incorporate evaluation findings in future project design. Finance, for its part, published a register of published evaluation reports. This is a ready-reference document which brings together brief details of findings which assist in widely disseminating information about evaluation purposes, methods and results. Add this to the requirements for all departments and agencies to produce published annual reports and that they develop managerial information and reporting systems that facilitate monitoring of performance, decision making and accountability and we have the beginnings of a learning system that aims for efficiency and is genuinely open.[71]

70 *Op cit*, MAB, fn 22, esp pp 359–61.

71 *Op cit*, MAB, fn 22, pp 353 and 369–70.

We have already seen that New Zealand demands greater openness in these matters than most countries; and for the most part the requirements are statutory. Outcome statements appear in the Estimates and departmental annual reports; outcomes are typically associated with individual ministers, who are accountable for them. Audited financial statements and consolidated financial statements are required annually under the Public Finance Act 1989. Departmental statements must also contain a report on performance in non-financial terms, through statements of objectives and service performance, which enable a comparison of the outputs produced with the objectives set at the beginning of the year. Departmental financial statements, contained in the annual reports, are extremely detailed.[72]

This leaves open the strategic focus of government decision making. For example, there is some evidence that a concentration on high quality outputs may disguise their lack of linkage with outcomes; there may be more efficiency, but less effectiveness. We shall return to this in a later chapter, but suffice it to say that a more pragmatic or learning approach may be desirable. For example, a focus on key outputs in relation to particularly desirable outcomes may be better than seeking to establish comprehensive linkages among different types of outputs and outcomes.

Evaluation strategies need to concentrate on both the effectiveness of policies adopted and their general acceptance by customers and citizens. This is a complicated dialectical process with information from a range of stakeholders intersecting, informing and altering both choices and strategies. NPM requires systematic enfranchisement of individuals, groups and interests. Policy formation and its monitored utility will be returned to from time to time, but there is ample evidence that present public management techniques are seriously flawed.[73]

> ... because of its neat fit with fiscal pressure and cutting-down-the-bureaucracy to size ... impulse, NPM has become a mixture of comfort-blanket and displacement activity for those who really have very little idea of what to do on the policy front.[74]

We shall leave firm conclusions and proposals until later, but a few problematics should be highlighted. First, evaluations are still more geared to quantitative than to qualitative data; secondly, since most programmes are complex and there are multiple stakeholders, there are divergent views to consider. This is exacerbated when governance produces policy and managerial networks, all of which have their own interests. This is to say nothing of regional and local governments, let alone supra-national entities.

72 See *op cit*, Office of the Auditor General of Canada, fn 16, p 43.

73 See *op cit*, MAB, fn 22, pp 376–77.

74 Hennessy, P, 'The essence of public service' (1997) 85 Canberra Bulletin of Public Administration 3, p 3.

Thirdly, though not exclusively, there is evidence to suggest that public sector employees do not regularly use evaluation information during the course of their job. This suggests that information generated by evaluations is not yet a key element in programme management.[75] More recently, there has been criticism that recommendations are being included without identification of priorities or likely benefits.[76] Evaluation has not been fully assimilated into the management cycle.

CONCLUSION

In general, the move towards governance has made Parliament even more marginal than it was before. However, governance and its changing face represents an opportunity for Parliament to reinvent itself. In New Zealand, where the changes have been largely statutory, public service reforms have enhanced the capacity of Parliament to hold government to account. Greater transparency, one of the successful elements of the reforms, financial statements based on the principles of accrual accounting, and audited statements of non-financial performance have all contributed to this renewal. Naturally, Parliament can never be an effective monitor of regular performance in the expanded public sector, but it should be sufficiently informed to put in train a series of accountability mechanisms which might perform these roles. It could make a start by ensuring that ministers are truly accountable for outcomes. This can only be done by recasting the contractual relationships between ministers and their advisers (public servants or otherwise), making them transparent and encouraging a wide range of stakeholders to engage them in their deliberations.

There is no doubt that managers must hold greater accountability for results than is presently the case. Ministerial responsibility has its place, but it presently obscures the pulses of decision making and cloaks incompetence. Furthermore, it is crucial that relevant and timely performance information and systematic evaluation programmes are made available both for manager, ministers and for Parliament. As an Australian source has put it:

> There are still improvements to be made in the quality of performance information managers and the Government use to make decisions about programs. This information has to be clearly relevant to program objectives, must address how well those objectives are being met from a client's perspective, and should include both quantitative and qualitative measures of effectiveness. Performance information systems should concentrate on recording the outputs and outcomes resulting from the implementation of government programs.

75 *Op cit*, MAB, fn 22, pp 376–78.

76 See (1997) *Canberra Times*, 1 October.

> The systematic evaluation of programs and regular relevant performance information and supporting systems need to be part of the tool kit of every line and program manager.[77]

Experience across the world shows that evaluation is central to the process of continuous learning and each reform must be seen as part of a system of continuous experiment and improvement. With the need to allocate clearer responsibility for results, something akin to contracts is probably necessary; at least, published information about responsibilities and the performance of those responsibilities is a necessity. This would represent the beginnings of a solution; no more. For example, it is clear that governance requires something in the nature of contractual relationships across the public sector/civil society divide, and, as has been seen, outcomes and purposes need greater attention than concentrating everything on specification performance. However, opportunities as well as hurdles lie ahead. In New Zealand, for example, the better information produced by the contracting model is beginning to change the way policy is made:

> Our current Cabinet now goes through a 'strategic management' process based at least in part, of [sic] the more coherent information our new contracting processes produce in support of the decision making process. Even five years ago this would have been unthinkable because of the unavailability of suitable information. Government now defines its three to five year desired 'strategic results' and these inform the contracted 'key results' of chief executives and thus departmental action.[78]

It is clear that public law values of openness and accountability are capable of contributing to the efficiency engendered by NPM. Although the general success of public management reform is widely accepted, the accompanying transparency and the sharing of experience has also given greater prominence to failings within the public service. This is associated with the phenomenon that no single actor, public or private, has the knowledge or information required to solve complex problems. Openness, sharing, recognised pulses of responsibility can, taken together, produce measurable advantages. The problem, so far unresolved, is how to structure optimum institutions within extenuated networks which render an effective account and encourage innovation and efficiency.

Those who take serious interest in these matters recognise that we are still seeking the appropriate balance between autonomy and accountability – something not susceptible to simple-minded blueprints. Once there is a move away from central prescription of official conduct, the ethic of accountability

77 *Op cit*, MAB-MIAC, fn 2, paras 3.2.3 and 3.2.4.

78 *Op cit*, MAB-MIAC, fn 2, p 8.

becomes more, rather than less important.[79] Something which has not yet been sufficiently stressed also needs to be brought into the equation. This is the issue of contracting between government and 'civil society'. There is increasing contracting with not-for-profit organisations, but we have not always paid sufficient attention to the fundamentally different cultures and purposes of government and voluntary bodies. It will not do to regard the relationship inevitably and simply as that of principal and agent. Areas of common concern and areas of genuine difference (including the need to bargain out differences) need to be given adequate attention.

The challenge is formidable. Engaging a broad range of actors, synchronising them towards desired objectives and policy outcomes, while allowing them relative autonomy and encouraging experiment is a fearsome proposition even without the global dimension. Ensuring that public values and overall legitimacy also prevail across a range of actors, private, voluntary, hybrid and unclassifiable is also a full time job for someone; for some public cadre. But the agenda is beginning to take shape.

One caveat is that new arrangements need to concentrate less on 'control' and more on accountability, always accepting, of course, that the latter goes hand in hand with helping government to carry out its objectives with increased efficiency. The search is for the optimum group of practices and institutional change that accompany this process. This is where old values and new challenges must learn to mesh.

A final few items need to be flagged up. The first relates to public service values. As there is a move away from central prescription of official conduct, public services ethics, including accountability, need to be re-examined and reinforced.[80] For all the changes being worked, the values remain more or less constant and need to be reasserted in new settings. A contract State places great financial responsibilities on the surviving policy core. Since they must handle large contracts to deliver government services, regular probity checks and transparent processes become essential. To prevent political interference or corruption, the policy core must have some measure of autonomy to act impartially as major public services are contracted out.

These matters are intimately connected to the ultimate nature of the public sphere. With so many functions off-loaded one way or another, there is a danger that we shall come to believe that government itself can be contracted out. In other words, we have to face up to the nature of the irreducible public sphere, a matter taken up further in Chapter 6. Although it will be necessary to return to this theme, it seems vital that some independent standing machinery is established to safeguard thinking in this area, since the day to

79 See *op cit*, Uhr, fn 52, p 60.

80 See *op cit*, OECD, fn 9, pp 21, 23, 34.

day pressures of politics may well cause the wood to be lost sight of in the process of chopping down the trees. Someone, for example, must take responsibility for the long term leadership of the State sector – for maintaining and enhancing the capabilities of the sector to meet the outcome objectives of current and future governments. Other issues which immediately spring to mind are responsibility for the system of government, for constitutional and legal matters, the machinery of government, strategic management, and so on.[81]

Finally, it is necessary to refer to political devolution. Governance is about off-loading, about partnerships, about strategic vision which allows the more knowledgeable to act. Whether we are speaking the language of subsidiarity or underlining the failings of command economies, it is now widely accepted that a marketisation of governmental structures has much to commend it. Unfortunately, in the UK, this has not been manifested in terms of political structures. With new assemblies in Scotland and Wales, a measure of devolution for London and a recognition that at least some form of regional structure is vital to socio-economic generation, the old wisdom about centralised politics is in decay. We shall need to produce institutional responses to the new state of affairs to ensure that transparency, fairness and enfranchisement accompany the process.

So far, inevitably, the issue of governance has been spoken to in general terms. From now on, it will be necessary to be more specific. Although NPM has already figured prominently, it needs more special attention on account of its centrality to the way government is compelled to operate in the new environment.

81 See, eg, State Services Commission, *Briefing Papers for the Minister of State Services*, December 1996, Wellington, p 25.

CHAPTER 3

NEW PUBLIC MANAGEMENT: A WORLD VIEW

The phenomenon of governance has been outlined and its various strands unpicked. One of those strands, to which little attention has so far been paid, is the reform of the public service. Since the complexity of delivering public services has increased, old-style bureaucratic management abated in favour of results-based, strategic management. This New Public Management (NPM) has been a necessary response to the changing roles of government. In consequence, a little attention must be paid to it here, although an enormous literature on the subject has been spawned and should be addressed by those wishing to know more.[1] At the outset, the UK experience will be the main concern, although later, some reference to comparative developments will be outlined.

Public service reform in the UK, as elsewhere, has been heavily influenced by managerial changes in the private sector. The emphasis has been on cost consciousness, better value for money, 'downsizing' and 'delayering', decentralisation and devolution, and a greater concentration on core business outputs and, to a lesser extent, outcomes. A key thrust has been delegation of authority from the Treasury and Cabinet Office to departments, from departments to accountable units such as agencies, and from personnel units and senior managers to line managers:[2]

> The most visible changes are the reduction in size of the service by over a third since 1976, improved resource management with more devolved to line managers, the setting up of executive agencies within departments (as part of the so called 'Next Steps' reforms), the launch of the Citizen's Charter initiative, with its emphasis on customer care, the opening of Government work to competition and the increase in private sector involvement in the provision of services. There has also recently been an increased emphasis on openness, and contact and communication with other sectors, and on setting a framework for the future for more devolved, focused and effective Government administration.[3]

The trigger for the first round of the reforms is usually agreed to be the Financial Management Initiative (FMI) in 1982. The aim was to improve management in the Civil Service by ensuring that all managers knew what their objectives were and how their achievements would be assessed; they were given well defined responsibilities for making the best use of their

1 See, eg, 'The New Public Management' (1991) Public Admin 69 (special issue).

2 See Cabinet Office, *Finding Your Way Round Whitehall and Beyond*, March 1997, Cabinet Office.

3 *Ibid*, Chapter 4; the main staging posts are listed on p 12.

resources; and the necessary information, training and advice to exercise their responsibilities effectively.

Managers were to be given much greater responsibility for managing their own budgets. Output was to be more carefully measured wherever possible, and cost-effectiveness of their work considered. As these reforms bedded in – and the reforms have been developed over a number of years – civil servants became more accountable for their work. Each department works within a limit for its total running costs.

As we shall see, these reforms have been broadened and deepened, but one point must be made at the outset. Management reality has altered, but, for the most part, accountability mechanisms have not. Remarkably, ministerial responsibility, threadbare at the best of times,[4] remains the central constitutional guarantee of responsible conduct for the citizen in this altered state. The responsibility of individual civil servants is proclaimed in graphic terms, while the convention of ministerial responsibility prevents Parliament from calling them to account.[5] As Sir Richard Scott makes clear,[6] the only effective way of finding out what happened in government is to ask the person directly responsible. That, incredibly, is just what we cannot do. This issue will be re-examined in Chapter 9.

NEXT STEPS (NS)

NS was launched in 1988 by identifying coherent areas of departmental work which could be grouped together into one operational unit under a single official who is accountable directly to the minister for delivering specific objectives, results and services. This initiative, which created quasi-autonomous executive agencies, has brought about major changes in the management structure and culture of the Civil Service. The following are central to this development:

- The application of the former 'prior options' exercise, as outlined in Chapter 1. Essentially this means that an agency is normally established only if the activities concerned cannot be abolished, privatised or contracted out.
- Central departments should concentrate on strategic management, which ought, if consistently followed, to have major implications for the policy process, including its evaluation.

4 See Chapter 1, fn 34.

5 See Lewis, ND, 'A Civil Service Act for the United Kingdom' [1988] Public Law 463, pp 463–88.

6 *Report of the Inquiry into the Export of Defence Equipment to Iraq*, HC 115, 1996 (the Scott Report).

- Appointing a Chief Executive (CE) to head up the agency. The best person to be appointed, either from within the Civil Service or outside.
- Encouraging the widest range of managerial freedoms and incentives and the delegation of operations to local management whenever possible.
- Setting up the agencies through 'framework documents', which although having no direct legal effect, may be seen as 'mini-constitutions'. The document sets out the aims and objectives for the agency, its anticipated outputs and outcomes in terms of quantity and quality, alongside explicit performance indicators.

The main thrust of the policy is that the agencies exercise day to day responsibility for providing goods and services under the direction of the CE, albeit within a framework whereby ministers impose clear targets, resource limits and the outputs to be achieved. The agencies are set financial and quality of service targets and possess the managerial freedoms necessary for their accomplishment. They publish an annual report and statement of account along commercial lines, which set out their achievements for the year against the published targets. An update of NPM was expected at the time of writing. It is seemingly aimed at moving targets:

> The preparations for the [forthcoming] White Paper are focused on Government from the user's point of view, seeking in particular to ensure that functions and services are designed to respond to and match more closely the needs of the user and the person affected, rather than the provider. Initiatives such as the re-launch of the Citizen's Charter, Access Business (on better regulation) and development and use of new technology should make it easier for citizens and business to access government and public services, by fitting them more closely to the way people live their life. In some cases, this will mean moving to more seamless delivery of government functions and services, or developing packages of services that people, such as the elderly and those caring for them, need at particular times, or that make sense in terms of life events or business events. The aim should be to organise work across several agencies so that everything the customer needs to do is, as far as possible, done through one contact point rather than needing to visit a succession of offices.
>
> Civil servants have a key role to play in bringing about these changes, particularly by working across organisational boundaries and working in co-operation with other public servants. They will need to develop new skills and working methods, to co-ordinate delivery of services across departments and provide services which are more responsive to users.[7]

One way in which NPM has been updated to embrace a number of the themes already outlined has been promoted by the Charter Unit[8] of the Cabinet Office; specifically, it is working on a project to provide better government for older people by bringing together the large number of agencies (central

7 *Op cit*, Cabinet Office, fn 2, p 14.

8 Since renamed the Service First Unit.

government, local authorities and voluntary agencies) that currently deal with and provide information about issues affecting older people.

Putting customers at the heart of public services is an expanding part of NPM across the globe. In the early 1990s, for example, the President of the US issued an Executive Order directing all agencies to develop a comprehensive programme of customer surveys, standard setting and benchmarking to enable government to deliver service 'equal to the best in the business'.[9] In Spain, in 1995, government created a 'negotiating table with the citizens' in which representatives of the consumer and user association participate with the Ministry for Public Administration in the discussion and assessment of the quality of public services.[10]

In the UK, of course, sub-national governments are not yet deeply embedded, and yet there are clear moves towards a versions of NPM at the lower levels. In Germany, on the other hand, where sub-national and regional governments are well established, the move to NSM (the so called 'new steering model') is almost a decade old. Most of the characteristics of NPM are to be found in these reforms.[11] Nearer to home, in the Republic of Ireland, there has been a recent review of systems for making decisions, allocating responsibility and assuring to the persons actually delivering the service, thereby delivering another blow to the fading convention of ministerial responsibility.[12] Indeed, similar developments are traced by the OECD amongst all its member countries, not forgetting to underline the notion of greater contestability and market competition within and for the public service.[13]

All of this leads, ineluctably, into budgetary processes and planning. For example, the 1995 Australian annual report to the President of the Treasury Board, *Strengthening Government Review,* underlines the importance of a management culture that is facts-based, results-oriented, open and accountable. In particular, performance measurement and review have been integrated into the new Expenditure Management System, policy development and programme delivery.[14]

9 OECD, *Issues and Developments in Public Management,* Survey 1996–97 on the US, PUMA, p 2.

10 *Ibid,* Survey on Spain, p 2.

11 *Ibid,* Survey on Germany, p 2.

12 Republic of Ireland Government, *Delivering Better Government,* 2nd Report of the Co-ordinating Group of Secretaries: A Programme of Change for the Irish Civil Service, 1996, Government of Ireland.

13 See, generally, OECD, *In Search of Results: Performance Management Practices,* 1997, PUMA.

14 *Ibid,* p 45.

BUDGETS, PLANNING, PERFORMANCE INFORMATION AND EVALUATION

NPM, as outlined here, has, in most OECD countries, been accompanied by more effective multi-year budgeting systems. However, as we shall see, this has too often reflected concerns over holding down total spending rather than developing long term investment strategies. Two of the countries which have attempted to overcome this short-sightedness have been Canada, with its Performance Review Programme, and Finland, which has regularly reviewed the implementation of management and budgeting by results. It is important to note, too, that in some countries Courts of Audit have a central role in these processes. Without wishing to dwell overlong on international comparisons, it is worth pointing out that some countries manage this budgetary planning process in a more inclusive and accountable fashion than others. The Swedish example is instructive.

A Framework Budget Model for handling budget proposals in the Riksdag has been introduced. The Parliament will first decide on the overall level of spending and then determine its distribution among various purposes. A decision has been taken that the government's budget proposals should come within a set expenditure ceiling for the public sector. This expenditure ceiling is defined in nominal terms, spans three years, and covers the entire public sector. For the State sector, it is divided into spending areas. As far as the municipalities are concerned, the expenditure ceiling rests on an agreement between the government and the municipal sector.

For some time, all the agencies[15] have been providing annual and interim reports, alongside monthly and quarterly monitoring of expenditure in real terms against the national budget. The annual reports include both performance reports and financial statements. The entire annual report is audited by the National Audit Office and an annual report for the State is submitted to the Riksdag annually. It is important to note that these changes have been accompanied by new budget laws and ordinances, as well as more informally adopted information mechanisms.[16] This reflects part of a more general movement to improve the strategic oversight by politicians over the business of government. The focus has been generally on financial management and budget cycles, on utilising some of the information now becoming available to review existing programmes critically, to identify the real costs of policies and programmes, on prioritising in a context of allowing medium term planning to occur.

These developments, however, raise the question of whether the public sector workforce needs long term reform. The widespread budgetary

15 It will be recalled that most Swedish government is managed through agencies.

16 See *op cit*, OECD, fn 9, Survey on Sweden and *op cit*, OECD, fn 13, Swedish Report.

stringency means that downsizing is commonplace. This requires not only critically examining the activities of the public sector, but also increasing productivity. Moreover, new skills and attitudes are needed to understand and react to issues raised by globalisation, technology and social adjustment. The consequent need for administrative structures to change will be addressed more fully in the concluding chapters. Even so, it is worth flagging up the fact that none of the changes being spoken to here can occur without more performance information, which is where issues of management efficiency meet the wider concerns of social democracy. The substance of planning exercises, for example, will need to be widely communicated within departments to check for fit, to adapt to suggestions for improvement and the like, whereas performance information is increasingly being required to be reported by all departments and agencies, usually in annual reports to Parliament.

Yet, none of this will mean a great deal unless it is subject to a rigorous process of review and evaluation, which again will place increasingly sophisticated demands on public management. It will be necessary to turn to this issue briefly, although it is addressed more extensively in later chapters. An overview of overseas experience will also be presented:

> It takes time to develop a performance measurement system and to integrate it into a management system ... The difficulty of the process reinforces the need for a permanent audit, review or evaluation of these systems by executive as well as legislative bodies. Indeed, review evaluation and audit of performance measurement systems normally improve their functioning.
>
> Audit of performance-related data and information is an essential step in the production of useful performance information. These audits are also an integral part of substantive performance audits, reviews and evaluations. Moreover, auditing can be applied to various stages of performance measurement. There may be a focus on performance information such as the choice of measures ... the standards and criteria for judgement, the interpretation and explanation of results ...[17]

The OECD then goes on to highlight the variety of approaches adopted in the various member countries. As for the UK, it refers to the role of the NAO, the NS Review and the Audit Commission, while underlining some of the limitations of the current system.

Issues of accountability and control may have an impact on the use and content of performance audits. For example, the use of market-type mechanisms – market-testing, contracting out, vouchers, etc – can influence accountability mechanisms such as audits. Performance audits are thought to be inappropriate for market mechanisms, and there can be argument as to how far NPM techniques stretching into the private sector are market as

17 *Op cit*, OECD, fn 13, p 19.

opposed to bureaucracy. If they are the latter, or indeed hybrid, then it can be asserted that inspection and contract control are all that are needed. In any event, democratic as well as organisational democracy needs to be jealously guarded.

The OECD survey discussed the relation between internal and external audits. There is little justification for monopoly internal audits and the UK, inter alia, mixes the two. One question to be posed, however, is whether the direction performance focus of the audits is converging or diverging. Both external and internal audit reviews are important in performance management, and external audits require well developed internal audits. Yet, if they develop in different directions, difficulties will arise.

Among NPM developments in some OECD countries is the move to performance budgets, or results budgeting. Indeed, in some countries, the running costs of all agencies have been allocated according to the results-budgeting system. However, in most countries, performance information does not directly affect the budget, although it may affect elements such as individual group pay levels and may influence flexibility in finance and personnel matters. In short, it can be said that performance information is being sought more and more widely – though, for the most part, in relation to outputs. Sophisticated evaluation of the relation between outputs and outcomes is rare and underdeveloped. This theme will be returned to from time to time. In the meantime, one or two examples of advanced NPM practices from around the world may be useful.

COMPARATIVE LESSONS

New Zealand represents a good place to begin, although little in the way of critical analysis is attempted at this stage. The major thrust of the reforms is well known and will not be repeated here. However, an independent review has recently concentrated on three major issues: strategic capacity, the resource base and accountability. Only the first and the last will be touched upon here.

As to the first, it found that the introduction of Strategic Results Areas (SRAs) and Key Results Areas (KRAs) has improved the government's strategic focus, although it is still too geared to short term outputs. This needs a little explanation. The starting point is a statement of the government's policy strategy for achieving a limited number of goals. This statement, which is essentially a political document, has been used in an endeavour to create a common vision for the country as a whole. On the basis of this vision statement, the government agrees a series of medium term goals for nine SRAs. These, in turn, have been used to encourage co-ordination between related groups of programmes and departments, and to inform the annual budget review of taxing and spending priorities. The SRAs also provide the framework from which more specific milestones – the KRAs – are derived. These then act as benchmarks against which departmental performance can be assessed. Thus, the system is intended to improve both the vertical integration between the political and managerial spheres and the horizontal integration and alignment across sectors, including the opening up and broadening of the policy process.

Accountability, according to the Report, has been the most successful aspect of the New Zealand management framework and, in particular, has been successful in 'making managers manage'. Accountability has not been an afterthought in New Zealand, as it has been in some other countries which have implemented reform. Instead, it has been robustly designed as an integral feature of the reformed public service. On the other hand, there is a suggestion that results-based accountability might have underplayed public values and concepts of service. It is regarded as vital that the government continues to exercise control and self-restraint and be fully accountable for its actions. The primary vehicle for this is the Fiscal Responsibility Act. This does not set any specific numerical targets, but does require governments to keep the public regularly informed about the true state of public finances, the government's medium term fiscal objectives, how they are to be attained and the key risks involved. What this means is that a government would be in serious trouble if it stepped outside the zone of acceptable fiscal conduct and, in effect, if it were seen no longer to 'own' fiscal policy.[18] Indeed, if one criticism of New Zealand figures more prominently than others, it is that the purchase role has dominated to the detriment of the 'ownership' role; that is, politics need to be re-asserted – the commitment to values whose impact can be effectively assessed.

The Republic of Ireland has been greatly influenced by the New Zealand experiments. The co-ordinating group which produced the 1996 Report recommend the adoption of SRAs as key priority areas of government activity and the means of implementing them. They should identify the key priority areas for government as a whole – for example, poverty, crime, long term unemployment and competitiveness, and specify attendant outcomes over given time-frames. One of the major benefits was seen to be to focus the attention of departments on their individual and joint contributions to achieving these pan-government objectives.

The individual departmental statements of strategy could then be placed in the context of a framework of SRAs, setting out their contribution to the achievement of government objectives. In particular, they set out how individual departments aim to achieve their SRA objectives. A key element in this process is the measurement of performance, so that progress in achieving

18 See Shick, A, *The Spirit of Reform: Managing the New Zealand State Sector in a Time of Change*, Report for the Treasury, 1996, Wellington State Services Commission.

the stated goals and objectives of the government programme can be monitored effectively. This process is believed to make for better quality policy formulation and decision making, and should ensure that work is prioritised and that programmes which no longer contribute to the achievement of goals can be wound down to allow higher priority work to be undertaken. There will be a significant degree of attention turned to cross-departmental issues.[19]

Finally, Australia. Like New Zealand, Australia has paid serious attention to management reform for well over a decade. Evaluation has been central to this process and has included the establishment of an Evaluation Task Force. Generally, it is fair to say that its primary finding was that evaluation was then still at an evolutionary stage.[20] The Task Force encouraged self-evaluation with a duty to report back and, in particular, to link evaluation priorities and outcomes more closely to the decision making process centrally and at the agency level. It is important to note that the Portfolio Evaluation Plans (PEPs) will normally be published.[21] This is very closely linked to the fact that progress was seen to be linked to the development of good performance information and management information systems and reporting requirements. Again, transparency and openness are seen to be as crucial for managerial purposes as they are for the general health of democracy. Even so, there was also the recognition that evaluation needed to take different forms in different contexts; for example, where some agencies are driven essentially by customer requirements and market pressures, then a central conceptual model for evaluation was less than helpful. Yet, even here, there was no hostility to evaluation or for the need for 'sufficient knowledge' to provide management with sufficient information to monitor and to improve performance. The overall finding was that improved evaluation procedures greatly enhanced accountability.

Other major findings include: a number of agencies believe that evaluation strategies have helped to focus staff on outcomes; evaluation has been incorporated into the culture and rhetoric of Australian Public Service management; that it is important that the various elements in the management cycle be linked and not treated independently – corporate plans, programme budgets, implementation strategies and monitoring and evaluation are all part of a seamless process.[22]

---

19 *Op cit*, Republic of Ireland Government, fn 12, Pt 1.

20 See Management Advisory Board, *The Australian Public Service Reformed*, 1992, Task Force on Management Improvement.

21 Some agencies go so far as to publish a 'lessons learned database' to provide a formal mechanism to incorporate relevant evaluation findings in future project design. See *ibid*, p 369.

22 The Corporate Plan was seen especially as a linking document which provides a statement of values and refers to the range of other planning documents: p 380.

These attitudes to NPM smack more than a little of JS Mill's 'experiments in living' and his espousal of free speech. Experiment and self-discovery are suddenly the buzzwords of NPM, of which New Zealand (and perhaps Ireland) are the leading examples. They seem to understand that not only is maximum transparency necessary for efficient and effective policy choice and performance, and that involved publics increase the range of information available, but that public management techniques need to take account of the long term difficulties of long term central planning. Thus:

> The distinguishing features of SRAs and KRAs are their selectivity and flexibility. For all the reasons that doom long term central planning, particularly the complexity and uncertainty of the future, it is not possible to come up with a complete set of higher level strategic objectives, finely specified. The best we can do is pick out a few objectives, which given our understanding of the systems in which they are embedded, are most likely to exert the desired leverage on those systems.[23]

As will be argued later, these are experiments to take on board in the course of the stakeholder debate. The UK recognises most of these problems, but its NPM is not as comprehensively reformed as some others, which is a little disturbing given how much more of public activities have been contracted out than in comparable jurisdictions. We are beginning to see special, cross-departmental units, and the Appraising Options has some of the characteristics of both the New Zealand, Irish and Canadian experience, but the approach is not yet sufficiently systemic, open or subject to legal codes which can act as yardsticks against which fully informed judgments can be made.

For the sake of completeness, it should be added that other OECD countries are adopting or have adopted many of the components of NPM as it has been described. NS-type agencies, performance management, regulatory reform, the modernisation of human resource management and delegation and responsibility centres all figure prominently.[24]

NPM AND PUBLIC SECTOR EMPLOYMENT

These changes will, of necessity, have enormous impacts on the nature of the public service: the move to managerialism, bringing in outsiders often unfamiliar both with public sector canons of accountability and with the intricacies of public service ethics, the move to managing contracts, greater personal responsibility with new relations to intra-departmental

23 State Services Commission, *Strategic Management in Government: Extending the Reform Model in New Zealand*, 1996, Wellington State Services Commission, p 10.

24 See, *op cit*, OECD, fn 9, Surveys on the Netherlands, France and Sweden.

accountability, etc. In the UK, the government has responded to this in a number of ways.

During the mid and late 1990s, the British Government sought to consolidate the changes brought about by NPM. This took various forms: a delegation of further management flexibility as the key to improved performance; the continued exploitation of competition through the privatisation and Competing for Quality (CFQ) programmes, but with less detailed central oversight; delegation of responsibility for pay and grading below senior levels as from April 1996. Added to this was the creation of the 'Senior Civil Service', which includes all agency CEs and others with substantial management and policy responsibilities. Members of the Service now have explicit, written employment contracts. Alongside this has been the introduction of a new Civil Service Code with an independent line of appeal to the Civil Service Commissioners. Formally, the Government expressed an open mind about giving statutory authority to civil service values. The Blair Government was committed, on coming to office, to legislate in this area, but currently shows no signs of enthusiasm. The manifesto commitment to a Freedom of Information (FOI) Act has been honoured in the letter, if not exactly the spirit.[25] What it is likely to do, however, because of its controversial nature, is to put the judiciary centre stage in this area.

CFQ remains strongly on course and this is, no doubt, as it should be. However, it is clear that important questions of transparency and accountability remain in this area,[26] a fact which has partly been recognised by the new Government. Thus, the Prior Options exercise is being replaced by the Appraising Options scheme, which shows early signs of recognising some of the democratic deficit which has been pointed up. However, these are still early days and much depends upon the culture of Whitehall being changed without the nudge of legislation.

Most OECD countries have responded to change by amending public service legislation, or at least amending codes and agreements. Sweden is typical in recasting general terms of employment to allow scope for modernisation, adjustment to local business conditions, less detailed regulations and simplification. Like many other countries, it provides for single agencies to determine their own level of pay rises and scope for pay distribution.

Germany recently amended its federal civil servant law. The cornerstones of the law include improvement of evaluation schemes, more flexible career paths, modernisation of remuneration regulations, limited, probationary, contract periods and an insistence on ongoing training and education. The

---

25 See Cabinet Office, *The Civil Service: Continuity and Change*, Cm 2627, 1994, HMSO and *Taking Forward Continuity and Change*, Cm 2748, 1995, HMSO.

26 See, esp, Goh, J and Lewis, ND, *The Private World of Government (occasional papers)*, 1998, Centre for Socio-Legal Studies, University of Sheffield.

promotion of managerial skills for senior civil servants, encouraging a consumer-oriented environment, and developing skills for working in an international environment have also all had high visibility in member countries. Added to this, the issue of public service ethics is so important that the OECD has made a special study of the problems which governance presents.

NPM AND THE POLICY PROCESS

Part of the *raison d'être* of NPM is the separating out of managerial and policy functions. This will be addressed more fully in Chapter 5, but some brief mention must be made of the issue at this point.

If responsibility for delivering public services is pushed down the managerial scale to the appropriate level, then it ought to follow that the Periclean few remaining on the Athenian slopes ought to be freer to concentrate on the policy process; and, indeed, more effective at it. However, most commentators feel that less progress has been made on this front than at the service-delivery level where considerable efficiency savings have been claimed. If improved services are to be provided by the market, or in a market-mimicked fashion, then a considerable burden can be seen to be placed on the framers or makers of policy. This is the old computer saw; 'junk in, junk out'. If inputs into the policy process are not of the highest quality, then severe policy failures are likely to result.

If NS and NPM are directed substantially to the business of delegating managerial powers to managers, then the objectives set out for them should be clear and ringing. They should also be intended to achieve clear objectives. As it is, there is often confusion between responsibility for inputs, outputs and outcomes; between what resources might require what measures to achieve what results. This is where the Citizen's Charter comes back in. Nothing could be clearer than that if yardsticks for service satisfaction are to be established and, say, compensation for breach available, prior questions relating to outcomes and resources must be posed. There is no doubt that separating out provider from purchaser, policy maker from management can produce very real advantages. Indeed the 'Contracting State' might indeed be an appropriate metaphor for the separation of powers in a changing world; but not if ministerial responsibility, which ordinarily conceals real responsibility, remains as the primary mechanism for democratic accountability. This will be a constant and recurring theme.

Policy making and evaluation is extremely difficult and by no means an exact science, but progress has been made in a number of countries, not least New Zealand, as we have seen, and the feeling is that much more needs to be done than is so far in prospect. A number of suggestions for change have been made,[27] including the idea of extending NS-type agencies into the policy process. As the previous Major Government stated:

> ... it [the Government] agrees that they [the NS principles] can, as recommended by the Select Committee, be extended to aspects of the policy process in core departments. In carrying out reviews of their senior organisation and staffing, departments will be looking for structures which reflect these principles.[28]

Not only have these ideas not so far been taken up by Government, but one of the most glaring deficiencies of the FOI Act 2000 is the effective exclusion of policy advice. There are ways in which matters might be improved by altered administrative practices and record keeping. We shall pursue this issue later. However, policy advice will, for the foreseeable future, remain hidden and sacrosanct, a matter which unfortunately seems to suit both ministers and their advisers. This way, nobody carries the can for failure. That this makes a nonsense of evaluating the policy process, as is now freely admitted in New Zealand, appears to carry no weight. As long as this attitude is maintained, then NPM will remain restricted to service delivery and will not grow as it needs to.

This is doubly regrettable given what has been said about complexity and globalisation. For example, governments are becoming subject to increasingly divergent policy tensions, often epitomised in the conflicting, sectoral interests of line ministries, which vie with each other for financial resources, while the budget ministry characteristically seeks to control outlays. In some countries, a degree of policy competition is deliberately maintained between line ministries, in order to ensure a level of creative tension, and to enhance the contestability of policy advice.

GOVERNANCE AND ETHICS[29]

The OECD recognises that a changing public management environment places potential strain on governing codes of public ethics. To this end, it has recently conducted a study of how nine member countries have addressed the issue and, in April 1998, it adopted a set of principles and recommendations that ought to be taken up if ethical conduct in the public sector is to be assured.

First, the changed managerial environment. Public servants are subject to greater public scrutiny and increased demand from citizens, yet they are also facing stricter limits on resources. They are having to assume new functions

27 See Lewis, ND, *How to Reinvent British Government*, 1993, European Policy Forum.

28 *Op cit*, Cabinet Office (1995), fn 25, para 3.14.

29 For the position in the UK, see *op cit*, Lewis, fn 5.

and responsibilities as a result of devolution and greater managerial discretion, the increased commercialisation of the public sector, a changing public/private interface, etc. While public management reforms have realised important returns in terms of efficiency and effectiveness, some of the adjustments may have had unintended consequences on ethics and standards of conduct. The nine countries, including the UK, reported considerable changes in ethics-related initiatives over the previous five year period.[30] The need to link ethics management to overall public management is becoming widely recognised.

The clearest finding was that reducing rules and controls (at the heart of NPM) allowed more opportunities for mistakes and impropriety. But, too many rules and controls may grind government to a halt; public servants will respond by avoiding risks and taking initiatives for fear of some degree of perceived impropriety. Conscious of this, the OECD adopted a set of principles which sought to strike a balance.

They began with a classic statement of the cornerstones of NPM. It involves greater devolution of responsibility, budgetary pressures and new forms of delivery of public services which have challenged traditional values in the public service. Globalisation and the further development of international economic relations, including trade and investment, demand high recognisable standards of conduct in the public service. Preventing misconduct is as complex as the phenomenon of the misconduct itself and a range of integrated mechanisms is needed as a response.

Twelve principles for improving ethical conduct were laid down, of which only a few, especially relevant to the arguments being advanced here, will be developed. Of particular significance is that 'ethical standards should be reflected in the legal framework'. Laws and regulations should state the fundamental values of public service and should provide the framework for guidance, investigation, disciplinary action and prosecution.

The second principle selected is that the decision making process should be transparent and open to scrutiny. Public scrutiny should be facilitated by transparent and democratic processes, oversight by the legislature and access to public information.

Thirdly, there should be clear guidelines for interaction between the public and the private sectors. This is particularly important in relation to public procurement, outsourcing or public employment conditions. More attention should be placed on public service values and requiring external partners to respect those same values.

Fourthly, public service employment conditions, such as career prospects, personal development, salary structure, etc, should create an atmosphere conducive to ethical behaviour. Using basic principles, such as merit,

30 OECD, *Ethics in the Public Service: Current Issues and Practice*, 1996, PUMA.

consistently in the daily process of recruitment and promotion helps operational integrity in the public service.

Fifthly, adequate accountability mechanisms should be in place within the public service. Accountability should focus on compliance with rules and ethical principles and on achievement of results. Mechanisms can be internal to an agency, government-wide, or can be provided by civil society.

Finally, appropriate procedures and sanctions should exist to deal with misconduct. Mechanisms for the detection and independent investigation of wrongdoing are necessary parts of an ethics infrastructure. These should include procedures for monitoring, reporting and investigating breaches of public service rules as well as sanctions to discourage misconduct.[31]

As well as the need to establish institutional structures to deal with the challenges affecting public sector management, the sheer complexity of many of the tasks requires a sensitivity in carrying officials with government in responding to the changes. There is a clear need to encourage public servants to understand why changes need to be made and to engage them in participating in the processes of change.[32]

NPM AND GLOBALISATION

The greys and the pinks of globalisation have been touched upon. However, it is having a considerable impact on the tasks and skills of public management.

Leaving aside for the moment the international aspects of the changes, globalisation has, as has been seen, implications for the internal balance of power in the advanced countries. It has altered the role of sub-national government, of pressure groups and even of civil society itself. Pulling together some version of the public interest, whether mediated or bargained or not, requires considerable managerial delicacy and knowledge of a kind which has not always been at the disposal of the public servant working at the national level. Communication skills, in particular, need to be finely honed if new ways of locking layers of politics together are to be found.

Moreover, citizens can use information about what neighbouring governments are or are not doing, in order to challenge or pressure their own governments. Globalisation allows groups, especially, to organise themselves

31 OECD, *Improving Ethical Conduct in the Public Service: Recommendation of the OECD Council*, 1997, PUMA. Note the international anti-corruption agreements summarised there, not least the Convention on Combating Bribery of Foreign Public Officials in International Business Transactions, 17 December 1997.

32 To some extent, an improvement has been affected by the establishment of the Committee on Standards of Public Life. Important work has been done by this Committee, but neither its remit nor composition is adequate to deal with all the issues raised here.

quickly and more effectively across national boundaries and can, accordingly, influence a policy debate in several countries at the same time. There is no doubt that this can be advantageous, can have the effect of re-democratising politics, but not only can it have the effect of complicating the policy process dramatically, it also re-asserts the concept of capture from an unexpected source. This places enormous cognitive pressures on both politicians and public servants, quite apart from anything else. The deft touch required to mediate and vindicate some version of the national interest will be even more difficult to achieve. And, assuming that central government has been able to assert priority policy goals, the difficulty of assuring their primacy or even their importance is going to be increasingly difficult to achieve.

The more obvious challenge of globalisation for NPM, however, is that policy processes are being driven on to the international level with increasing frequency, even disregarding the increasing autonomy of the European Union in the UK's affairs. Not only does public management have to sew in domestic partners to the international presentation of the nation's preferred position, but it is extremely likely that Parliament will wish to establish greater oversight of the international activities of their governments. One strand of the problematic has been well stated recently:

> ... countries must invest more in building effective and legitimate international organisations that are capable of delivering results, while maintaining democratic values. A range of procedures are [*sic*] needed, including: new negotiation, mediation, and dispute resolution; mechanisms for building trust and mutual confidence between countries; and assessment and revision processes. Building international institutions that are fair and well respected poses a challenge to all parties involved in international policy making.[33]

It is not just the building of institutions and procedures that requires the most delicate of managerial skills, but also the servicing of those institutions and procedures. The OECD has described various approaches for re-examining roles which impact on both NPM and the institutional side of politics – or the machinery of government. They include special policy reviews, more comprehensive processes to review roles, budgetary or service quality initiatives and regulatory reform. They also recommend the desirability of ongoing processes to call roles into question or promote review – such as a challenge function at the centre, advisory councils or institutionalisation of a review process. Substantial re-examination, they argue, requires a central focal point, linked to political leadership, with professional support.[34]

All this has to be taken on board while pursuing the preferred strategy of focusing on objectives and accountability while maintaining basic reporting and professional requirements. Over and above these difficulties, it has to be

33 OECD, 'Globalisation – what implications for democratic decision making?', in OECD, *Strategic Management and Policy-Making*, 1996, PUMA, p 4.

34 *Op cit*, OECD, fn 9.

stressed that performance measures have their limitations and must be treated as helping in the decision making process. However, measurement will never replace judgment. All in all, the challenges for public management are formidable.

The international focus has another aspect. Individual governmental institutions – in particular, the sectoral specialists who work in them – are themselves adapting to a globalised environment by developing their own transnational linkages. Line ministries and finance ministries now routinely manage international contacts and the international dimensions of their policies. As such, new international networks are developed between policy makers – who are linked as much by common policy interests as by national loyalties – while foreign ministries are progressively losing their monopoly in external relations. By blurring institutional and policy boundaries, globalisation is challenging governments' capacities to provide effective and coherent policy responses. A challenge for public management; a challenge for the machinery of government. Again, the OECD mounts a challenge while making a forceful observation:

> When individual ministries develop relations with foreign counterparts or negotiate in international fora, there are few guarantees that their actions will reflect the 'national interest' or a national position, as opposed to a narrow sectoral perspective. This is especially a risk where the issues at stake are of a technical nature and managed by 'experts'. Pursuing narrow interests might even undermine the actions carried out by other ministries. For example, environmental officials may support the linking of environmental protection with trade sanctions, and labour officials the linking of labour standards with trade sanctions. Yet, not surprisingly, trade officials will insist on the maintenance of an open world trading system as the most beneficial system for all. Inter-ministerial disputes, and jostling for turf, common in the domestic setting, are thereby transferred to an international setting where the stakes are arguably higher and the possibilities of policy failure more dramatic.[35]

In this situation, how do national governments ensure that the right hand knows what the left hand is doing? And how are public servants supposed to respond? The need to react quickly to fast-moving events exacerbates the dilemma. Part of the needed response is openness, which in turn increases the complexity of consultation processes. When the way in which decisions are made changes, it is, of course, extremely likely that the decisions themselves will be affected.

There is a danger that public management is being and will be increasingly constrained by the globalisation of the world economy. All the foregoing issues raise serious problems about public values and the ability to take political decisions. These are difficulties which will not go away.

---

35 OECD, 'Globalisation: what challenges and opportunities for government? The need for structural and institutional change', in *op cit*, OECD, fn 33, p 2.

NPM: A CRITIQUE

The FMI and NS initiatives in the UK were explicit attempts to move public services into the mainstream of NPM, and, although the implications for political and constitutional science were not always broadcast, the changes have, for the most part, been welcomed. However, there have been other changes, less explicit, which took some little time to make their impact felt. In particular, CFQ was submerged in the public mind under the claims made for the Citizen's Charter. It has been remarked elsewhere that as the latter developed, a congeries of changes were occurring which, for a while, appeared to be looking for a philosophy.[36]

In fact, the Charter was a symbol of the changes which were being worked. It embodied and embodies much more than improving service to the customer/citizen; it is also about improving efficiency, which is itself embedded in other considerations. One of them is that a stage has been reached in the liberal democracies where taxpayer resistance to funding public services, in part based on a concept of citizen autonomy or freedom, means that the improvement demanded by government and citizen alike must be delivered at constant or diminishing cost to the Exchequer. The belief has been fostered that freedom from being over-taxed is premised on individuals making their own choices rather than having them foisted on them by the State. This, in turn, means that not only must management become more efficient, but more imaginative and innovative, so that choice in the remaining public services is maximised.

When NS was introduced in 1988, the commitment to multiple providers, competition and the emerging value of the citizen as volunteer had not become clarified. At its inception, the expectation of multiple providers, public, private, voluntary, partnerships had by no means become set. On this basis, NS was merely a staging post between an older and a newer concept of government. That newer concept of 'governance' has already been outlined and it clearly poses very great challenges to the way governments work and to the tasks facing public management professionals.

Let us return briefly to the contracting out of public services to third parties. It is indefensible to regard these contracts as simply an illustration of the common law genus of contracts; the contracting out, say, of economic forecasting from the Treasury has little in common with a contract to purchase widgets.[37] Contracts which let public services are more like delegated legislation than commercial contracts. They are often difficult to draw, as they

36 See Lewis, ND, 'The Citizen's Charter and Next Steps: a new way of governing?' (1993) 64 Political Quarterly 316, pp 316–26.

37 For the way contract law is increasingly becoming a realm of regimes, see Brownsword, R, *Contract Law: Themes for the Twenty-First Century*, 2000, Butterworths.

seek to describe public purpose; performance indicators will be established, arrangements for inspection and monitoring put in place, and, presumably, provision for crisis management. The prison service is an obvious example, but we do not possess all the contractual information we need to call those responsible effectively to account. There is, in short, a need for a new constitutional settlement. Without attempting a blueprint here, it will be useful to trail some of the difficulties which need to be addressed.

TOWARDS NEW MECHANISMS FOR NEW GOVERNANCE

First, a summary of the institutional problematics. The establishment of a strategic policy framework is a pre-condition, in order to ensure that individual policies are consistent with overall goals and priorities. This necessitates, at the least, a central overview and co-ordination capacity to ensure horizontal consistency among policies. Alongside this, there is the need to provide mechanisms for anticipating, detecting and resolving policy conflicts early in the process to avoid inconsistencies and budgetary imperatives. Such mechanisms need to be clearly 'political' rather than legal or independent, although this begs the question of the need for standing institutions to identify gaps in the machinery of government. There is also an obvious need for a systematic dialogue between different policy communities.

Various approaches are available for re-examining roles. They include special policy reviews, more comprehensive processes to review roles, and public management initiatives that may have the effect of re-examining roles. It is clearly vital to combine budgetary with policy or programme perspectives. It may be at this point that some more 'constitutional' approach needs to buttress purely managerial initiatives.

Short-termism is the particular enemy of the British political scene, and points to the necessity of providing ongoing processes which call roles into question and/or promote review. This may represent a 'challenge function' for the centre, which is still the hub of British constitutional politics. The institutionalisation of a review process is greatly needed and, and, at the very least, some kind of broad-based advisory council should be introduced. The OECD seemed to favour something of a separation between national institutional necessity and raw politics in saying that 'Substantial re-examinations require a central focal point, linked to political leadership, with professional support'.[38] Their view appears to be that developing and testing better ways to deliver public services needs to proceed alongside ways of informing the public and engaging it in a discussion of the future. In other

38 *Op cit*, OECD, fn 9, p 1.

words, some kind of think-tank (insulated from party political influence), with the duty to consult broadly.

This relates to other recent phenomena which are at the heart of governance, if not NPM as such. Privatisation, in its more limited sense of the direct sale of previously public assets, has recommended itself to governments across the world in the past 15 or so years, and the UK has been a market leader in many respects. Yet, however the success of privatisation is to be judged, many mistakes have been made. This must, in no small measure, be the result of a lack of institutional reflection. Privatisations started in the UK at the pragmatic level and then continued at one of ideology. In neither case was any real exercise in national cost-benefit-analysis undertaken. If the best value for money is to be obtained for the Exchequer, and if the best services are to be delivered against a clear set of policy objectives while holding firm to essential public values, then some alteration of an institutional nature is necessary over the way in which these matters are to be decided.[39] Indeed, the same argument can and should be made over the whole contracting out and market-testing programme.

The difficulty can be traced as well to the regulatory processes adopted for the privatised utilities. The role of the regulators has been adopted and adapted very much *ad hoc*, with each statutory regime displaying marked differences as well as similarities. Criticisms can be made that the regulatory process is not sufficiently transparent, characterised by public hearings or other desirable forms of accountability. There is no clear identification of the responsibility to promote social aspects of policy or to cost them.[40] In other words, no rigorous theories of regulation have been developed within government. There have recently been rumblings within government about the need to regulate not just for competition but for wider social goals. This is clearly reflected in the Utilities Act 2000, and the move towards giving consumers priority. This theme is taken up in Chapter 7.

The rate of change in the State sector is now very rapid. Demands for modernisation and greater economy have helped to bring about major changes in the organisation and functioning of the State more rapidly than at any time in the recent past. Such changes have involved abolishing, amalgamating and corporatising government agencies. This has involved the task of finding the right forms for State activity. It also raises the question as to the role of legal or paralegal institutions in supervising the changing shape of the State and our public services. This will be returned to in Chapter 9.

---

39 See *op cit*, Lewis, fn 36, esp p 323. More generally, see Prosser, T and Graham, C, *Regulating the Privatised Industries*, 1991, OUP.

40 And see Veljanovski, C, *The Future of Industry Regulation in the UK*, 1993, European Policy Forum.

NPM is but one part of the governance revolution, although it is very much core. The UK seems to have gone from there (the old governmental system) to here (governance) without ever having had a very clear idea of why, let alone developing a coherent philosophy of the needs of changing times. At last, however, both the distinctly Blairian 'modernisation project' and Gordon Brown's more rounded approach to the way public services are managed[41] indicates a more proactive approach to the future.

Public Service Agreements (PSAs) are the flavour of the month and will remain so for the foreseeable future. The PSAs published in early 1999 were said to be 'at the cutting edge' of a revolution in the way public services are managed. The focus is to be on outcomes rather than inputs, with funding for modernisation tied to results. PSAs set clear targets (if perhaps rather too many at this time) which public services will deliver in exchange for extra investment. The targets laid down are complex and varied, but include promises to consumers about accessible information and redress. Indeed, there is a push to consumer protection in all services, public and private. Government asserts that consumers need good information on products, services and their rights. The influence of the New Zealand model is clear. It should be added that larger outcomes have been added to the more restrained outcome lists: for example, the New Commitment to Regeneration, the establishment of the Social Exclusion Unit within the Cabinet Office, and so on.

Much of the current Government's thinking in relation to NPM is to be welcomed. Real management reform is taking place and it brings with it real constitutional reform. To some extent, the 'dignified' parts of the constitution have changed, but the pragmatism of the British constitutional experience looks set to continue. It is also clear that, dignified devolution aside, area-based programmes are part of the future. It is doubtful if they can be ultimately played out without greater legal definition. There is currently a discernible tension between management theory and constitutional theory. The sinews of the modernisation project need stiffening by entrenching the essential principles of democracy through a considered re-examination of the relationship between public power and public law.[42]

41 See, especially, HM Treasury, *The Government's Expenditure Plans 1999–2000 to 2001–2002*, Cm 4218, HMSO and *Public Services for the Future: Modernisation, Reform and Accountability*, Cm 4315, 1999, HMSO.

42 And see Lewis, ND, 'Modernizing government: management theory or constitutional theory?' (1996) 6 EPL 201, pp 201–16.

CHAPTER 4

NETWORKS AND CIVIL SOCIETY

INTRODUCTION

> One of the greatest challenges stems from the interpenetration of domestic and international issues, brought about by several concurrent trends: some towards globalisation and the reinforcement of multilateral trade arrangements and regional groupings of companies; others towards fragmentation, brought about by decentralisation, and by the rising importance, in many countries, of subnational levels of government. These developments compel governments to find better ways to manage layers of policy making without losing sight of their own national policy agendas.[1]

We have noted this before. The OECD is right to point out the significance of these changing patterns, but perhaps underestimates the difficulty of holding together such a dissipated chain of policy actors. A tranche of difficulties is encountered in this new world of policy making and management. Coherence is perhaps central; how does one primary actor seek to hold together what it sees as primary purposes in light of the heterogeneous interests involved? Indeed, can it? The likelihood is that initial policy will be filtered through opposing or different points of view and consequently altered; sometimes, no doubt, for the better, but sometimes there are bound to be charges of undue influence. Furthermore, how does government secure the representative nature of the groups in the loop and what are the dangers of exclusion? All these are real issues which require close attention.

Governments have never governed unaided. Indeed, from time to time, they even pay attention to elected parliaments. This aside, we have experienced government as a gesture towards pluralism, we have seen the rise and fall of corporatism, of the dominance of sectional interests and the like. But, what is now almost universally occurring is different. Government as a series of networks or partnerships has become part of the warp and woof of statecraft. There are many reasons for this, which should not detain us for too long. There is, of course, the problem of rationality. How can the centre ever possess enough information, regularly renewed, to know what is good for the sticks or the Seven Seas? This claim to being all-knowing has been rightly termed the 'synoptic delusion' and finally won over waverers after the collapse of the control and command economies. No single actor, public or private, has all the knowledge and information required to solve complex, dynamic and diversified problems. Furthermore:

1 OECD, *Strategic Management and Policy-Making*, 1996, PUMA, p 2.

> Public finance will no longer be able to support the public sector and the Civil Service as they have done for so long. We must summon all the instruments at our disposal, such as regulation, market forces, dialogue, action by non-governmental organisations, improved information, direct public services and so on. We must draw on this whole arsenal to find the best and most advantageous courses of action ...[2]

Important though bureaucracy remains for certain policy areas, its limits are increasingly recognised and attempts at imposing central commands are as capable of provoking avoidance and confrontation as promoting co-operation. A careful balance has to be struck.

The global explosion of information has also played its part and allowed many of the former disenfranchised rapid access to information and the consequent ability to mount informed campaigns at a timely stage. Flattening out or the hollowing of structures of all sorts is killing off 'one size fits all' and paying homage to the expertise of specialists who are bought into projects for their special knowledge. New Public Management (NPM), as we have seen, shows government working increasingly with and through the private sector.

Add to this the rise and rise of the voluntary sector, renowned for adding both value and compassion, and the move towards communitarianism and the broth begins to come to the boil. Across the world, we see the inevitable rise of Non-Governmental Organisations (NGOs), sometimes one-issue groups, but often not, and the unerring rise of community groups which has been given a boost by the move towards sub-regional systems of government.

It goes without saying that not only single levels of government must learn to tackle salient issues across departmental boundaries (social exclusion, crime, etc), but must learn to live with lower levels of government, with business (increasingly) and other partners and, of course, supra-national bodies, not least, but not exclusively, the European Union. Quite apart from the fact that a congeries of forces has combined to re-make this collaborative world, the intellectual tide has recently turned back to the concept of 'civil society' and the many advantages of intermediate bodies to enrich democracy and the entire decision making process. The move away from bureaucracy towards civil society has been, perhaps, late in re-asserting itself and cannot be traced to any one single source or event, but the tone is caught by David Green's justly influential book *Reinventing Civil Society*.[3]

PUMA has summarised recent developments succinctly by saying that the ship of State is becoming a flotilla. This is an international development and by no means confined to the UK.[4] What is interesting, however, is how these trends are interpreted by different countries. In the Irish Republic, for

2 OECD Symposium, Ministerial Symposium on the Future of Public Services, 1996, p 39.

3 1993, Institute of Economic Affairs, Health and Welfare Unit.

4 See, eg, Republic of Ireland Government, *Delivering Better Government*, 1996, Government of Ireland, p 11.

example, partnership is seen as offering the promise of greater openness and the opportunity of building deeper relationships between the several parties. Furthermore, there appears to be a greater willingness to legislate for accountability in the changed conditions than is currently apparent in the UK. We shall have cause to ponder from time to time whether partnerships – especially in the policy making area – can effectively occur without a genuinely expansive commitment to freedom of information.

It is clear that effective networked politics involves not only co-operation in the policy building process, but also in the tricky business of managing cross-cutting policy issues. In all events, new tricks will have to be learned. Increasing the number of actors involved in the governing process often means creating new mechanisms, or adapting existing ones, in order to give the new actors a voice, while maintaining the government's capacity to guide the process towards coherent results. Traditionally, the British State has been exceedingly centralist and yet now, it has to spread itself much more thinly in order to be effective. Centralisation, of a changed sort, needs to co-exist with fragmentation and interdependence lest 'policy intentions drown under their unintended consequences'.[5] As we shall see, co-ordination is rapidly becoming a central challenge.

Orchestration, then, is a challenge for government. It is argued that networks cannot ordinarily be created by policy *diktat*. They tend to the organic and social. Even so, there is a large potential role for public activism to help promote collaborative networks and clusters, either along supply chains, or in regions. As Leadbeater points out, even networked companies are becoming increasingly common. He cites Visa, which 'is not really a company at all, but an alliance of banks, brought together into an international settlements system'. He continues, 'Visa has no assets more durable than its brand and a set of relationships: a network'.[6] Yet, given all this, government can and does promote and encourage industrial development, as well as seeking to regulate it. Granted the form of preferred regulation is self-regulation – by concordat and voluntary codes rather than legislating the bottom line – government nevertheless retains the legitimacy of the democratic stamp of approval with its attendant obligation to uphold public values.[7]

Central government is not any longer, if it ever was, a line manager or transmission belt for public purposes. Even so, it will remain the primary unit for expressing public purposes for some time to come and will seek to exert direction and influence where possible, albeit being conscious both of its limitations and the need for carrying its partners with it in complex

5 Rhodes, RAW, *Understanding Governance: Policy Networks etc*, 1997, OUP, p 4.

6 Leadbeater, C, *Living on Thin Air: The New Economy*, 1999, Viking, p 128.

7 See Cabinet Office, *Self-Regulation: A Substitute for the State?*, Better Regulation Task Force, 1999, HMSO.

enterprises. The world is changing faster and more unpredictably than ever before. But the global challenges are not only to government, but to business in substantial measure. This is most obviously true in the case of sustainable development. It is now widely assumed that eco-efficiency and the 'social licence to operate' will shortly become standard items on the agenda of most business organisations.[8] This is clearly not something to which the world's elected governments can remain indifferent. Corporate social responsibility is something which, hopefully, is voluntarily assumed by the business community, but it would be foolish to believe that government, national and supra-national, did not have a major input. The role of public and private in this area is something to which we shall have cause to return. Even so, it will be helpful to conclude this introduction by reference to just a few initiatives which are illustrative of the consciousness of government of its dependence upon networks, partnership and collaboration.

In early 1999, the British Government launched the second Invest to Save Budget which comprises a competition to gain access to funds totalling £230 million over a three year period for projects which look for new ways of delivering public services through joint working between public sector bodies. This enables public health authorities, local authorities, etc, to bid for funds alongside government departments. So, also, the Cabinet Office is encouraging Local Business Partnerships as a forum for dialogue between the local business community and the local enforcement community. The voluntary sector, too, is encouraged to participate. The *Modernisation* White Paper, also 1999, announced the setting up of a number of 'Integrated Service Teams' to identify the practical problems faced by people in using public services. The teams were to look at seven of the most common 'life episodes' – for example, leaving school, retirement, bereavement, etc. In addition, we have seen the launch of 'Access Business' (a partnership of ministers and representatives from business and local government), national citizen-focused programmes, group-focused programmes, area-based programmes, etc.

In conclusion then, one of the cardinal features of governance is that centralisation (steering, strategic guidance, etc) co-exists with fragmentation and interdependence. Partnerships and networks add value, but pose considerable questions of accountability for the constitutional lawyer. Indeed, increasing the number of actors involved in the governing process means creating new mechanisms or adapting existing ones, in order to give the new actors a voice, while maintaining the government's capacity to guide the process towards coherent results. All this is tied to both national and international governments' ability to communicate with actors and partners who might be in the process of seizing either initiatives or opportunities or both. It ties into their relationships with consumers' organisations and other

8 See, eg, WBCSD, *A Challenge for Today's Business Leaders*, 1997, WBCSD.

NGOs and, most particularly, has repercussions for open access to information and for consultative devices.[9] However, there is more to it than this. Again we find the old meeting the new.

GOVERNANCE AND CIVIL SOCIETY

One of the hallmarks of a deeply embedded democracy is the existence of a set of social institutions intermediary to the State and the citizen. It was ever thus, as we can recall from Plato. The absence of such institutions is one of the reasons for the failure of post-communist Russia to embrace democracy as we understand it or, in any event, for democracy to run much deeper than the wafer-thin layer of elected politics. In the past few hundred years in the West, it seems that bodies intermediate to the individual and the State not only contribute to pluralism, but also help to counter the dissipation of neighbourhoods by successive waves of industrialisation:[10]

> Where the State is the only environment in which men can live communal lives, they inevitably lose contact, become detached, and thus society disintegrates. A nation can be maintained only if, between the State and the individual, there is intercalated a whole series of secondary groups near enough to the individuals to attract them strongly in their sphere of action and drag them in the way, into the general torrent of social life.[11]

History also suggests that both market and State operate more successfully in civic settings. Social capital and trust, common standards and networks can improve the efficiency of society by facilitating co-ordinated action and fostering partnerships of various sorts.[12] This is old wisdom rejuvenated by the emergence of governance. It is reassuring how ancient certainties re-assert themselves from time to time after years of appearing to fall into desuetude; the importance of civil society is one such. We have already looked at the constituent features of governance and seen how important networks are. Let us bring the argument up to date:

> Governance blurs the distinction between State and civil society. The State becomes a collection of inter-organizational networks made up of governmental and societal actors with no sovereign actor able to steer or

9 See, National Council for Voluntary Organisations, *Meeting the Challenge of Change in Voluntary Action into the 21st Century*, 1996, Commission on the Future of the Voluntary Sector and Campbell, D and Lewis, ND (eds), *Promoting Participation: Law or Politics?*, 1999, Cavendish Publishing.

10 See Lewis, ND, *Choice and the Legal Order: Rising Above Politics*, 1996, Butterworths, esp pp 88–100.

11 Durkheim, E, *The Division of Labour in Society*, 1933, Free Press, p 28.

12 For the important role of Friendly Societies in Britain in the 19th and early 20th centuries in the UK, and for important lessons to be drawn therefrom, see the seminal work of Green, D, *Reinventing Civil Society*, 1993, Institute of Economic Affairs.

> regulate. A key challenge for government is to enable these networks and seek out new forms of co-operation.[13]

The assertion of the inability to steer is contestable, but the general thrust of the argument is unexceptionable. In any event, this issue will constitute the main burden of this chapter. For the moment, the role of civil society, and indeed community politics, needs closer examination. It is important to stress that although politics is not at an end, there are limits to its influence. This means that networks cannot be confined to different layers of politics – supranational, national, regional and local – but must embrace non-elected groupings who are nevertheless representative, in a looser or stronger fashion, of significant interests. The final link in the network chain is perhaps community politics/community groups. But, we are scarcely there yet and have certainly not formulated a sophisticated political theory of networks that runs the spectrum from high politics to community groups.

The argument for devolved politics has been outlined and will be resumed later, but it is necessary to concentrate for a moment on community action as an important feature of civil society. Community development involves the formation of ordinary people in their localities to give collective expression to their concerns. This was recognised in the UK in the 1960s and 1970s following the US War on Poverty programme, but community development was discredited by Marxist entryism so that its liberating potential was never realised at that time. However, local authority outreach programmes and the commitment of successive governments to self-management schemes are part of the same logic.

An important part in this movement is currently played by the Community Development Foundation, a not-for-profit organisation which works directly in and with the community, provides and communicates examples of best practice and feeds 'hands-on' experience and knowledge into new programmes and policy proposals. It sees partnerships as the key to supporting community efforts and works closely with local people and groups, local authorities, Training and Enterprise Councils, business, the voluntary sector and health authorities as well as central government.

The voluntary sector, or 'third force' as it is frequently called, is crucial to the way modern governments deliver policy, but the voluminous literature existing in this area will not be addressed here.[14] However, it may be worth noting how the voluntary sector, through its accredited NGOs, is now increasingly walking the stage at an international level. Take the Council of Europe, for example. The Council recognised their importance as early as

13 *Op cit*, Rhodes, fn 5, p 57.

14 For a summary of history and dilemmas, see *op cit*, NCVO, fn 9.

1952, but in recent years their influence has increased considerably and they are now represented at all levels of the Council's structure. They appear as consultants, contribute to the work of intergovernmental committees, prepare memoranda for the Secretary General, make representations to the Congress of Regional Authorities and so on. Of particular significance is the signal role now given to recognised NGOs in the new system of collective complaints operated by the Council under the European Social Charter.[15]

The last few years have also witnessed a remarkable increase in interaction and collaboration between the World Bank and the NGO community worldwide. Through enhanced policy dialogue and operational collaboration, this relationship has evolved into a complex and important one for both parties. To give some indication of this expansion: in 1988, only 6% of Bank-financed projects involved NGOs. In 1993, this had risen to one-third and in 1994, to one-half. Their particular contributions lay primarily in their strong grassroots links, field-based expertise, ability to innovate and adapt and their participatory methodologies. This is very much the nub of community-driven development; reversing control (and accountability to some extent) from central authorities to community organisations in their initiation, planning, implementation, operation, maintenance and evaluation of projects with NGOs or voluntary organisations playing a supportive role.

On the other hand, an experienced community observer has remarked that communitarianism has been given short shrift, given the 'balkanisation' of identity which has accompanied the rise and rise of the market. If this view is correct, it is not only lamentable in itself, but makes the realisation of medium and long term government policies difficult to deliver. Even the pessimistic view of community action accepts, however, that there are successes and that they tend to spring up spontaneously. What such initiatives have in common is that they are organised by people who have experienced problems first hand, and who have lost faith in conventional political systems to deliver solutions:

> In many cases, action is intended to create a new and alternative lifestyle for a diverse group of people so that a broad based organisation is formed. For the most part, organisations remain outside the grant and contract culture used by the traditional community and voluntary sectors ...
>
> One of the best organised ... is called 'citizen organising'. This is a technique that locates and trains community leaders, strengthens communities and contributes to civil society through building a broad base of people able to take part in local politics.[16]

The author goes on to ask a series of vital questions. Can the new politics meet the old? Will the old politics be re-invigorated by the new? Or will it try to

15 See Council of Europe, *Europe Through Its Associations*, 1999, Council of Europe.

16 Knight, B, 'Community politics', in *op cit*, Campbell and Lewis, fn 9.

crush it? Will the old politics accept the new and vice versa? Can those in conventional politics harness the energies of those in community politics for the greater good and reform the character of politics in favour of greater conclusion?[17] The answers lie somewhere in the future and, although tension can always be expected between elective politics at various levels and grassroots activity, the need to bind together all those who can make a positive contribution to public policy is more important than ever. To a considerable extent, government will be judged on how far it can help to deliver community support for all the reasons which make governance the force it is.

Tenant participation is one way in which governments have pursued empowerment in a UK setting. Central government has encouraged local housing authorities to ballot their tenants to approve sales to social housing organisations. These social companies are normally comprised in equal parts of councillors, tenants and independent board members from charities or business. The motives for such initiatives are mixed, and include the passing of financial burdens, but at least the level of tenant involvement in such elections and schemes has been uncharacteristically high. In June 1999, a major initiative was developed in the form of the National Framework for Tenant Participation Compacts. These are agreements between local councils and their tenants which set out how tenants will be involved collectively in local decisions on housing matters which affect them. These agreements will be based on the core standards set out in the national framework. In like vein, the Government, in June 1999, offered people living in some of the country's most deprived areas a chance to help re-build their communities. Seven New Deal for Communities (NDC) organisations were given the go-ahead to start developing long term strategies to regenerate neighbourhoods and deal with problems such as crime, educational underattainment, limited job prospects and poor health. £800 million was earmarked over a three year period. Detailed long term strategies for delivering change are being drawn up in partnerships which include 'non-traditional' organisations, such as the community and voluntary sectors.[18] The Government sees such developments as part of a larger commitment to putting *Modern Government in Touch with the People*.[19]

This commitment is actively concerned with promoting the well being of communities. The Government's public position is that community leadership is at the heart of the role of modern local government.[20] Nonetheless, local government is expected to play the pivotal role in unlocking the potential of local communities through partnerships of various sorts:

---

17 *Op cit*, Knight, fn 16, pp 180–81.

18 DETR, *New Deal for Communities*, 21 June 1999.

19 June 1999, DETR.

20 See DETR, *Modern Local Government In Touch with the People*, 1999, DETR, Chapter 8.

> ... councils are ideally placed to work with government, their communities and the wide range of public, private and voluntary sector bodies who operate at local level and who need to come together if these challenges are to be successfully addressed.

It is for this reason that Government has introduced legislation to place on councils a duty to promote the economic, social and environmental well being of their areas and to strengthen councils' powers to enter into partnerships. This new duty provides an overarching framework for local government. It enshrines in law the role of the council as the elected leader of their local community with a responsibility for the well being and sustainable development of its area. In taking decisions affecting their area, councils will have to weigh up the likely effects of a decision against three objectives: economic, social and environmental. To this end, there is perceived a need for greater coherence of all those whose efforts can affect local communities. In consequence, there is a now a duty to secure the development of a comprehensive strategy for promoting the well being of the area. This must be developed with local people, local business, and with public and voluntary sector bodies who operate in the area. This follows on the well known Local Agenda 21 strategies developed by many councils and the 'new commitment to regeneration', to which it will be necessary to return. These strategies will increasingly form the backdrop to locally based bids for further resources from central government and elsewhere. Interestingly enough, the Government does not believe it would be appropriate for these new partnership arrangements 'to alter the formal lines of responsibility of other public bodies'.

Quite how far this fits with the legislative discretion to engage in partnerships with other bodies in the area is not immediately clear. However, the powers provide for the pooling or sharing of resources, accommodation and IT staff, and encourages the delegation of responsibility for decisions within an agreed framework or plan. These new powers are intended to encourage the establishment of joint arrangements with both statutory and non-statutory bodies and to clear up uncertainties about councils' abilities to establish and participate in companies. There is also power now for the Government to establish a basis for the best performing councils to be freed from some of the constraints which previously limited what they could do and which stood in the way of improving service to the public. These powers will be available both to 'Beacon' and non-Beacon councils provided that they can show that they are running their affairs effectively and in an innovatory capacity.

So, although many of the most effective community organisations seem to be a spontaneous reaction to dissatisfaction and perceived injustice, the Government view is clearly that local authorities should encourage and facilitate co-operation with local groups of all sorts. This is a challenge which will be followed with considerable interest and, in itself, poses a challenge both to traditional politics and to traditional patterns of accountability. It is a crucial face of governance.

This goes at the political level a little further than the New-Right attitude towards governance which tended to target consumers rather than citizens. Most entrepreneurial governments promote competition between service providers. The only sense in which control is pushed out of the bureaucracy into the community is as a body of consumers who are seen as market players in the area of public services. However, in reality, the citizen-as-consumer has little opportunity to make real choices even when case managers (as in social services) help the client to make choices and are paid performance bonuses.

The present Government in the UK is committed to market mechanisms, including 'best value' approaches to buying services, but also sees the need to go a little further and adopt the approach advocated by Osborne and Gaebler, whose vision of entrepreneurial government is one which seeks to push control out of the bureaucracy into the community, to concentrate on outcomes rather than inputs or outputs and to embrace participatory management.[21] As the OECD has argued, governments increasingly realise that they are unable to conduct policies if there is no effective citizen support for implementation, especially in the area of long term challenges. Governments' interlocutors, they believe, are increasingly diverse and represent a broad swathe of civil society. To embrace them fully, they point out that legally established information policies are being introduced across the world. However, the next step, they believe, is a more 'proactive and comprehensive information and participation policy' to provide citizens with better quality information, and to improve two way communication between government and citizens. Participation in the design and organisation of better services is also a necessity:

> For some governments, improving service delivery is sought through alternative solutions, such as partnership with (for profit or not-for-profit) private sector (for instance in the management of hospitals or schools), through the introduction of competition between public and private service delivery (giving citizens a choice) and in some cases through privatisation. Whatever the management solution chosen, however, one of the crucial challenges is to identify and respond clearly to citizens' needs. This has prompted a strong decentralisation and devolution movement in recent years, empowering public managers at the local level, where the government is closer to the citizens.[22]

This, in a sense, summarises the whole thrust of governance and NPM, but it confirms the contemporary emphasis on partnerships and the need to re-awaken the concept of civil society. Although much citizen involvement will remain spontaneous, it is clearly the function of government to facilitate and

21 Osborne, D and Gaebler, T, *Reinventing Government*, 1992, Addison Wesley Longman.

22 PUMA, *Responding to Citizens*, Emerging Market Economy Workshop, Session 3.

encourage open channels of communication and to make participation in them worthwhile. This can only be done through a process of genuinely open dialogue and participation, structured from time to time by obligations imposed by constitutional and administrative law.

This leaves open an important question, viz, whether community organisations will, in the future, have to be dealt with more as equals rather than patronising them. Is a serious surrender of powers unavoidable if the stock of social capital is to be increased and provided through neighbourhood networks? David Green's answer would seem to be in the affirmative. Experiment and best practice, and the need to avoid rigidity, must be the aim. A re-examination, and probably a reassertion, of the role of sub-national governments will be called for during this process.

At the time of writing, several competing models seem to be on offer. The new Local Government Act 2000 indicates the way the Government wishes sub-national government to go, not least through its emphasis on government-by-cabinet and elected mayors. However, this model has its challengers. In Liverpool, where the mayoral idea has considerable support, there is nevertheless a view that Whitehall's proposals are over-prescriptive. The 'Democracy Commission', set up to find a way forward for the City's governance, favoured a radically streamlined council plus the creation of 25 neighbourhood councils in a tier below that of the City Council in order to bring government closer to the people. This appeared to indicate creeping scepticism about a modernisation agenda hatched by Downing Street. Other forward looking local administrations have emphasised their commitment to less adversarial politics and a greater tolerance of opposition points of view.[23]

SUB-NATIONAL GOVERNMENT

We have seen that among the most significant partnerships are those between the various layers of government itself. And, part of the drive to modernity and governance is the recognition that subsidiarity has a crucial part to play in delivering effective government. Although that concept takes various forms, it is becoming almost axiomatic across the developed world that central government must increasingly share its powers with the elected periphery. Thus, we are witnessing a resurgence of local government, often suppressed at least in the UK in recent years, as well as a burgeoning of regional government and other forms of sub-national government. Most of this discussion will be left open until Chapter 9, but a few words are needed at this point:

23 See Hetherington, P, 'Lame mayors' (1999) *The Guardian*, 10 December.

> Policy co-ordination is usually conceptualised as a top-down process, typically led by the centre. Top-down management assumes that the top has enough information to produce policies that are mutually consistent at the delivery level. The bottom-up alternative suggests that allowing ministries to negotiate among themselves might result in programme delivery that is better-adapted to the needs of clients. The bottom-up approach corresponds to the 'empowerment' ideologies now being implemented by many governments. It implies a higher degree of managerial autonomy to interact with client constituencies.[24]

Correctly defining cross-cutting issues (in particular) requires, according to this view, a high level of interaction between the top and the bottom. Those who are actually working with clients probably have a greater understanding of their needs than do those higher up the governmental chain, although it is important that their views are fed back into the evolving policy process at national level. In most countries, sub-national governments play a role in the delivery of services. They are often agents for the implementation of central government programmes. This applies to unitary as well as to federal States, although the latitude of sub-national governments in federal States tends to be greater. The approach of dealing with problems at the level of intergovernmental relations presents one of the greatest challenges of our time for the business of public management. Some countries, such as Germany, depend heavily upon a strong legal framework, while others, such as Australia, operate a strong set of fiscal incentives – not that they are mutually exclusive. It is interesting, too, that the Maastricht Treaty wrote the role of regional and local government into the official Treaties of the Union by setting up the Committee of the Regions. This may ironically be seen as offering UK local authorities a stronger constitutional role in Europe than they are accorded at home.

There are clear problems of accountability raised in the new politics. Who is responsible for expenditure? The central or the local level? Are different programmes at different levels involved and, if so, how are expenditures connected to specific programmes, and how are co-ordination and integration achieved? Furthermore, the clients of programmes can provide feedback and apply pressures to provide more consistent and coherent approaches. Where this happens, there is a tendency to see clients as increasingly indispensable partners in the governance process. This approach is applied in the Scandinavian countries, where ministries have advisory committees, composed of representatives of other ministries and outside groups, to which significant policy initiatives are referred for review. This is happening increasingly in the UK, but without the level of openness associated with

24 PUMA, 'Managing cross-cutting issues', in *op cit*, OECD, fn 1, p 3.

some partner countries. However, there are signs that things might be improving. For example:

> Local government must be an equal partner in our drive to modernise government. We want to encourage initiatives to establish partnerships in delivering services, by all parts of government in ways that fit local circumstances ... We will continue to involve other groups too, including business and the voluntary sector ... We are exchanging ideas with other countries on policy making ...[25]

The White Paper makes constant reference to the need to embrace local government and increasingly to welcome it as a partner in major initiatives. This will be watched with interest, but already it is clear that this Government, like its predecessors, also welcomes industry and commerce as a significant partner in the governance process.

NETWORKS: WHO IS INCLUDED?

The fall of the Berlin Wall finally put paid to the idea that there was a viable alternative to market economics. It is hardly surprising, therefore, that governments of all stripes seek to work constructively with business. The Labour Government post-1997 is indistinguishable from its predecessors in seeking to work with business and to operate in partnership with it at all levels of the economy. The range of activities and associations is too great to list, but a few initiatives will serve to illustrate the point. One of industry's greatest gripes is the issue of regulation, an area discussed in Chapter 7. However, it is difficult to envisage a scenario where industry is more involved directly than in discussions about the desirability and extent of regulation. In April 1999, the Cabinet Office announced a new partnership with the business community as a new approach to regulation was announced. Not only is the Better Regulation Task Force dominated by representatives of business and industry, but the new Cabinet Office-based Regulatory Impact Unit has taken on secondees from industry and commerce while 'more openness in the development of the regulatory process including greater consultation with industry and commerce' was announced.[26] This is scarcely surprising, although consumer and labour representatives often feel, with some justification, that they are paid less attention.

The other area worth mentioning is the PFI or PPP – Private Finance Initiative or Public/Private Partnerships.[27] It is probably true to say that the Labour Government has been even more committed to this controversial initiative than its predecessors. It is a central plank in Labour's economic and

25 Cabinet Office, *Modernising Government*, Cm 4310, 1999, p 12.

26 CAB 96/99, 27 April 1999.

27 See Goh, J and Lewis, ND, *The Private World of Government (occasional papers)*, 1998, Sheffield: Centre for Socio-Legal Studies, University of Sheffield, esp Appendix 1.

social programme, so much so that most structural projects are now funded by the private sector in one kind of deal or another. PPPs can take a number of forms and there is little point in describing the range here, but the central feature is that public works projects which used to be undertaken by the public sector (in most important respects, anyway) are now operated as well as built by the private sector for an extensive period of time. No comment on the merits of this development is necessary here; it is a semi-permanent feature of the landscape. As usual, the questions to be asked are whether the processes used for any particular project optimise the efficient use of public resources and whether they are sufficiently inclusive to satisfy the canons of accountability. On both levels, serious questions remain to be answered. This issue will be left hanging here and re-addressed in Chapter 9. However, some of the complaints have had an effect. In late 1998, a Treasury Taskforce announced that trade unions will, in future, be told of the options under review and will receive public sector comparator information unless this would damage the tendering process. Unions are to be invited to meet the businesses tendering for PFI/PPP contracts and to submit their views to government on those companies. The Taskforce accepted that historically, the process had been too secretive.[28] The fact remains that the partnerships are a crucial part of the Government's governance options.

In spite of this, serious commentators have begun to be highly critical of PPPs. It is claimed that they hold back private investment rather than increasing it. Schemes for 1999 ran at only 40% of the intended level while, when comparisons are drawn with the public sector, efficiency savings are exaggerated in order to win approval for projects and it is, of course, the private sector consultants who will be used for assessing projects. It is also alleged that corners tend to be cut on public works – most notably in hospital projects – while there is a general lack of flexibility. An alternative might be to use public interest companies and trusts which could borrow from the market and drive projects forward.[29] Again, there is a lack of genuine transparency in this area and it remains to be seen how far s 43 of the FOI Act, which exempts information which would or would be likely to prejudice the commercial interests of any person, is interpreted.

While Government relations with private industry are extremely cordial, organised labour feels less included in the various strands of partnership arrangements than they would wish. Although the Government delivered on its manifesto pledges of the minimum wage and union recognition, the TUC has expressed its disappointment with the Government's rejection of a European style social dialogue – the idea of people working together under ministers to draw up strategies for the economy and the labour markets. So

28 See (1998) *Financial Times*, 21 October.

29 See, eg, Hutton, W, (2000) *The Observer*, 3 December.

far, there has been little public enthusiasm for a new Companies Act which compels business to recognise interests other than those of shareholders.[30] This is an area of the utmost importance given the impetus from the international community for business to become active partners with governments for the promotion of social and environmental goals. This is the area where partnerships now need to blossom if organised life is to be fashioned for the benefit of citizens the world over.

The Brundtland Commission summarised the challenges as far back as 1987.[31] Sustainable development, upon which the future of mankind depends, crucially depends on a partnership between governments and industry. This has since expanded to embrace what is often called the 'triple bottom line', which underscores that business must increasingly focus on integrating its targets and performance against the economic, social and environmental dimensions of sustainable development.[32] This requires a degree of corporate social responsibility about minimising the company's adverse impact on the social and physical environment. It is sometimes argued that only by acting in partnership with all stakeholders to promote these ends does a company enjoy a 'social licence to operate'. Brundtland had made it clear that development cannot be said to be sustainable if it is not equitable, or if it does not meet the pressing needs of the majority of the inhabitants of the globe. Although markets will play an important role in the sustainability transition, the world's poorest nations and peoples are generally unable to express their needs through markets. This is why establishing effective government policies in developing markets is a critically important element of sustainable development initiatives. These concerns have also been recognised by the Prince of Wales's Business Leaders' Forum, a global network of business leaders which seeks to encourage partnerships among business, government, communities, NGOs and aid agencies as a means of promoting sustainable development.

These issues, though critical, tend to be glossed over in the search for profits. No one suggests that the task of governments in advancing these necessary partnerships will be easy, as the differences of opinion expressed between, say, the WTO, World Bank, IMF, ILO and others indicate. Nonetheless, governments at different levels must be an equal if not more important driver than business interests. As well as strengthening conventional regulation, it must create a regime where many environmental costs are internalised. Companies will need a mix of positive incentives and tough penalties to achieve environmental performance. Effective governance then, at this level, is a function that is necessarily performed by a wide variety of public and private, State and non-State, national and international

30 See (1999) *The Observer*, 12 September.

31 The UN Commission of Environment and Development, *Our Common Future*, 1987, UN.

32 WBCSD, *Corporate Leadership and Governance: Securing the Social Licence to Operate (The Challenge Brief)*, 1997, Chapter 7.

institutions and practices. However, there is presently no overall body with the legitimacy and authority to ensure that sustainable development happens around the world. Indeed, the Common Agricultural Policy (CAP) of the European Union is driven by production rather than sustainability, so the way ahead will be long and hard. *The Challenge Brief* summarises best practices and outlines steps that could and should be taken if sustainability ends are to be met. One thing is clear: the commitment to environment and development must be built into the fabric of the major corporations. Only genuine partnerships between industry and the other stakeholders have a hope of success. Although 'solutions' are for the future, there is no shortage of suggestions as to the way forward.[33]

As things stand, the WTO, in particular, has been the subject of fierce criticism by consumer groups who believe that it is the mouthpiece of business interests rather than citizen-business partnerships. Consumers International, an umbrella body for consumer organisations around the globe, insists that the threat of trade sanctions is being used to dismantle consumer protection in favour of corporate interests. WTO disputes panels have, more than once, undermined action taken by national governments seeking to protect health and welfare. What is needed to redress the balance, they argue, is greater input by NGOs and an equal participation in negotiations by all countries, coupled with safeguards in areas such as food security, health and competition.[34]

In all these matters, international regional groupings have a vital part to play. The European Union should be a major player in securing equal partnerships with business interests. It is already impossible to understand EU policy making internally without a working understanding of the role played by partnerships of various sorts. It is clearly desirable that the EU turns outwards as well in helping to construct policies across the globe, taking into account the interests and roles of a tranche of players. This issue is taken further in Chapter 10.

GIVING VOICE TO PARTNERS

There is no doubt that the instruments of governance place parliamentary, even democratic, government in considerable jeopardy. This can be left over for the present time. What cannot is the relationship of government properly so called and both its partners and those outside the partnerships, but whose interests are nevertheless at issue.

---

33 And see, further, Chapter 8.

34 CEPR, *Trade Policy and Economic Growth: A Sceptic's Guide to the Cross-National Evidence*, 1999, CEPR.

As could be expected, this is becoming a worldwide phenomenon. In the US, we have seen 'performance partnerships' in areas such as health, rural development, education and training, housing and urban development and transportation. Federal agencies are giving their State counterparts more freedom in how to spend Federal dollars, in exchange for a commitment to be accountable for achieving measurable results. The Environmental Protection Agency has given communities the assistance and flexibility to implement their own community-designed strategies for greater environmental quality. In 1995, the Spanish Ministry for Public Administration established a 'negotiating table with citizens' in which representatives of the Consumer and User Associations participate with government in the discussion and assessment of the quality of public services.[35] These examples are taken at random, but they raise theoretical issues about government and citizenship. Who provides local questioning to the partnerships is another, neglected, item.

In the past, there has been a tendency to discuss policy networks as forms of private government, which clearly poses problems of exclusion and legitimacy. The task, perhaps, in the expanded universe of multi-layered, multiagency partnerships is to ensure, through public law techniques, *inter alia*, that traditional democracy is buttressed by more inclusive forms of discourse. Some argue that it is possible for citizens to regain control of government through their participation in networks as users and governors.[36] This will not happen unaided and the problem of 'who is invited to the party' remains as surely as it did when corporatist arrangements characterised much of the decision making process of some of the advanced economies in, say, the 1970s. Increasing the number of actors involved in the governing process often means creating new mechanisms, or adapting existing ones, in order to give the new actors a voice, while maintaining the government's capacity to guide the process towards coherent results.

That said, it is widely claimed that the information explosion had multiplied the number of actors engaged in public policy making. The influence of the information society has increased the influence of the mass media and multiplied the number of interest groups and NGOs asserting the right to play a greater role in the governance process. But it has also added to the external pressure on governments to steer policy developments. We have not yet satisfactorily traded off the advantages with the downsides. Enhancing the contestability of policy device is, in general, a good thing; but so also is the ability of the elected government to make informed value choices unhindered by overrepresented lobby interests and to ensure that less well organised interests are somehow registered. One thing is clear; the maximum

35 OECD, *Issues and Developments in Public Management*, Survey 1996–97, PUMA.

36 See, eg, Fox, CJ and Miller, HT, *Postmodern Public Administration: Towards Discourse*, 1995, Sage, esp p 149.

information about policy backgrounds and options must be available if these dilemmas are effectively to be addressed. We have seen that there is a greater concentration on outcomes than formerly; another generally desirable move. But connecting inputs, outputs and outcomes is notoriously unscientific and demands, at the very least, open access to all available information by all critics. These are not merely legal problems, but also organisational. While the most liberal FOI regime is a necessary condition of effectiveness and accountability, it is not sufficient; the compartmentalised structures of line ministries need to be broken down, since they have traditionally limited information flows.

The UK Government has recently pinned much of its faith in its MAPPs initiatives. This is an attempt to use performance targets to help the public sector work in a more coherent fashion. There are to be vigorous drives to consult and involve the local community in the work of partnership initiatives and setting local targets which is to be accompanied by a summary of best practices. It is too early to predict the outcome of these developments, but they will repay close monitoring.

We shall return to the institutional responses necessary to relegitimate politics in the new environment in later chapters. The other problem, already touched upon, is the coherence of policy stances in the world of governance.

COHERENCE AND ORCHESTRATION

It is clear that just as networks provide rich opportunities, so they also produce problems for government at the centre:

> Interdependence in networks was always asymmetric; for example, central government could always unilaterally change the rules of the game. It did so regularly in the 1980s, selectively activating new actors to bypass the professions and local government. This exercise of power had marked and unintended consequences. Central departments eroded their nodal position in the networks. Networks became more numerous and complex. Steering was more difficult. Some of the new actors, for example, business, were even less amenable to central steering than Labour-controlled local authorities. Governance, or self-organizing interorganizational networks, were a major unintended consequence, challenging elites to substitute indirect management for control.[37]

The *Modernisation* White Paper is short on specifics for addressing this particular problem, speaking mainly of establishing partnerships that 'fit local circumstances'. It is inconceivable that the Government is unaware of these problems, but less certain how it intends to proceed over the short term.

37 *Op cit*, Rhodes, fn 5, pp 22–23.

PUMA has spoken of the need for a strong strategic capacity at the centre of government, the need for organisational flexibility and for effective information gathering and processing systems. They are clear that the paramount tool of coherence is informed decision making. There is a heavy concentration on tools of coherence, though few of them are sufficiently concrete to be identified as markers for those troubled by the process. They include commitment to political leadership, the existence of a central overview and co-ordination capacity, mechanisms to identify policy conflicts early and an administrative culture that promotes systematic dialogue between different policy communities in order to strengthen policy coherence. At this level, they appear more aspirational than inspirational.

Speaking of networks in the business sector, Leadbeater remarks that they take a great deal of patient management. 'They only work with a strong sense of common values and rules. If an organisation becomes too decentralized it will find it difficult to take concerted action when needed.'[38] This will be true in spades in the public sector, which depends on its moral legitimation from citizens. Public sector networks will also be less concerned at the centre with monitoring and checking, more with setting standards and goals, communicating values, identifying challenges and risks and lifting ambitions to wider horizons. As the Ministerial Symposium on the Future of Public Services put it: '... the Political authorities have the legitimacy and the responsibility to remain the central driving and decision making force in this process.'[39] The belief was expressed that clear political leadership was required, as was vision and the long term view. More concretely, they proposed constructive consultation with partners, transparency and openness, balanced participation of concerned parties and more effective and active relationships with the media.

The social and political communities fostered by the new economy are increasingly likely to be regional – or even City-based. And, increasingly, contests between partners are bound to emerge. One very clear recent example in the UK involved a clash between the South East England Development Agency and local authorities in the area, the latter currently having statutory planning powers. The clash arose over the contest between those who wished to see the region explode exponentially in terms of growth and those who wish operate a more restraint-based approach.[40] It is crucial for government at the national level to impose some sort of order on these disputes in the name of cohesive national politics. The limits on government action in relation to the economy are often remarked upon, but it is possible for government to impose policy restraints on innovation and advance. Furthermore, it is necessary to produce the right degree of political

38 *Op cit*, Leadbeater, fn 6, p 135.

39 *Op cit*, OECD Symposium, fn 2, p 25.

40 See, eg, (1999) *Financial Times*, 24 May.

intervention at the right level as partnerships develop sub-cultures and satellite dishes of community unanticipated in recent times. Leadbeater cites Silicon Valley as one such development where the business community recognises that it needs a public policy machine to address the problems which the region's growth has thrown up.[41]

CONCLUSIONS

The phenomenon of governance presents a formidable challenge to traditional notions of democracy. The issues of networks and the role of civil society highlight this challenge in a vivid fashion. It instantiates the concept of a 'differentiated polity' where the Westminster model of government is seriously challenged. Ministerial responsibility, seen by many as a busted flush, is being replaced by interdependence, 'a segmented executive, policy networks, governance and hollowing out'.[42] This view is echoed by Paul Hirst, who has remarked that traditional representative governments deliver low levels of accountability and public influence on decision making. This democratic deficit, and the emergence of 'new tribes', show the need clearly to develop new forms of democracy, outwith the constitutional orthodoxy.[43]

Rhodes seems to have a point when he says that effective accountability lies in democratising 'functional domains'; that is, looking at particular policies, projects or activities and seeking to make them informed and inclusive rather than reforming the dignified parts of the constitution:

> Accountability can no longer be specific to an institution but must fit the substantive policy and the several institutions contributing to it.[44]

This is not to say that the centre has no role to play; on the contrary. For all its limitations, it remains at any given time the primary source of democratic legitimacy. Its role, however, is changing and will change further. Nevertheless, it will remain the one actor in the piece which is both entitled and obliged to engage in the authoritative allocation of values. There is a potential conflict between the tenets of accountability in a representative democracy and participation in networks which can be open without being accountable. Rhodes again:

> These differing views of networks pose different challenges for the public manager. Is their role to regulate networks (in the sense of maintaining relationships)? Do they act as guardians of the public interest? Do they still have the authority and legitimacy to claim a privileged position in the

41 *Op cit*, Leadbeater, fn 6, pp 143–44.

42 *Op cit*, Rhodes, fn 5, p 7.

43 Hirst, P, *Representative Democracy and Its Limits*, 1990, Polity.

44 *Op cit*, Rhodes, fn 5, p 59.

network? Can they be privileged actors in the network without undermining the discourse?[45]

In fact, the answer to all but the last question appears to be 'yes'. And that question can probably only be answered on a case by case basis. The important point is a high level of transparency, reporting and monitoring. The networks must also be as open and representative as possible so that the centre, in exercising its functions, does so in the fullest knowledge of the interests of all those on whose behalf it seeks to act. Sub-national government must be allowed to play a fuller part than in the past and it, in turn, must respect the views of local communities:

> The philosophy for the virtuous triangle needs to be developed. In the process the State must find its own level; must respond with an adequate concern for subsidiarity; must find a level at which its constituency can relate but at the same time make it possible for dialogue to occur between it and a wide range of forms of community expression so that the basic goods of the constitution – the floor of rights to which all are committed – can be most appropriately delivered.
>
> This new triangular relationship should ultimately produce a more mature form of politics since the present is dominated by a handful of political activists and a mass of the politically inert who have lost their faith in active politics. Community self-awareness should serve, as it always has done in minority faiths, as an introduction to political awareness. Given that a pluralistic society is the only truly democratic society, then the reconstruction of the State from a dozen different points of entry represents an opportunity to revise and re-affirm the political compact in a modern setting.[46]

Nations across the world are experimenting with new forms of constitutional accountability and with machinery for ensuring the effective delivery of public policies. Most are agreed that address needs to be made to functional domains rather than simply refurbishing traditional institutions. Outcomes are being paid more attention than previously and there is a transformation taking place in the way that agencies are administered and programmes managed. Task forces and agencies are increasingly preparing strategic plans that are built around their missions and clearly outline their goals. Methods are being increasingly adopted to track their progress in achieving goals. Annual performance reports are particularly helpful in this respect in order to assist the public in understanding how government generally is spending public money and seeing what is being achieved. Performance-based intergovernmental partnerships, for example, are being used in the US to identify goals and the progress being made towards attaining them.

45 *Op cit*, Rhodes, fn 5, p 58.

46 *Op cit*, Lewis, fn 10, pp 99–100.

The differentiated or dissipated polity has arrived. This requires explicit accountability in multiple forms and forums. For effective discourse there must be the maximum amount of information available and open channels of access, directly or indirectly. An Administrative Procedure Act for the 21st century is urgently required to lay down basic minimum standards and to encourage the publication of best practice. We shall return to this issue in Chapters 9 and 10.

CHAPTER 5

POLICY AND IMPLEMENTATION

INTRODUCTION

Throughout the development of the modern State, it has been convenient to talk of the necessary distinction between policy and its implementation. This is evident in much of the literature and argument surrounding the separation of powers – it is a distinction traditionally recognised by the courts and, to a very considerable extent, it has been recognised in the development of the institution of ombudsmen. Ombudsmen are primarily established to examine failures of administration and, for the most part, keep well shy of policy issues. One could go on.

Much of the post Second World War literature has been characterised by arguments about the impossibility of making such callow distinctions. This literature is too extensive and too well known to need citation here. However, New Public management (NPM) and concomitant developments have given the old debates a new twist.

Enough has already been said about the impact of NPM, but the contemporary status of the policy/implementation issue requires special attention. This will constitute the theme of this chapter.

THE ISSUES

The emergence of the Next Steps Agencies and the somewhat earlier purchaser/provider split provides a useful starting point. The latter, at least in the UK, was, to a substantial extent, based upon ideological considerations. Public bad – private good seemed to represent the spirit of the times and the logic was the farming out of public services – preferably to the private sector, failing which the voluntary sector. At best, this movement required the public agency to assume overall responsibility for the delivery of services while leaving the means and day to day operations in the hands of those who were thought to be better equipped to operate at the sharp end. They would be more efficient, less hide and culture bound, more innovative, more sensitive (in the case of the voluntary sector) and so on. At the further extreme, public institutions would be privatised and the public sector, sooner or later, banished from the equation.

The NS agencies constituted a different part of this logic. If services were not suitable, for one reason or another, to be 'privatised' (in the generic sense), then the agency formula would mimic the contracting out solution to the nearest extent possible. Government departments would concentrate on policy formulation and the agencies on delivery of services according to targets or service agreements.[1] Although this is to simplify a complex issue, it is probably fair to say at this point that the delivery of policy and standards of public service have received more detailed attention than the policy process. The reforms appear, at this point in time, to have been more successful in relation to the former than the latter.

As has been seen earlier, although in the UK these trends were almost certainly driven by ideological considerations, much of the change in management styles and modes of governance have been adopted across the world and by governments of differing political persuasions. Some version of the modern policy/implementation divide is here to stay and, in consequence, its main features fall to be examined in more detail.

THE BACKGROUND

If NS is, to a large degree, about delegating managerial powers to managers, then the objectives set for them should be clear and ringing. They should also be intended to achieve clear objectives. As it is, there has often been confusion between responsibility for inputs, outputs and outcomes: between what resources might require what measures to achieve what results. It must be said that clarity in the arrangements has not always characterised public administration in the UK. This is not least since the processes for moving from one end of the policy spectrum to the other have seemed to be part of a seamless web, so that responsibility for failure is insufficiently highlighted. Resignations for policy/delivery failures are rare, and when they do occur, have tended to produce both acrimony and obfuscation as to where accountability truly lies. The resignation of Derek Lewis as Head of the Prison Service under the last Major administration is a case in point. The disagreements between Lewis and the Home Secretary largely revolved around what constituted policy and what managerial issues, with allegations too that the Home Secretary had tried to micro-manage Lewis's territory. In the event, Lewis was dismissed and he sued for wrongful dismissal, a claim which was settled out of court, thereby denying the public the opportunity to inspect the discovered documents which would almost certainly have told us a good deal more about our governing arrangements than we currently know.

For Next Steps, read also one of the main thrusts of the Citizen's Charter or Service First Programme. Nothing could be clearer than that if yardsticks for service satisfaction are to be established and compensation for breach

1 See, Rhodes, RAW, *Understanding Governance: Policy Networks etc*, 1997, OUP, esp Chapter 5.

available, prior questions relating to outcomes and resources must be posed. What do the objectives delivered by public agencies amount to? Can they be achieved within current resource constraints? This issue has become one of burning importance within the Health Service over the question of 'rationing'. One of the suggestions currently being made is for a wider debate over the question of priorities within a service that simply cannot provide universal remedies. Is the balance between service deliverers and policy makers adequately struck and is it sufficiently transparent to allow a broader public debate? The issue becomes even more urgent when multiple service providers are involved, as the *Modernising Government* White Paper has recognised:

> This emphasis on management reforms has brought improved productivity, better value for money and in many cases better quality services – all of which we are determined to build on. On the other hand, little attention was paid to the policy process and the way it affects government's ability to meet the needs of the people. Although there are areas, such as foreign and security policy, where effective co-ordination and collaboration are the norm, in general too little effort has gone into making sure that policies are devised and delivered in a consistent and effective way across boundaries – for example between different government departments, and between central and local government. Issues like crime and social exclusion cannot be tackled on a departmental basis. An increasing separation between policy and delivery has acted as a barrier to involving in policy making those people who are responsible for delivering results in the front line.[2]

The OECD has affirmed these sentiments, arguing that governance includes the effectiveness of the policy making machinery, the provision of information, the relations between levels of government and the consequent implications for the interaction between government and the rest of the community. They add that it is very difficult to achieve reductions in government programmes or regulations without good policy analysis and intervention which demonstrates that government action is not having its intended effects or is not achieving them effectively or efficiently. In effect, experience suggests that expenditure and regulatory reduction must be shown to reflect 'good policy' at the micro-level as well as in terms of its macro-economic impact if it is to be sustainable.[3]

A lot more remains to be said about improving the policy process after we have discussed the issue of management and delivery, but a further word needs to be said here about the relationship between information systems and effective policy. In a number of Commonwealth countries, for example, the quality of information used to support policy development is closely related to budgetary and financial reforms. Essentially, the shift to a focus on results has required programme objectives to be more clearly established and to

2 Cabinet Office, *Modernising Government*, Cm 4310, 1999, HMSO, p 15.

3 Keating, M, *Public Management Reform and Economic and Social Development*, 1997, OECD.

measure indicators of performance to be developed against which the efficiency and effectiveness of progress towards those objectives can be assessed. In Australia, New Zealand and Sweden, for example, the reporting requirements for budget systems must now include references to outputs and outcomes and, although there is still room for improvement, the quality of information is gradually being improved.

Improvements to the quality of performance information coming forward by whatever means are not only intended to meet the immediate needs of policy makers: they should also underpin the new emphasis on accountability for the results obtained. This new accountability emphasis is an important feature of the public management reforms, representing an essential *quid pro quo* for the devolution of authority to managers under the reforms. In the longer term, the public availability of improved performance information should, however, also support better policy, both by drawing on a wider circle of informed advice and by keeping the public services up to the mark.

In the UK, especially, ministerial responsibility has, as we have seen, too often been a cloak for hiding individual responsibility. The *Modernisation* White Paper shows itself to be aware of this, although disguising current and past failures is a lost opportunity to address problems of the modernisation agenda. In particular, it argues that ministerial responsibility and accountability has failed to take account of the fragmentation of decision making so that scrutiny has been confined to individual departments and agencies rather than overall governmental strategy. In other words, the failings of the traditional doctrine are likely to have been considerably exposed in the new world of partnerships, networks and joined-up government. The more players there are in the game, the greater the possibility of accountability gaps and an inclination to pass responsibility for failure on to the next link in the chain:

> Policies too often take the form of incremental change to existing systems, rather than new ideas that take the long term view and cut across organisational boundaries to get to the root of a problem. The cultures of Parliament, Ministers and the civil service create a situation in which the rewards for success are limited and penalties for failure can be severe. This system is too often risk averse.[4]

This is, of course, the Government's celebrated commitment to 'joined-up government', but, important though it is, it fails to accept that responsibility for decision making has always been obscured and remains obscured. Of course, policy and implementation are intimately connected, but now responsibility for both can be strung out along a very long continuum, even if ultimately responsibility for both decision making and orchestration must rest at a pivotal, identifiable, pulse. This is one of the greatest problems of modern

4 *Op cit*, Cabinet Office, fn 2, p 16.

politics and public management. It is the essential dilemma of governance.[5] Let us now turn to strategic issues.

POLICY AND IMPLEMENTATION: A STRATEGIC OVERVIEW

The search for 'best value' is at the heart of governance. In the UK, the *Modernising Government* White Paper spoke of the need to identify the *best supplier* for all central and local government activities. This is to be done by consulting widely with users, benchmarking and open competition. The focus is to be on end results and service standards, rather than simply on processes. Winning suppliers will need to offer improved quality, as well as better productivity and lower costs:

> And because public service needs do not stand still, we expect best suppliers to prove they can manage change and offer the public continuous improvement. We will mount a co-ordinated programme across the public sector based on common principles, embracing the Better Quality Services initiative for central departments and agencies, and Best Value in local government.
>
> To make sure we get the best supplier, competition will be considered seriously as an option in every case. Where internal restructuring without competition emerges as the preferred solution, then for larger government services, this will be subject to prior scrutiny by the Cabinet Office and Treasury. The Government will take decisive action to deal with failing services, whether supplied by the public or the private sector. A Committee of Ministers (PSX) will monitor the performance of Departments in delivery of Better Quality Services, *ensuring that reviews are robust and generate continuous improvements in quality and cost.* (*Modernising Government*, Cm 4310, 1999, p 41 – emphasis added.)

In local government, this heralds a change in approach. Compulsory Competitive Tendering (CCT) and market testing have led too dogmatically to the use of private sector suppliers. Although CCT delivered savings and efficiencies, 'this was sometimes at the expense of quality'. An open mind is to characterise future choices of supplier. In February 2000, the Cabinet Office produced a *Guide to Quality Schemes and Best Value* as an aid to improved performance by local government.[6] This embraces, too, the EFQM Excellence Model, being a framework to help assess an organisation's performance, both in its results and the processes needed to achieve them – and to identify where improvements are needed.

Best Value is one of the key means of delivering the Government's modernising agenda in local government. Best Value is defined as a duty to deliver services to clear standards, covering both cost and quality, by the most

5 And see Perri 6 *et al*, *Governing in the Round: Strategies of Holistic Government*, 1999, Demos.

6 CAB 75/2000.

economic, efficient and effective means possible. As from April 2000, local police and fire authorities had a statutory duty to provide Best Value to local people, local taxpayers and the wider community.

At the level of central government, the central document is *Better Quality Services: A Handbook on Creating Public/Private Partnerships Through Market Testing and Contracting Out*,[7] which replaces the previous Government's *Guide to Market Testing*. The new document embraces the 'Appraising Options' exercise, which is a variation on the Prior Options exercise dedicated to determining, at five-yearly intervals, the ongoing need for any particular service and the optimum form of providing it where a case is made out.

The robustness of the reviews has already been touched upon. There is little doubt that in the past, the exercise was nothing like as transparently performed as it should have been. Parliament is clearly unable to conduct an effective scrutiny of the process so that some ancillary device is necessary for democratising the process. The Public Administration Committee has commented on these procedures and recommended that the review team, when commencing a 'Prior Options Review' (*sic*), should invite responses via the department or NDPBs' websites. This has been accepted and reflected in the new guidance for quinquennial reviews.[8] The Government also accepts that most NDPBs, at least, should publish their reviews and that an 'independent' member should be attached to the team. We shall have to wait to see how things work out in practice, but it would be an additional improvement if all comments submitted were kept in a record for public inspection.

Effective policy making ought to bring effective performance in its wake. Since the NS agencies were established, there have been noticeable improvements in performance,[9] although the salient criticism levied has been that established targets do not measure the key issues which matter to people. (It should also be remembered that 'Executive Agencies', as the Government now prefers to call them, are the main delivery arm of central government.) The Government is extremely sensitive to this criticism and has put in train a number of reforms intended to rectify the position. As yet, it is too early to assess their impact. At the time of writing, however, improvements in the performance of a raft of government bodies were being reported. NS agencies were hitting 75% of targets and NDPBs 69%. Even so, there is much to do and the Government is committed to adopting robust customer satisfaction targets

7 Cabinet Office, 1998, HMSO.

8 Select Committee on Public Administration, *Responses to the Sixth Report from the Select Committee on Public Administration (Session 1998–99) on Quangos*, HC 317, Session 1999–2000, 1st Special Report, paras 3–5.

9 Companies House, for example, has reduced its unit cost by 33% since 1991 while maintaining or improving all its service standards. This is only one of many success stories.

and setting targets so that service standards rise year on year.[10] In fact, the PSAs, introduced in 1998, set out firm targets for improving services over a three year period. This was intended to shift the focus decisively from inputs to outcomes that matter most to users of public services. Following the 2000 Spending Review, new PSAs were published which included key commitments on the management of public services. Following the New Zealand experience, there is now a recognition that sufficient focus needs to be placed on key priorities.

Action on the *Modernisation* White Paper has included a report showing the performance of government departments and agencies against the six service standards for central government. These set minimum standards in such areas as correspondence handling and waiting times. Government has also published the aims and objectives of all departments which together add up to a comprehensive statement of what the Government has set out to deliver.[11] Increasingly, as indeed has happened around the world, there has also developed the practice of asking departments to fund new initiatives through reallocation of existing funds, thus creating an additional incentive for efficiency.

The UK is following best practice adopted in several other countries with similar traditions. The New Zealand experience has already been noted, but the US is also very much in the game. Using the Performance and Results Act 1993, the administration is working to transform the way agencies are administered and programmes are managed. Under the Act, agencies prepare strategic plans that are built around their missions and clearly outline their goals, and develop measures to track their progress in achieving the goals. They publish annual performance reports to enable Congress and the public to understand more clearly the progress government is making.

It should be added that seeking the best supplier sometimes means seeking out the most appropriate partners with whom the allotted tasks can be shared. Identifying partners is increasingly becoming a central feature of reformed governance. The constitutional problems associated with partnerships have already been observed, but it is also important that, where partnerships have been established, agreements that they are performance-based are vital. Again, the US has recognised this through adopting the Federal structure of government to modern management methods. So, for example, in exchange for commitments to specific performance levels, State and local governments receive more administrative flexibility on how to achieve those levels. In 1996, the President sought to consolidate 271

10 At the time of writing, there was some suggestion that the new PSAs were proving cumbersome and inoperable. They were too detailed and too numerous. Instead of an average of 30 targets per department, a reduction to nine was thought more suitable: Cabinet Office, *Executive Agencies 1999 Report: Focus on Achievement*, 2000, HMSO.

11 Cabinet Office, *Modernising Government: Action Plan*, 1999, HMSO, p 4.

programmes into 27 performance partnerships in areas such as public health, rural development, education and training, and so on.[12]

Strategic management should also involve 'steering at arm's length' instead of by detailed rules, through output and consumer orientation, transparency of output, costs and impacts, replacing control through performance contracts and decentralised structures, all of which are directed to increase managerial freedom and bringing administrative action closer to citizens. To be fair, a good deal of this is happening under the Blair administration, but it needs to be buttressed by a wider public debate culminating, ideally, in a broad-based Administrative Procedure Act which would turn good ideas and occasional administrative practice into a set of enforceable obligations.

It is also becoming increasingly understood that policy making and policy management must, in future, be much more closely aligned. In other words, more attention should be paid to learning from experience. Government, as the White Paper on Modernising Government makes clear, should regard policy making as a continuous learning process, not as a series of one-off initiatives. There is some sign that the Government is now improving its use of evidence and research, the better to understand the problems being addressed. It is also making more use of pilot schemes to encourage innovation and to test their efficacy. All policies and programmes need to be clearly specified and evaluated, and the lessons of success and failure communicated and acted upon. Feedback from those who implement and deliver policies and services is essential. The need is now acknowledged to apply the disciplines of project management to the policy process. The newly established Centre for Management and Policy Studies should help this hoped-for transformation.

In terms of making policy, the New Zealand Government is much praised for the reforms it has introduced into strategic management. Its thrust is so important that it is worth quoting the official position in some detail:

> The starting point is a statement of the government's policy strategy for achieving a limited number of goals. This statement, which is essentially a political document, has been used in an endeavour to create a common vision for the country as a whole. On the basis of this vision statement, the government subsequently agrees a series of medium-term goals for nine 'strategic result areas' (SRAs). These SRAs have in turn been used to encourage co-ordination between related groups of programmes and departments, and to inform the annual budget review of taxing and spending priorities. The SRAs also provide the framework from which more specific milestones known as 'key result areas' are derived, which then act as benchmarks against which departmental performance can be assessed. Thus, the system is intended to improve both the vertical integration between the political and managerial

12 OECD, *Issues and Development in Public Management*, Survey 1996–97 on the US, PUMA.

> spheres and the horizontal integration and alignment across sectors, including the opening-up and broadening of the policy process.
>
> At the same time, it is recognised that it is vital that the government continue to exercise control and self-restraint, and be fully accountable for its actions. The primary vehicle for this is the Fiscal Responsibility Act. This Act does not set any specific numerical targets or immutable boundaries, but it does require governments to keep the public regularly informed about the true state of public finances, the government's medium-term fiscal objectives, how those objectives are going to be attained, and the key risks involved. In effect a government would be required to face the music if it stepped outside the zone of acceptable fiscal conduct, and a result the government no longer 'owns' fiscal policy.[13]

Not only is this a rationally integrated system worthy of close attention in the UK, but it is worth noting that the whole edifice is underpinned by legal obligations of the sort which successive UK governments have sought to avoid.[14] The OECD has seen fit to relate the reform process to wider democratic expectations. One of the primary lessons of the reform process is that it is necessary to communicate openly, clearly and often about the problems which the reforms will address and the staging posts on the way to full implementation. Communication should be across government, to Parliament, to affected individuals and groups, the media and beyond to the wider public. A management culture that is fact-based, results-oriented, open and accountable is also being actively pursued in Canada.[15] Delegates to the Ministerial Symposium in Paris, March 1996, also:

> ... stressed the importance of constructive consultation with stakeholders, transparency and openness, balanced participation of concerned parties, and more effective and active relationships with the media. There was a clear recognition that real change will not occur without political leadership, vision and a longer term view, rather than *ad hoc* reaction.[16]

Everything which drives the modern political world is making short term decisions less relevant than in the past. Structures are changing rapidly and a considered response is necessary for contemporary governments to adapt to the social consequences of change. Managing change is no longer a short term option. This presents problems for the ordinary life cycle of politicians, but they are coming to understand that their influence can only be judged in the long term. For them to be successful in this new framework, they not only have to take bold political initiatives, but they need to carry publics with them through effective stakeholding relationships and consultation which is less

13 OECD, *The New Zealand Approach to Strategic Management, Public Reform and Economic and Social Development*, 1998, PUMA, p 61.

14 Note, however, that New Zealand does not have a statutory obligation on ministers to report on outcomes.

15 See OECD, *In Search of Results: Performance Management Practices*, 1997, PUMA, p 45.

16 OECD Symposium, Ministerial Symposium on the Future of Public Services, 1996, p 43.

perfunctory and more effective than in the past. Before turning to this issue, a recurring theme of this essay, one or two policy issues need to be tidied up.

First, a reconsideration of the connections between policy making and implementation needs to be made. There is a general and a particular problem. The general is that just as there can be no clear-cut distinction between the two on the ground, so there needs to be a two-way process of feeding operational experience into revising the policy process. The policy process must also balance the feasibility of high-sounding promises against the available resource-base. The particular is the overwhelmingly British experience with ministerial responsibility, which has already been touched upon. The fact that there is a real danger of no one taking responsibility for anything must be addressed. The literature in this area is enormous, much of it recent. And, although the Derek Lewis case is the one most often quoted as an illustration of the failure of the doctrine, it is not because it is the exception, but rather that it highlights the problems of routine relationships between ministers and their advisers. More recently, however, has been the Passport Agency fiasco of the early and mid-summer of 1999.

The Guardian newspaper used the Code of Practice on Access to Government Information to uncover the facts behind what was a clear failure in terms of delivery on promised targets and performance indicators:

> The fact that the agency met the 20 working day deadline is the only good news. If you thought the government would come clean about how they wrecked the holiday plans of over half a million people, dream on. On every key fact that would throw light on this disgraceful episode, Jack Straw is prepared to cover up at any price.

Clearly, part of the problem was yet another computer system failure. This time, the contractor was Siemens:

> The kernel of the saga lies in the answer to four questions: how did Siemens get the contract to do the work; how did a separate demand for children's passports overload the system; how did Siemens get in such a mess in the pilot runs in passport offices in Liverpool and Newport, Gwent; and who takes the financial blame ...?
>
> On each and every key point, Jack Straw has invoked the same discretionary powers that he will have under the FOI (Freedom of Information) Act to stop the public getting the truth. In one of the most extraordinary aspects of the case – the ill-fated trial runs in Liverpool and Newport – Jack Straw has actually sold the information on the disaster to the private company running the show. As David Gatenby, the outgoing chief executive of the agency put it: 'Agency staff reviewed, agreed and took part in test programmes, but ownership of test documentation rests with Siemens Business Systems ... I am afraid that I cannot pass on the information requested. You may wish to approach Siemens to see if they are prepared to waive this commercial confidentiality.'[17]

17 Hencke, D, 'Your stunt is a sham, Mr Straw' (1999) *The Guardian*, 30 July.

Through the Private Finance Initiative (as it then was), the Home Secretary has 'turned himself into the company's servant rather than its master'. Siemens, elected by no one, decided what the country could be allowed to know and what not.

Hencke continues. As for finding out what recorded decisions led to the disastrous introduction of child passports at such a critical time – or what the options were for putting things right – the Home Secretary invoked the same blanket ban on 'policy advice' as is prominently enshrined in the FOI Act. This effectively allows him, just like his predecessors, to hide his lack of judgment.

This episode speaks volumes about the level of transparency and responsibility which British Governments are prepared to tolerate. Where policies and their implementation are successful, it will be in spite of, not because of, the system. Even so, what constitutes success in the absence of an open process is almost impossible to judge.

WHAT NEEDS TO BE DONE?

While an adequate response to these dilemmas is contested, most countries are in the process of reforming – the UK no less than elsewhere as noted from the Modernisation initiative. The Irish Government, which has borrowed so many British traditions, is clear that ministerial responsibility as practised can represent a liability. To that end, it has looked sympathetically to assigning responsibility and authority to the persons who actually deliver a service. Furthermore, action has been taken to provide protection to those appearing before Select Committees and the provision of a statutory framework within which civil servants, while acting *bona fide* in the public interest, may legitimately disclose information.[18]

At the present time, the UK Government has not gone this far, its predecessor being unsympathetic to clarifying the roles of ministers and Agency Chief Executives, although an understanding was reached as to the appropriate role for Select Committees where an individual civil servant was subject to disciplinary proceedings.[19] Much, however remains to be done.[20]

One suggestion made is that, as well as executive agencies, there should be established policy agencies, operating with a high degree of transparency. So there might be a Family Policy Agency, an Energy Agency, a Transport Agency and so on. These new agencies might well include both ministers and external policy advisers. They should take a lesson from their Federal US

18 See Republic of Ireland Government, *Delivering Better Government*, 1996, Government of Ireland, esp pp 1, 14.

19 See Cabinet office, *Government Response to the Second Report from the Public Service Committee (Session 1995–96) on Ministerial Accountability and Responsibility*, 1997, HMSO, esp pp xi and xiv.

20 See Lewis, ND, 'A Civil Service Act for the United Kingdom' [1998] PL 463, pp 463–88.

counterparts and be under a legal obligation to trawl for facts and opinions in the wider community. The Cabinet Office does presently, of course, have a number of cross-cutting bodies operating under its aegis, most famously, perhaps, the Social Exclusion Unit, which has done much important work. It has also brought in outsiders and trawled for opinions. However, its working methodology is very much traditional Civil Service and not exposed to the public in a way that would identify responsibility for options chosen and rejected. Indeed, public scrutiny and accountability to publics have been considerably undervalued in the UK. Things are undoubtedly improving, but they still require a constitutional nudge or two.

To begin with consultation. Consultation, especially as Parliament weakens, is both a democratic necessity and a valuable tool for effective governance. The Blair Government clearly recognises the need for doing more. Indeed, the *Modernisation* White Paper, in a sub-heading entitled 'What must change' speaks directly to 'involving others in policy making'. Rather than defending policies, government should lead a debate on improving them. This means developing new relationships between Whitehall, the devolved administrations, local government and the voluntary and private sectors; consulting outside experts, those who implement policy and those affected by it early in the policy making process so that they can develop policies that are deliverable from the start.[21] We shall return to these issues in a more general setting in Chapter 9, but the emphasis on being part of a national team, albeit the lead player, in taking social life forward rather than stubbornly defending the indefensible would represent a sea change in attitudes and habits. History will be the judge, but again, it is difficult to see how this can be achieved wholeheartedly when secrecy in the policy process is being defended and when ministerial responsibility as a doctrine remains undiluted. Even so, the shift is genuinely perceived, albeit that the means are not always willed to achieve what is desired. The approach replicates that adopted for changes in systems of governance by the most advanced practices across the world. We are therefore talking ideal-type consultation, and the real world must be measured according to how it shapes up to the paradigm.

It is a central theme of this essay that the new needs to embrace older democratic ideals and, in the modern world, given the limited compass of individual parliaments, this means, at least in part, that constitutional and administrative law should play a greater part, both in enfranchising citizens, and in stiffening the resolve of governments which, in times of crisis, are prone to backsliding. Granted that the UK culture is historically rooted over a long period and that its autonomy must be respected, it is nevertheless important to underline that it is out of step with its partners and friends in underplaying the role of the law. Certainly, most of the OECD countries take a

21 *Op cit*, Cabinet Office, fn 19, p 16.

more robust view. In an influential paper prepared for PUMA, one of the accompaniments of the move towards new systems of governance is seen to be strong institutional reform of a quasi-constitutional nature:

> ... there has been a very substantial development of administrative law. People are now much more willing and able to contest government administrative decisions through a plethora of appeal bodies which have been established for this purpose and ultimately through the courts. *Whereas once the authority of the State was largely accepted as a given and without question,* now decisions can be questioned precisely because they were made by or on behalf of the State. Associated with this process of administrative review is a much more transparent and open process of decision making. Citizens now enjoy considerable rights of access to information regarding themselves, and in some countries (including Australia, Germany, France) they can demand statements of reasons for decisions affecting them or their business.[22]

Now clearly, although not all problems of governance can be legislated away, it is interesting to see how far the British Government has been prepared to impose statutory duties of a general nature on local government, particularly throughout the 1980s and 1990s. These can be of a general or a specific nature, the former being backed by negotiated codes and notes of guidance. The Local Government Act 2000 is a radical document which has not been welcomed in all quarters. However, it represents a genuine attempt to modernise local government and to address the problems thrown up by networking government. However, what is sauce for local politics should be sauce for the centre. In other words, a greater role for the imposition of statutory duties on central government as well should be envisaged – preferably through a broad ranging Administrative Procedure Act.

Although the issue of FOI runs through everything that is being said here, this is perhaps the place to elaborate a little on its implications for the policy process in particular, but also for the effective monitoring of public management systems. The FOI Act 2000 in the UK is fiercely complex and it is not yet possible to assess its impact when its main provisions come into force. However, it is clear that for policy to be properly evaluated, the greatest amount of information on the policy forming process needs to be disclosed. However, that does not seem to be a view shared by the framers of the Act. Although there are both absolute exemptions and 'balancing public interest' exemptions (for the Information Commissioner to determine in the first instance), most fall into the latter category. They include information relating to the formulation or development of government policy and ministerial communications, although generally, statistical information will be released at a later stage. There is also an exemption for information which is 'prejudicial to the effective conduct of public affairs' as determined in the first instance by

22 *Op cit*, Keating, fn 3, p 26.

a minister of the Crown. This is openly directed at protecting 'collective responsibility' and the 'free and frank provision of advice'.[23] It would be foolish to forecast how the Act will be interpreted and how fearless and active the Commissioner will be, or as to the frequency of her being overruled by the minister.[24] However, the overall thrust of the Act looks to be directed at protecting government from a close examination by the people and the national press. Once more, the position of New Zealand seems infinitely more acceptable to those of a democratic disposition. A recent example will serve.

On 21 November 2000, *The Dominion* newspaper in Wellington carried the news that the Finance Minister chose to ignore a Treasury warning that his proposed superannuation fund was likely to result in New Zealanders saving less, according to a released Treasury document. The document, obtained under the Official Information Act 1982, differed from information made public by the Government when it unveiled its $100 billion superannuation scheme on 10 October 2000.

When the Government unveiled its proposed fund in October, the Minister issued an earlier Treasury paper from June of the same year which reported that it was unclear 'whether the establishment of the fund will affect household saving'. The newly disclosed document, however, cited research from the US and Australia, which appeared to indicate that the more certainty people have about their investment income, the less they will save. The following day, the same newspaper reported that the Minister had claimed that the Treasury advice 'is clearly wrong'. A Treasury spokeswoman said the papers had all been released, the Minister had considered his advice and, as with any other advice such minister 'makes his or her own decisions'.

Set the 1982 Act against what has just been noted of the UK FOI Act and the differences in cultural approaches are striking. New Zealand is, of course, well known for its reforms of public management and, in particular, for its practice of forcing Chief Executives (the UK Permanent Secretary equivalent) into written contracts where they are held responsible for specific outputs. This never had the effect of shoring up the retarded doctrine of ministerial responsibility, as had been anticipated, for reasons which are too complex to explore here. However, the Official Information Act, as it operates under the keen watch of the current Commissioner, Sir Brian Elwood, gets to the parts other reforms can't reach.

Sir Brian operates against a background which, in short, appears to restrict the release of policy advice. In practice, however, he interprets this to mean that such advice is only exempt until a decision has been reached. After that, most things can be revealed. He protects certain sorts of inter-personal communications, but insists that policy options discussed will be revealed. As

23 FOI Act 2000, ss 35, 36.

24 *Ibid*, s 53.

the superannuation discourse clearly shows, life can be breathed back into the faded doctrine of ministerial responsibility if a sufficiently robust FOI regime is in place. What emerges from this discourse is that the minister responsible for the decision can be fingered. It is much more difficult in New Zealand than in the UK to shelter behind the symbiotic relationship of civil servant/minister when no one accepts responsibility. It is interesting that the current UK Government appears to believe that UK citizens are not mature enough to interpret the signals passed between public actors taking policy decisions with sensitivity and judgment. The Derek Lewis affair reminds us that transparency in public affairs would cast light on issues perhaps more serious than pension issues. However, this must all be looked at in the light of the Government's new arrangements for written consultation on major policy issues.

Systems of consultation in the UK have improved and are improving. We have progressed beyond questionnaires administered to the random public into much more intensive qualitative consultation. However, this is still very much left to the discretion of individual administrations without there being a continuous constitutional duty through successive governments as part of the expression of democratic sentiments. Only the law of the constitution possesses that moral authority and suasion. It is comforting to hear that the agenda is less being set by government than the result of constructive engagement by a raft of partners. However, the institutional relationships are still out of balance. Nonetheless, the Code of Practice on written consultation, published in November 2000, and which applies to consultation documents issued after 1 January 2001, appears to be a genuine step forward. The criteria in the Code are described as follows:

> Though they have no legal force, and cannot prevail over statutory or other mandatory external requirements ... they should otherwise generally be regarded as binding on UK departments and their agencies, unless Ministers conclude that exceptional circumstances require a departure.[25]

The details of the Code will be passed over here, but the Government has made it clear that consultation exercises require 'proper feedback' from government after a consultation exercise, 'including an explanation of why particular options were, or were not, favoured'. This is a genuine improvement, although not going as far as US Administrative Law requirements or the New Zealand Act. No code, subject to ministerial interpretation, is a substitute for a truly effective FOI Act. Would the UK Treasury, for example, really implode if the New Zealand experience were repeated here? This ought to be a rhetorical question for one of the world's oldest democracies.

25 Code of Practice on Written Consultation, Cabinet Office, November 2000.

In 1999, the UK Government also set up a Project Board, chaired by the Permanent Secretary of the Cabinet Office, to oversee the Modernising Government programme, focusing particularly on the strategic drivers for making it happen and driving forward change in these areas. It contains just a few outside experts. Its reports will be welcomed, but it would be better were its working papers released for comment, along with progress reports, so that the Modernisation Project was examined in the context of a truly national debate, as its significance demands.[26]

What is being addressed here is the whole machinery of government. It would be churlish to deny the significance of the changes being worked. Traditional policy processes remain important, though they need to be constantly updated and improved, but various forms of public participation are now a necessary complement to them. We are talking about the optimum range of ancillary devices to dovetail with both the dignified parts of the constitution and its customary components. There is a danger, as the Government recognises, that consultation is seen as limited to informing the policy debate rather than controlling the policy debate with the government in the end weighing up the various views and taking the final decision. Yet, we are still a long way from achieving that aim, especially in knowing how government has weighed the advice which it receives from various quarters and how it prioritises it. There is still too little openness in the policy process.

In light of the general finding that there has been a decline in public confidence in government with citizens less willing to trust governments, there is a shift to a more open and participatory process in a number of OECD countries, in particular. It is becoming increasingly clear that governments must take the people with them, especially in creating safe social environments for both business and pleasure. There are ways and ways of doing this, but it is worth noting that an increasing number of countries have established constitutional or legal rights for public consultation, including Finland, Portugal, Sweden, Switzerland and the US.

With the right institutional background, much of the Modernisation agenda could herald a genuine improvement in the way the UK is governed. The Government understands the seamlessness of the policy process full well:

> Government should regard policy making as a continuous, learning process, not as a series of one-off initiatives. We will improve our use of evidence and research so that we understand better the problems we are trying to address. We must make more use of pilot schemes to encourage innovations and test whether they will work. We will ensure that all policies and programmes are clearly specified and evaluated, and the lessons of success and failure are communicated and acted upon. Feedback from those who implement and

26 And see below, Chapter 9.

> deliver policies and services is essential too. We need to apply the disciplines of project management to the policy process.[27]

Furthermore, serious attempts are being made to sew individual policies into the government's overall philosophical tapestry. So it has published the aims and objectives of all departments, which taken together represents a comprehensive statement of what the government has set out to deliver. As to what has been promised, the Performance and Innovation Unit will complete a report showing how they are to reform current accountability arrangements and incentive systems to help government departments work together to provide seamless services for their customers.[28] The constitutional scholar is always a little wary of what a UK government means by accountability, but we shall see.

To reprise, greater transparency of information not only assists decision making and reinforces necessary budget discipline, but is potentially a valuable tool for accountability, broadly conceived. Multiyear budgeting frameworks mean that both ministers and the public are fully informed about the total costs of new proposals rather than just the first year costs, which can be misleadingly low. Furthermore, performance information not only helps to improve the management process, but makes effective policy that much more achievable. So, improved quality performance information not only meets the immediate needs of policy makers; it should also underpin the new emphasis on accountability for the results attained. This new accountability emphasis is an important feature of the public management reforms, representing an essential *quid pro quo* for the devolution of authority to managers under the reforms. In the longer term, the public availability of this improved performance information should also support better policy, both by drawing on a wider circle of informed advice and by keeping the public service up to the mark.

TOWARDS A MODERN INSTITUTIONAL RESPONSE

Sweeping progress has been made in the years since the Next Steps initiative in the UK. In particular, there has been a marked improvement in public service management; the implementation of policy has been more effective. Customer concerns have been paid attention to with attendant yardsticks and service standards promoted against which ordinary users of public services can judge how far their expectations are being met. It is true that, until recently at least, the standards and targets have been more usually set by the management regimes themselves than by citizens or their representatives.

27 *Op cit*, Cabinet Office, fn 2, p 17.

28 *Op cit*, Cabinet Office, fn 11, p 5.

That is in the process of being changed, and progress will need to be monitored closely.

The *Modernisation* White Paper, alongside the Government's other initiatives in broadening and deepening consultation practices, promises a more open and responsive approach to policy making. There is a renewed understanding that monitoring current systems and practices and funnelling them back into the policy process has distinct and rational advantages. All these are pluses, although it is too early yet to make a mature judgment. In addition to traditional difficulties associated with public management, modern governments are now grappling with two new-ish issues. The first concerns the increasing use of partnerships for service delivery; these partners include devolved levels of government as well as the private and voluntary sectors. At the moment, there are real difficulties in determining the pulse of decision making within the partnerships. There is an understandable reluctance by the centre to let go in circumstances where, nevertheless, the 'synoptic delusion' of control from the centre is understood. These are problems facing public administration across the world and yet the feeling is that the centralist traditions of the UK may be hampering progress more than in some other places.

Secondly, there is the problem of 'joined-up' government, where cross-cutting issues are effectively pulled together at some kind of control point.[29] We are still very much in the early stages of a learning process over this dilemma. However, what is important for the whole exercise of weighing, monitoring and judging the effectiveness of programmes and their delivery is adequate institutional machinery which is not owned by the government of the day. Such machinery should exist to deliver its own judgment on, particularly, institutional and managerial deficiencies without at any stage seeking to second-guess government's judgment about what is desirable and what is not. Again, it has to be repeated that only the freest possible public information regime will be acceptable if things are to be as good as they should be and judged to be so. At the moment, considerable reservations on this score must be registered. Furthermore, institutional/constitutional supervisory machinery is not as strong in the UK as, say, Australia, the US and elsewhere. Chapter 9 takes up this theme in greater detail.

Although Parliament alone cannot fill the gaps being identified here, nevertheless, the Select Committee system, in particular, has a valuable role to play, in spite of the recent spat between their members and the Leader of the House.[30] In recent times, it has begun to display a little more independence than has been customary. Furthermore, there has been some improvement in the way government Bills have been presented to Parliament during the

29 For the problems and some of the solutions see *op cit*, Perri 6 *et al*, fn 5.

30 And see below, Chapter 9.

current administration, not least as a result of the role of the Modernisation Committee. In the past, Select Committees have only been encouraged to concentrate on *post hoc* examinations of government conduct. They are now being encouraged to play a more active, forward looking role in the policy process. The Government has begun increasingly to publish legislation in draft to give Departmental Select Committees an opportunity to comment on and help shape legislation at a formative stage. This is greatly to be welcomed and brings the UK more into line with the practice of parliaments elsewhere.

As the OECD has recognised, public management reforms are not in any direct way responsible for increasing democratic deficits. In fact, they ought to be part of the solution. Across the world, such reforms are assisting the participation of a more informed public, not least in the way so much emphasis is placed on transparency, which has led to the provision of far more useful information than ever before regarding government policy, programmes and activities. Elsewhere, but not to the same extent in the UK, the authority of elected politicians has typically been reinforced, with the role of expert advisers being more clearly understood. In a number of jurisdictions, both of these aspects of the reforms have strengthened democratic accountability. Again, the emphasis on service quality, the decentralisation and devolution of decision making affecting the delivery of services, and the associated strengthening of public consultation are increasing the opportunities for public involvement in those activities of government which most immediately affect people's daily lives.

As far as the UK is concerned some, but by no means all, of these advantages are in evidence. Certainly, there is greater transparency, but the policy process is still far too clouded and the responsibility of ministers versus their advisers not at all well highlighted. Decentralisation has occurred through the Scottish Parliament, the Welsh Assembly, the London Mayor and Assembly and, hopefully soon, through the English regions. The tensions which will inevitably occur have yet to be fully played out. And yet all these developments – and partnerships in all their forms – will be less effective and more centralised unless information surrounding the policy process is released quite extensively. There is no immediate prospect of this occurring in the UK at the time of writing. Indeed, even the Select Committees still do not receive information about agencies and their establishment or review outside the normal announcement of Prior Option Reviews. In other words, they enjoy no special advantage in commenting on proposals in advance of publication. Furthermore, although there have been important constitutional law developments, there has still not been the commitment to reform through administrative law that is so common in the OECD countries. Modernisation of management has occurred at a different pace from the modernisation of our system of public law.

Separating out provider from purchaser, policy maker from management (to some extent) can provide genuine advantages. But, only if the respective competences and responsibilities are clearly defined and only if ownership is admitted, thereby making accountability a reality. There is still some way to go in this respect. The UK is currently reforming public management with a genuine will. It has still some little way to go in reforming its constitutional structures. These themes will be re-addressed in later chapters.

CHAPTER 6

THE PRIVATE WORLD OF GOVERNMENT: PRIVATISATION AND CONTRACTING OUT

> Privatisation is not a rigid ideological policy of marketisation, rather a shorthand for a group of policies able to assist in the transition of the inefficient into the productive.[1]

In this view, privatisation is a generic concept and an article of faith about the proper nature and scope of government. The UK, however, has arguably gone further than other nations in actively seeking to privatise government itself and not just the appurtenances of government. This has taken the form of contracting out, market testing, partnerships between the public and the private sector (albeit with the private taking the lead in ownership and management of resources) and the extensive use of private consultants, not just in the traditional way, but to supplement or even replace advice formerly tendered by civil servants. This will be re-examined later, but the celebrated purchaser/provider split provides the opportunity for readdressing the optimum role of the State in the matter of governance and for focusing its responsibilities more sharply. Leaving aside the crucial issue of releasing slimmed-down government to concentrate more forcefully on policy issues, and in particular the making and evaluation of policy, the redefinition of roles requires a close scrutiny of accountability mechanisms which Parliament, 'willy-nilly', has largely abrogated.

Recent administrations appear to endorse the underlying philosophy of the 'private world of government', well expressed in the following official communiqué from the Executive Office of the President of the US:

> In the process of governing, the Government should not compete with its citizens. The competitive enterprise system, characterized by individual freedom and initiative, is the primary source of national economic strength. In recognition of this principle, it has been and continues to be the general policy of the Government to rely on commercial sources to supply the products and services the Government needs.[2]

Although this sentiment has considerable contemporary resonance, it is clear that this does not amount to what Rhodes calls 'governing without government'.[3] Contracts have to be managed, while partnerships are just that

1 Ward, G, 'Reforming the public sector' (1993) 64 Political Quarterly 301. Much of what follows in this chapter is taken from Goh, J and Lewis, ND, *The Private World of Government (occasional papers)*, 1998, Sheffield: Centre for Socio-Legal Studies, University of Sheffield.

2 Circular No A-76 (revised), OMB, Washington DC, 4 August 1983. This national policy was promulgated through Bureau of the Budget Bulletins issued in 1955, 1957 and 1960. OMB Circular No A-76 was issued in 1966 and revised periodically.

3 Rhodes, RAW, *Understanding Governance: Policy Networks etc*, 1997, OUP, Chapter 3.

– with the public partner remaining in charge of the overall direction of projects. Furthermore, even 'retained' government has, in a sense, been privatised since there has been a distinct movement towards fostering a change in management culture within the public sector so as to function, to the maximum extent possible, as if it was within the private sector. To promote a performance orientation, the system is subjected to market disciplines such as competitive tendering and contracting out, cost recovery, and accrual accounting (including capital costs). This means that traditional administrator-dominated bureaucracies are being replaced by manager-dominated and market-oriented organisations. Practices in the UK highlight that two elements – letting managers manage (increased flexibility) – and making the managers manage (accountability by central mechanisms) must be present for a successful incentive system.[4] User-pay regimes for intra-government transactions are also part of this general drive.

Mimicking the private sector has become increasingly significant in the UK and a marked upping of the ante was evident under the Major Government, whose emphasis, expressed as recently as *Competing for Quality*,[5] was particularly marked. Of course, even before that, the Local Government Act 1980, extended by the 1988 legislation, introduced compulsory competitive tendering (CCT) into a range of local authority services, the only example of such compulsion identified up to this point. More recently, CCT was introduced into areas that are arguably managerial as opposed to policy-oriented and include the management of council properties, such management including dealing with tenant problems and, to some extent, even allocation.[6] Although CCT is in the process of being abolished and replaced by the Best Value (BV) initiative in local government and Better Quality Services (BQS),[7] the post-1997 Labour Government has scarcely resiled from its predecessor's preference, as evidenced by partnership arrangements for the Channel Tunnel Link, the London Underground and, indeed, its reaffirmation of PFI, now rebranded as Public Private Partnerships (PPP).

With the development of policies for private finance, market testing, contracting out and internal markets, government departments are doing more of their business than ever through procurement as opposed to direct provision. Even in 1995, the annual spend was around £40 bn a year, with purchasing authorities in the former NHS internal market accounting for another £20 bn. Since *Competing for Quality* was introduced, the involvement

4 OECD, *In Search of Results: Performance Management Practices*, 1997, PUMA, p 10.

5 Cm 1730, 1991.

6 See, eg, *Market Testing Bulletin*, Vol 2, No 7, May 1995, Business Information, p 17.

7 Cabinet Office, *Better Quality Services: Handbook on Creating Public/Private Partnerships Through Market Testing and Contracting Out*, 1998, HMSO.

of the private sector in the provision of services previously undertaken by civil servants increased significantly. Between April 1992 and March 1995, work with an estimated value of £1.3 bn had been contracted out either directly or as a result of market-testing exercises.[8] PPP, as noted, has added a further dimension to the Private World of Government (PWG).

The pace of 'privatisation', then, has quickened. This has occurred in the fields of information technology, telecommunications, prisons and court escort services. Even where in-house teams win market tests (and often, in the past, they were precluded from tendering), they are increasingly managed by departments in much the same way as external providers, with their responsibilities set out in service level agreements. Although the major concentration here will be on central government, the trend is clear in local government too. The management of council properties has been noted, but even mediation services for neighbour disputes have been added to the list.[9] The homelessness legislation was revised with a view to increasing the role of private landlords, private consultants are being increasingly used for the privatisation programme itself, for the roads programme, for the evolving nature of Next Steps, while partnering or partnership sourcing whereby customers and suppliers collaborate closely to deliver cost reductions, improvements in quality, etc, have come on apace. All these developments have much to recommend them, but both the decision making process itself and subsequent arrangements for transparency and accountability pose vital questions for the constitutional lawyer.

It is not clear how far the goal of genuine competition drives the process,[10] although in the US, for example, the Competition in Contracting Act 1984 requires Federal Agencies to open their bidding process to all qualified firms by eliminating advertising restrictions and non-competitive bidding procedures. However, four years after the passing of the Act, a government report recorded the existence of in-built bias in favour of the status quo.[11] Better Quality Services, while committed to genuine competition in the Appraising Options process, retains closed or limited tendering lists in a number of instances. The main restrictions are imposed by EU procurement regulations, of which more later. However, it is necessary to flag up that the general lack of transparency in so called 'commercial-in-confidence' matters presents a serious and continuing problem.

There has always been procurement in government, but it is the contracting out of public services themselves that is relatively new. As might be anticipated, it goes back a little further in the US. The programme was

8 *Government Opportunities Special Report*, 27 June 1995.

9 See, eg, *Government Opportunities*, Vol 1, No 1, July 1995, p 38.

10 For some ambiguous statistics on efficiency in the process, see, esp *op cit*, Goh and Lewis, fn 1, p 6.

11 OMB, *Enhancing Government Productivity Through Competition*, 1988, OMB, p 13.

initially formalised in 1955 when the Eisenhower administration issued the Bureau of Budget Bulletin 55-4. In 1966, the Bureau of the Budget introduced the policy as the now-celebrated Circular A-76, a policy supported by successive administrations. As in the UK, opinion in favour of contracting out has hardened so that all new activities that can be performed by private sector commercial sources must be acquired from such sources, except where a statute, or national security interests require government performance or where private industry costs are manifestly unreasonable.[12] Although there has been some dissatisfaction with the state of the law in this area, there is at least more law regulating the process than is the case in the UK. This is particularly true in the arena of the adjudication of complaints by disappointed seekers of government contracts,[13] an arena where accountability mechanisms are being developed in the UK largely as a result of EU Directives.

Although much contracting out is impelled by efficiency savings, the practice, where it has been closely investigated, is not always as clear-cut. Thus, for example, the Wolds Prison, the first to be contracted out, has been subject to an audit investigation by the CAG which revealed serious contractual deficiencies and cost overruns which were not anticipated.[14] It is also important to note that not only was the successful bidder not the lowest tenderer, but subsequent events cast doubt on the quality standards which it had promised to deliver. Contracting out public services is a notoriously difficult matter, but it is undoubtedly more difficult to judge the effectiveness of the process in the absence of greater transparency than is currently the case in the UK. Furthermore, there are cases, freely admitted, when placing business with a supplier having a near-monopoly of provision 'appears to be the lowest cost of best quality solution, at least in the short term'. In such circumstances, the government will attempt to gauge the short term advantages against the long term risk to both sides where government might become over-dependent on a single supplier or the supplier over-dependent on government business. Exactly how this exercise is rationally conducted is less than clear to the independent observer. This applies equally to attempts by the government to ensure that it is not captured over the long term by a supplier who develops an effective monopoly. Indeed, effective repatriation to in-house teams, according to 40 years of American experience, is a rarity. There are circumstances, too, for example, the procurement of defence equipment, where competitive procedures are not always possible. This is

12 For a review of one particular area, see Lundenburg, WV, 'Contracting out by the Federal Government for legal services: a legal and empirical analysis' (1988) 63 Notre Dame L Rev 399, pp 399–491.

13 See Administrative Conference of the United States, *Government Contract Bid Protests*, 1995.

14 For the mixed results of the then PFI see *op cit*, Goh and Lewis, fn 1, Appendix 1.

perhaps inevitable; what is not inevitable is the closed nature of the procedures accompanying the process.[15]

There is no objection being made here to PWG or the Contracting State.[16] The point being made is that these developments are constitutional issues which have not been properly addressed by our system of constitutional accretion. As Harden makes clear, there is much potential in this relatively new way of delivering public services, not least the highlighting of different responsibilities in functional terms. However, contracts of this sort are often not like commercial contracts, but much more like delegated legislation. They should, then, be subject to a different regimen from their purely commercial counterparts.

At least the Blair Government affects to a pragmatic, non-ideological approach in such matters. This means looking hard – but not dogmatically – at what services government can best provide itself, what should be contracted to the private sector, and what should be done in partnership. It has developed a number of levers to drive up standards in public services. They are, in particular, first, the Comprehensive Spending Review, which establishes a new approach to improving service delivery. Secondly, the new Public Service Agreements (PSAs), which set out in detail what people can expect for new investment and, thirdly, three year spending plans for departments to allow rational forward planning. All this should help to make public bodies more 'competitive' when compared to private sector models. At the heart of the new approach will be the concern to seek best value for service delivery, regardless of ownership. We shall return to this theme shortly.

However, there are those who believe that in seeking genuine competition, innovation and best value, the public sector alternatives have not always been allowed to operate on a level playing field. Certainly, there has been no attempt in the UK to imitate the New Zealand experience of corporatisation. However, at the time of writing, one interesting public sector initiative was being taken seriously. The Government was reported to be considering giving Manchester's council-owned airport powers to invest in rail franchises and in Railtrack, as well as in other commercial ventures. The airport is on the verge of taking a multimillion pound stake in Greater Manchester's Metrolink supertram system.

Although the Government has lifted restrictions on the airport borrowing on the open market, directors claim it is still prevented from using its considerable assets to invest outside its core business. These developments will be followed with considerable interest.

---

15 See, in particular, the role of the Review Board on Government Contracts: Birkinshaw, P, Harden, I and Lewis, ND, *Government by Moonlight*, 1990, Hyman Unwin, esp pp 169–72.

16 See Harden, I, *The Contracting State*, 1992, OUP.

However, a word about PPP, the former PFI, is called for. It is intended to provide an effective means of harnessing private sector management skills in the delivery of capital projects and associated public services:

> Departments will consider private finance options for their capital projects whenever it is possible to transfer control over the project and the associated risks to the private sector without disproportionate cost. Many projects across Government will pass this test and hence invitations to tender for them will be on the basis of private finance. When private finance proposals are received, they will be treated like other forms of procurement and assessed on VFM criteria, taking into account the costs and benefits of transferring risk and management responsibility to the private sector.
>
> Where capital investment is not a major consideration, Departments will continue to explore whether there are areas of work suitable for market testing or contracting out.[17]

PPP, according to government, shares much in common with, and is an evolution of, privatisation and contracting out. It 'sits between privatisation and contracting out, bringing the private sector into areas which have previously been considered to be wholly the preserve of the public sector. PFI is focused on the provision of capital assets which underpin services delivered presently, by the public sector'.[18]

PPP is now government's preferred method of procurement for major capital projects so that all capital spending schemes will be required to demonstrate that private sector alternatives have been fully considered before public finance is made available. There is even legislation in the form of the New Roads and Street Works Act 1991 to facilitate the process, while the government also argues that access to world capital markets allows projects to proceed which would otherwise be unaffordable from the public purse.[19]

The Blair Government has continued the upward spiral of commitment to the PPP. For example, in 1999, it announced plans to privatise the projects arm of the PFI/PPP Taskforce. This is now known as Partnerships UK, which will provide private sector expertise and funds to the public sector to define and develop PPP projects before they go to the market. Partnerships UK is a private sector company, part-owned by government, which will make its money either by taking equity stakes in the projects it backs or by charging a fee to the public bodies whose projects it takes on.

---

17 *Setting New Standards*, paras 2.15-16. Whatever the original intention, the Treasury Select Committee has come to the conclusion that PFI is a substitute for public expenditure rather than representing an additional injection of funds into public services. *The Private Finance Initiative*, 6th Report, HC 146, 1995–96, para 7.

18 Cabinet Office, *PFI Initiative: Report on the NIRS2 Project*, 1995, CCTA, Pt 1.

19 Ministers have made it clear that most new hospital building for the NHS in future will have to be privately financed. In 1997, the government gave the go-ahead to 14 privately financed hospitals with a capital value of £1.3 bn.

Some larger points about privatisation generically should be made. First, the ideological case for:

> Whereas reform of the public sector through cost cutting and restructuring merely delays the reassertion of monopolistic and inefficient practices, a direct break with the public sector through privatisation frees the entity to identify and then to engage in what should be its primary function, the efficient delivery of a given service or product.
>
> The most important aspect of this process is in reacquainting the unit, be it the airline, a trucking firm or a steel plant with its commercial objectives. No longer under political control, it will be able to build plant where it is most cost effective to do so, raise capital on the open market without the need to consider the budgetary constraints of government, and set prices at a market level rather than as a result of political sensitivities to consumer response.[20]

However, there are opposing contentions. Some believe that there is no reason to suppose that merely transferring a natural monopoly from public into private hands will produce an output more valued by consumers or that gains in allocative efficiency will only come about via gains in internal efficiency. Support for privatisation, therefore, should rest on the increased internal and dynamic efficiency imposed by capital market competition. It has been well argued[21] that the effects of ownership on allocative efficiency are indeterminate, and that it is increased competition rather than changes of ownership *per se* which generates gains in internal efficiency.

This would suggest that it is not possible to assess efficiency in abstraction from the social ends of economic activity which cannot simply be reduced to market-enforced commercial objectives. Although the separation of the State and the economy is generally desirable, it is equally true that the mixed economy has evolved as a means of managing the social inadequacies of unrestrained market mechanisms, so that any significant shift in the mix can be expected to ameliorate one set of problems only by exacerbating others. Currently, the UK, like most other countries, has no reflective and dispassionate mechanisms to make balanced recommendations on what the mix should look like at any given time.

Privatisation has been a central phenomenon in recent political history and is part of a huge constitutional shift which, regardless of the merits of the changes worked, has been such as to merit the kind of constitutional debate which current institutional arrangements do not permit.[22] New Zealand, on

20 *Op cit*, Ward, fn 1, p 299.

21 Williams, M, 'The political economy of privatization', in Holland, M and Boston, J (eds), *The Fourth Labour Government: Politics and Policy in New Zealand*, 2nd edn, 1992, OUP, p 149. The treatment of 'efficiency', pp 149–60, seriously calls into account much of the recent conventional wisdom on the economic benefits of privatisation.

22 Lewis, ND, 'Regulating non-governmental bodies: privatization, accountability and the public-private divide', in Jowell, J and Oliver, D (eds), *The Changing Constitution*, 2nd edn, 1989, OUP, pp 219–46.

the other hand, has been more open and principled. Annex 4 to the 1988 Budget statement lays down the government's objectives, principles, criteria and guidelines for asset sales. They include reducing public debt, subjecting State-owned enterprises to professional business management, avoiding future demands for government cash and minimising commercial risk and enabling ministers to concentrate on economic and social policy. Each sale is assessed on a case by case basis with the overriding objective of maximising both economic welfare and revenue to the Exchequer.

It has been made quite clear that the case for privatisation is separate from the case made for efficiency. There are publicly owned enterprises in New Zealand which are efficient by any standards. Of course, both privatisation and corporatisation seek to improve efficiency not only in the affected markets, but also in the markets in which the industries become actors. Furthermore, privatisation must not impede the government's broader macro-economic or social policy. This implies that the cost of any particular asset sale must include those of making good any degradation of objectives, including social objectives – for example, employment considerations.[23]

Nevertheless, there remains something in the argument that private enterprise may be generally preferred. In a private enterprise, both internal control by the shareholders and external control by the capital market provide incentives to avoid inefficiency. Shareholders monitor managers to ensure that they maximise income and failure to do so will lead to the sale of shares with other managerial groups bidding for control of the company in the belief that they will be able to obtain a better return for the company's resources. In a public enterprise, capital market monitoring does not work, while internal monitoring will by performed by politicians who are not necessarily interested in how efficiently managers allocate resources. This is the bottom line justification for private market enterprise, and to modify it requires careful justification. Instinctively, however, the feeling persists that rail privatisation in the UK was ideologically driven, has proved to be consumer unfriendly, and is likely to have been economically damaging to the economy in the round, especially taking into account environmental considerations. This highlights the fact that, in real terms, genuinely constitutional issues do not receive appropriate institutional deliberation.

The justification for privatisations in the UK has never been made clear and empirically would seem to have shifted over time. No grand theological debate has taken place; not is there an obvious theatre for such an event.[24] How, then, are decisions to privatise taken and what criteria should be employed?

---

23 And see *op cit*, Williams, fn 21, p 146.

24 And see Lewis, ND, *Choice and the Legal Order: Rising Above Politics*, 1996, Butterworths, Chapter 7.

BETTER QUALITY SERVICES

First, a word should be said about *Government Opportunities*, formerly the *Market Testing Bulletin*, fittingly enough published by the private sector. The publication aims to facilitate communication between government and business. It is a 'comprehensive guide to contract opportunities' arising from the Competing for Quality programme and the PPP initiative. *Inter alia*, it includes both contract awards and contract notices; however, the information afforded for the award of contracts is not only sparse, but reasons for decisions are ordinarily expressed through a standard *pro forma* which, as far as the general public is concerned, is not especially informative. Although it is normal to disclose the number of tenders received, details are not disclosed nor, except in the most technical of cases, is the successful bid. This is in spite of the government *pro forma* contract award notice referring to the price or range of prices paid.[25] The award criteria are invariably rigid and opaque. However, following upon the requirements of GATT (now the WTO) and European directives, a procedure for 'debriefing' has now been adopted. Debriefing occurs on request when unsuccessful tenderers are informed of the reasons for their elimination from the exercise.

A fundamental basis of the contracting out process is the 'prior options' review which was first set out in the *Government's Guide to Market Testing*, but which has now changed and has been renamed 'Appraising Options' with the publication of *Better Quality Services*. First, it is asked whether any particular activity needs to be performed at all or whether it should be wound up. If it does need to be performed, is it a suitable candidate for privatisation? Where government wishes to retain responsibility for the service, it will consider whether competition for its provision should be introduced and the possibility of establishing a NS agency will be canvassed at the same time. In considering how to ensure competition, a key decision will be whether for policy or management reasons the work should be done by the private sector, or whether to have a genuine 'market testing' exercise complete with in-house bid.

Privatisation, at least in the general sense, remains very much part of the Government's agenda. No view is taken on this matter except to say that it is not blindingly obvious that the UK possesses the institutional machinery to conduct a cost-benefit analysis of proposed schemes.[26] If the best value for money is to be obtained for the Exchequer and if the best services are to be delivered against a clear set of policy objectives, then some alteration in the way these matters are presently decided is clearly called for. Without wishing

25 *Government Opportunities: Guidance and Proforma*, 1995, GOI, Annex 111e.

26 And see Lewis, ND, 'The Citizen's Charter and Next Steps: a new way of governing?' (1993) 64 Political Quarterly 316, esp p 323.

to be overly prescriptive, the example of the French Conseil Constitutionnel might be re-examined,[27] although other countries, for example, Canada, Finland and Holland have revised their arrangements for the consideration of these matters. Holland, in particular, has particularly sophisticated procedures for both assessing these issues, for monitoring and evaluating effectiveness and efficiency and for the relationship between strategically core ministries and the satellite organisations.[28]

Many of the key issues have again been laid out by the OECD.[29] For detail, reference should be made to the text, but several points are worth noting here. In particular, where the State's responsibility is principally to ensure equitable access to quality services at a reasonable cost, the scope for contracting out should rest heavily on:

- how far it is possible and desirable to specify all the relevant considerations in the contract;
- the State's capacity to monitor the contract and apportion accountability obligations between the contracting parties to the satisfaction of all concerned;
- creating incentives so that it is in the contractor's interest to fulfil the spirit as well as the letter of the contract; and
- providing meaningful sanctions to enforce the contract provisions if necessary.

Although writing contracts with an external supplier can, therefore, represent a challenge and the transaction costs can become significant, it also needs to be remembered that many of the same issues should be addressed if the alternative of providing the service internally were adopted.

Although the previous Government was convinced that 'privatisation' was already producing improvements in meeting consumer demands, there was considerable evidence that CFQ was driven more by a search for efficiency savings than for improvements to consumer services:

> It is also clear that CFQ does not always work in the way intended. Thus the CAG revealed serious contractual difficulties and cost overruns in relation to the Wolds prison, while contracting with near-monopolies has meant that government appears over-dependent on a single supplier. Public accountability is also too often pinned on the NAO whose occasional reports have been most informative. However, they are necessarily spasmodic and do not provide for a constant and consistent flow of information. *Setting New*

27 See, eg, Prosser, T and Graham, C, *Regulating the Privatised Industries*, 1991, OUP.

28 See, esp, OECD, *Issues and Developments in Public Management*, Survey 1996–97 on The Netherlands, 1997, PUMA.

29 See OECD, *Contracting Out Government Services: Best Practice Guidelines and Case Studies*, Public Management Occasional Papers No 20, 1998, OECD.

Standards demands a clear audit trail for all these contractual relationships, but such matters are difficult for the public to assess.[30]

Of course, the present Government has introduced *Better Quality Services* and *Best Value*. Although Best Value provisions for local government have been much more publicised, the BQS initiative, announced in 1998, is of considerable importance, replacing, as its does, the Government's *Guide to Market Testing*. It sets out how governments, agencies and quangos should go about achieving better quality services at optimal cost to taxpayers. As a key component in the strategy for improving government services, BQS stresses recognition of people as a key asset, encourages public/private partnerships, confirms the Government's commitment to competition as a tool, covers retendering, and offers guidance for the first time on insourcing.

The guidance is a significant repositioning on market testing. Departments are encouraged to make clear-cut choices between internal restructuring and contracting out whenever possible, rather than the halfway house of market testing, which has often caused uncertainty for staff and customers in the past. Departments will consult their staff, service users and the private sector before making their choice. Although greater information is now available than formerly, there is still a failure to meet US-style administrative law mechanisms aimed at improving genuine accountability.

Best Value for local government is provided for in the Local Government Act 2000.[31] Even so, BV partnerships had been in place for some two years before the Act came into force. Some considerable number of authorities had been identified where specific policies were already in place at both the corporate and departmental/service levels. Nearly three-quarters of all local authorities had BV review programmes up and running by early 1999. The main division appeared to be between authorities that have chosen an all-services, authority-wide approach from the outset and those who were looking at BV across a range of specific services or themes. There have, to date, been a range of approaches to BV which include:

- production of draft community plans by the authority alone or in partnerships with other agencies;
- review of member and officer decision making and implementation structures at a corporate level;
- commencement of a corporate review of policies and strategies;
- devising of processes for organisational health checks;
- commencement of formal consultation with local people, business, the voluntary sector and others;

30 *Op cit*, Lewis, fn 26, para 10.2, p 60.

31 And see below, Chapter 9.

- arrangement for formal employee involvement in development of BV
- details of criteria used to select services for Fundamental Performance Reviews,

and so on.[32]

It is too early at this point to assess the significance of BV initiatives, but early signs are promising. However, it is critical, as New Zealand has constantly shown, to measure outputs and indicators in a meaningful way; in a way which is directly related to the quality of policy advice:

> The Public Service harbours substantial policy development and advisory capacities – more, probably, in terms of resources invested and people employed than at any other time. This capacity, however, needs to be focused upon the public policy issues of today in the same way that resources were focused on economic policy in the 1980s. The major public policy issues today include health, welfare, education and training, and Maori affairs. Improvement of the policy development and advisory performance of the Public Service is a priority.[33]

THE MECHANICS

Achieving value for money, effectiveness, improving customer service and the like depends at least in part on the mechanics adopted for involving the private sector in the delivery of public services. This is, in part, about institutional/constitutional matters, but also about a raft of associated items.

Best Value will frequently be judged to be best delivered by the private sector, either singly or in partnership. All work which is to be 'market tested' in the broadest sense will be advertised to ensure that the full market potential is explored. BQS is directed to achieve that end and, as has been noted, it is a little early to say how far it is being effective. It is clear, however, what the deficiencies of its predecessor were, and therefore, it is not difficult to identify some of the pitfalls it must seek to avoid. Previous detailed work on CFQ presents something of a mixed picture concerning accountability and effectiveness.[34]

Advertisements will be placed in *Government Opportunities* and the Official Journal of the European Communities. The stages which follow are described in *The Private World of Government*. The specification should contain the scope and type of work to be required, outputs, quality standards, work

32 See Bailey, M and Sutcliffe, J, 'Exacting the most out of Best Value' (1999) 29 Local Government Management 8, pp 8–9.

33 Report of the States Services Commission, New Zealand, presented by the Commissioner and tabled in Parliament October 1997.

34 Most of what follows is taken from *op cit*, Goh and Lewis, fn 1.

measurement, the respective responsibilities of the parties, a schedule for the supply of the service and continuing responsibilities on completion. Sometimes pre-tender meetings are arranged with bidders and occasionally first hand visits made to contractors' premises to ensure a first hand assessment of facilities and systems. The findings and conclusions will be carefully documented in a consistent format in order to provide a clear audit trail, but any such information will be treated as commercial in confidence. Nothing in the Freedom of Information Act 2000 has changed this.[35]

Although there has traditionally been a general lack of transparency, occasional glimpses of the process can be gleaned from the reports of the NAO. The report into the testing of the Home Office's ED5 Division, which provided information technology services,[36] indicated that the government's general claims about the conduct of the process had been followed. Two proposals were received, one from the in-house team, but the private sector was preferred. What was important to note, however, from such observations was the preponderance of such exercises in favour of the private sector bidder by reason of the fact that cost reductions such as redundancy payments or lower wages were matters that the in-house team may not necessarily find easy to assess. By contrast, the private sector bidder was able to show projections which were more accurate and in line with private sector practice, or indeed was more able to absorb the additional costs of the contracts within its established system of operation.

The whole area is one where the EU is having and is likely to have considerable influence. There are different requirements for supply contracts, public works, and services. The value of contracts to which the Directives apply will be passed over, since they will be amended from time to time, but where they do apply, contracts may be awarded by 'open procedures', 'restricted procedures', whereby only those service providers invited by the authority shall submit a tender, 'negotiated procedures', whereby authorities consult service providers of their choice and negotiate the terms of the contract with one or more of them. The circumstances for using particular procedures are laid down in the Directives, with some degree of flexibility retained for the national authorities. The detail is too complex for a work of this kind and attention to the *ipsissima verba* of the Directives will need to be paid by the authorities concerned.[37] Although the open procedure is said to

35 Indeed, in September 2000, John Prescott, the Secretary of State for Transport, etc, was reported to have barred the Home Office Minister in charge of freedom of information from access to the financial details of a deal to build Britain's first private toll motorway. 'Commercial secrecy' was the main reason put forward: (2000) *The Guardian*, 18 September. The protection of sensitive commercial information is now primarily protected by FOI Act 2000, s 43. Again, the way it is interpreted will be crucial.

36 Report of the Comptroller and Auditor General, *The Market Testing of ED5*, Session 1995–96, HC 281.

37 See Council Directives (92/50), (71/305), (89/440), (77/62), and (80/767).

be the best assurance of the establishment of equal conditions for participating in public contracts in all Member States, there is some considerable leeway in practice.

The contract notices themselves will often contain useful information both for potential applicants and the general public. They will, for example, specify the procedure to be adopted, indicate the maximum number of tenderers to be invited, the proposed length of the contract, and will usually ask for a description of the service provider's measures for ensuring quality, a copy of the last available audited financial accounts, and so on.

A few words must be said especially of the EU Directives' requirement on the publication of contract notices. An extensive body of case law is beginning to emerge and, in a sense, it represents an attempt to structure the discretion of Member States or contracting authorities in procurement. The rule is that contracts which exceed the thresholds laid down in the Directives must be notified and published in the Official Journal. An example of intervention by the Court of Justice is *Commission v Spain*,[38] where the question arose as to whether the single tender procedure was exempted from the general requirement to notify under Directive 77/62 on Public Supplies Contracts. The ECJ, in accepting the right of contracting authorities to invoke the exemptions under the Directive, decided that the use of any exemption must be construed restrictively. In addition, it made clear that the burden of proof lay on the party seeking to rely on the derogation. This line of argument is consistent with its earlier jurisprudence and, particularly in public procurement, the cases of *Commission v Spain* and *Commission v Italy*.[39] The requirement of publication also applies to 'framework agreements'[40] which are 'no more than a structure within which numerous contracts are to be awarded'. This was so established in *Commission v Greece*.[41] In addition to this limited number of cases on publication after the award of contracts, the Commission has also taken interim action against a contracting authority for failure to comply with the publication requirement. In *Re the Dundalk Water Service Commission v Ireland*, the Commission successfully obtained the suspensory remedy under Art 10 of Directive 71/305 on public works contracts prior to the award of the contract so as to ensure, as the ECJ reasoned, 'that the application for interim measures is not prejudiced by the existence of a *fait accompli*'.[42]

38 Case C-328/92 [1994] ECR 1-1569.

39 Case 71/92 [1993] ECR-1-59233 and 199/85 [1987] ECR 1039.

40 See *op cit*, Goh and Lewis, fn 1, pp 34–35.

41 Case C-79/94 [1995] 1-1071; closer to home, see *R v Secretary of State for Home Department ex p London Borough of Harrow* (1996) 2 CMLR 524, which concerned the refusal of the Minister to approve Harrow's decision/notice of tender because of non-compliance with Directive 92/50.

42 Case 45/87R [1987] 2 CMLR 197, p 199.

Compliance with the publication requirement has never been the hallmark of contracting authorities of Member States, although the record of the UK has been good. Disregard for the requirement is frequent. Yet, unless the Commission is apprised of the material procurement information through publication, particularly the value of contracts so as to determine whether the Directives apply in the first place, enforcement against the contracting authority in default is necessarily imperfect. An inquiry by the House of Lords' Select Committee on the European Communities revealed, *inter alia*, that a difficulty of enforcing compliance was down to the fact that 'the information to [the Commission] on specific cases of non-observance is normally second-hand, and random in character'.[43] Dependence on unsuccessful bidders to supply the material information is itself dependent on these bidders having access to the relevant information – very much a vicious circle – and to lodge a complaint. In the summary of the *Guide to the Community Rule on Government Procurement*, the Commission observed in respect of the first Directives that 'despite the progress they have not matched up to expectations, because of improper transposition into national law in some cases and widespread abuse of exception clauses'.[44] Little has changed since. A recent review by the DTI on public procurement revealed abuses of a similar nature; the lack of publication, particularly the value of contracts. It also noted that the system of enforcement through national courts is virtually non-existent. Informal complaints was the preferred method of redressing grievances among unsuccessful bidders. This was due principally to the fear or risk of jeopardising future business, the difficulty of proving damage as required by the Directives and national legislation transposing those Directives, and the costs and uncertainty of outcome arising from any pursuit of formal redress.[45] Any legal proceedings are usually commenced under the Art 226 (formerly 169) procedure by the Commission, which has no fear of reprisals. Be that as it may, there is a growing juridification of procurement activities by Member States and contracting authorities. Where appropriate, the Commission has been ready to initiate action against non-complying parties. The challenge now for a more effective regime of procurement law must be to depart from the declaratory remedy of the Court of Justice and the simple award of costs towards a penalty system where fines will far outweigh the gains of non-compliance. This is both essential and unavoidable as the procurement world widens and deepens.[46]

---

43 House of Lords' Select Committee on European Communities, *Compliance with Procurement Directives*, Session 1987–88, HL 72, para 50.

44 Case C-358/87 (1987) OJ C358/1.

45 Single Market Compliance Unit, *DTI Review on Public Procurement*, 1994.

46 For GATT/WTO rules, see *op cit*, Goh and Lewis, fn 1, p 15.

THE AVAILABILITY OF DOCUMENTS AND INFORMATION

The imperfections and uncertainties of the FOI Act have been touched upon. However, the point to underline is that, especially in the current context, the FOI Act is severely circumscribed by the provisions relating to, especially though not entirely, matters said to be 'commercial in confidence'. However, a considerable body of information is available in the form of government or government-sponsored publications, press releases, PQs and the like.

PQs are, of course, an established form of information release and much information concerning contracting out, etc, can be gleaned from searching the columns of *Hansard*. In procedural terms, the handbook on *Better Quality Services*[47] is the bible, although a number of documents are available containing bibliographies of the procurement and contracting out process. The handbook contains valuable sources of information, including contact points for the contracting out process and a helpful glossary, although it lacks the model forms of contract which was contained in its predecessor. Of particular value are the lists of CCTA and Central Unit on Purchasing Procurement (CUP) guidance and publications.

From time to time, individual documents are issued which add to the stock of knowledge, an important example being the *Market Testing Bulletin* Special Report, January 1995, which provided systemic information on CFQ reviews. *Government Opportunities* is seen as the definitive source of all information relating to the market testing programme, including PFI/PPP initiatives.[48]

As far as contractors and the interested general public are concerned, individual contract specifications would be expected normally to be available for inspection in addition to being available for purchase, while individual contract notices and invitations to bid are available through *Government Opportunities*. The contract specifications define the service which the purchaser wishes to buy, the scope and type of work to be undertaken, frequency of inspection, equipment to be provided by the purchaser, etc. There are also Treasury model documents from which departments may derive specifications for particular purposes.

Empirical work indicates that, in the past, departments have generally been reluctant to disclose prices in contract award notices for diverse reasons: for example, that price may not be the overriding consideration and will yield to quality of service or, as may be expected, on the grounds of commercial sensitivity. In particular, prices are not disclosed for fear that the practice

47 *Op cit*, Cabinet Office, fn 7.

48 There is copious public documentation available on the PFI. See, eg, PSP, *Public Sector Procurement and Finance*, first published in 1995. It was announced that it would appear 10 times per year.

might lead to collusion between contractors in future bids. In spite of this, the First Division Association (of civil servants) has alleged that there has been collusion 'between certain private sector companies that for each contract only one of them will make a realistic bid, with the result that contracts would eventually be shared out amongst them'.[49] It is interesting to note, however, that BQS states that a robust contract, which would reduce the risks of things going wrong, 'should not contain any undertaking not to reveal the contract price'.[50] Thus, on paper at least, a sea change may be in store, although the question of whether this bold step will translate into practice inevitably remains.

Some departments earlier disclosed that if they wished to let above the EU thresholds, then procedural rules regarding price must be complied with *unless the contractor expressly asks that the price be withheld*. It also appeared that suppliers of goods ask for this protection rather more frequently than suppliers of services. However, a recent CFQ Policy Review by the Office of Public Service has suggested that departments should ordinarily disclose prices, and so has the handbook on BQS, which states that departments must act on the presumption that 'contract prices may have to be disclosed'.[51] Certain requirements under EU Directives also exist as to the details of contracts which must be disclosed, though it appears that few departments are prepared to go beyond these minimal conditions. It is rare for a contract in its entirety to be published; herein lies the danger. On the other hand, several departments said that *Government Opportunities* was a door to wider information and the contact officer named may be prepared to go further than the published details. The DETR has already committed itself to greater openness in the contracting process with the promise that 'all DETR contracts signed in the future would, as far as possible, be publicly available documents'.[52] This, however, is the same DETR which, in September 2000, refused to disclose details about Britain's first private toll road.

There is the same patchy disclosure here as with the Appraising Options exercise. One of the research contacts made during *Private World of Government* explained the reluctance to publish in full, and in doing so made out the case for a strong FOI Act as clearly as it could possibly be made. One good reason immediately followed by a bad one. Full disclosure, it was said, could be sensitive on account: (a) that it might disclose the price which an agency might be sold for or which a contract might be let for and (b) that it might disclose policy advice to ministers, including which lobby groups might be upset. Sensitive materials can always be excluded (the document can be 'redacted' in legal parlance). The second reason is simply an indictment of the British policy process writ large.

49 FDA News, July 1995.

50 *Op cit*, Cabinet Office, fn 7, para 8.8; original emphasis.

51 *Op cit*, Cabinet Office, fn 7, para 2.10.

52 Press Release 619, 23 July 1998.

Transparency, or the absence of it, has been, as we have seen, a constant feature of British government, in spite of the manifest improvement in recent years. The move to contract, with its inevitable association with confidentiality, scarcely improves the situation. Indeed, the informality with which government can enter into contracts underwrite Dicean concepts of the public sphere, and in particular, that the law applies equally to both the public and the private domains. The notion of a distinctly *public* law of contract, whereby contractual terms effectively bear the hallmark of legislation, has been consistently opposed. It takes an investigation by the PAC to highlight just how unsatisfactorily drafted some contractual terms can be.

There is a general reluctance to release information as a matter of course, even if it would not be objectively regarded as commercially sensitive. The onus seems to rest heavily on the individual seeking the information, including unsuccessful tenderers. While BQS marks a more promising future, there is already the suspicion that the Blair government can be as secretive as its predecessor. The Audit Commission's report in 1993 still rings true in finding that the evaluation of contractual performance is made difficult given that contractual specifications are not for public consumption.[53] Others have expressed the concern that the whole contractual culture is being used to manage the tightening constraints on public expenditure, so that spending problems become budget and contract, rather than political issues.[54]

The position with contract specifications appears to be that generic specifications (a kind of template) are available, but that detailed specifications are not. The bidders naturally receive a general specification in order to allow them to prepare their bids and, to that extent, an interested party could obtain copies. However, specifications are not made public as such, and contractual details are more or less sacrosanct. It will be rare for information other than that disclosed in *Government Opportunities* to be disclosed.

BQS had said that the public has a right to know how much government services cost, no matter who provides them. At the time, it urged that the Code of Practice on Access to Government Information should be interpreted as liberally as possible. In particular, the permitted exclusions should require a robust assessment of harm, rather than intuition. This means that departments should be prepared to reveal contract prices for services unless it can be shown that real harm would result to the department's, the contractor's or an

53 Audit Commission, *Realising the Benefits of Competition: The Client Role for Contractual Services*, 1993, HMSO.

54 Deakin, N and Walsh, K, 'The enabling State: the role of markets and contracts' (1996) 74 Public Administration 33, p 44. What is also of interest is how little detail on market testing is contained in Departmental Annual Reports. Procurement Manuals for most departments are, however, available on request.

identified third party's competitive position. Commercial confidentiality 'must never be used as a cloak to deny the public's right to know how much Government services cost'.[55]

POST-CONTRACT ISSUES

It is not only at the tendering stage that issues of accountability and public concern arise, matters which are well understood in the EU, which is seeking to promote as much openness as is consistent with canons of commercial confidentiality. Government sources accept the impact which EU Directives are already having and, less plausibly, appear to welcome the formal mechanisms of redress for those disappointed in the selection process. The Government accepts that the Directives cumulatively require that decisions on the selection of bidders are objective and award decisions are based on objective criteria, made known in advance to personal contractors, and that the results of the tendering exercise must be published. Under most circumstances, there are requirements for debriefing for unsuccessful applicants. These now appear in BQS. The government's own *Guidance and Pro Forma* also states that the format for all contract notices and awards supplied is that prescribed by the EU procedures, most usually following the 'restricted procedure' formula, even though Brussels has made it clear that the open procedure 'best assures the establishment of equal conditions for participating'.[56]

Debriefing has been touched on and is further described in the *Private World of Government*. However a word must be said about reasons for decisions. BQS speaks to the duties imposed on the tender evaluation panel which must produce a detailed record of their decisions and the reasons for them, and evidence that the competition has been approached in a transparently open and fair manner. This should be in a 'commercial in confidence' note to managers including a wide range of detail. All selection details will be recorded to ensure 'accountability' (that is, within government) and to inform those responsible for monitoring and re-letting the contract the rationale underlying the decision.[57]

What emerges is that there is a considerable gap between what the government knows and what the citizen is allowed to know and is, generally, wider than in partner countries. EU Directives are constantly moving in the direction of greater openness. However, in the UK, reasons for contractual

55 *Op cit*, Cabinet Office, fn 7, para 38. FOI Act 2000, s 3 refers to other persons holding information on behalf of a public body. They are *prima facie* covered by the provisions of the Act.

56 88/295 EEC, Preamble. For further information on the Directives and their operation in the UK, see *op cit*, Goh and Lewis, fn 1, pp 20–22.

57 *Op cit*, Cabinet Office, fn 7, para 7.27.

awards will hardly ever enter the public domain. Furthermore, there is ordinarily no disclosure of evaluation criteria to bidders who have been shortlisted. There are two exceptions to this state of affairs: first, where the EU Directives apply, and secondly, where there is a single overriding objective, it may make sense for the purchaser to inform bidders of the evaluation criteria.

The TSC, reporting in late 1994, received evidence expressing concern about the impact of the *Competing for Quality* programme on accountability. The Civil Service unions argued that contracting out would dramatically reduce the accountability of service provision to the public and Parliament by severing the direct administrative link between the providers of the service and the ministers. With most contracts not published, the standards laid down in them were not publicly known. One proposed solution was that all contracts should be subject to parliamentary proceedings, involving scrutiny by a Joint Committee and a power for either House to annul a contract. The Government, for its part, told the Committee that they saw no reason why service standards in a contract should not be in the public domain 'subject to the requirements of genuine commercial accountability'.[58] The Guidance on the Code of Practice on Access to Government Information lists information which should normally be made public, including the identity of the successful tenderer, the nature of the job, service or goods to be provided, the performance standards set and the criteria for the award of the contract.[59] The FOI Act is not specific on these matters, and researchers will need to follow up such issues in the future with due diligence.

ADVICE AND CONSULTANCY

The phenomenon of privatisation and contracting out has not simply increased the role of the private sector in the delivery of services or provision of goods previously undertaken directly by the State. Consultants, typically management consultants, have been drafted in to provide advice on a variety of issues, and sometimes have even been seen to replace advice from the Civil Service. There are potential problems of accountability associated with this practice. Although replacing Civil Service advice is one matter deserving further attention, it is the transparency of the advice, the manner in which consultants are appointed, the details of their contracts and so on which are of considerable importance. It is true that advice by civil servants is not

58 *Op cit*, Goh and Lewis, fn 1, p 27.

59 And see *op cit*, Cabinet Office, fn 7, paras 11–16. Contracts, of course, need to be managed. This involves project management, monitoring and evaluation, responses to unsatisfactory performance and retendering. These issues are all crucial for NPM and are considered in *op cit*, Goh and Lewis, fn 1, Chapter 3.

transparent in the ordinary course of events. However, consultants' 'commercial-in-confidence' claims appear to compound the problem.

During the Thatcher and Major years, the pace of the use of consultants quickened considerably. Between 1979 and 1995, some £320 m was spent on advice relating to privatisation and market testing alone.[60] An answer to a PQ in the summer of 1996 disclosed that consultant fees for the privatisation of British Rail had been in the order of £450 m. Member firms of the Management Consultancies Association (MCA) increased their income from government sources consistently between 1985 and 1990 and seem to have remained more or less constant since. The Institute of Management Consultants (IMC) is the other main body representing these interests, and was established in 1962.

No one doubts the value of expert consultants in the abstract, but again, questions of accountability and VFM are necessarily posed. The government's own Efficiency Unit had insisted that VFM had been obtained under the privatisation programme, although they were quick to add that 'there may be no realistic way of apportioning their particular contribution'. From the public lawyer's point of view, this is hardly reassuring and it is difficult to believe that a public contracts commissioner, whose appointment is argued for shortly, would not get a little more purchase on constitutional essentials than the conclusions of the Efficiency Unit.

Naturally, much of the use of consultants is politically uncontroversial, for example, in relation to information systems – even if their track record in the IT field has not always been a shining example to others. On the other hand, rail privatisation, the market testing exercises and more general research and policy advice is not merely technical, but offers the opportunity for considerable differences of opinion, which are unlikely to be systematically aired in a commercial-in-confidence atmosphere.

The 1994 Efficiency Unit Report on the use of consultants carried mixed messages. In particular, it noted that too many projects were let by a single tender and that follow-on work sometimes vastly exceeding the value of the original contract – is afforded to the successful bidder. The EU Services Directive now governs the issue to a considerable extent and the *Treasury Guide on Government Accounting* also lays down stringent rules for securing fair and open competition 'unless there are convincing reasons to the contrary'. However, there are exceptions which include the situation where one firm or individual has specialist knowledge which is required, where the cost of tendering would outweigh the value of the contract or where continuity of knowledge with previous work is important. The Efficiency Unit also indicated that single tendering was widespread where the consultants were well known to the person letting the contract. It seems clear that

60 For this and other matters under discussion, see *op cit*, Goh and Lewis, fn 1, Chapter 4.

inadequate safeguards currently exist in relation to single tender practices and, indeed, occasional criticisms of the tendering process more generally have emerged from the PAC.

There are a number of evident concerns about the use of consultants in the public sphere, with too little clear thinking, too little publicity and too little public accountability. Again, the EU might be expected to bring a little order into the proceedings. The Services Directive (92/50) came into force in the UK in July 1993 and has been implemented by the Public Services Contracts Regulations 1993 SI 1993/3228, which set down common procedures by public authorities when awarding contracts for services. There are various rules laid down about the criteria to apply when awarding contracts. There are several different procedures, which vary in the range of services providers that need to be invited to express an interest, or to tender for the work, and in the timescale laid down. There are exemptions, for example, related to national security, banking, financial services and the like.

The procedures laid down are likely to be cumbersome where departments have a continuing need for specific types of service, and where needs crop up unexpectedly. As a result, several government bodies make use of Framework Agreements with particular consultancy firms which eliminate the need to advertise individual contracts in the Official Journal and 'the inevitable delays'.

Conflicts of interest are potentially extremely important in the case of consultants who may be interested in distorting future competition in their direction or in the direction of other firms in which they have interests, direct or indirect. To this end, both the MCA and IMC have issued codes of conduct which deal, *inter alia*, with conflicts of interest and the impartiality of advice tendered. So, also, have the Cabinet Office and one or two other departments.

Even so, considerable accountability concerns remain. First, consultants' reports are overwhelmingly not made public and are normally said to be commercial in confidence. At this stage, the FOI Act seems set to make little difference to this state of affairs. Naturally when official policies have hardened, parts of a consultant's report will emerge, although almost always anonymously. It is the same problem which observers have with the opaqueness of the policy process in Whitehall more generally.[61]

It may be noted that in New Zealand, annual reports of the Ombudsman have demonstrated the growing use of consultants as a source of government advice and the associated problems of openness and availability of information. The Ombudsman has noted that 'the more the consultants become involved in the actual decision making process, the more they must expect to disclose information'.[62] Consequently, a claim for withholding

61 See, eg, Lewis, ND, *How to Reinvent British Government*, 1993, European Policy Forum.

62 New Zealand Ombudsman, *Annual Report 1989*, p 30, and *Annual Report 1992*, p 30.

information 'will require strong evidence of unreasonable prejudice to these consultants' commercial position [and] even then the public interest ... may well outweigh any interest in withholding'.[63]

He also held that there was little reason to withhold consultants' fees unless there are special circumstances. In the UK, details of such fees are normally withheld.

ADVISE AND CONSULT

External sources of advice have always been relied upon by government, but in recent years, the trend has increased considerably in the UK. Indeed, there has been constant concern expressed that independent advice has begun to replace Civil Service advice. Be that as it may, advisory bodies and the use of consultants has begun to pose constitutional questions since the area is so little burdened by legal niceties.

In the US, the significance of advisory bodies has led to legal obligations which seek to ensure public awareness, openness and scrutiny. The Federal Advisory Committee Act (FACA) 1972 is the most important regulator in the field, and contrasts starkly with the almost total absence of formal constraints in the UK. Not only does the legislation require balanced membership, but it insists that each advisory committee or body (broadly defined) registers a charter before it is allowed to operate. Most meetings are held in public, minutes are available and there is a wide degree of consultation.[64]

There have been some especially important advisory bodies in recent years which appear to have had a significant impact on government thinking. The Southgate Committee[65] was amongst the most significant, having as its remit the review of the organisational structure and functions of the Treasury. Again, during the Major years, of critical importance was the *Review of Police Core and Ancillary Tasks* which examined the most cost-effective way of delivering core policing services and to assess the scope for relinquishing ancillary tasks. The final report was published in 1995 and recommended, inter alia, the 'civilianisation' of certain liquor licensing functions and contracting out of immigration escorts across the country.[66] The whole CFQ exercise was also buttressed by the Private Sector Forum which acted as a channel of communication for the private sector in relation to Prior Options, etc, exercises. It enjoyed no formal terms of reference, its meetings were occasional and from time to time its membership was disclosed through PQs.

63 *Op cit*, New Zealand Ombudsman, fn 62.

64 See, eg, Democratic Audit of the United Kingdom, *Advisory Bodies in the UK*, 1995.

65 See, also, the Treasury's *Fundamental Expenditure Review*, 1994.

66 Home Office, *Review of Policy Core and Ancillary Tasks*, 1995, HMSO.

'Record notes' of its meetings were normally available on request from the Efficiency Unit. Again, of considerable significance has been the Deregulation Task Force, which published its first annual report in September 1995. Its task was to advise government on how to remove unnecessary regulation and to reduce the burden of necessary regulation. It was believed to be influential in the framing of the contentious Deregulation and Contracting Out Act 1994. Under the Blair administration, it has been recast as the Better Regulation Task Force under the chairmanship of Lord Haskins.

In fact, 'ruling by task force' has been a central feature of the Labour Government since 1997. A leading observer of this phenomenon has even been moved to remark:

> No sooner had the Nolan Committee on Standards in Public Life proposed reforms to minimise partisan appointments to quangos and other public bodies, than new creatures appeared in the *demi-monde* of Whitehall in the form of Task Forces, Advisory Groups and Policy Reviews.[67]

In spite of their being described as a genetically modified form of quango, such bodies have been around for centuries. It is their proliferation under Blair that has concerned students of the constitution who worry that the whole business of government is being privatised, or 'croney-ised' as the argot has it. No one denies the value of independent advice, but the concern is that such bodies prosper and proliferate without wide public input and policy debate. If they are part of an attempt to 'modernise' government, then this may be no bad thing, especially if input is genuinely open to all, through, for example, the internet.

The Barker review found that since May 1997, government was known to have set up 318 task forces and external advisory bodies. About a dozen appeared to have led to the creation of standing bodies, adding to the number of new advisory and executive quangos which Labour had created.

Barker concluded that task forces do create a more inclusive and focused advice-gathering process than previous practice in consulting interested parties by government departments. He emphasised the functional nature of the process and the role of task forces in providing practitioner experience or in mobilising outside interests in support of government objectives. He recommended the more open creation and operation of advisory groups. Constitutional issues would be at stake if ministers seemed to cut out alternative sources of advice while arranging privileged access to the favoured; an accusation which could, with some justice, be made against the predecessor administration. As always, the lesson is that 'efficient' government must not be achieved at the cost of democratic and accountable

67 See T, Smith's Preface in Barker, T *et al*, *Ruling by Task Force, Democratic Audit of the United Kingdom*, 1999, Politico's.

government. Adopting the US system of administrative law protection seems by far the surest way to marry a series of desirable objectives.

The public/private 'divide' is, in fact, a continuum with partnerships, as we have seen, increasingly occupying centre stage. Yet there are still philosophical/constitutional arguments to be had. How much is enough? When is the State in danger of evaporating? Should it wither away, or should there always be a core?

CORE GOVERNMENT

The OECD Ministerial Symposium on the Future of Public Service posed the question starkly. There is a need for a fundamental analysis of the role and scope of government, including analyses of what should be provided by other sectors and what should remain in the public sector. Although the State has redefined its relationship with the private sector, government cannot absolve itself from responsibility for the delivery of core services. However, the definition of 'core' is unclear. Is the State, in some measure at least, 'irreducible'? These are, in fact, constitutional matters, but have too rarely been treated as such, although some guidance is institutionally afforded by States which are essentially federal in nature. If these issues are, in fact, seen as constitutional, then for the public to have no voice in what constitutes services to which they are entitled is the greatest act of disenfranchisement. When we canvas the privatisation of the Treasury and the Ministry of Defence, it is time to ask what are the remains of the State. Where does the 'long march through Whitehall' end? Whatever the answer is, it is clear that citizens should be empowered to make those decisions. Currently, they are not.

Most advanced countries are struggling with this issue. In France, for example, some certainties have been underlined:

> Ministries now have responsibilities which they alone can perform: analysing public priorities and the strategic challenges facing the central government, bringing measures before Parliament and providing it with information, and overseeing the central government's local offices.[68]

In The Netherlands, there has been active discussion of restoring the 'primacy of politics', perhaps an echo of recent developments in New Zealand over the red/purple zone theories. In the former, as part of the effort to restore the primacy of politics, the government has laid down in legislative instructions the requirements to be met by statutory regulations, and administrative authorities with autonomous powers are being established. Policy documents

68 Turc, A, 'Accountability in public organisations: responsiveness to political authorities, users and market forces', in OECD, *Democratic and Political Accountability*, 1997, Public Management Service, p 7.

have also been published; one of them, Towards Core Ministries, has called for the formation of smaller, strategic administrative centres.[69]

A 1986 UK Treasury Report may seem a lifetime away, but its arguments still need to be taken seriously in arguing that the 'core' could not function adequately if so called 'peripheral' services were contracted out:

> There are no theoretical limits. In principle, contractual relationships could be established everywhere in the Civil Service. In practice, however, some relationships are more easily and more efficiently handled informally, in-house, instead of being formalised into contracts.[70]

This approach has been buttressed in the US, where the OMB's arrangements with individual agencies as to what is regarded as commercial and what not is a major part of the policy making process, in which interested publics are heavily involved.[71] The A-76 Circular is more expansive than anything which exists in the UK. There are naturally disputed categories, but some are described as inherently governmental. They include activities which involve the use of discretion or value judgments, criminal investigations, prosecution and judicial functions, the conduct of foreign relations, the selection of programme priorities, the regulation of natural resources and of industry and commerce, food and drugs, monetary transactions and entitlements and the conduct of research and development. The revised circular also contains illustrated examples of what constitute purely commercial and what governmental activities.

The area is mined with difficulties. Although most would accept that traditional patterns of service delivery are not sacrosanct, the concern is that the baby might be thrown out with the bathwater. The one area where these larger issues has been raised was the investigation of the former Treasury and Civil Service Committee into the Role of the Civil Service.[72] A number of witnesses appearing before the Committee expressed unease at the unfolding of events. The provisions of the Deregulation and Contracting Out Act which promote a version of inherently governmental functions are unargued, went undebated and are self-evidently inadequate. Government, while agreeing that there was a 'spinal cord of State which cannot be under the private sector', was sceptical about these matters being determined other than by the government of the day from time to time. This is to adopt the view that there are no constitutional foundations and that the constitution is whatever the elected politicians of the day say it is. This is a view which is so heavily dependent on ministerial accountability as the only democratic requirement

69 *Op cit*, OECD, fn 28.

70 HM Treasury, *Using Private Enterprise in Government*, 1998, para 8.

71 US President's Council on Management Improvement, *Study of OMB Circular A-76*, 1990, Inter-Agency Task Force.

72 Lewis, ND, Evidence to the Treasury and Civil Service Committee on the Role of the Civil Service, Session 1993–94, HC 27-1, HMSO, Vol 11, esp Chapter 9.

as to be unsustainable. Public Accountability and ministerial responsibility become elided in this view.

Worryingly, the last major debate in the House on contracting out occurred over draft regulations allowing statutory functions to be discharged by contractors regarding the registration of companies.[73] Even so, the level of debate was not what was needed under the circumstances. It took merely 20 minutes, in the first use of the power enabling contractors to discharge services previously provided by public servants, to debate the proposed legislation in the House of Lords.

There is currently no constitutional apparatus which is equal to providing a serious debate with argument tested by counter-argument, the very least which could be expected when the very remains of the State are being picked over. As for so many other issues, the establishment of a Standing Advisory Committee or Conference on the machinery of government offers the best hope of instilling some form of institutional rational discourse into the UK governmental system.

CONTRACTING OUT AND COMMERCIAL CONFIDENCE

For governments to be democratic, they need to be as open as possible. When the private sector becomes a part of government, in one sense or another, their dealings, too, ought to be opened up as much as possible. The defects of our public law have been dwelt upon sufficiently, but the whole privatisation phenomenon has brought to centre stage the need for greater openness in the way public affairs are conducted. The private sector resents and is uncomfortable with the accountancy conventions ordinarily adopted by government. But, commercial confidentiality goes beyond this unfamiliarity; it is a genuinely felt concern to ensure that commercial rivals do not gain from a voluntary disclosure of the inner workings of their business. As a result, a claim of commercial confidentiality tends to occur as a more or less reflex action rather than anything else and the tendency of UK governments to accept that state of affairs has been regularly noted. In the new circumstances of modern partnership governance, this is simply not acceptable.

Unfortunately, *Better Quality Services* is not particularly helpful in this respect. The tender evaluation panel must produce a detailed record of their decisions and the reasons for them, 'and evidence that the competition has been approached in a transparently fair and open manner. This should be in a "commercial-in-confidence" note to senior managers'. Contract award notices

73 Contracting Out (Functions in Relation to the Registration of Companies) Order 1995, and for the problems raised by Pt 2 of the Contracting Out and Deregulation Act 1994, see [1995] PL 21.

'in the prescribed form' should be despatched to the appropriate authorities.[74] The new arrangements do contain a 'contents of contract' section which must include 'information for customers/users, including complaints procedures',[75] but it is interesting that that provision is entirely separate from, and therefore presumably unconnected with, the requirement to state the 'service required and the outcome to be achieved'. It must be stressed that these are still early days for the new arrangements, but earlier empirical work suggests that too much information is still being shielded from the general public.[76] However, some advance has been made, although it is not possible to give a detailed assessment at this stage of our knowledge. The following, however, is potentially important.

Service components of contracts or SLAs should be published in order to keep customers/users informed of the service and standards they should expect. Customers/users should be actively involved in contract management arrangements. Formal arrangements should be made for them to offer feedback on contractors' performance or on changes in their requirements. If relevant, there should be arrangements for complaints and redress in individual cases when services do not meet contract/SLA standards. The degree of customers/users' participation will depend on the nature of the customers/users and services in question. For example, where there are a large number of geographically dispersed customers/users involved, user groups may be the best way of canvassing their views.[77]

All this depends, at the end of the day, on the government's attitudes to FOI. Until the passage of the FOI Act 2000, departments were bound by the Code of Practice on Access to Official Information, overseen by the Parliamentary Ombudsman. Government policy was expressed to be that the Code should be interpreted 'as liberally as possible'. What is also noteworthy is the following provision. Departments must:

> ... not use commercial confidentiality as a cloak to deny the public's right to know. But departments need not publish or disclose information which would (*on the basis of firm evidence*) harm the legitimate commercial interests of the Department, a supplier, or a third party ...[78]

The accompaniment to *Best Quality Services*, the *Guidance for Senior Managers* deferred generally to the public's right to know, including the statement that departments should be prepared to reveal contract prices unless real harm could be shown. However, these documents were drafted by Dr David Clark, who was dropped from the Blair Cabinet early on when FOI was handed over

74 *Op cit*, Goh and Lewis, fn 1, paras 7.27 and 7.30.

75 *Op cit*, Goh and Lewis, fn 1, para 8.7.

76 *Op cit*, Cabinet Office, fn 7, para 8.8 says 'the contract should not contain any undertaking not to reveal the contract price'. This, of course, does not dispose of the matter.

77 *Op cit*, Cabinet Office, fn 7, para 8.17.

78 *Op cit*, Cabinet Office, fn 7, para 2.10.

to the Home Secretary, who exhibits a far less open policy than his predecessor. The Select Committee on Public Administration's 1998 Report on FOI was, predictably, much more robust than government spokesmen. In July 1998, the DETR had announced a more open policy than its government counterparts arguing that, with inevitable exceptions, all DETR contracts signed in future would be publicly available documents.[79] Unfortunately, it has been noted that the DETR has, at the time of writing, somewhat blotted its copybook in this respect. It should also be stressed that the Select Committee Report just referred to had described a series of very different practices running across Whitehall. Although some were relatively open, most 'argue strongly that the scope for disclosure of contracts or hire agreements is limited'.

The record of the Ombudsman in seeking to disclose commercial information over recent years has been most honourable.[80] At the time of writing, the number of complaints made to the Ombudsman about the refusal to release information remains low. Only five cases were reported in the six months in question:

> If any lessons can be drawn from so few investigations, it is, perhaps, that some information in sensitive areas such as crime prevention and national security can be released safely if departments take a realistic view of potential harm in relation to the public interest in disclosure.[81]

Nonetheless, most experts in the area are agreed that commercial in confidence claims are capable of representing a serious constraint on the public's right to know:

> The movement to government by contract and the use of private consultants to advise government is inevitably protected by commercial confidentiality clauses. There is a great danger that this is just another device to remove government from public scrutiny and to revert to unjustified secrecy. I would like to see safeguards that helped to ensure that the exemption was properly established and which restricted the wide extent of the current exemption. I take comfort from the PCA's general approach on the question of onus and quantum of proof.[82]

---

79 See DETR Press Release 23 July 1998, No 619.

80 For some of the more interesting cases and observations, see *op cit*, Goh and Lewis, fn 1, pp 55–56.

81 Parliamentary Ombudsman, *Investigations Completed April–October 2000*. Access to Official Information, HC 494.

82 Birkinshaw, P, Evidence to the Select Committee on the PCA, *Open Government*, 2nd Report, Session 1995–96, HC 84, Appendix 2, para 12.

ACCOUNTABILITY AND CONTRACTING OUT

The issue of the evaluation of programmes and initiatives is a notoriously difficult exercise, but one which is a core function of modern government. It is not one which has always been conducted well in the past; certainly not at the local government level, according to the Audit Commission. For example, in 1994, it was reported that health and local authorities were spending around £1,000 per day on management consultants but were often failing to ensure value for money. Local authorities, in particular, omitted to evaluate 70% of their products and the Commission found that poor project management meant that consultants were not being used efficiently or effectively.[83] Hopefully, much has changed in the intervening years, but experience indicates the need for very close attention to both efficiency and accountability.

The 'enabling' State has highlighted problems about monitoring and evaluation as part of the arts of government which went substantially unaddressed in the past. The Treasury and Civil Service Committee, in its 1994 Report, commented upon evidence it had received concerning the evaluation of the policy process, too, and remarked that all was not as well as it might be. Criticisms were made from several quarters, not least from former Permanent Secretaries, which led the Committee to recommend piecemeal reform. In particular, it urged that the policy tasks of an agency be specified in annual performance agreements and that they should be subject to evaluation other than by the parent department. It also argued for a search for improved methods of auditing policy implementation.[84] Some improvements have been effected since that time, but there is still a long way to go. Although the policy process has been touched on from time to time, there is still evidence that it is not as scientifically approached as the managerial side of contracting-out.

Constitutionally, there is a long way to go before the UK comes to terms with the phenomena of NPM and governance. The author would retract nothing from statements made some little time ago to the following effect:

> There is an acute need for reinventing the doctrine of the separation of powers. Contract can assist this by clarifying what government expects from service providers in pinpointing responsibility and thereby improving accountability. Instead of distinguishing between legislative, executive and judicial functions, there is a need to concentrate on separating out purchaser and provider functions. But public law 'contracts' will often have to be different from the commercial variety and to embrace constitutional values in terms of formation of terms, pricing and dispute resolution. Public law contracts will often need to be based on common values which are difficult to express. In defining the best form of service delivery, there is a need to avoid the failures and the evasions

83 And see generally, *op cit*, Lewis, fn 24, esp pp 172–77.

84 Op cit, Lewis, fn 72, 5th Report, paras 205–11.

> of ministerial responsibility. Contract can be used for the pursuit of political objectives through individual rights and freedom of choice. Yet in making decisions about what to produce and in ensuring efficiency in the process of supply, the commercial-style contract will have to be re-examined for constitutional fit.[85]

It is doubtful whether the present system of public law could deal easily with the transition to more marketised services. The point has been raised in another jurisdiction by a judge of the New Zealand Court of Appeal, Sir Ivor Richardson, who has expressed the view that the model of administrative law which seeks to control the Welfare State in a largely regulated economy is nowadays inappropriate. A more market-oriented State has rendered it in part obsolete. However, as Professor Mike Taggart has responded:

> The fundamental values of public law – openness, fairness, participation, impartiality and rationality – not only provide a yardstick against which to measure the activities of privatised enterprises with market power, but should be embodied in the design of institutions and regulatory schemes at the outset. In speaking up for these values, administrative lawyers perform their most important role.[86]

This is the old meeting the new with a vengeance. And, it is clear that many other countries have begun to adapt their legal orders to the new circumstances in a way which the UK has yet to follow with any conviction.[87] The High Court of India, interpreting a written constitution with unaccustomed vigour, has shown what it is possible for courts to do without second-guessing the political process.[88]

It is possible to envisage much of the government of the future as a series of contracts, compacts or partnership arrangements. These must meet the requirement of customers, but it must be remembered that citizens are more than mere customers. They require a quality of public life and guarantees of debating the terms of that public life. It will be necessary to concentrate hard on policies and strategies, to judge what the market will bear and what it will not, to guard against unnecessary monopolies and to protect the public purse. All this, however, requires an organising framework and a new legal settlement, whereby adequate machinery for monitoring, for evaluation and for standard-setting are put in place.

An evaluation technique is needed which can be regularly, if not routinely, applied to questions concerning service initiation, continuance, amendment or expansion. The strengths of privatisation, contracting out, franchising, vouchers, user fees, public-private partnerships, etc need to be considered as a

85 *Op cit*, Lewis, fn 72, p 173.

86 'The impact of corporatisation and privatisation in administrative law' (1992) 51 Aust J of Public Administration.

87 See, eg, *op cit*, OECD, fn 28 and *op cit*, Goh and Lewis, fn 1, esp Chapter 5.

88 See, eg, the *Cellular Telephones* case (1994) *The Times of India*, 5 August.

set of general principles and then applied to particular delivery systems once policies have been determined. This should happen in conjunction with users, carers, professionals of all sorts, bearing in mind the commitment to 'hard-looking' the decisions ultimately taken. The users of services must be regularly consulted on their views of the service with a commitment to change either the service itself or the delivery system where appropriate. Where public bodies deliver services, comparators can be developed with other public bodies delivering similar public services. There is a great deal to be done in all of these areas, in spite of considerable improvement made since the Blair Government came into power in 1997. It is almost certainly the case that legislative support for some of these sentiments would reinforce commitment to them.

Market mechanisms alone, presently characterised by inadequate information and an emphasis on cost are, of themselves, unlikely to solve the problem of providing equitable, high quality and more efficient public services. Contract has a valuable role to play, but within a broader constitutional and legal framework which encourages a more open and considered set of consultative practices throughout both the policy and management processes. Structured competition cannot always be regarded as a substitute for reasoned policy and planning.

It is clear that, as in the US, so in the UK, the balance between 'liberty and justice' has not yet been achieved. Private enterprise encapsulates a belief in freedom, competition, autonomy, etc, yet the public world seeks to embrace co-operation, fairness and accountability. Considerable work needs to be done to ensure that the latter set of objectives is not submerged. It is clear that, in the new circumstances, it will not do to claim that accountability is preserved by the accountability of ministers to Parliament.[89]

A number of much-needed legal and constitutional reforms have been touched upon on the way and, in Chapter 9, the themes will be brought together. However, in relation to contracting out as such, one particular reform needs urgent consideration. This, strongly urged in the *Private World of Government*, concerns the role for a Contracts Commissioner.

CONCLUSION

Contracting-out, along with partnerships, is here to stay. However, it is clear that accountability mechanisms and the constitutional architecture are in need of improvement to address the inevitable issues which arise from modernised

89 For examples of unsatisfactory progress see, esp, *op cit*, Goh and Lewis, fn 1, Chapter 6. In particular, the comments on the need for stronger provisions for consultation and transparency remain just as valid at the time of writing.

government. In particular, it is clear that a Contracts Commissioner (or ombudsman) needs to be established to oversee the whole field of government contracting. The remit would be to enhance efficiency and accountability. He should report to, and be an aid to, Parliament.

In his evidence to the Australian Select Committee, the Commonwealth Ombudsman recommended that his powers be extended to establish a specialist team to enhance its ability to oversee tendering procedures.[90] This is obviously one area where the new Commissioner should have jurisdiction. Others include recommendations as to when contracting-out should not be used; monitoring the underlying causes of complaints and comment on individual complaints procedures; identifying service failures and undesirable practices by contractors, and ensuring that government remains ultimately responsible for the oversight of the public interest and standards.

The Commissioner should produce codes of practice in numerous areas, for example, in relation to compensation for customers. To take an illustration, Australia Post makes a compensatory payment to customers where a complaint arises, and has contractual powers to recoup the sum from the contractor. Best practice in a number of areas should be highlighted by the Commissioner. He should also insist that the development of service standards and charters be regarded as a prerequisite before contracting out public functions.

These recommendations are made against a backdrop of a rapidly changing area of public administration, especially since governments are driven to seek innovative ways to involve the private sector in public services and activities. They are simply part of the necessary drive to put the private world of government in the sunlight rather than the moonlight.[91]

90 *Op cit*, Goh and Lewis, fn 1.

91 And see *op cit*, Birkinshaw, Harden and Lewis, fn 15.

CHAPTER 7

REGULATION AND MARKETS

INTRODUCTION

> Leaders of Government and business continue to have choice. So let us choose to unite the power of markets with the authority of universal ideals ...[1]

Markets are the preferred form of economic organisation (if that is the correct word) across most of the developed world. There is also an argument for saying that markets as ideal-types are a form of free speech in that they allow individuals to send out their signals/preferences to others who, in turn, will speak back to them by providing for those preferences in a form of economic ideal-speech situation. That is to say that they will afford information on prices, product reliability, shelf life, repair and replacement costs, etc. An ideal-type, ideal-speech marketplace. Regardless of how far real-world markets differ from the ideal, such a view of markets is about freedom as surely as is political emancipation and universal suffrage. It is unsurprising, therefore, that some of the newer constitutions of, say, central and eastern Europe, contain in their constitutions commitment to a market economy. Reference to its primacy in a foundation document is, in effect, a claim that undermining the market is an interference with liberty – a claim given added force since most of these constitutions have been drawn up under the supportive supervision of the Council of Europe. The Council has, since the end of the Second World War, been Europe's leading advocate of both human rights and the West's cultural traditions. Thus, for some, markets *pur sang* are a part of the human rights package; in any event, they are much more than a preferred economic mode and more than the most effective engine for growth, which in turn needs to be seen as a means of advancing both material and spiritual fulfilment.[2]

Now, it will come as a surprise to no one that markets as described here are an extreme rarity in the real world. Hence, if the language of human autonomy, freedom and rights is to have any meaning, restraints on real-world economic formations will have to be imposed by the political process. The portmanteau term for those restraints is regulation. We shall see that even conceptually, regulation is much more complex than is normally supposed.

1 Annan, K, address at the World Economic Forum in Davos, January 1998, quoted in (1998) *Financial Times*, 2 April.

2 See, eg, Lewis, ND, 'Markets, regulation and citizenship: a constitutional analysis', in Brownsword, R (ed), *Law and the Public Interest*, 1993, Franz Steiner Verlag, pp 109–37.

However, it is high on the agenda of all those who are interested in governance and no discussion of that phenomenon would be realistic which did not address at least some of the regulatory arguments.

If this were a different type of work, more time would be spent on markets and political and moral theory. As it is, they will be subsumed under the general dilemmas of governance, and both markets and regulation will be discussed against the twin concepts of efficiency and accountability.

GOVERNANCE AND REGULATION: THE NEW WORLD

As the OECD Symposium made clear, public management is a changed creature. No longer is its primary concern designing administrative structures to carry out public programmes efficiently, faithfully executing laws, etc. Instead, it is concerned more with policy and decision processes, management of resources and 'the techniques for carrying out policies such as market-type mechanisms and regulation'.[3] The old problems of government's mandate to the people remain in the face of the newness. The dilemmas are well summarised by the OECD:

> ... the use of market-type mechanisms (for example, market testing, privatisation, contracting out, vouchers) may influence accountability mechanisms such as audits. Because the market paradigm assumes a 'natural' performance, some observers argue that government should not require performance audits in market environments. They argue that inspections and contract regulations are all that are needed to ensure the focus on clients. Any government requirements outside the marketplace would be dealt with by directives set out in performance agreements or results targets. They argue further that non-market-based budget allocations such as intra-governmental contracts (individual and institutional), decentralisation, devolution, or subsidiarity require performance audits because they lack the 'natural' mechanism to focus on performance and guide managers. These issues can also be applied to a wider policy debate concerning political accountability.[4]

There are, as yet, no clear answers to the questions implicit in this assessment and the OECD will be returning to the subject from time to time. However, using regulation as a generic term, NPM and governance simply pose more complex problems of supervision than formerly, even though the issue of regulation has been centre-stage for most of the last century in one guise or another. The US is, perhaps, the classic example where regulation and its study has been an industry in itself. We shall see that *effective* regulation is threatened by globalisation, but the *optimum* form of regulation addressed to the problems of governance is in its infancy.

3 OECD Symposium, Ministerial Symposium on the Future of Public Services, 1996, p 7.

4 OECD, *In Search of Results: Performance Management Practices*, 1997, PUMA, p 20.

In OECD's work, regulatory reform refers to changes that improve the quality of regulations in enhancing performance, cost-effectiveness, etc. Reform can mean revision of a single regulation, removing and rebuilding of an entire regulatory programme and its institutions or improvements of processes for making regulations and managing reform. Deregulation is seen as a subset of regulatory reform and refers to complete or partial elimination of regulation in a sector to improve economic performance. Although reference is also made to the social benefits of regulatory reform, and even the promotion of policy goals such as environmental quality, health and safety, etc, as yet the OECD's approach to regulatory reform seems to underplay the accountability end of things.[5] As if none of this was enough, the development of new technology is challenging notions of what constitutes a natural monopoly. Flux, then, everywhere. However, before returning to the overall problems posed by governance, it is worth pointing out that regulation and its purposes and functions have always been more sophisticated than many would have us believe. A brief excursus on this issue may be helpful.

REGULATION: A MANY-HEADED THING

There is a view of regulation that its rationale is essentially economic and not one of social engineering since, *inter alia*, consumer satisfaction will flow naturally from economic efficiency. Almost all serious study, however, shows that both in concept and actuality, regulation tends to have mixed motives and achieves mixed outcomes.[6] Moreover, even the concept of 'economic' regulation is more complex than appears at first sight. Thus, Prosser, in his seminal work, says of the regulation of telecommunications in the UK that:

> It is thus clear that price control is anything but an automatic process subject to occasional review, and involves an extensive degree of discretionary judgment by the regulator ...[7]

In the same place, he remarks of the experience of gas regulation that it became, almost inevitably, concerned with the promotion of energy efficiency from an early date.[8] Furthermore, the inevitable discretionary freedom afforded to regulators has, in practice, allowed considerable scope 'for the political values of the regulators to influence the decision making process', even to the extent of undermining government policy.[9]

---

5 See, eg, OECD, *Report on Regulatory Reform*, June 1997 and *Regulatory Reform: Overview of OECD's Work*, 1998, OECD.

6 See, esp, Prosser, T, *Law and the Regulators*, 1997, Clarendon, and the literature referred to there.

7 *Ibid*, p 67.

8 *Ibid*, p 111.

9 *Ibid*, p 113.

This aside, it is clear that, the world being organised by human beings to gratify their own inner needs, social considerations will rarely be absent from any regulatory regime. Again, much of what follows is taken from Prosser or the works referred to there.

To take the regulation of electricity supply, regardless of recent events, it is notable that there is a very long legislative history of universal service and other regulatory duties. On the other hand, the recent gas legislation gives special protection to the vulnerable in the inner cities and even opening up the market to competition has not resulted in the end of social obligations. They have simply become implemented in new ways; through, for example, licence conditions drawn up by government with the regulator's advice and incorporated in all licences.[10] It is also important to see that even those who advocate deregulation and regulatory reform recognise that this has to be done without sacrificing important policy objectives.[11] As part of the same study, the Dutch experience is quoted in support:

> The main feature is the linking of economic and judicial aspects. By promoting market forces and competition, political objectives can sometimes be achieved more effectively than by imposing compulsory rules. On the other hand, more transparent and consistent rules, which are easier to enforce, will strengthen competition. Another important feature is organised political commitment. At the start of every project, documents are drawn up in which the minister responsible states his commitment to the project.[12]

Prosser is clear that not only are we unlikely to see an end to regulation, but that that which remains 'will become increasingly concerned with two themes: policing competition and enforcing social obligations'. The pattern which emerges is the 'free economy and the strong State'.[13] These findings merge clearly with the argument in the introduction to this chapter and will be returned to from time to time.

One more point should be added concerning the relationship between market and State. It is that while competitiveness is a particularly pressing requirement in a global economy, it is too often viewed from the standpoint of the private sector alone. However, since the public and the private sectors clearly depend upon each other, competitiveness is a joint concern shared by both sectors. The standard and efficiency of public services determine the quality and dynamics of the environment in which business operates.[14] This is

---

10 The Secretary of State has also retained strong reserve powers in addition to those of the regulator.

11 See, eg, OECD, *Issues and Developments in Public Management*, Survey 1996–97, PUMA, Executive Summary, p 4.

12 *Ibid*, The Netherlands Survey, p 4.

13 *Op cit*, Prosser, fn 6, pp 110, 152.

14 See Lewis, ND, 'Good governance: the UK experience' (1998) XLIV (Special Number) Indian Journal of Public Administration 616, pp 616–25.

not only to broaden the meaning of regulation but to show the interconnectedness of the various strands of governance, not least in relation to those issues described in Chapter 4.

REGULATORY REFORM AND GOVERNANCE

Regulatory reform is currently on everyone's agenda. In response to the British Government's Green Paper on reform of utility regulation, a joint paper by the regulators appeared to accept Prosser's central argument by explaining that their main concerns were to ensure the continuation of effective competition and the protection of customers through arrangements which are clear and effective. The Office of Electricity Regulation, however, regarded its primary concern as to protect consumers through competition and insisted that government rather than the regulators have the primary responsibility for social or environmental measures.[15] The Government's response to the consultation exercise was produced in July 1998 and spoke to all the concerns addressed here. It accepted that ministers should give statutory guidance on social and environmental objectives, but also said that consumer protection should be the regulators' primary duty, though independent consumer councils should also promote consumer interests.[16]

Although the original intention of the Government was to take a comprehensive, if not holistic view to the regulation of the major utilities, in the event their big picture was compromised and the result was the Utilities Act 2000 which deals primarily with gas and electricity markets. A new, unified, body was set up to regulate these markets and has been christened OFGEM. As well as a joint regulator, the Act establishes a joint Consumer Council and empowers the minister to give guidance to the regulator on social and environmental matters.

When the new Authority was set up in December 2000, the Energy Minister announced that the interests of consumers would, from now on, be the first priority for OFGEM. She announced the appointment of new members of the authority, the first board to replace one-person regulation:

> Today's new board for OFGEM is a crucial element in the new system of regulation. Regulation is changing, and for the better. By making regulation and the market work more openly, these new arrangements will ensure all consumers are confident they are getting a fair deal.[17]

The key objective of the Board is to put consumers first, although the Government is looking to the market for assistance in this objective. Other

15 *Response to the Green Paper on Regulation*, Press Release R39/98.

16 DTI, *Modernising the Framework for Utility Regulation*, 27 July 1998.

17 Liddell, H, P2000/857, DTI.

social and environmental obligations are present in the Act and it will be instructive to see how both the minister and the Board interpret the interlocking nature of the obligations.[18]

The UK has, nevertheless, to a considerable extent, been playing follow my leader; the OECD has stated clearly that regulatory reform is high on their list of cross-cutting efforts to improve the efforts of governance.[19] The OECD literature is too rich to be treated with the respect it deserves here, but a few of the salient research findings should be mentioned. Regulatory Impact Analysis, the systematic assessment of positive and negative impacts of regulation, can help reduce regulatory costs while maximising the effectiveness of needed government action. Concrete best practices were identified in areas such as applying analytical methods and including cost-benefit analysis, consulting with the public and enhancing the ability of government to produce high quality analysis. They recommend a balanced mix of policies involving regulation, deregulation, re-regulation, institutional reform and co-ordinated reforms in other policy areas.

A research paper prepared for the OECD has pointed out that the traditional focus of regulation has been on control of process, whereas the starting point in designing regulations under NPM is that the focus should be on the outcome to be achieved. Until recently, there was no regular review of regulation and its costs similar to the way in which expenditure problems are reviewed in the annual budget. Although a large number of countries have put plans in place for regulation review, there was a need, argued the author, to give the process a new impetus and more teeth. One possibility is to have a sunset clause, which requires regulations to be resubmitted for review from time to time. It can also help if the review process is independent of those responsible for the particular body of regulation in order to minimise the chances of regulatory capture.[20] The main OECD 1997 Report had made the startling, to some, claim that effective regulatory reform could improve GDP 'in the long run' from between 1% and 6%, depending on national circumstances. But all of this needs to be set against the background of the ends to be achieved – or the 'outcomes', in the argot. In other words, there is nothing incompatible between regulatory efficiency and reform as a part of the move towards good governance and the ancient ideals of justice, fairness, openness and democracy. The trick is to devise processes and procedures which will marry these objectives in changing times.

One present danger to this enterprise is the power of multinational corporations. Although the MAI has presently been put on hold, there is the

18 This initiative must be seen, however, against the background of the Regulatory Reform Bill which is generally directed at deregulation in the interests of British business.

19 Its range of publications in this area is extensive and enlightening.

20 Keating, M, *Public Management Reform and Economic and Social Development*, 1997, OECD, p 25.

continuing likelihood of pressure being exerted to establish something similar in nature and scope. The ability of governments to regulate in the public interest is seriously limited at the present time by the ability of the big companies to control investment decisions in the absence of a community of interest by regional government groupings. This central contemporary problem for the new public lawyer is further addressed in Chapter 10.

REGULATION AND PUBLIC INTERESTS

Markets at best are a form of economic democracy; so, therefore, regulation must be directed at enhancing the democratic process – both in the political and the economic sense. That is how it should be judged.

In fact, as Prosser shows, many of the themes of modern regulation – including the deeper, if disguised, issues touched on here – had been anticipated in the 19th and early 20th centuries.[21] Although the claims are not as grandiloquent as the instant ones, the similarity of approach is striking:

> A central theme is that both the legal mandates and the operational practice suggest that regulation is a complex task, irreducible to a single goal of efficiency maximization. In particular three different regulatory tasks should be recognized: regulating monopoly, regulation for competition, and social regulation, especially in the form of universal service. These different tasks may have contradictory policy implications; as a result it is necessary to conceive of regulators as 'governments in miniature' whose decisions cannot be pre-determined by rules or by economic technique.[22]

Regulation, at the very least, must serve the ends, not only of limiting monopoly power, but of creating and policing the conditions for effective competition – to regulate markets into existence, so to speak. However, as the OECD has made constantly clear, it is necessary to ask whether private sector models invariably incorporate social concerns. The unspoken answer is 'no' and implicit is 'not very often'. Since governments, of necessity, must incorporate social concerns, regulatory arrangements, howsoever described, must be put in place. Thus, the new Financial Services Authority is expected to be given a specific statutory duty to promote consumer understanding of financial services. This is a new aim for financial regulators.[23] Other proposals include those of the DGFT to tighten up the law against 'rogue traders' in order to protect consumers.[24] This is further discussed in Chapter 8.

---

21 *Op cit*, Prosser, fn 6, p 40.

22 *Op cit*, Prosser, fn 6, p 269.

23 See FSA's Press Notice FSA/PN/41/98.

24 OFT Press Notice 39/97.

Public interests need to be 'regulated' in other fashions, too. So, for instance, even though governments increasingly contract out public services, consumer/citizen interests need to be protected both through the terms of the contracts themselves and procurement and other regulations, as was seen in the previous chapter. Furthermore, the need for some degree of protection or regulation is even more obvious in the case of market-mimicking initiatives within government itself. Thus, the need for quality charters as a set of promises/guarantees to the public on performance standards and delivery, a matter further developed in the following chapter.

There is, in fact, a view that effective regulation is a win-win exercise. Effective regulation, as the OECD points out, needs to reinforce democratic expectations. Open dialogue and communication are an indispensable part of the regulatory process:

> It can strengthen the voices of those who support and will benefit from reform. Important allies in the reform process include businesses which will gain from low cost, high quality goods and services inputs; consumers; and employees and their representatives in fields in which job creation and wage growth are constrained by unnecessary regulatory restrictions.[25]

Prosser also makes the point that if effective regulatory structures are not created, disputes 'will inevitably end up in the courts for resolution'.[26]

There are, then, inevitably a range of public interests which will need to be protected by some form of regulation, although there is not always agreement as to whether it should always be government rather than the regulators themselves who should take responsibility for social or environmental measures which have significant implications for customers or companies. Whatever the arrangements, ancillary protection of interests is possible through, for example, the creation of consumer councils to promote consumer interests and to work closely with the regulator. As Prosser points out, the French have developed the concept of service public where, for example, public service concessions have been granted to private concerns. He also points up the plethora of examples of accountability methodologies available with reference to overseas experience. He summarises thus:

> The problems of utility regulation in the United Kingdom are not unique, but mirror much older problems elsewhere and overseas experience is important as a means of learning how to resolve the problems effectively. In particular, case law in other nations has dealt more explicitly with two particular problems: in the United States procedural questions have been dealt with much more coherently, and in continental Europe there has been a fuller recognition of the plurality of regulatory goals through the establishment of a relatively sophisticated case law dealing with the social requirements of public

25 *Op cit*, OECD (1997), fn 5, Introduction.

26 *Op cit*, OECD (1997), fn 5, p 271.

> service, and suggesting that there is something different about basic services linked to citizenship.[27]

This leads naturally to the question of the accountability of regulatory regimes and, in particular, the role of law, broadly defined, within them.

ACCOUNTABILITY OF THE REGULATORY PROCESS

Granted the need for regulation, how open should the regulatory process be and, in particular, what role should law play in the process? Well, in one sense all regulation is law, especially if we adopt a broader concept of law than is usual.[28] In a democracy, regulatory regimes need to be accountable; the question becomes how, and through what institutions.

There is, within British public administration, a traditional hostility to law, lawyers and, especially, the courts. Some of this hostility is misplaced, some not. However, to argue for greater accountability in the regulatory process is not necessarily to argue for a greater role for the courts, as Prosser makes continuously clear in his major study of regulation. Nevertheless, he is equally clear that, at least as far as the regulation of the utilities is concerned, the British regulatory experience has, until now, been one of highly personalised regulation, and that legal controls over the regulators are far more relaxed, in both procedure and substance, than is the case, say, in the US.

Prosser also points out that regulation in Britain is very long established, and can certainly be traced back at lest to the time of the Stuarts and Tudors. Key regulatory areas were foreign trade, markets, prices, quality of products, employment education and land use. However, most would associate regulation with the 19th century, where experience was, to say the least, mixed. Nevertheless, this does not mean that lessons have been well learned:

> ... the rejection of legalism in the creation of the new regulators rested on an assumption that legalism had been the chief reason for failures of earlier regulatory models, yet in fact there was a large number of different reasons for such failures, of which legalism was only one.[29]

Nevertheless, he is right to say that a mistrust of legalism has been a central theme in the design of British regulatory institutions. To take the regulation of the railways as a signal example, the story was one of regulation by Parliament, then by the courts of common law and finally by regulatory commissions, often involving proceedings with a high degree of legal

27 *Op cit*, Prosser, fn 6, p 292.

28 But see, eg, Lewis, ND, 'Towards a sociology of lawyering in public administration' (1981) NILQ 89, pp 89–105.

29 *Op cit*, Prosser, fn 6, p 32.

formality.[30] Prosser, commenting on the history of transport regulation in the UK, has this to say:

> This sorry tale makes it clear that the adjudicative model of regulation based closely on the procedures of a court of law is totally unsuitable for a regulatory institution deciding matters of general principle such as price control; reasons for this include delay. Nevertheless, the avoidance of adjudicatory models does not mean avoiding law; as we have already seen, there is inevitably a vast body of law applying to any utility regulator.[31]

Again, it is hard to quarrel with this position. Although they were commenting on the unsatisfactory nature of the monopolies legislation, a Parliamentary Select Committee might have been commenting on regulatory models more broadly in arguing that there was, in particular, a need for greater openness and transparency.[32] Even where consultation procedures have been innovatory, we are still a long way from a fully fledged FOI regime. Thus, in relation to water regulation, an innovative consultation procedure was criticised as being used to inform the industry and consumers rather than to create a dialogue, because the results of the consultations were not published as such and because too much discretion was given to the companies as to how they undertook consultation. It has been observed, too, that the expectation that the electricity regulator was in a position to obtain accurate information was misplaced, while the powers for him to require information were themselves inadequate. There must be some forum in which information can be properly tested through criticism and debate; in other words, some form of hearing. Prosser found, after a searching analysis, that the accountability record of the regulators was mixed. A strikingly large amount of information is now made available in, for example, price reviews, but devices such as hearings to test opposing views have not been used and there has been criticism of lack of access to all important consultants' reports.[33]

There have, of course, been public hearings by the UK regulators, though none of them adequate enough to satisfy all of Prosser's accountability requirements. OFGAS, for example, has not used hearings as such, although it has sought an 'independent' third view in the form of consultants' reports. This helps, *inter alia*, in reducing the regulator's reliance on information from the regulated company.

---

30 At this point in time, the role of the courts in supervising the regulators is unclear; compare, eg, *R v Independent Television Commission ex p TSW Broadcasting Ltd* [1996] EMLR 291 and *Mercury Communications Ltd v Director General of Telecommunications* [1996] 1 All ER 575.

31 *Op cit*, Prosser, fn 6, p 185.

32 Trade and Industry Select Committee, *Government Observations on the Fifth Report of the Trade and Industry Committee*, Session 1994–95, HC 748, paras 2–3.

33 See, eg, *op cit*, Prosser, fn 6, p 116.

Another important development in opening up the regulatory process can be seen in the case of water. As well as innovative attempts at assessing customers' views, the Director General (DG) has involved the Customer Service Committees in important ways. He has made the confidential business plans of the companies available to the Chairmen of Committees and they were present at the formal meetings between the DG and the companies to hear the representations of the latter on them.[34] But, as has been said, the record is patchy and a Select Committee has supported the concept of public hearings, as well as the practice of giving reasons for the decisions of the regulator, a recommendation not supported by the government of the day.[35] The new Utilities Act goes some way to meeting these criticisms, but there is still a distance to go. However, since governments have been feeling along in the dark, it may well be that the authority will conduct itself in a thoroughly radical fashion that successive governments may feel confident enough to build on.

We have seen already that effective regulation does not mean over-specific regulation which can lead to rigidities, selective application, etc. Interpretation and effective implementation of individual regulations requires a degree of discretion. But, as the OECD has pointed out, this discretion needs to be balanced by administrative procedure legislation and external reviews of decisions, appeal mechanisms, judicial review, ombudsmen, etc.[36] Few jurisdictions yet seem to have the balance right.

As to the regulators in the UK, several of them have gone a long way to opening up the regulatory process without any single one having produced an 'optimum' model, while too much process discretion is given to individual regulators and there is too little legal guidance. OFTEL's US-style 'notice and comment' procedures have received much favourable comment. Alongside a decision to give reasons, public hearings and a waterfall of freely available information, the notice and comment provisions require responses to consultation to be made publicly available as part of a US-style record; confidential representations may be withheld, but can be expected to have less probative value and therefore to carry less weight.[37] There is little doubt that some of the US Federal Administrative law requirements are cumbersome and over-weighted, but the majority of rule making procedures are not unduly onerous and few are as overblown as the Monopolies and Mergers Commission procedures in the UK. The major OECD publications on regulation, while stressing the need to avoid undue delay of business

34 Note the criticism that the Electricity Regulator has been less open in the decision making process than his colleagues: *op cit*, Prosser, fn 6, p 177.

35 See Trade and Industry Select Committee, *Aspects of the Electricity Supply Industry*, Session 1994–95, HC 481, and the Government's response.

36 OECD, Emerging Market Economy Forum Workshop, 10–11 December 1998, Session on Promoting Good Governance.

37 OFTEL, *Consultation Procedures and Transparency*, 1995.

decisions, is clear that democratic safeguards and procedural protections are a vital ingredient of regulatory regimes. So where does this leave us?

SOME PROPOSALS

Prosser says this:

> If, then, OFTEL gives us a model for regulatory procedures on the US pattern, the energy regulators have gone some way to enunciating the sorts of social concerns which have characterized *service public* in Continental Europe ...
>
> OFWAT has offered other lessons. First, the requirement of independent monitoring of information through the use of external reporters could usefully be adopted by other regulators, as could the degree of openness shown through the publication of letters from the Director General to the companies. Secondly, the pattern of consumer representation in water did permit a closer involvement of consumer representatives in the price-control process, and it seems that this affected outcomes in important ways.[38]

Democratic and accountable procedures will still be needed if nations move towards 'enforced self-regulation' which involves negotiation between the State and individual firms to establish appropriate standards and regulations, which can then be publicly enforced.[39]

There are a number of regulatory reviews now taking place in the UK and their recommendations will be received with interest. However, it is difficult not to agree in broad terms with Prosser's overall assessment, viz, that procedural questions have been dealt with more coherently in the US, while in continental Europe there has been a fuller recognition of the plurality of regulatory goals through the establishment of a relatively sophisticated case law dealing with the social requirements of public service, and suggesting that there is something different about basic services linked to citizenship.

CONCLUSIONS

Central to concerns about good governance are the encouragement of market institutions, both in the traditional sense and in that of quasi-markets within public settings, promoting efficiency, regulation at the optimum level to ensure both efficiency and democratic ideals, and an increasing concentration on the incidents of citizenship. This latter is about building up constituency support for government policies and for economic growth and protecting

38 *Op cit*, Prosser, fn 6, pp 296–97.

39 See, eg, Michael, DC, 'Federal agency use of audited self-regulation as a regulatory technique' (1995) 47 Administrative L Rev 171, pp 171–253.

human rights, not least through informed participation and being rendered a meaningful account. The problems and the opportunities are vast and will need to be worked at diligently over the years to come. A great deal more work has been done in the field of regulation in recent years than in relation to some of the other considerations raised here. The general principles can be stated with some degree of general support anticipated, though a deal of work still needs to be done in terms of comparing best practices and laying down basic standards. After all, as the OECD research makes clear, economic and social policies should be mutually supportive.

Regulatory reform that sharpens competitive pressures provides powerful incentives for firms to become more efficient, innovative and competitive. These improvements can boost the productivity of entire industries and bring sharp and swift price reductions and improvements in the quality and range of products and services, to the benefit of consumers and user industries. Reform that reduces business burdens and increases the transparency of regulatory regimes supports entrepreneurship, market entry and economic growth that, in turn, should produce high paying, high quality jobs. Reform that reduces red tape and paperwork burdens for ordinary citizens – particularly in their role as taxpayers – frees up valuable time and individual initiative. In turn, more productive, innovative, and flexible economies are in a better position to meet other public interests and to help governments deal with issues such as social cohesion and environmental quality.[40]

Because regulation is such an inexact term and applies not only to the utilities, it will be returned to again in Chapter 8 regarding competition policy, corporate governance and the protection of consumer interests.

This approach recognises, but underplays, the primacy of social purposes by which all economic activity should be judged. Thus, it would be well to recognise that in defending markets, what is really being defended is a set of human freedoms – the flipside of democratic politics. Jobs, profits and growth are all desiderata for a healthy society – providing that they are not bought at the cost of social exclusion or a serious imbalance of private power.

40 See, eg, *op cit*, OECD, fn 36, Workshop on Regulatory Reform.

CHAPTER 8

COMPETITION, CONSUMERS AND CORPORATE GOVERNANCE

Competition is at the heart of modern systems of governance, so much so that, as has been seen, the public sector seeks to mimic markets as far as possible and to engage in competitive exercises with the private sector, with a view to determining which form of service delivery is best suited to the public sector. Indeed, the whole Citizen's Charter/Service First initiative is built around the notion that service standards and targets are a necessary counterpoint within public agencies to the improvement of cost-effectiveness and service quality in the private sector by competition. What is thereby achieved is a kind of quasi-market within the public realm. Many of these issues were touched upon in Chapter 6. In Chapter 7, one of the defences of regulation is where market competition fails. Indeed, one of the central roles of economic management these days is to encourage competition and remove any barriers to it. 'Perfect' competition is supposed to protect consumers by providing choice in a number of settings and naturally involves easy access to information on price, quality and a number of other variables. Where it does not, then government clearly has the duty to protect consumers through some form of regulation.

Recent developments in NPM have been described already and there is little doubt that the changes worked in these matters have improved services in the public sector to a considerable degree and moved them closer to private market models. However, the flipside of the concern to protect consumers is not so frequently commented upon, viz, competition and fair trading policy by the private sector as a primary concern of government itself. This is just as crucial a 'governance' issue as any other, although it is treated far less prominently, at least in the public law literature. However, the view taken here is that competition and fair trading policy have compelling public law dimensions – at least as far as the public agencies vested with the task of promoting these issues are concerned. Equally of significance to public law scholars should be the procedures adopted by these agencies in dealing with the private sector under their statutory remit.

In spite of popular opinion, the Citizen's Charter is about more than performance standards for public bodies, important as they are. Both the government's own annual reports and associated publications, and a closer inspection of its overall philosophy indicates that the Charter is shorthand for a liberal market-based credo. A central feature of these beliefs is a commitment to the protection of the customer/citizen (although the terms are by no means synonymous) by market process, by competition or its approximation (market-mimicking). The ruling sentiment of choice, suffusing as it does so much of the Government's rhetoric, compactly summarises everything that lies behind the Charter and its inspiration. If the market is all important in providing citizen choice and standards, it has to be a properly functioning market. To this extent, competition policy is crucial, as is being increasingly recognised within the European Union, whose directives can be expected to become more influential with the passage of time.

The other point to make by way of introduction concerns the issue of corporate governance. This is important in itself, but the importance is compounded by the phenomenon of globalisation whereby a small number of very large companies – upon whom much of the opportunities for growth and future wealth lies – possess an influence denied to many governments. They also possess the potential for limiting political choices around the world. It is for this reason that the issue of corporate governance is now high on the agenda of democratic governments everywhere. Governance, then, must include a concern for corporate governance and it is for this reason that it has been linked with competition as one of the central themes of this chapter.

THE CITIZEN AND COMPETITIVE MARKETS

> I take it that the objective of competition policy, in economic terms, is to secure the optimal allocation of resources in the economy, through the interplay of independent decisions by producers and consumers, in the interests of providing, at minimum cost, the goods and services which consumers value most highly.[1]

If public services operated in this way, there would be no need for charters – according to one view. In fact, genuinely open markets are a relative rarity and thus, governments need to pursue competition policies to ensure fairness for consumers in their dealings with businesses. No one should doubt the genuine difficulties in pursuing policies which protect consumers and strike a balance between short term and long term economic efficiency. Yet, Aaronson describes the relative dearth of significant action taken by the authorities to restore competition or maintain it. Indeed, just a few short years ago, the Director General of Fair Trading (DGFT) was able to describe the UK competition regime as 'very much showing its age'.[2] Some expert opinion believes that there is at present insufficient incentive to prevent firms from behaving in an anti-competitive way.[3]

Apart from deficiencies recently recognised by the government, it needs to be said that only two to three mergers per year have been blocked, only around six monopoly situations are found to be against the public interest

1 Aaronson, R, *The Future of UK Competition Policy*, 1996, IPPR, p 1.

2 Bridgeman, J, speech to the Law Society Commerce and Industry Group, 27 April 1996.

3 See, eg, Cave, M, in *op cit*, Aaronson, fn 1, p 18.

(and even here, the action taken is rarely proportionate), the tripartite system of control produces substantial inertia, and much of the work of the competition authorities is directed at quite minor infractions, leaving the larger players free to roam as they wish. Part of the reason for this is that, until very recently, legal powers were better suited to reacting to complaints than proactively to search out priority sectors.[4]

It is because of this that attention has recently been turned to updating the jurisprudence in this area. This is not the place to explore competition law in detail, but some outline of the Competition Act 1998 is necessary. The Act only came into force in March 2000 so that, at the time of writing, it is too early to say much about its impact. Nevertheless, its main thrusts were to prohibit anti-competitive agreements, such as price fixing or market sharing cartels, and also to prohibit the abuse of a dominant position in the market – for example, if a business with a large market share imposes unfair trading conditions on suppliers. The Act gives to the Office of Fair Trading (OFT) the power to impose a financial penalty for breaches of the Act of up to 10% of a company's UK turnover, greater power to seize information from companies suspected of acting anti-competitively, and the power to stop suspected anti-competitive behaviour while investigations take place. Significantly, one hopes, the Competition Commission replaces the Monopolies and Mergers Commission.

Abuse of a dominant position is somewhat complicated and technical, but the position adopted in the Act is based upon Art 86 of the Treaty of Rome. The European Court has defined a dominant market position as:

> ... a position of economic strength enjoyed by an undertaking which enables it to prevent effective competition being maintained on the relevant market by affording it the power to behave to an appreciable extent independently of its competitors, customers and ultimately of consumers.[5]

The Act does not set any market share threshold for defining dominance. Although market share is an important factor, it does not, of itself, determine whether an undertaking is in a position of dominance. The European Court has stated that dominance can be presumed in the absence of evidence to the contrary if an undertaking has a market share persistently above 50%.[6] The DGFT considers it unlikely that an undertaking will be individually dominant if its market share is below 40%, although dominance could be established below that figure where the circumstances indicate. Entry barriers will also be evidence of dominance.

The Act, again following EU law closely, goes on to discuss the second test, that is, abuse. Without going into great detail, it can be said that the test

4 And see Lewis, ND, 'The Citizen's Charter in the round', written evidence to the Public Service Select Committee, 3rd Report, HC, Session 1996–97, The Citizen's Charter, pp 53–64.

5 Case 27/76, *United Brands v EC Commission* [1978] 1 CMLR 429.

6 Case C-62/86, *AKZO Chemie BV v Commission* [1993] 5 CMLR 215.

refers primarily to the following: excessively high or discriminatory prices, predatory behaviour, vertical restraints, or refusing to supply existing or potential competitors. Vertical restraints cover a multitude of sins, but resale price maintenance is perhaps the best known. There may be benefits attached to vertical restraints which preclude the arrangements being seen as an abuse of a dominant position, especially since they can operate to overcome failures in the workings of the market.

It is naturally not possible to compile an exhaustive list of when market or competition abuses might occur, but the main criterion is whether the conduct either exploits the undertaking's customers or reduces existing or potential competition. On the other hand, an objective justification may be legitimately raised.[7]

The penalties attached to the Competition Act are fairly severe. As has been seen, companies found to be infringing the new Act will be liable to a maximum penalty of 10% of UK turnover. It is now possible for the DGFT and the utility sector regulators to impose penalties on companies of up to 10% of UK turnover for each year of the infringement of the prohibitions, up to a maximum of three years.

Under ss 46 and 47 of the Act, such decisions taken by the DG or other regulator may be appealed to an Appeal Tribunal of the Competition Commission. The tribunals may confirm, set aside or vary the DG's decision, or make any other decision that the Director could have made. A further appeal on a point of law or on the amount of any penalty lies to the Court of Appeal. Following the appointment of the first President of the Appeal Tribunals, Sir Christopher Bellamy QC, it was decided that the most appropriate model for the Appeal Tribunal rules was the procedure used by the Court of First Instance of the EU, which deals with appeals from the competition decisions of the European Commission. Draft rules of procedure went out for consultation between October and December 1999 and resulted, after modifications following representations, in a statutory instrument which came into force on 1 March 2000. The framework adopted breaks new ground in terms of traditional court procedures following the recommendations of the Woolf reforms.

The OFT has increased powers of information gathering and investigation under the Act. A major weapon against cartels will be the 'leniency policy', similar to that successfully operated in the US. Providing that they meet the conditions set out in the OFT's guidance, total immunity from financial penalties will be offered to any member of the cartel who is the first to provide evidence of the existence and activities of a cartel and who co-operates with the OFT throughout its investigation. There are other aspects to the leniency policy which will not be pursued here, but it is important to note that the

7 See Office of Fair Trading, *The Chapter 11 Prohibition*, 2000, OFT.

policy has been fairly successful in the US in flushing out secret deals which damage competition and increase prices to consumers and to business. Two applications per month for leniency are currently being made to the US Department of Justice. As the DGFT remarks:

> The UK has waited a long time for punishment to fit behaviour which damages and distorts the marketplace. I intend to see that the Competition Act is effective.[8]

The omens are promising, but only time will tell how much improvement in competition and in the lot of consumers can be expected. However, it is crucial that the systems and processes by which competition law is operated be as open and consultative as possible. In previous years, the situation has not been remotely satisfactory.

During the first year of the Commission's existence, it initiated a wide ranging consultation exercise on its procedures. This took the form of a series of interviews conducted by consultants with lawyers, other advisers, government officials, regulatory offices, consumer organisations, trade unions and others with a direct interest in their work. This was supplemented by a written consultation paper available to the public generally. The search for transparency was, however, not universally popular. This is because some of the information needed by the Commission is necessarily commercially sensitive. In 1999, the Competition Commission held its first public hearing into an alleged monopoly. It should be said that the fact of a public hearing is a great advance and one greatly to be welcomed. However, the car manufacturers, the subject of the investigation into price fixing and the manipulation of the market, decided to boycott the inquiry. Instead, they delegated responsibility to a three-man team from the Society of Motor Manufacturers and Traders, the trade body for the industry. The manufacturers were perfectly willing, they said, to be open and frank with the Commission in private session.[9] In the event, the Commission found 'a complex monopoly situation' which was detrimental to consumers.

A second open hearing was held on planning-related issues arising on a supermarkets inquiry held in Birmingham. The Commission believes that these hearings demonstrated the value which public discussion can bring. However, they were keen to stress that open hearings will never replace the need for private hearings where commercially sensitive matters can be explored. This is clearly right, but most research indicates that confidentiality is claimed in circumstances where a 'substantial harm' test would result in much more information being publicly disclosed. This is a matter which requires close attention.[10]

---

8 Office of Fair Trading, *Guidelines on the Calculation of Penalties*, 2000, OFT.

9 See (1999) *Financial Times*, 21 July.

10 And see Competition Commission, *Annual Review and Accounts 1999–2000*, HMSO.

Mergers present a different problem, and most empirical research shows that they rarely produce tangible benefits for consumers. Nevertheless, they are allowed to occur without relative hindrance on account of what many see as the deficiencies of UK company law. It is, clearly, now time to take seriously the argument that mergers should be controlled unless the parties can show that the public interest is served rather than that the merger is not against the public interest. As Aaronson persuasively argues:

> If there are effective means of removing inefficient management short of a takeover, a requirement to show positive benefits ... could well be a desirable policy, since only mergers with demonstrable synergy benefits would then be allowed.[11]

At the time of writing, although the 1998 Competition Act was in force, the law relating to mergers as described here is largely unchanged. Some unease has been expressed in relation to acquisitions and mergers which does not appear to be adequately addressed at the moment. For instance, it has been suggested that the OFT be given a considerable boost in its dealing with company acquisitions and mergers. At the moment, the DGFT has a duty to identify mergers which have taken place or are about to happen. Once he is aware of a merger, he may carry out an informal inquiry looking into the possible effects on competition and other matters of public interest. If there appear to be reasonable grounds for believing the merger could have a detrimental effect, the DG can advise the Secretary of State to refer the case to the Competition Commission. Broadly, a merger qualifies for investigation if it involves the acquisition of gross assets worth £70 million or more, or the creation or enhancement of a share of 25% or more in the market for goods or services of any description in the UK or a substantial part of it. In 1998, the OFT considered 425 merger cases; of these, eight were referred to the MMC.

For some time, there has been active discussion concerning the desirability of merging the OFT with what is now the Competition Commission, thus producing a single authority for judging merger decisions. Instead, the Secretary of State recently announced a compromise. This is that ministerial involvement would largely be removed from the control process. The OFT will normally refer directly to the Competition Commission and the minister will accept its recommendations to refer 'in all but exceptional cases'. Competition assessments should be made by independent bodies charged with clear competition objectives. The move is a significant step back from the radical restructuring of merger authorities outlined by the Government as part of its competition policy review. The decision not to create a 'super OFT' has not been universally acclaimed. The Mergers Task Force in Brussels carries out both stage one and stage two investigations and some concern has been expressed that it is too powerful; hence the reluctance to allow the OFT

11 *Op cit*, Aaronson, fn 1, p 14.

to follow suit. However, in July 1999, the Government published a consultation document outlining proposals for reforms to the merger control regime. The most significant changes proposed were that ministers should relinquish their role in considering mergers, save for cases raising exceptional public interest matters such as national security. Moreover, the test under which the independent competition authorities would assess mergers should be changed from the present 'public interest' test to one focused on competition.

The Government stresses that the OFT has gained considerable new powers under the Competition Act – including the power to raid company offices – and it is to gain control of deciding when mergers should be investigated under a competition test. Under the present arrangements, the Secretary of State decides which mergers should be referred to the OFT. In addition, he can modify Competition Commission decisions, by, for example, blocking mergers which are cleared with conditions attached.

Consumer dissatisfaction surveys indicate that citizens are by no means receiving the quality of service from the market which they are entitled to expect. This is partly because of failures in competition policy prior to 2000, and partly because even with an adequate level of competition, the struggle between consumers and business is often unequal. As Aaronson points out, half a million inappropriate pensions have been sold to the British people in recent years while poor repairs are routinely undertaken on cars in the UK. He believes that consumers need proactive protection through a new institution which pulls together the powers held by many different institutions. This would be a statutory consumer watchdog with broad powers of intervention.[12]

Most consumer protection issues are essentially the province of the DTI and its shadow Select Committee. However, the impact on consumers and citizens is not currently addressed by any particular public agency which sees these things in the round and which directly addresses the disjunction between the market at large and the interests of consumers.

The OFT has both a Director of Competition Policy and a Director of Consumer Affairs who, at least theoretically, ought to be closely linked. Following the prevailing economic philosophy, the Office is committed to the view that promoting competition is perhaps the best way of furthering the interests of consumers. There have, however, been a number of recent initiatives which have sought to embrace a wider role for consumer interests.

Regulation, as has been seen, is one of the major tools of modern governance, though there are different schools of thought about the need for 'lightness' of touch – or a greater degree of social and environmental regulation. Not enough thought has been given to the old values of openness,

12 *Op cit*, Aaronson, fn 1, pp 22–23.

participation and accountability – yet, given the relative weakness of those values in informing the overall conduct of government in Whitehall, that is hardly surprising.

Many of the sentiments expressed by Prosser over the balance of interests in the regulatory field[13] carry across to all consumer issues; after all, consumer protection and enhancement is, to a considerable extent, about regulation, albeit not being seen in the traditional fashion in which the problems of utilities are addressed. Citizenship and participation are vital concepts which need to be instantiated within modern governance systems, while large corporations must be made to serve the ends of justice rather than simply pursuing growth and profits. At the moment, it can scarcely be said that the consumer is truly king.

Although reform proposals to strengthen consumer rights have been in the air for some time, there is still considerable dissatisfaction. Shortly after the election of the Blair Government in 1997, the DGFT made a series of proposals to the DTI to tighten up the law against rogue traders. He expressed the view that it was time to update standards of consumer protection to bring the UK into line with good practice in many other countries, including Australia, Canada, Germany and the US. In particular, he sought powers to allow the OFT and trading standards departments to require a trader to discontinue a practice deemed 'unfair'. Recourse would be had to a Fair Trading Tribunal.

In his final annual report in June 2000, the DG, John Bridgeman, claimed that a combination of weak law and long term apathy has allowed disreputable and irresponsible business to flourish at the expense of UK consumers. Some of his remarks are worth quoting in full:

> Global trade and e-commerce are increasing the financial risks to consumers. Cowboys, frauds, confusion selling, misleading claims and the hidden pitfalls of long term investments are among the problems which demand a new approach.
>
> This Government has moved swiftly to overhaul and modernise competition law to stop price fixing and abuse of monopoly power. The next step is to reform consumer protection legislation and restructure the agencies delivering it. I am encouraged by ministers' assurances that the OFT will play a major part in this, but it will need sufficient resources to do it.
>
> For too many years both the law and funding of central and local consumer protection have been inadequate – the OFT has just £10 million a year for this work ...
>
> The Government has proposed new consumer protection legislation. It has also accepted the need for reform of the Trade Descriptions Act – something urged by the first Director-General in 1976. I hope both of these will be pursued with some urgency ...

13 Prosser, T, *Law and the Regulators*, 1997, Clarendon, esp pp 268, 292.

> My time at the OFT has convinced me that the consumer's interest has been neglected by past Governments and too long abused by business. It needs to be much nearer the top of the agenda of both to enable the OFT and local trading standards departments to safeguard the public interest.[14]

Granted that the DG left his office at odds with the DTI, his words represent a stinging rebuke to the current regime for the protection of consumer interests. Given the adoption of a liberal market philosophy by all governments presently on the scene, it appears clear that there is too great a leeway granted to business in delivering on notions of citizenship to which, given their specially accorded status, they must now be seen to be fully committed. This is part of the so called 'social licence to operate', a matter which is increasingly on the agendas of company law reform and is an issue which will need increasingly to be addressed as 'governance' becomes ever more globalised.

For their part, the Government in the 1999 White Paper promised action across a range of activities and has outlined a 'consumer strategy' to help consumers become better informed and more demanding. Finally, the consumer strategy consultation process has gone online with the Government listing, in particular, eight areas on which consumer comments are sought – though without prejudice, of course, to any general remarks which contributors may wish to make.

There are also slightly more radical reform proposals in the air which would not go as far as the proponents of 'stakeholder capitalism' would like, but would, at a stroke, give all consumers a stake in the capitalist enterprise. Samuel Brittan is but one who believes that spreading capital ownership more widely early in life would represent a huge stride in making capitalism more acceptable. Brittan, it may be recalled, had argued that, during the great privatisation sell-off of the 1980s and early 1990s, shares in the nationalised industries should be distributed 'free' to all adult citizens. This would have been both a nest egg and a way of accustoming people to handle financial capital. He now appears to approve what he describes as 'a further step forward' in recommending the findings of two left-of-centre think tanks, the Institute for Public Policy Research and the Fabian Society, both of whom favour some form of capital endowment for all. This is not the place to pursue these ideas in detail, but some readjustment of the relationship between consumers and capital would seem to enjoy general support.[15]

Before examining the crucial issue of corporate governance, a word should be set about the reform of UK company law, although much of the argument is relevant to what will be said later about corporate governance. At the time of writing, a review of UK company law had been ongoing for a couple of

14 Director General of Fair Trading, *Annual Report of the Director General of Fair Trading 1999*, 2000, HMSO.

15 See Brittan, S, (2000) *Financial Times*, 15 March.

years. A consultation paper published in March 1998 outlined the scope and arrangements for the review. The Review Steering Group's first consultation document, *The Strategic Framework*, was published in February 1999. In October of that year, the Group issued three further consultation documents building on the results of the earlier consultation process. The topics covered by these documents are company formation and capital maintenance, reforming the law concerning overseas companies and company general meetings, and shareholder information. For present purposes, the most significant consultation document was issued in March 2000.[16] This document analysed and made proposals on key areas of governance of companies and on small and private companies. Only the first of these two issues will be touched on here.

First, it should be said that the current framework of company law is essentially constructed on foundations which were put in place in the middle of the 19th century. Although there have been numerous additions, amendments and consolidations in the intervening years, what exists is a patchwork of regulation that is both immensely complex and seriously out of date. The primary consolidating measure is the Companies Act 1985. It should by now be obvious that governance at the larger level is now hugely different from the circumstances obtaining when UK company law was first conceived, and it is now generally accepted that the wealth upon which we all depend in future will be primarily generated by the private sector. This provides benefits and potential pitfalls. The benefits are obvious, but there is also a downside. It is that big business can at worst outflank government choices or at least cause them to be severely constrained. Furthermore, business is increasingly becoming the partner of government in numerous endeavours of critical national importance, and finally it must not be overlooked that markets and business can produce serious externalities, not least, though not exclusively, severe environmental damage. It is obvious, then, why the Brundtland Commission spoke of companies needing a 'social licence to operate'. It is obvious that companies owe obligations both to their 'host' governments (if they can any longer be clearly identified) and to a wider range of interested parties or 'stakeholders', to adopt the fashionable argot.

It is against this background that the central proposals of the Consultation Paper must be assessed. First, there is the issue of what the Group terms 'scope'; that is, in whose interests should companies be run? Their answer is a compromise, but with the position of the shareholder still dominant. It argues that the overall objective of wealth generation and competitiveness for the benefit of all can best be achieved through the twin components of:

16 DTI, *Modern Company Law for a Competitive Economy: Developing the Framework*, 2000, HMSO.

- an 'inclusive' approach to directors' duties which requires them to have regard to all the relationships on which the company depends and to the long, as well as the short, term implications of their actions, with a view to achieving company success for the benefit of shareholders as a whole; and
- wider public accountability: this is to be achieved *principally through improved company reporting* (emphasis added), which for public and very large private companies will require the publication of a broad operating and financial review which explains the company's performance, strategy and relationships (for example, with employees, customer and suppliers as well as the wider community).

Under the proposals, public and very large private companies would include in their full annual report a new statutory operating and financial review, which would enable the user to assess the performance and prospects of the business – *including its wider relationships,* its reputation and its impact on the community and the environment. The content of the review would be partly prescribed by statute, *with the detailed requirements being laid down in standards.*

The Group canvassed what necessary changes would accompany broadening the duties of directors to embrace stakeholders other than shareholders. The obvious way to achieve this would be through a two tiered board system on the German model. This they rejected, favouring transparency and public accountability of the company as a means of ensuring that the community could hold not only directors, but also shareholders, to account for the external impact of its operations.

The main change in the status quo would be the obligation for public and listed companies, at least, to publish as part of the full annual report an Operating and Financial Review. This would cover all that is material in the directors' view for users to achieve a proper assessment of the performance and future plans and prospects of the business. It would include, where relevant, its relationships with employees and others. This would be a statutory version of the current OFR already adopted by the best run companies. In cases where information was thought necessary in the public interest, the Secretary of State would have power by regulation to require its inclusion in a supplementary statement if not included in the OFR (as it would be if the directors regarded it as material). Note that the detailed contents of the OFR would be a matter for standards developed by an approved body. It would enable shareholders and the community as a whole to monitor performance of the broadly expressed duty, and for all concerned to develop flexible and responsive standards for reporting on the matters covered and to provide appropriate feedback to the company. 'This in turn would affect its reputation.'[17] Furthermore, 'it should not be unduly burdensome or inflexible ...'.

17 *Op cit,* DTI, fn 16, para 2.20.

Leaving aside the difficulty of discussing 'future plans' openly when 'commercial in confidence' is almost always the order of the day, the Steering Group's, and indeed the DTI's, philosophy is best captured in the following:

> It may be asked whether this proposal is an 'enlightened shareholder value' or a 'pluralist' one. The overall objective should be pluralist in the sense that companies should be run in a way which maximises overall competitiveness and wealth and welfare for all. But the means which a company deploys for achieving this objective must take account of the realities and dynamics which operate in practice in the running of commercial enterprise. It should not be done at the expense of turning company directors from business decision makers into moral, political or economic arbiters, but by harnessing focused, comprehensive, competitive business decision making within robust, objective professional standards and flexible, but pertinent, accountability.[18]

It remains to be seen how this will work out and whether the Review is too conservative and too lacking in its understanding of the role modern business already plays against the larger governance picture. There is much here that is forward looking, but some of the analysis is a little shaky. For example, it appears to ignore the fact that company directors already take enormous moral and political decisions without any direct social or collective responsibility. It also inclines to the view that the politics of the driven market place are somehow not politics at all.

One issue is clear. Mandatory change to reflect wider stakeholder concerns 'would not be justified'. However, faced with hostility from its traditional backers in the face of an imminent general election, the Blair Government is reported to be prepared to review the issue further. Although still resistant to a new EU Directive on workers' rights which would compel companies to consult the workforce over proposed redundancies, the Prime Minister is said to have agreed to set up a review of the procedures on company mergers and closures.[19]

It is necessary to underline that socio-industrial organisations are often State-dependent, worker-dependent and, indeed, dependent on a raft of institutions of civil society to which they often pay scant democratic respect, pleading instead the legitimacy of the market. For example, it is widely accepted that governments increasingly provide 'public goods', such as education and training, in which industry is often too short-sighted to invest. Not only are such goods increasingly important in the new technological era, but an insight into our proper priorities is afforded when skills and education are described as 'human capital', for this makes it clear that it is human needs

18 *Op cit*, DTI, fn 16, para 2.21 and, indeed, Chapter 2 at large.

19 See (2000) *The Guardian*, 10 July.

that must be respected, rather than man-made institutions which are the product of history and accident as well as of genuine desiderata.[20]

It is by no means clear that the imperatives of 'private fiefdoms' coincide with those of the governments which host their activities. For instance, investment is often thought by politicians to be inadequate given the longer term needs of national economies. To take one instance: the ratio of dividends to R and D spending in the UK is three and a half times higher than in the US, 10 times higher than Germany and 13 times higher than Japan.[21] Furthermore, in the global free market economy, the ownership of industries once thought to be strategic is passing to those whose interests are very different from those of the previous owner. It is important to restate some of these larger ideas in the face of those who believe that life is too fast moving for governments to seek to intervene in order to reassert principle.

The role of employees in the corporate sector is woefully out of sync with almost any concept of personal dignity. This is an issue which cannot be pursued in any depth here. Suffice it to say that, for any version of governance to be acceptable over the longer term, citizens have to be taken seriously into account. This is essentially a matter of human rights. It is not possible at this stage to predict how events will unfold, but the EU is potentially the most active player. The 'social partners' are a fact of Community life, with their roles potentially far reaching. Currently, of course, those partners must be consulted by the Commission when proposing labour and social policy initiatives which take their impetus from Art 118 of the Treaty of Rome, as amended by the Single European Act. There are fashions in social policy, and some see the Working Time Directive as a sign of the re-emergence of the radical version of worker rights set out in the Paris Treaty which established the European Coal and Steel Community.[22] It may, perhaps, be the case that this sign points ultimately to a 'social constitution' for the EU. There are clearly prime movers who envisage an active, combined labour/social policy, as was suggested by the Green Paper on the future of labour policy in November 1993. This Green Paper speaks the language of participation in decision making processes and, most notably, the language of 'reconciliation' between work and home life. This is a concept with dramatic potential, not just for work, but for the whole spirit of community.

In light of this, the issue of corporate governance – seen particularly against the background of global governance – needs to be addressed further.

---

20 See Thurrow, L, *The Future of Capitalism*, 1996, Nicholas Brealey; Lewis, ND, 'The constitutional implications of participation' and Parkinson, JE, 'Participation and corporate governance', in Campbell, D and Lewis, ND (eds), *Promoting Participation: Law or Politics?*, 1999, Cavendish Publishing, pp 1–30 and 319–48.

21 See TUC, *Your Stake at Work*, 1996, TUC, p 10.

22 See Bercusson, B, *European Labour Law*, 1996, Butterworths, pp 346–47.

GOVERNANCE AND CORPORATE GOVERNANCE

Although the partnerships through which governments choose to operate include a wide range of actors, the private sector is increasingly involved. Private companies, then, to this extent, become vehicles for delivering public purposes. Furthermore, the end of the Cold War has seen the acceptance of the private sector as the primary engine for both economic and social regeneration. Its position of dominance, both nationally and globally, necessitates that the people's elected representatives pay close attention to its system of governance; to the way it organises its affairs and to the effects which that organisation produces for the common weal.

Corporate governance means more than just the constitutional framework which States impose through company law. It means regulation of various sorts – competition law, consumer and unfair business practice law, and the regime adopted by individual companies and sectors for promoting their several purposes. Some of this is best described as 'soft' law. Increasingly, it has an international or global dimension and embraces accords of various sorts struck between regional and international agencies and the corporate sector. The experiments have only just begun. They have much further to go.

The issue of corporate governance has come to non-philosophers relatively late. The power of multinational or transnational corporations has been apparent for some time and was much written about in the early 1970s, but time has moved on. Telecommunications, information or multimedia, automobile production, banking and other financial services are being largely developed through private companies that operate on a multinational stage. Their concerns are necessarily with the totality of their business operations rather than with any one country. Thus, although only private corporations can produce the wealth on which the world depends, they are in danger of being answerable to no one. Correspondingly, it is becoming increasingly accepted that, while it is impossible and undesirable to second-guess the major investment decisions of large corporations, a system of checks and balances has to be established to ensure that business operates, on a global level, within a wider framework of social responsibility.[23]

'Sustainability' is a case in point. It presents a paradox. Clearly, big business can strip out the planet and produce the most horrendous environmental problems. At the same time, corporations are the only organisations with the resources, the technology, the global reach, and, ultimately, the motivation to achieve sustainability. The resolution of the dilemma clearly lies in the concept of partnership between business and government(s). Government support is necessary to encourage research on

23 And see the Commission on Global Governance, *Managing Economic Interdependence*, 1995, UN.

energy efficiency since market-based incentives are inadequate and the long payback of such research seldom provides sufficient attraction for business. It is felt that the answer is for governments to build policies on properly designed market-based approaches, eliminate counterproductive subsidies and establish incentives for exploring and promoting highly efficient technologies.

The influential Brundtland Commission[24] urged business, in partnership with government, to play its part in promoting not only sustainability, but also in changing the quality of growth and protecting human rights. So also, in the UK, the Prince of Wales Business Forum has encouraged partnerships between business, government, communities, NGOs and aid agencies as an effective means of promoting sustainable development and to raise the awareness of the value of corporate responsibility.[25] The WBCSD was clear that many transnational companies now accept that the social licence to operate will become the third key issue board members will have to take account of when steering the company – that is, in addition to the economic and ecological dimensions.[26]

Given the commitment to a free market, global economy, corporate governance is becoming a crucial factor in efforts to restructure governing institutions. This is a hot topic internationally, given that the big investment funds have gone global, and the legitimacy of the conduct of large corporations is beginning to be called into question. Until now, governments in the UK have given public companies every opportunity to reform themselves.[27] In fact, it is not just in the UK that the whole field of corporate governance is being reassessed.

There is a growing mood that private sector organisations need to incorporate social concerns.[28] The need for change is being widely canvassed:

> The fact that public services are currently undergoing significant change enhances that need for extra vigilance and care to ensure that sound systems of corporate governance are both set in place and work in practice.[29]

A matter of the clearest importance, given the privatisation/contracting out phenomenon, is whether it is possible to delegate responsibilities for managing public services while maintaining equity. How far are the core

24 WBCSD, *Corporate Leadership and Governance: Securing the Social Licence to Operate (The Challenge Brief)*, 1987, WBCSD.

25 World Bank and the UN Development Programme, *Business as Partners in Development*, 1996, World Bank.

26 John Parkinson seems to adopt a similar position in arguing for maximisation of the value of a company's total assets, which includes the value of its relationships. See 'In whose interest should the directors act?' (1998) 1 Corporate Governance International 44.

27 *Ibid*. For the view that self-regulation behind the scenes may be effective see Holland, J, 'Self-regulation and the financial aspects of corporate governance' [1996] J Bus Law 127, pp 127–64.

28 See, eg, *Ministerial Symposium on the Future of Public Services*, 1996, OECD.

29 *Corporate Governance in the Public Services*, 1994, CIPFA, p 6.

values of the public service, including accountability, being heeded by the private sector in contracted out activities? Well, some of this is going to depend on the terms of the contracts struck by governments in their dealings with the contractees, and how far the public interest is sewn into the terms and conditions to be respected. As has been seen, in the UK, privacy and commercial confidentiality are too often the norm in contracts for public services so that not only is there a pressing need for a truly effective FOI Act, but also that a 'Contracts Commissioner' should be established to supervise the whole area. (S)he will need strong powers of social and democratic audit over the companies concerned. Anything less will set back the progress of democratic government to a considerable degree.[30]

It should be added that, quite apart from the standard contracting process, government, not least in the UK, is promoting a range of partnerships, including, naturally, the private sector. Most recently there have been Education Action Zones, Regional Development Agencies, Agenda 21 and the like.[31] It is inevitable that industry will have to learn to understand the needs of all its partners, and just as business has so much to contribute, it must also accept its wider responsibilities, not least to the voluntary sector.[32]

Over and above these concerns, competitiveness is a particularly pressing requirement in a global economy, but too often it has been seen from the standpoint of the private sector alone. However, since the public and private sectors depend crucially upon each other's resources, competitiveness is a joint concern. The standard of public services determines the quality and dynamics of the environment in which business operates. This is quite apart from the increasing competitiveness of the public services themselves, both at central and local levels, where benchmarking is increasingly important.

All the foregoing issues raise serious problems about public values and the ability to take political decisions. However, problems of accountability are placed in stark relief. The UK, historically, deals with problems, especially affecting public administration, as and when they arise, but traditionally without recourse to legislation. At the moment, a number of government reviews affecting this area have been undertaken, some resulting in legislation and some not. An assessment of the effectiveness of these interventions will be undertaken in Chapter 9.

30 See Goh, J and Lewis, ND, *The Private World of Government (occasional papers)*, 1998, Sheffield Centre for Socio-Legal Studies, University of Sheffield.

31 See, eg, Alexander, Z, 'Public partners' (1998) 25 Local Government Management 14, pp 14–15.

32 See, eg, National Council for Voluntary Organisations, *Meeting the Challenge of Change in Voluntary Action into the 21st Century*, 1996, Commission on the Future of the Voluntary Sector, for the suggestion, *inter alia*, that members of the voluntary sector should be co-opted on to company management boards.

In any event, corporate governance can no longer be seen in a vacuum. Quite apart from the stakeholder debate and questions of sustainability, the larger issue of 'overall governance' kicks in. Representative democracy, which has always been more hollow in the UK than in comparable democracies, has now to be re-examined seriously. With 'governance-as-networking', government has to be opened up to civil society, decentralisation has to spawn new accountability structures and democratic devices need to be more localised. In the UK, we can expect the following to impact on corporate governance: individual laws and regulations to deal with externalities – many of them prompted by the EU; the wide ranging review of company law; the FOI Act and a more open regulatory process. In addition, 'contracts' of various sorts will be struck within partnerships which will include business, and contracts between individual governments and companies and/or sectors. Of course, all this must be set in the context of globalisation.

GLOBALISATION AND CORPORATE GOVERNANCE

Globalisation has implications in the internal balance of power in nation States, including between levels of government, between parliaments and the executive, between groups of countries, citizens, the media and interest groups – not least some of the most powerful drivers of policy in the modern world – corporations. As a result, some sub-national governments are seeking direct representation in international decision making fora. Furthermore, national governments will need ways to improve co-operation with other levels of government through better communication and consultation so as to reconcile national and sub-national governments in the global policy environment. This has enormous potential for both the culture and the practice of corporate governance:[33]

> As more decisions are taken at the international level, there are also likely to be demands for more transparency and greater accountability in national fora. Citizens at the local level will demand to know who is driving the debate at the international level, and under what authority. These demands apply to both governmental and non-governmental policy actors.
>
> Whatever the future institutional arrangements, democracy, transparency and openness will need to feature alongside effectiveness as important considerations in the development of the structures of global governance.[34]

Questions have been raised, within the OECD in particular, as to whether the current arrangements for consultation with business and labour should be

33 See, eg, OECD, 'Globalisation – what implications for democratic decision-making?', in PUMA, *Strategic Management and Policy-Making*, 1996, PUMA.

34 *Ibid*, p 3.

augmented by procedures to consult with other interests such as consumer and environmental groups. It is worth repeating that global governance is not only a public sector activity, given the impact of multinational companies. Indeed, there is a danger that public management is being constrained by the globalisation of the economy. In particular, it is forced to react quickly in a manner that tends to hamper traditional consent procedures.

While accepting that corporations must pursue sharply focused economic objectives, any substantive concept of democracy requires that the interests of other affected parties should not be left out of account. The question becomes more one of how they can be taken into account. It would be absurd to expect that private companies, any more than government, should wish to take decisions without identifying all relevant facts. To that extent, not listening to stakeholders would be foolish. Whether they will necessarily do so voluntarily is unclear, although experience within the EU suggests that some degree of regulation is necessary. Be that as it may, many companies believe that the social licence to operate mandates a commitment to the environment and to development, including a budget designed to support not-for-profit environmental activities.[35]

The challenge for global corporate governance in particular is the 'triple bottom line':

> Both the dynamism and the instability of the process of global economic integration are linked to the fact that it largely originates in the private sector. Future stability requires that a carefully crafted balance be struck, nationally and internationally, between the freedom of markets and the provision of public goods. The pace of globalization of financial and other markets is currently outstripping the capacity of governments to provide the necessary framework of rules and co-operative arrangements to ensure stability and prevent abuses of monopoly and other market failures. National solutions to such failures within a global economy are severely limited.[36]

It is not government's job to manage business; it must, nonetheless, ensure that it can help create the optimum structure for resolving tensions between differing claims. Every country wants the firms within its borders to flourish and grow in such a way as to provide employment, wealth and satisfaction, not only to improve standards of living materially, but also to advance social cohesion. At the international level, there is no single body with the legitimacy and authority to ensure that sustainable development (quite apart from social justice) happens around the world. The resistance of some national governments to develop more federal regional government structures, such as exists in the form of the EU, suggests that it will be some time before strong

35 See, eg, WBCSD, *Corporate Leadership and Governance: Securing the Social License to Operate (The Challenge Brief)*, 1987, WBCSD, Chapter 29, for examples of companies with progressive practices in this regard.

36 *Op cit*, Commission on Global Governance, fn 23, p 2.

international government systems can play their part in marrying the concerns of legitimate governance and legitimate corporate governance.

Until then, business must work with such partners as there are: the UN, OECD, WTO, the World Bank, etc, to ensure that appropriate systems, standards and controls are in place. At the national and local level (and in the case of the EU, regional levels too) there are growing demands for governance that provides some basic standards. There have been impassioned pleas at the international level, as witness, for example, the Brundtland Commission and the emergence of Agenda 21 as an important initiative emerging from the Rio Summit. Even so, it is clear that business holds the key to resolve not only economic issues, but social, ethical and indeed political issues – the so called 'triple bottom line'. Nonetheless, other global institutions need to be seen as global players too.

Historically, global governance has occurred without global institutions. A degree of governance through empires has been replaced with self-regulating, but unstable, markets, and unilateral action by powerful nations. This is no longer acceptable and the belief is emerging that rules and a sense of order are necessary for assuring the public goods which are not likely to emerge automatically from free market arrangements. This explains why corporate governance has been on board corporate agendas in recent years. The matter is taken up more fully in Chapter 10.

The UN has a long way to go, although it makes important contributions to, for example, water management and the general environmental programme. True, attempts are being made at the supranational level to address these problems, but because of the general absence of appropriate democratic institutions, some of these initiatives are under attack by representatives of those most at risk. This was seen in terms of the successful opposition to the OECD Multilateral Agreement on Investment (MAI), referred to elsewhere, and the failure of the WTO summit at Seattle in 1999. Nevertheless, the WTO, in particular, remains an organisation that is viewed with caution bordering on hostility by many NGOs in particular, and by much of the third world, who see it not so much in terms of liberalisation but as offering a *carte blanche* to Western multinational corporations.

Regional groupings, such as the EU, represent the beginnings of a way forward in bringing the contributions of multinationals into partnerships with public needs, even though, at present, the focus on production in the EU's Common Agricultural Policy (CAP) is a setback to sustainability. New 'set aside' laws and 'environmentally sensitive area' designations are clearly more appropriate. However, so far only the EU has created both a durable system of regional trade liberalisation and a strong commitment to political co-operation of the sort capable of having an influence on corporate governance.

Corporate governance reform requires a mix of voluntary action by the private sector, partnership agreements of various sorts, and regulation.

Regulation of whatever kind presumes a market economy, though the nature of the regulation has to be thought through. A uniform EU Company Statute still lies on the Commission's shelves awaiting Member State backing, while, as we have seen, the UK is engaged in a process of fundamental rethinking of company law. New, more systemic, forms of governance may emerge as a result of these initiatives and it is possible that they may be reflected or even mirrored in other supranational assemblies. More likely is that individual acts of regulation aimed at the triple bottom line will emerge without being of the detailed, control and command version now, quite rightly, out of fashion. Undoubtedly needed will be voluntary codes or 'contracts' agreed between governments, national and supranational, and companies or sectors.

A number of industry sectors have formulated voluntary codes of conduct. Among them are the chemical industry's Code of Ethics on the International Trade of Chemicals, and the banking industry's Statement by Banks on the Environment and Sustainable Development. On the other hand, there are a growing number of regulations, produced after extensive discussions with the industries concerned. They include CITES, the Montreal Protocol, the Basle Convention and the International Tropical Timber Agreement, while the WTO is now responsible for bringing some order into the relation between trade and the environment. Environmental groups are and will continue to be involved with the EU, NAFTA and WTO.[37] The Challenge Brief has charted the movement away from prescriptive legal controls on industry towards voluntary agreements; they include notably, in The Netherlands, 'covenants' in industry sectors to reduce emissions and control environmental performance, the EU's 'environmental agreements', not least through the Auto/Oil programme, and the EPA in the US with more than 50 voluntary partnership programmes with different industry sectors.

Negotiated agreements often appear to reach commonly stated goals more easily than regulations, mainly because they require an open dialogue about goals and priorities from the outset. Voluntary agreements take place between the regulatory authorities and industry sectors to achieve clearly stated goals within an agreed time frame, failing which traditional legislation may be substituted. There is flexibility in such arrangements, since the authorities set up the framework and targets jointly with the other stakeholders, who are then free to choose how to attain those targets.[38]

Another thing to be encouraged is transparency through social and environmental reporting, modelled very closely on annual financial reports

---

37 'Global trade', in *op cit*, *The Challenge Brief*, fn 35. For an interesting partnership, see the Keidanren Nature Conservation Fund in Japan, which has promoted social partnership and has helped build a network which includes NGOs, the World Bank and the World Conservation Union.

38 Partnership approaches were given a major impetus by Agenda 21, one of the key outputs of the 1992 Earth Summit.

and accounts. Various broad-based standards on the supranational level are emerging to make the data included more comparable across sectors. Companies will increasingly have to deal with a growing variety of stakeholders, which will require constructive relationships. Public reporting is a cornerstone for such trust and is becoming a necessary source of information both for customers and investors who seek to track the management of environmental risk. There have been a number of policy responses. The UN has taken early steps in its Initiative on External Environmental Reporting: the EU's Accounting Advisory Forum is preparing an opinion on how to improve reporting on the environment in annual reports and accounts, while a number of the Scandinavian countries have been working on green accounting. Individual companies have begun to respond and are at the cutting edge of environmental reporting.

The most recent development in the field has been the OECD Guidelines for Multinational Enterprises, adopted by the governments of the 29 member countries and of Argentina, Brazil, Chile and Slovakia at the OECD Ministerial Meeting on 27 June 2000. They are, of course, merely recommendations which provide voluntary principles and standards for responsible business conduct consistent with applicable laws. The Guidelines aim to ensure that the operations of these enterprises are in harmony with government policies, to strengthen the basis of mutual confidence between enterprises and the societies in which they operate, to help improve the foreign investment climate and to enhance the contribution to sustainable development made by multinational enterprises:

> Many enterprises have responded to these public concerns by developing internal programmes, guidance and management systems that underpin their commitment to good corporate citizenship, good practices and good business and employee conduct. Some of them have called upon consulting, auditing and certification services, contributing to the accumulation of expertise in these areas. These efforts have also promoted social dialogue on what constitutes good business conduct. The Guidelines clarify the shared expectations for business conduct of the governments adhering to them and provide a point of reference for enterprises. Thus, the Guidelines both complement and reinforce private efforts to define and implement responsible business conduct.

Before turning directly to the Guidelines, it should be observed that the OECD encourages the use of international dispute settlement mechanisms, including arbitration as a means of facilitating the resolution of legal problems arising between enterprises and host country governments. Arbitration, or the new *lex mercatoria*, as it has been recently dubbed,[39] will probably become increasingly important in the years to come and there is a real interest in injecting public values into the process. Bodies such as the OECD have the capacity to make important contributions to ensuring that arbitration

39 Twining, W, *Globalisation and Legal Theory*, 2000, Butterworths, eg, p 51.

decisions with global repercussions take place against a backcloth of principle and process that receives wide scale approbation.

The General Policies laid down by the OECD's Code on Multinationals includes contributing to sustainable development, respecting human rights, close co-operation with local communities, not seeking exemptions from the regulatory framework affecting health, safety, labour and taxation issues, protection for 'whistleblowers' and the encouragement of 'business partners' of various stripes to comply with the Guidelines.

Enterprises are urged to disclose material information on:

- the financial and operating results of the company;
- company objectives;
- major share ownership and voting rights;
- members of the board and key executives, and their remuneration;
- material foreseeable risk factors;
- material issues regarding employees and other stakeholders;
- governance structures and policies.

Enterprises are also 'encouraged to communicate additional information' of a more concrete and demanding kind. There are further references to trade union rights, non-discrimination of a comprehensive nature and the like, all, unsurprisingly, 'within the framework of laws, regulations, etc, in the countries in which they operate'. Yet, it is in the field of environmental protection that the guidelines are most detailed. These are greatly to be welcomed, but the limited nature of their overall authority remains a problem so that binding international conventions must be the preference over time.

For the sake of completeness, it should be added that the Guidelines include reference to consumer protection, including adequate complaints procedures and a list of necessary criteria for ensuring genuine competition, including the kinds of prohibitions found in the UK Competition Act referred to earlier.

The Whitehall Trade Minister has praised the new Code as being a significant move forward, which was achieved in spite of rigorous opposition to central features made by the Mexican delegation. NGOs were, however, disappointed that there were no sanctions and that the OECD had not adopted a tougher stance. In fact, it was never likely that a UK Government which appears set to reject stakeholder obligations in its domestic legislation would bring pressure to do more on the global level. On the positive side, there is the expectation that other non-OECD member countries will sign up to the Code of Conduct, thus offering the promise that these Guidelines will become an example of international best practice for responsible multinational enterprises operating around the world.

There are a number of other important initiatives occurring in this area. For example, in July 1999, the International Chamber of Commerce argued that the UN should play a bigger role in setting the rules of the global economy for the benefit of workers and the environment. Both the ICC and the UN adopted the position that the WTO should not tackle social and environmental standards. The US and the EU have been pressing the WTO to adopt minimum labour standards while the ICC has brought its influence to bear against that position, instead backing the developing countries by endorsing a greater role for the UN's social agency, the ILO. In the same year, the UN, under the guidance of its Secretary General, Kofi Annan, launched a Global Compact intended to give a human face to the global market. This is again, naturally, a voluntary agreement on good practice which the UN itself does not have the resources properly to monitor. However, its website exposes the specific pledges made by multinational corporations and encourages NGOs publicly to challenge companies which appear to be in breach.

One vital issue should be added. It was fleetingly referred to in the preface to the OECD's Code, viz, there is more to be concerned about than the power of TNCs. As they make clear, strategic alliances, and closer relations with suppliers and contractors, produces tendency to blur the boundaries of the enterprise. Business alliances are very much part of the future of the global landscape. Some label it 'the extended enterprise', which necessitates looking at a company and all its suppliers and associates as one unit. The resulting creature in the corporate zoo has sometimes been termed 'the trillion dollar enterprise'. These come about as customers, suppliers, unrelated companies and even competitors come together to accomplish big, risky and expensive jobs in, say, the oil industry, telecommunications and aerospace. Companies have been struggling to deal with a business world that was irreversibly globalising, just as nations are forming blocs and protecting their borders. The development of huge enterprises linking independent companies together is becoming the solution adopted by business to deal with these two seemingly incompatible developments:

> The potential power of a trillion dollar enterprise to sidestep laws, create cartels, dominate industries, and overrun sovereign nations is great. Its size and economic power could easily translate into political power, but could also spur massive economic development. The possibility of a new form of cultural imperialism is clear, as consumers across the world buy and adapt to products, media, and entertainment from these global giants.[40]

One thing this development threatens is traditional concepts of competition. Not only will competitors feel the need to come together to advance risky and expensive projects, but the larger alliance or network might well need to bring

40 Freidheim, C, *The Trillion Dollar Enterprise*, 1998, Perseus, p xiii. Much of the following analysis leans heavily on Freidheim.

on board civil society (consumers to some extent) in its endeavours. This is 'the ability to promote co-operation' and, whatever the role of governments, industry will frequently be the prime mover. Business will need to be not only multinational in the understood sense, but at home in many countries, an advantage where governments are protecting local industry and are tapped into local talent, resources and funding. One size fits all regulatory regimes (including competition regimes) will almost certainly be outflanked. On the other hand, these developments must not be seen as wholly inimical to the public interest. For example, it was only by co-funding and general co-operation that the major US motor manufacturers have been able to conduct research which is beneficial to an improved environment; the catalytic converter is merely the most obvious example.

It is necessary to embrace globalisation as a concept, but to go beyond it. It is arguable that the world has entered a new era; the era of collaboration. A relationship enterprise, it is argued, will actually operate more like a political federation than a business alliance. At this stage of development the pros and cons of such alliances make a cost-benefit tally difficult. It can be argued, of course, that they increase investment and opportunity in far-flung reaches of the world and even that the logic is to favour attractive living conditions in order to attract talented managers and employees (which necessitates support of cultural, civic and recreational institutions). On the other hand, they may represent a threat to a number of legal and regulatory frameworks and might use excess leverage to change laws in their favour. This is an oversimplification of a highly complex phenomenon, but some such as Freidheim pose polar opposite solutions; the creation of a global antitrust police-force on the one hand, or a *laissez-faire* approach on the other.

Let us first make the case for global alliances as forcefully as possible:

> Biotech will enable us to feed the additional 10 billion people and ensure a healthier and longer life. Electronics will enable us to educate, communicate, and advance the productivity of the masses. Other technologies will save our environment, extend our natural resources, provide our energy, and make life easier and more fun.[41]

But this scenario also invites the end of all politics. This cannot and must not be so. The search for a 'global constitution' of some sort is inevitable and urgent. At the present state of our knowledge we can do no more than warn and urge increasing vigilance. The public lawyer must go global and help to devise a form of governance that is both ethical and realistic.

41 *Op cit*, Freidheim, fn 40, p 235.

CONCLUSIONS

Governance is not just government. But, elected governments (at various levels from the local neighbourhood to the world community) must be the orchestrators of governance, albeit increasingly through striking partnerships and alliances, and by empowering groups to forge alliances and networks themselves in order to increase added value both in terms of economic and social capital. These issues run through all the arguments being made here. However, there are clear duties on government in the regulation of business in spite of the fact that corporations represent the only real opportunity to increase wealth and benefit the world's citizens.

Markets need to be regulated, citizens and consumers empowered, competition encouraged and adequate systems of corporate governance put in place. Public and administrative law have historically been attached to values of openness, consultation and accountability and, more recently, to assuring human rights. The focus has traditionally been on government properly so called, but as the world changes it is not just elected governments that need to conform to public values, but also to their partners, not least simply because they are their partners. They are sharing in the business of government.

It follows that much more attention than formerly must be paid to both the values and processes of commerce and industry. This is the entitlement and the duty of elected governments. The justification for markets is freedom and choice. They must, therefore, operate to enhance those values and they will not convince unless their processes are open, transparent and inclusive. The State – though increasingly a contested concept – is the necessary guarantee of both the market and civil society. As the world has changed, so the State changes with it; the need for constitutional and administrative law reform changes with it and the necessity for an intensive understanding of developing power structures becomes ever more obvious. The 'public law' relating to consumer protection and corporate governance is currently, for example, seriously underdeveloped.

Nowhere is this more clear than in the space where the need for governance and the fact of globalisation collide:

> At a global level, what model of decision making should an emerging system of modern governance adopt? It will have to draw on lessons from regional and national levels and from business organizations ... Multilayered decision-making systems are emerging that depend on consultation, consensus, and flexible 'rules of the game'. Inter-governmental organizations, however, still face basic questions as to who should set the rules and according to what principles.[42]

42 Commission on Global Governance, *Global Decision-Making*, 2000, UN.

One thing is clear: the role of law is necessarily circumscribed, though, flexibly applied, crucial. However, governments should build policies on properly designed market-based approaches, eliminate counterproductive subsidies and establish incentives for exploiting efficient technologies. As well as strengthening conventional regulation, government should create a regime where, for example, many environmental costs are internalised. Companies will need a mix of positive incentives and tough penalties to achieve the requisite goals.

None of this will be easy, but reform is necessary. The SEC in the US, for example, is making a greater demand for information disclosure from publicly listed companies, as is the Swedish Government. The EU is considering similar provisions. Each of these interventions needs to be agreed with stakeholders, including, of course, industry itself. Contracts and agreements between various levels of government and various levels of industry represent part of the future. All major companies should have the issue of corporate governance firmly underlined on their agendas. But, at the end of the day, there is no obvious objection to legislation to compel the issue of corporate governance to be brought on to board agendas, or to requiring companies to render accounts which take note of environmental and social impacts. This will increasingly need to be done at the supranational level, leaving national governments, in the interests of subsidiarity and flexibility, to operate to a large degree as monitoring authorities.

Finally, to avoid the ongoing proliferation of weak codes of conduct and certification and reporting systems, it is important that there be some degree of harmonisation and adherence to higher standards. This implies a greater role for international codes and frameworks, which use as benchmarks internationally agreed standards contained or implied in such documents as Agenda 21 and ILO and human rights conventions. There should also be a role for independent verification of codes of conduct, environmental management systems, and perhaps UN-business partnerships.

CODA

Given the economic reality of the times, it is absurd to believe that listed companies can, in any real sense, be regarded as private entities. Their historical inclinations have ineluctably been towards monopoly – hence, for example, the centrality of anti-trust legislation in the US, most recently exhibited in the litigation involving Microsoft. No State can turn a blind eye to monopoly or its potential for abuse, and competition law continues to be at the heart of the State's relations with commerce and industry. However, as we have seen, co-operation, partnerships and other alliances pose new dangers as well as holding out new promise. This, and other developments necessitate innovative relations between the public and private sector:

> Public legitimacy is a vital intangible asset. A successful company has to reproduce its licence to operate. The knowledge economy will deepen the interdependence between the public and private sectors, between consumers and producers. Companies will be less like neatly bounded organizations. They will depend more on knowledge assets which lie outside them, in universities, for example, or the ideas of their consumers. The ability of life-sciences companies to exploit their new ideas – for example, for genetically modified crops – will depend on securing public legitimacy for these new products. Companies that want to marshal publicly provided knowledge for commercial use will need to show that they can be trusted. Companies are increasingly dependent upon assets such as knowledge which they cannot themselves own.[43]

Indeed, it is possible that knowledge-intensive industries will require radical innovation in the way basic economic institutions are owned. It seems likely that when new company law is produced in the UK, it will already be out of date. The EU will probably be the forum where new institutional relations between politics and economics will be forged. The old constitutional certainties will need to be reworked to deal with the new and the constantly changing.

---

43 Leadbeater, C, *Living on Thin Air: The New Economy*, 1999, Viking, p 85.

REINVENTING PUBLIC LAW AND THE CONSTITUTION

INTRODUCTION

Governance absorbs New Public Management (NPM), it embraces the purchaser/provider split, it tends to favour deregulation, celebrates privatisation as a broad phenomenon and is increasingly identified with a search for effective partnerships. It reaffirms the value of civil society and is logically compelled towards subsidiarity. All these developments are identifiable in the UK, as elsewhere, although the mix of governance 'components' – defining features – is different from all of its contemporaries and allies. Above all this, however, towers the role of politics. This disaggregated system of steering and guiding nations and blocs does not, in any way, diminish the centrality of collective purposive action. Rather, it makes its reaffirmation more urgent. It certainly requires more imagination in the matter both of statesmanship and statecraft than the former ideal-typical model of government as a delineated set of grand institutions. This former model has been a fading, long-in-the-tooth, incubus which has obscured the real business of governing for many years, especially in the UK.[1] The governance revolution makes it both inevitable and desirable that legal, institutional and constitutional re-address moves rapidly up the national agenda:

> Governance relies on more than efficient and effective public management. It also relies on the ability of democratic institutions to function well in the modern environment of rapid economic change, global communications, and well developed interest groups. Finally it depends on the capacity of public administration to attract and retain first class talent. Despite the extensive efforts at reform discussed at the Symposium, the process clearly needs continued improvement.[2]

In the UK, aspects of governance have been developed over a period of 15 or so years; the Blair Government has added a smattering of constitutional reform while undertaking a significant change in the shape of local government and has pinned enormous faith onto its 'modernisation' programme. These are significant achievements which still suffer from the

1 A point which the author sought to make some years ago; see Harden, I and Lewis, ND, *The Noble Lie: The British Constitution and the Rule of Law*, 1986, Century Hutchinson.

2 OECD Symposium, Ministerial Symposium on the Future of Public Services, 1996, p 5.

English vice of responding to genuine constitutional need by administrative and managerial shifts rather than coherent constitutional revision.[3]

The *Modernising Government* White Paper marked a coherent and forward looking commitment to sound business principles, to respect for the market and also for consumers. The Government understood that, for the consumer to be king, the private sector needs effective, though streamlined, regulation and that where the public sector or its partners deliver services, then certain incidents of citizenship must be respected. This would constitute no mean achievement, and the next five years will be a testing time. What is still missing, however, is the larger constitutional view. It may be strange to argue that a reforming constitutional administration, such as the Blair Government could claim to be, should be challenged for not having a joined up attitude to constitutional theory. Yet, that appears to be the case. The modernisation project is in its early stages, but some signposts are missing.

Modernising Government in its various manifestations is a radical, holistic programme. The rhetoric is substantial and seeks to connect various strands of the Government's agenda:

> Modernisation is a hallmark of the Government. We are rebuilding the National Health Service. We are raising standards in education. We are modernising our constitution and local government.[4]

The claims are exceedingly strong – relating, as they do, not only to managerial improvement but to citizen emancipation through responsive public services and longer term policies in the public interest. The Government is encouraging citizen participation in the development of policy and service objectives and the establishment of partnership with community groups and the voluntary and private sectors to find strategic answers to important social problems and to sustainable development. However, not all the Government's actions match the claims.

There is a huge gap between what is claimed and the contents of the Freedom of Information (FOI) Act 2000. How do central and local government work in partnership when much of the information which the partners need is being withheld? The Prime Minister speaks consistently of the twin aims of constitutional reform and the modernisation of the effectiveness of government as if they were separate items. They are, in fact, inextricably linked and depend on an overarching commitment to openness and inclusiveness. This requires both constitutional and administrative law reform. The sinews of the modernisation project need stiffening by entrenching the essential principles of democracy through a reconsidered examination of the relationship between public power and public law.

3 See Lewis, ND, 'Modernizing government: management theory or constitutional theory?' (1996) 6 EPL 201, pp 201–16.

4 Cabinet Office, *Modernising Government*, Cm 4310, 1999, HMSO, para 3.

Improving service delivery is core to NPM and the governance agenda, and in recent years this has been achieved, to a considerable extent, through 'alternative' solutions; that is, alternative to traditional public sector mechanisms. However, whatever the management solution chosen, one of the crucial challenges is to identify and respond clearly to citizens' needs. In many countries, as will be seen, this prompted a strong decentralisation and devolution movement which empowers public managers at the local level, where the government is closer to citizens. In the UK, only partial progress has been made in this respect, through devolution to the Scottish Parliament, the Welsh Assembly and the Greater London Authority, Mayor and London Assembly. Regionalisation and local government reform will be revisited shortly, but one thing is clear. There is no coherent movement towards genuine subsidiarity within the UK. At the moment when the Blair Government is pressing for just such a solution within the European Union, there is intellectual chaos at best on these matters within the Kingdom. Granted, there is no real popular mandate in this area – merely undirected rumblings and expressions of discontent – there is also a marked absence of intellectual political leadership. The essence of subsidiarity – that decisions should be taken at the point where most effective action can be expected – is intellectually unassailable. It is also logically implicit in the pragmatic groping for effective partnerships. Yet, it currently has no real resonance in UK political leadership.

This is all really part of a parcel which comprises genuine accountability by government to its citizens. It is no exaggeration to say that the management reforms of recent years (which have often considerably improved the sharpness of public management as well as the delivery of services) have so obsessed the reformers that they have spent too little attention on reforming constitutional delivery mechanisms. The insistence that an unreformed Parliament with tag-on extras is a satisfactory concomitant to a genuinely revolutionary managerial and delivery regime is as absurd as it is unsatisfactory. This manifests itself in a number of ways.

Although considerable advance has been made in seeking consumer satisfaction with public services, there is no doubt that the policy process in the UK remains unsatisfactory and, while this is the case, there will be a large hole at the heart of governance:

> What is fairly clear is that it is very difficult to achieve reductions in government programmes or regulations without good policy analysis and evaluation which demonstrates that the government's intervention is not having its intended effects or is not achieving them effectively or efficiently. In effect, experience suggests that expenditure and regulatory reduction must be shown to reflect 'good policy' at the micro-level as well as in terms of macro-economic impact if it is to be sustainable.[5]

5 Keating, M, *Public Management Reform and Economic and Social Development*, 1997, OECD, p 2.

This is as true in one policy area as another. The riddle of the democratic constitution is accountability, and revised forms of accountability lie at the heart of reconciling governance with the spirit of democracy. Although recent years have witnessed considerable ingenuity in devising new forms of internal or managerial accountability, the other side of the coin has tended to lie face down.

The traditional emphasis was on hierarchical accountability structures capped by the minister's political obligations to the legislature. To these have been added the demands for external accountability to customers (or consumers or clients). And in the past decade or so increased resort to the market to improve performance in delivering publicly funded goods and services has highlighted another dimension:

> At the centre of any system of public accountability is the amount and quality of information available to citizens or their agents. Information that provides the true costs of publicly produced goods and services is essential if optimal allocation of resources is to be achieved and if organisations are to be managed efficiently and effectively. If this information is publicly available citizens are able to participate more effectively in the decision making process and to monitor the performance of agencies. Such transparency also assists in locating responsibility when things go wrong. But, of itself, good information will not automatically assign responsibility. That will depend on the law and conventions operating in particular jurisdictions.[6]

Many of the improvements in managerial accountability in the UK and elsewhere have already been noted. Martin, however, underlines the need to rethink 'normative' accountability and it is in this respect that overall performance of the UK in its attitude to governance must be judged. It has already been observed that there is a lack of willingness to embody accountability notions in legislation and where the need for legislation is conceded, its content has not always been congruent with citizen expectations. This is the charge levelled at the FOI Act 2000 in the UK.

PROGRESS AND DISAPPOINTMENT

It has been observed on more than one occasion about the UK that secrecy is the cement of the constitution. As long as this state of affairs remains, it is difficult to see how British governments can expect the new ways of governing to be either policy effective or normatively acceptable to its citizens. Unfortunately, old habits seem to be an unconscionable time a-dying. This is particularly true in relation to governments' relations with business and their

6 Martin, J, *Changing Accountability Relations: Politics, Consumers and the Market*, 1997, Public Management Service, OECD, pp 1, 3.

willingness to accede too readily to pleas for confidentiality. Furthermore, this is not simply an issue of citizens being able to seek and secure documentation, but probably more importantly being about government's willingness to disclose information about its conduct and relationships *as a matter of course.* The FOI Act does empower the Information Commissioner to approve schemes for the publication of information by public authorities and may indeed approve, in appropriate cases, model schemes. Even here, the legislation is peppered with exemptions and discretion and it remains to be seen how far the Commissioner will be able to use her undoubted clout to produce a change in the culture of openness within Whitehall.[7]

Shortly before the time of writing, yet another deeply worrying incident in the saga of secrecy was revealed by diligent investigative journalism. It concerned British Nuclear Fuels which was alleged, *inter alia,* to have buried important safety information – with the knowledge of the DTI – on the running of nuclear waste trains. MPs in both Ireland and the UK were the objects of what appears as a conspiracy against the public's right to know.

An Irish MP had written to the Prime Minister expressing her concerns about BNFL, only to be sent a response from a junior minister telling her that her fears were unfounded by copying a paragraph from BNFL's own publicity presentation. More disturbingly, BNFL staff had 'buried' vital information about the dangers of trains which carry highly radioactive waste hundreds of miles across Britain, a matter apparently conveyed to officials at the DTI. Another secret memorandum indicated that the DTI encouraged BNFL to keep quiet about its failure to comply with reporting requirements on accidents and other hazardous incidents.[8]

It is possible that such conspiratorial secrecy is rare, but there is no way of knowing. The enormous secrecy described in Sir Richard Scott's Report on *Arms to Iraq*[9] does not bode well. In a comprehensive report which makes uneasy reading, one remark made by a senior official seemed to summarise everything that is wrong with the secret world of government. Having been found to have given unfounded information, he famously replied: 'I simply misled myself.' This cavalier attitude seems to have carried over into Westminster's first FOI Act. It is not just 'commercial in confidence' issues which undermine a genuine regime of frankness, as can be seen by the remarks of the Chairman of the Committee on Standards in Public Life.

In June 2000, Lord Neill, in evidence to the Commons Select Committee on Public Administration, attacked the Bill upon which the Act is based as setting up 'formidable obstacles' to prevent disclosure of secret meetings between government ministers, civil servants and lobbying companies. Lord Neill's

7 FOI Act, ss 19, 20.

8 (2000) *The Guardian,* 13 April.

9 See, eg, Lewis, ND and Longley, D, 'Ministerial responsibility: the Next Steps' [1996] PL 490, pp 490–507.

Committee had called for Britain to follow the US and Canada in keeping public registers of meetings with lobbyists and for the discussions to be fully minuted. The Chairman of the Public Administration Committee, Dr Tony Wright, pointed out that such procedures would be thwarted by at least five exemptions in the Act. These include prevention of disclosure of any procedures in ministerial offices, discussions of public policy and confidential communications between outside individuals and government. Lord Neill said that just two of these restrictions – the supply of information in confidence and discussions about public policy – created 'formidable obstacles' to the introduction of his reforms.[10]

One of the leading scholars researching 'joined-up' government has stated clearly that 'holistic working will erode secrets and remove information barriers between central and local systems'.[11] Others working in the field have expressed the belief that integrated knowledge is ultimately more important than integrated budgets. At the time of writing, it seems totally uncertain as to how far holistic government will be undermined or unravelled by the tightly drawn provisions of the FOI Act. Its letter, if not its spirit, will have to be broken if partnerships are to be genuinely interdependent and open. For that to happen, the traditional ways of Whitehall will have to be broken open and genuine political partnerships between citizens and their representatives introduced. This is an enormous challenge, which future British governments will have to confront. This is the logic of the world we now inhabit:

> All organizations should be willing to commit themselves to be judged on open information about their performance and impact on society. That commitment should be a measure of whether they are genuinely part of a democratic, open society. Consumers of NHS hospitals, for example, should have far more information about the comparative costs and performance of different doctors and operating theatres, to know which are underperforming. Companies should be under an obligation to provide far more information on the impact of their activities on the environment, both social and environmental. As far as banks are concerned, for example, this should include information on their lending policies and performance in poorer areas of our cities and to ethnic minorities. A willingness to be open with information in an era when there are few technological constraints on acquiring and distributing information should be the first and most fundamental mark of a trustworthy organization. Companies are closed, secretive organizations in a democratic era awash with information. If they are to inspire our trust in future, as they acquire even more power, they have to be more open with information we can use to hold them to account.[12]

10 See (2000) *The Guardian*, 8 June.

11 Perri 6 *et al*, *Governing in the Round: Strategies for Holistic Government*, 1999, Demos, p 40.

12 Leadbeater, C, *Living on Thin Air: The New Economy*, 1999, Viking, p 164.

In recent times, governments have provided more and more information and yet, it is still far too selective. They have also been far too willing to concede claims of confidentiality to private organisations. Until this culture is reformed, many of the advances in service delivery will remain tarnished.

However, advances for consumers/citizens are generally proclaimed and periodically delivered on. One of the most promising has been announced for the NHS. It involves giving patients' representatives a central role in a Modernisation Board to oversee radical reform in the service. They are to be given one-third of the seats on the Board to be known as the National Council for the NHS. It will monitor implementation of the National Plan and help shape the way care is delivered and ensure the standards patients can expect. The Board will be linked to task forces overseeing priority programmes of reform, such as cancer services. It has been claimed that key decisions about hospital mergers and bed places will in future be taken by an independent panel of doctors, nurses, managers and patient representatives. The proposal was announced as an example of decentralisation of decision making.[13] The rhetoric is impressive, but it remains to be seen how such a radical promise can be delivered inside the insider Whitehall culture and whether it is a genuine attempt to push decision making, or at least influence, further down the policy chain. If so, it is what needs to happen if governance is going to be effective, or indeed possible.

Such initiatives, on the other hand, are not uncommon elsewhere. Yet, crucially, such countries traditionally operate in a significantly more open fashion. The OECD again describes developments:

> The clients of programmes and services, if they are given a sufficient voice in the process, can provide feedback, and apply measures to encourage more coherent approaches. By engaging outside actors in the process, the government sends out the signal that they are no longer simply clients or constituents, but increasingly indispensable partners in the governance process. This approach is applied in the Scandinavian countries, particularly in Norway, where ministries have advisory committees, composed of representatives of other ministries and outside groups, to which significant policy initiatives are referred for review.[14]

There is a constant stream of political journalism which speaks about the disaffection with politics expressed by citizens at large. This is not the first time it has been observed, and it would be a mistake to believe the old political order was thereby under threat. However, there is a considerable body of evidence to indicate that placing too great a distance between political authority and the governed can lead not only to disaffection but something more destabilising. This can be detected over voter attitudes towards the EU,

13 (2000) *The Guardian*, 4 September.

14 OECD, 'Strategic management and policy-making, in *Building Policy Coherence*, 1997, OECD, p 3.

the rise of NGOs in relation to global issues, consumer resistance to genetically modified food, in the UK Countryside Alliance, the protests over fuel prices in the autumn of 2000, and the like. Taken together, this suggests that it is not enough to concentrate on market-style mechanisms to re-enfranchise the citizen as consumer, crucial though that might well be. More active styles of participation – either directly, or probably through their representatives – is almost certainly needed to reassert a sense of civic identify in the face of both dissipated governance (often seen as networks of the elite) and the disproportionate influence of industrialists and bureaucrats.

The successes should not be understated. Successive governments' concerns with targets, performance indicators and comparators can lead not only to improved efficiency, but more effective delivery of public services carried on the back of such indicators can be, and have been, genuinely beneficial for consumers of public services. Government literature in the UK is replete with instances of targets satisfied and performance improved, whatever may be the public perception. The change in management culture is that the search for continued improvement is almost certain to continue. One small example. The Strategic Rail Authority is in the process of telling the 25 railway companies that they will not be offered extensions to their franchises unless they get rid of overcrowding and improve punctuality and performance. This should, for example, guarantee commuters with a daily journey time of more than 20 minutes a seat to work.[15] The fact of the climate and rail crises of late 2000 should not obscure the importance of strategic oversight of major services, or the value of tightly set, though realistic, standards.

The most striking institutional development in this area in recent times has to be the Public Service Agreements (PSAs) attached to the Comprehensive Spending Review for 1999–2002.[16] The PSA aim to set demanding, but realistic targets for improvement in a range of key services to update the interim targets previously announced. The focus is on outcomes rather than inputs. It is money for modernisation with funding tied to results. The PSAs set clear targets which public services will deliver in exchange for the extra investment they are receiving. They are expressed to be 'a contract with the people'. At the outset, the Government published in the form of Output and Performance Analyses the indicators to be used for monitoring and measuring progress against the targets. An example should help to explain the Government's philosophy towards service delivery and accountability mechanisms.

Sure Start will serve to illustrate. It is a programme about working with families with very young children to help them thrive when they get to

15 See (1999) *The Guardian*, 28 December.

16 See HM Treasury, *Public Services for the Future: Modernisation, Reform and Accountability*, Cm 4315, 1999, HMSO.

school. The Government's plans involve a mix of outputs and outcomes, but it needs to be stressed that the longer term effects of children being ready to thrive will show in a number of outcomes, including better behaviour and performance at school, a reduction in criminal behaviour, a reduction in teenage parenthood, etc. Such outcomes will only be measurable over many years. A major evaluation programme is being planned to assess the effects of *Sure Start* on families and their children in the medium and longer term.

The Government can only be congratulated on taking such a long term view of empowering its citizens through a mix of improved managerial systems and the direct involvement of those immediately affected. In the first year or so, however, there has been criticism that the Government has been chasing too many targets when a smaller, more achievable and easier-to-evaluate set would be preferable (as has been the New Zealand practice in recent years). There is a larger problem with PSAs too. It relates to who can be blamed when things go wrong, not least since the Government is moving in a holistic, joined up, cross-departmental fashion. *Sure Start*, again, serves the illustration well. The economic environment in which children from poor families are forced to operate is, to a large extent, the product of the very same Treasury which is a party to the PSAs and is the ultimate judge of whether the moneys have been well spent or whether they should be withdrawn. Who is best placed to make the judgment? No immediate answer is yet in sight.

There has clearly been a greater attempt in recent years to assess the public's satisfaction with the state of public services. Although the institutional response is by no means as strong as it should be (relying, yet again, on administrative fiat rather than legal obligation), the Cabinet Office has sought to co-ordinate the customer/consumer voice over a range of initiatives. The People's Panel is one such innovation introduced by the Blair Government, as is the establishment of a 'consumer champion' within all central departments and agencies, whose responsibility is to ensure improved services to reflect consumers' needs.[17] The responsibilities for local government are even higher and under the *Best Value* regime, all local authorities will collect and publish performance information allowing people to see how their council is doing compared with others.

It should be added in the interests of completeness that the Citizen's Charter was upgraded in 1998 as *Service First*.[18] The upgrade includes a commitment to greater consultation with users of services, more independent review within complaints procedures, greater choice of provider of services and greater influence to the People's Panel itself, which operates through novel consultation techniques including surveys, workshops and citizens' juries.

17 See Cabinet Office, *What We Want from our Public Services*, CAB 326/00.

18 Cabinet Office, *Involving Users: Improving the Delivery of Local Public Services, Service First*, June 1998, Consumer Congress and National Consumer Council.

However, at the end of the day, it is by no means clear how successive governments have judged or balanced the relationship between citizens and consumers. Bringing the delivery and management of public services up to the best standards in the private sector has been long overdue and, in so far as the gap between them has been closed, NPM and the governance bandwagon have rolled in the right direction. However, at certain nodal points, the incidents of public and private services diverge and the rights of citizens trump those of raw consumerism. To that end, the revolution in privatised government – the 'private world of government' – should have been accompanied by at least a screw's turn of administrative law reform. It was inevitable that hiccups, at the very least, would occur when the traditions of public service delivery were turned upside down, and hiccups there have been. The issue was addressed directly in Chapter 6, but its importance needs to be restated. Two, quite disparate, criticisms point up the issue. First, the Public Accounts Committee has recently condemned, in the rawest terms, governments' purchasing policies for IT systems. It described 'a decade of blunders' during which basic errors were repeated time and time again. The report highlighted 25 projects which failed to deliver promised improvements to the public, most critically perhaps in the NHS, with inevitable repercussions for patients.[19] Even more significantly, the Treasury Select Committee has recently raised serious doubts as to whether the PFI/PPP initiative is delivering the benefits claimed by its adherents. It went so far as to suggest that it was an idea whose time was past, especially under the new financial framework announced by the Chancellor of the Exchequer, which makes it easier to provide publicly funded investment.[20] Whatever the judgment which should ultimately be made, there is no effective institutional arrangement for making it. There is no Contracts Commissioner or Ombudsman and no Standing Administrative Conference to conduct systemic investigations.

All of this must be seen against the more measured backdrop of the *Modernising Government* White Paper, which is very centrally concerned with holistic policy making and service delivery. In particular, integrated service teams, national citizen-focused programmes, group-focused programmes and area-based programmes have all been introduced. With an extensive programme of future action announced at the time, it is clear both that the Government is attempting a new, more comprehensive approach to building public services and that it is too early, yet, to gauge how successful it has been. Nonetheless, as must continually be expressed, they have too often denied themselves the means to bring new concepts of governance and new machinery of government into kilter. Perhaps a blueprint for a proper

19 Political Action Committee, *Improving the Delivery of Government IT Projects*, 1st Report, HC 65, Session 1999–2000.

20 Treasury Select Committee, *The Private Finance Initiative*, 4th Report, HC 147, Session 1999–2000.

constitutional response to the challenge of governance could not be provided at this time. What is clear, however, is that the necessary thinking from first principles is not taking place. Yet again, when faced with change, the British response is pragmatic rather than principled.

One way in which this is exhibited has been the perhaps excessive concentration in recent years on the citizen as consumer. The role of civil society, in particular, in the UK has been consistently underplayed. In many ways, the UK was the classic home of civil society – certainly from the 18th century to the early 20th century.[21] It is, of course, a realm of existence which is private, but grounded in notions of equality before the law and the right of free association and, as such, the contribution of various groups and associations over the years has been immense. The 1980s and 1990s, in particular, saw an excessive concentration on atomistic individualism as the market was rediscovered and people struggled to find its optimum contribution to the commonweal. During that period, especially in the UK, the trades unions, the most visible and powerful manifestation of the phenomenon, were marginalised while attempts were made to forge an ideology from the centre which sought to undermine sites of opposition; or, in other words, pluralism.

The past decade has seen a huge impact made by NGOs, both of the grass-roots variety and those with an international presence. In very recent times, they have been most prominent in relation to their responses to the forces of globalisation, a crucible in which the nature of their legitimacy has been seriously contested. However, it is fair to say that there has been no serious attempt in the UK in the intervening years to promote the role of civil society in the space between the individual and representative government. Individual groups, some powerful, some disruptive, have emerged, prospered and sometimes disappeared again, but there has been no real attempt to promote tenant and credit unions, for example, let alone to find an institutional role for other representative groups. There is a real need to facilitate the emergence of community groups for the resolution of local problems, as well as to inform the business of policy making.

Added to this, were consultative processes to be given the kind of administrative law backing which exists in the US and which is beginning to appear all over Europe, community and voluntary groups would find an institutional niche in which to inform the policy and decision making process. To some extent, one can expect a lack of institutional opportunity to inhibit the emergence of groups with genuinely important points of view to bring to the decision making table.

One interesting contribution to this debate has recently been made outside the UK: improbably, perhaps, in East Africa. In Arusha, on 30 November 1999,

21 See, eg, Green, DG, *Reinventing Civil Society*, 1993, Institute of Economic Affairs.

the Treaty for the Establishment of the East African Community was ratified by the respective partners, Tanzania, Kenya and Uganda. To some extent, it is modelled on the European Union Treaties, but there are some important differences. For present purposes, what is of interest is Chapter 25, which specifically refers to the role of the 'private sector and civil society'. Although it is clear that the private sector is seen as the primary partner, civil society has not been left out of the picture. The relevant passages are as follows:

> The Partner States agree to promote [an] enabling environment for the participation of civil society in the development activities within the Community...
>
> [and]
>
> The Secretary General shall provide the forum for consultations between the private sector, civil society organisations, other interest groups and appropriate institutions of the Community.[22]

These are, of course, early days, but the fact of legislating for the interests of civil society and providing a legislatively authorised forum ought not to be lost on the UK and its own partners.

Administrative and constitutional architecture has few adherents within the British establishment. The ombudsman is a good example. In fact, its very historical emergence was the result of a fudge by the Wilson Government of the mid-1960s which missed the opportunity to establish a royal commission on administrative law. In spite of the success of the phenomenon on British soil, the ombudsman has never been placed in a rounded context of administrative justice as happened, for example, in Australia in the mid-1970s. Interestingly, one of the few solid institutional accountability mechanisms referred to in the *Modernisation* White Paper is that same ombudsman system. In a substantially unfounded claim that the Blair modernisation process was committed to ensuring that all public bodies are properly and fully accountable to the public, it announced a review of the organisation of the public sector ombudsmen in England (*sic*). The review was an internal Civil Service exercise which, although widely advertised, was less than transparent by the standards of modern administrative law. More significantly it was, in reality, a response to largely managerial concerns expressed by the ombudsmen themselves. Although it will hopefully result in more radical change than the Government could have anticipated, it is extraordinary that it occurred in such a blind fashion. Almost contemporaneously, parallel, though largely unconnected, reviews were announced of both the system of administrative tribunals and the procedural aspects of judicial review.[23] Joined up government, it appears, does not embrace joined-up justice.

---

22 Treaty for the Establishment of the East African Community, Art 128, paras 3 and 4.

23 See, eg, James, R and Lewis, ND, 'Joined-up justice: the reform of the UK Ombudsman system', in *International Ombudsman Yearbook 2000*, 2001, Kluwer.

This latter concept ought to be a natural concomitant of holistic government. The present administration is undoubtedly doing more than its predecessors to ensure effective co-ordination of policies and services. Its achievements have been recently charted.[24] From an institutional point of view, one of the most important developments has been the emergence of holistic auditing. The four national audit agencies, the NAO, the NI Audit Office, the Audit Commission and the Accounts Commission for Scotland have established the Public Audit Forum to provide a focus for development thinking in relation to public audit. The main role of the Forum is consultative and advisory. It is not able to direct the national audit agencies and other bodies involved in public audit. As well as building on the existing co-operation between the national agencies, it provides a strategic focus on issues cutting across the work of the national audit agencies. Early in its existence, the Forum identified a number of major implications of 'joined up' government, including the need for new forms of accountability, the challenge of assessing value for money where more than one body is involved, and the importance of co-operation between auditors.

Accountability is the issue which will be taken up here. Partnership government involves more services being delivered by a wider coalition of bodies – in the public, charitable, voluntary and private sectors, and both centrally and locally. This may:

> ... blur the accountability to Parliament and other elected representatives of the bodies delivering joined up services ... Public sector management needs to ensure that a clear governance framework, and accountability and reporting arrangements, are established at the outset of Modernising Government initiatives setting out who is accountable to whom and for what. Audit is an essential part of the corporate governance arrangements, *which include the constitutional and legal framework* ... (Emphasis added.)

At the very least, the sharing of responsibilities needs to be agreed and set down. There is equally a need to obtain sufficient evidence about the way bodies are delivering services to enable them to assess whether the funding bodies have established a framework for control and performance and whether this has been effective. The Forum was also at pains to stress that auditors will sometimes need to form a view on whether the outcomes used to justify a new regime can be adequately measured. This would be made easier if the outputs and outcomes expected from the programme were clearly defined and that arrangements were in place at the start of initiatives to measure achievement. Public sector management should also establish performance measures which give some indication of progress against the ultimate intended outcomes.[25] The dilemma has been more broadly stated:

24 *Op cit*, Perri 6 *et al*, fn 11, esp p 17.

25 Public Audit Forum, *Implications for Audit of the Modernising Government Agenda*, 22 April 1999.

> Central government will have to construct a framework for the monitoring, audit and accountability of holistic governance. It will need to introduce reforms at many levels; how the House of Commons holds the executive to account; how ombudspeople and systems of audit work; how accountability within the executive works, for example in the design of cabinet committees, and the roles of senior civil service accounting officers; and most difficult of all, how central government holds local government to account.[26]

In 1998, the OECD was able to say that, although many public/private partnerships have been criticised for lacking democratic legitimacy or not being subject to effective monitoring of performance, there is no systematic research on the accountability management of public service partnerships.[27] As has been noted, the *Modernising Government* White Paper largely identified accountability issues with reform of the Ombudsman system. It is not enough.

THE OLD IN SEARCH OF THE NEW

Governance has happened and government is chasing events. The nature of politics – short-term and opportunistic – is such that Periclean thinking about the nature of the polity is lamentably absent in Whitehall and Guildhall. *Modernising Government* may be the nearest thing to a big picture painted by recent British governments, but it is still a case of trying to catch a tiger by the tail. What is lacking is a testament of belief about the nation's purposes to which instrumentalities should bend. The world has a habit of running ahead of our predictions and to that extent politicians can be expected to play catch-up. But they ought to bring an informing spirit into play which demands of a changing world that it owes obligations to primary purposes. It is no longer fashionable to talk about politics in a constitutional setting; no longer fashionable to reason that public life exists to liberate the spirit of countless individual lives. In the UK, even more than elsewhere, first principles are not the currency of the politician's trade. Even when the Human Rights Act 1998 was introduced, it was explained in relatively technical terms; never in the ringing tones of human expression. It should, therefore, not be surprising that modernisation, partnership and governance should all be embraced without passion. There is not even a live debate about the need for an Administrative Procedure Act to infuse the business of governing with the elementary principles of fairness that the developed world insists should inform the basic texts of new Council of Europe members. While it is true that the political culture and history of the UK has grown in the soil of tolerance and fairness, the solid constitutional achievements have almost always been a response to

26 *Op cit*, Perri 6 *et al*, fn 11, p 42.

27 PUMA, *Accountability Management of Public-Private Partnerships*, 1998, PUMA.

failure, actual or imminent. Big picture statements about the worth of the individual have been largely absent. Were it to have been otherwise, the Pilgrim Fathers would never have left these shores.

This is not to say that achievements have been minimal. The rule of law, for all its ambiguity, embodies real virtues. Disinterestedness, rational discourse and equality can never be regarded as devalued coinage. But, the nation has to be painted into a corner before these virtues are asserted. Governance is a serious challenge to democratic values and they are nowhere being systemically addressed. A few years ago quangos were under siege for being institutionally unaccountable – as if the rest of public life were. However, the public mood demanded alteration and, to an extent, it has occurred.[28] Nevertheless, the opportunity was lost to express faith in the traditional values of fairness and accountability in a generic fashion. Quangos were reformed, but precious little else was affected. An Administrative Procedure Act asserting basic principles for the whole of the governmental machine never entered the collective head. And now that government is joining up with industry and commerce in a previously unanticipated fashion, pragmatism still informs whatever responses to the changing times emerge.

The idea that large industrial configurations were merely an instantiation of individual freedom, and that the market was simply an aggregation of free-choosing citizens' need, never stood up to close scrutiny. However, when industry becomes an active agent of government, and when transnational corporations have the global clout to affect the destiny of nations, it is extraordinary that governments, not least that of the UK, does not express a philosophical position on corporate governance. As we have seen, the review of company law is exceedingly unlikely to rise to the challenge. As for partnership within industry, the UK has always limped along behind the European Union. Constitutional architecture is as lacking here as in the rest of the polity.

However, it is subsidiarity which represents the biggest challenge, and where most of the work is to be done. The UK is a highly centralised State and power needs urgently to be devolved. It is often said that Westminster is too big to be effective at the local level and too small to be effective at the international level. Hence the support for an enlarged European Union of the regions. Starting from basics, it should be emphasised that representative politics is normally second best. An inevitability in a complex world, but still a substitute for choosing exercises made by individuals or groups on their own behalf. Once that case is ceded, the core of a central State should be a shrunken thing. In the UK, it is not, and the disparities between the regions are overblown and untenable. The basic building block should be the local community with larger political arrangements justifiable on a rational basis.

28 See, eg, Cabinet Office, *Quangos: Opening Up Public Appointments*, 1998, HMSO.

Whitehall has historically displayed a superiority complex when it comes to lower levels of government, so much so that it can be authoritatively rebuked for not putting enough effort into adopting lessons learned from the most innovative local initiatives and applying them to the great departments of State.[29] However, the Blair Government has undoubtedly been innovative in this area, not only in relation to the widely hailed devolutions, but also in its reforms of local government. At the time of writing, the Local Government Act 2000 had just received the royal assent and it is clearly too early to make any mature judgment on its likely effects. However, it introduces new political structures, encourages bringing decision taking closer to local communities, significantly enhances duties to consult, especially through community plans and achieving best value through performance review and the development of local performance plans, and introducing a new ethical framework. Promoting the well being of local communities and provisions for consultation are potentially the most far reaching of the changes.

The Act includes a duty placed on local authorities to promote the economic, social and environmental well being of their areas and to strengthen their powers to enter into partnerships. This includes a requirement to secure the development of a comprehensive strategy for promoting the well being of their areas with local people, businesses, voluntary organisations and so on. It will also be expected to graft on to the economic strategy for the region prepared by the new Regional Development Agencies. All this must be set against the Guide to Consultation at the local level issued by the Cabinet Office.[30] A number of local authorities already possess highly effective consultation practices and it remains to be seen how far best practice will become common. The nascent regional development movement, however, is the concept to watch over the years to come.

Right across Europe, inter-governmental structural changes have primarily taken the form of creating new intermediary levels and of local rationalisation. Few countries have eliminated a level of sub-national government. Local level rationalisation has taken place in many countries, usually in the form of aggregation aimed at creating larger units capable of providing a wider range of local services more efficiently. These changes have usually resulted in a more decentralised hierarchical structure for making and implementing decisions. 'These changes have modified roles and the relations between central and sub-national governments, as well as blurring lines of accountability.'[31]

29 *Op cit*, Perri 6 *et al*, fn 11, p 27.

30 *Op cit*, Cabinet Office, fn 18.

31 OECD, *Managing Across Levels of Government*, PUMA on Multi-level Governance, 1998, OECD, p 2.

Numerous redistributions of responsibility have been made – some big and some small – and usually downwards to sub-national government. Change has often taken the form of greater sharing of tasks and a greater mix of financing and implementing responsibilities, leading to more interdependence. There has also been a growing interest in result-oriented management and inter-governmental partnerships encouraging more consultation to agree on objectives, standards and cost-sharing arrangements. In those countries with long traditions of local self-government, there tends to be more diversity in the methods of control used, with *ex post* review and the role of courts becoming more important. At the same time, countries with a tradition of detailed controls over sub-national governments are becoming less interventionist due to the increasing complexity of the tasks undertaken. Finally, the move towards performance management based on targets and results, and away from detailed regulation and control of inputs, is encouraging the shift from specific grants in favour of general grants.

Accountability mechanisms have inevitably been affected. For instance, fiscal arrangements involving the use of shared taxes, joint financing of projects and equalisation formulae to distribute funds among sub-national units of government all oblige different levels to consult and negotiate. There is some evidence of this occurring within the UK although, as might be expected, it is not quite as patterned as elsewhere. Furthermore new results-based managerial styles tend to the bottom-up rather than top-down approach to service delivery. Top-down management assumes that the top has enough information to produce policies that are mutually consistent at the delivery level. The bottom-up approach corresponds to the 'empowerment' ideologies now being implemented by many governments and implies a higher degree of managerial autonomy to interact with client constituencies.

There is no doubt that recent years have seen a substantial devolution of power to lower levels of government, particularly affecting the education, health and welfare sectors in countries as diverse as Canada, Denmark, Finland, France, Sweden and the US.[32] The intellectual case has also increasingly been made out in the UK in recent years, although progress has been somewhat slower than elsewhere for a number of reasons. The commitment to Scottish and Welsh devolution is long standing and, to a considerable extent, free standing, with no necessary commitment to an England of the regions. However, leaving London to one side, some progress has been made.

Only recently, a poll indicated that those in favour of an elected assembly in their own region outnumber those who oppose the idea in six out of nine English regions. However, substantial majorities backed the idea only in London, which of course voted in favour of an assembly in a referendum in

32 See *op cit*, Keating, fn 5, p 58.

1998, and the North East, where a Scottish-style constitutional convention was established to press for devolution. The poll indicated that there was no majority in favour of an assembly in Yorkshire and Humberside.[33] It is widely believed that the Deputy Prime Minister was actively supportive of creating powerful regional assemblies to match those of Scotland and Wales, but that he lost the battle within the Cabinet. Predictably, however, there were the inevitable opponents who were concerned that regional assemblies might become alternative power bases which would threaten traditional Whitehall supremacy.[34]

In the event, what has been established is a series of Regional Development Agencies which, it is hoped, will unlock the regions' economic potential and narrow economic disparities between them. These were formally launched in April 1999, and have the following statutory purposes:

- to further economic development and regeneration;
- to promote business efficiency, investment and competitiveness;
- to promote employment;
- to enhance development and application of skill relevant to employment; and
- to contribute to sustainable development.

Their specific functions include formulating a regional strategy, regional regeneration, taking the lead on regional inward investment and seeking out European funding. The Government has issued statutory and non-statutory guidance to the RDAs on the formulation of their regional strategies which were presented to and largely welcomed by the Government in October 1999. Government Offices, nevertheless, retain important responsibilities in the regions while local authorities have a significant stake in the work of the RDAs, with four of the 13 board members drawn from local government. Although the Agencies are responsible to central government, there are also arrangements in place to ensure that they are responsive to regional views. To this end, regional chambers, comprising businessmen and councillors, have been designated under powers in the Regional Development Agencies Act 1998. They must be consulted by the RDAs on their strategy and other key documents such as the annual report and corporate plan.

In July 2000, the Government launched a national consultation document, *The Regional Development Agencies as Strategic Drivers of Economic Development*, which proposes a stronger economic development role for the RDAs. The Government's apparent confidence in the RDAs was endorsed in July 2000 with the announcement of an additional £500 million by 2003–04 in the Comprehensive Spending Review. Significantly, they are also to have greater

33 (1999) *Financial Times*, 26 March.

34 See, eg, (1999) *The Guardian*, 4 August.

flexibility over how to spend their budgets, as their funding will be brought together in a single cross-departmental budget to which the DTI, DETR and DfEE will commit funds. The RDAs will, thus, be more powerful than they were in the first year of operation.[35] As well as increased funding, the Chancellor promised greater freedom from Whitehall to secure more jobs, redevelop derelict land and improve rundown neighbourhoods. The eight RDA heads were urged to pursue a more strategic role embracing housing, transport and higher education. The move came two weeks after delegates at Labour's national policy forum decided that the next Labour Government should commit itself to directly elected regional government in England 'where there is a demand'.[36] At the time of writing, there were some signs of greater support for regional government and indeed, also, for 'neighbourhood empowerment',[37] though little resembling a coherent approach can be detected. To some extent, the way forward has recently been signposted by the West Midlands RDA, which launched a new representative office at Brussels on 27 November 2000. At the time it issued a statement that old approaches to regeneration – for example, emergency or other capital injections – were inappropriate, and that from now on, regeneration needs to operate bottom-up rather than top-down and be driven by local needs and competences. Interestingly, it recognised that the new ways require greater accountability and scrutiny.[38]

Finally, there is an informed view that regards effective devolution as a necessary response to the process of globalisation:

> The internal balance of power in the OECD is being affected by globalisation. As noted above, some sub-national governments are, as a result, seeking direct representation in international decision making fora. The rationale behind this is that executive government is entering into agreements that have serious implications for their given functions and responsibilities. For example, environmental treaties set limits on sub-national governments' capacities to manage local land and resource use. From the other side, globalisation is used as an argument for national unity – that when national governments speak with one voice, the collective interests of government will be maximised – as was used in Canada, with respect to the debate on Quebec separation. In any event, national governments will need to develop ways to improve co-operation with other levels of government through better communication and consultation – so as to reconcile national and sub-national interests in the global policy environment.[39]

35 DETR, 21 July 2000. For the considerable developments in devolving power in Sweden in recent years, see OECD, *Issues and Developments in Public Management*, Survey 1996–97 on Sweden, PUMA.

36 (2000) *The Guardian*, 22 July.

37 (2000) *The Guardian*, 3 November.

38 (2000) *The Guardian*, 13 December.

39 *Op cit*, OECD, fn 14.

It is clearly time to reverse the over-centralised nature of the British State. A beginning has been made and, as and when elected regional government is established, it can be expected that the legal order will have a more substantial role to play than has been the case up until now.

NEW SYSTEMS OF ACCOUNTABILITY

It is not at all clear that accountability issues have been clearly thought through in the UK in the changed climate. Ministerial responsibility has always been very largely a fig-leaf, but with so many decisions being outsourced or 'partnered', there is a clear need for auxiliary mechanisms. The ombudsman system, as has been noted, is being re-examined, if not with the level of institutional thoroughness necessary. Complaints procedures are taken much more seriously within government these days than formerly, yet we know far too little at this point in time about accountability gaps within the new systems of governance; not least multi-layered partnerships. A certain unease exists in relation to arrangements for contracting out, and it would be surprising if the concern was not justified across a broader canvas. However, as we have seen, there is accountability and accountability, and it is not clear that the 'managerial' variety has been optimised in the new partnership arrangements:

> An overly rigid culture of accountability is in large part responsible for undermining learning. Goals, outcome and performance measures are set too early on and then become immutable; there is no room for the recognition that innovative initiatives may well change, grow new purposes, be successful in new terms – or that there are lessons to be absorbed from the shift away from the original aspirations. The use of taxpayers' money demands public accountability; poor performance must attract sanctions. But traditional practices of accountability applied in haste are in danger of making the best into the enemy of the good. Lessons learned units might boost managers' confidence to make the case to politicians (at all levels) for developing more appropriate systems of accountability.[40]

One unanticipated source of modern accountability has recently surfaced in the form of the International Consortium of Investigative Journalists. This is made up of journalists from the UK, the US, Spain, Columbia and beyond, who have combined to open up the machinations of some of the globe's biggest and most penetrating international players:

> ... globalisation is not a trend for the Microsofts and Starbucks alone. The media, too, can globalise – using the internet to work across borders, drawing on diverse, international talents to invigilate those who operate globally. If

40 *Op cit*, Perri 6 *et al*, fn 11, p 79.

> corporate power is now exercised across the world, then journalism must do the same to keep tabs on it.[41]

Although there is a lot of advice available on the need for new systems of accountability in the world of governance, there is considerable variation in the visibility and openness of the systems in operation. In particular, the use of law is extremely variable, even though the OECD has argued that a legal framework allows a 'mandatory and comprehensive' approach to accountability.[42] They are also clear about the need for fresh thinking in this area:

> Over the past decade, the role of the State has been shifting from that of a dominant actor toward that of a strategic enabler and co-ordinator of other actors in public policy processes. Increasing the number of actors involved in the governing process often means creating new mechanisms, or adapting existing ones, in order to give the new actors a voice, while maintaining the government's capacity to guide the process towards coherent results.[43]

There is a dilemma here. New forms of accountability are a necessity, but the primacy of politics also needs to be restored. For instance, to some extent, international relations and events are more visible and transparent than formerly, although the policy process is more complex. But, does greater access to information and greater participation in policy processes by an increasing range of policy actors make those processes and their outcomes more legitimate, responsive and democratic? Or is it possible that policy processes are captured by powerful interests with special access to information and its dissemination? For instance, although there is a greater willingness among governments to involve NGOs in the policy process, is there a danger that in any given case, they might be unrepresentative and over-influential, especially when they can act with others at speed to influence the turn of events?

THE PRIMACY OF POLITICS AND THE ROLE OF THE LAW

There was a time in the 1990s when the primacy of politics was being seriously questioned. There was such a commitment to privatisation, hiving off and a belief in the superiority of the private sector that a genuine ownership of the State was being called into question. That tide appears to have passed, and yet there remains some uncertainty about both the place of politics and the larger shape of the State. The OECD recently singled out the

---

41 (2000) *The Guardian*, 31 January.

42 OECD, *In Search of Results: Performance Management Practices*, 1997, PUMA, p 27.

43 *Op cit*, OECD, fn 14, p 1.

Netherlands as a country which had recognised the nature of the problem and had sought to take action.

This did not take the form of 'repatriating' public services, but rather involved the reformulation of requirements to be met in respect of steering and supervision by the administrators concerned and improving the manner in which account is rendered to elected representatives. As part of the effort to restore the primacy of politics, the government laid down in legislative instructions the requirement to be met by statutory regulations, and administrative authorities with autonomous power were established. The existing autonomous authorities were screened with the intent to review the manner in which the government task concerned was carried out and to improvements in steering, supervision and organisation. The system of advisory bodies was also reviewed with a view to gearing up more effectively to political requirements and to focus on strategic questions and the main policy elements. The creation of more strategically oriented core ministries was advanced by improving the steering and supervisions of semi-privatised bodies, the progressive transfer of tasks to other levels of government and the reorganisation of the system for providing strategic advice by setting up bodies for that purpose.[44]

What was encouraging about this exercise was first, that the move to governance was accompanied by a thorough revision of the government machine and secondly, that much of the change was brought about by legislation, thus marking up and highlighting lines of responsibility and accountability. For all its merits, the *Modernising Government* White Paper in the UK was not in such a heroic mould. Ministerial responsibility is still seen as the lynch-pin of accountability mechanisms in spite of the way the modern world has emerged. In New Zealand, individual officials in positions of bureaucratic authority are increasingly being named and their actions subjected to sharper scrutiny by committees of the legislature and other forms of inquiry. There has also been considerable liberalisation of similar conventions in OECD countries through various constitutional means in the knowledge that times have changed:

> ... confidence in government may require clarification of the respective accountability obligations, which can become blurred in a more devolved system of public management. There have been some instances where it has been difficult to establish who is responsible for what and to whom, especially where separate agencies are set up at arm's length from the Minister. In order to avoid confusion, which can damage good management as well as accountability, the underlying principle should be that the most senior person is to be held accountable if he or she were involved or should have been involved. Specifically, this means senior management is not necessarily held

44 *Op cit*, OECD, fn 35, Survey on The Netherlands.

> accountable for an isolated instance of wrongdoing or poor service by a subordinate, but senior management would be held accountable if this were systemic, and especially if senior management did not take adequate preventative action. Once accountability is clarified along these lines, it should be possible to reconcile the need for proper accountability with devolution of responsibility.[45]

These are issues which have still not been satisfactorily resolved in the UK, any more than it has made really serious attempts at modernising Parliament. Pre-Bill inquiry has undoubtedly improved, but much else remains unchanged. Again, as the OECD has remarked, parliaments and other institutions need to change to complement changes in public expectations or styles of administration. 'They will not necessarily do so easily.' Even so, some governments, it was noted, were anxious to involve their parliaments, including opposition members, in the development of long term policies. Others seem keen to shield strategic planning from the daily political arena as much as possible.[46] There is a strong body of opinion which favours Parliament playing a more independent role by making increased use of its committees to review policy in the future.

In the UK, the most important contribution to this debate in recent times has been the Report of the Parliamentary Liaison Committee.[47] The Committee, which includes all 33 select committee chairmen, recommended stronger powers to scrutinise Whitehall budgets, extra back-up staff and ways of breaking the control of party whips on who gets appointed to plum committee posts – often a reward for loyal service. While welcoming the Report, the Government also managed to reject it in effective terms. The Government's line was that, while it supports the Committee's aim of strengthening the Committee system, it may differ about how that can be achieved. In particular, the Government was not persuaded that 'a radical change' to the current system of appointment was needed.[48] What lay at the heart of the Liaison Committee Report was the belief that making law and policy is a consensual business, in which MPs are partners and not mere subordinates. Led by Giles Radice, the MPs wanted to build an alternative career path, with good MPs making a name for themselves not as ministers, but as scrutineers. By rejecting the proposal out of hand, the Government was signalling that it had no intention to weaken party discipline in the House. One of the proposals had been to discipline ministers who came to a committee and gave 'a sub-standard response'. The implication, according to

45 *Op cit*, Keating, fn 5, pp 56–57.

46 See *op cit*, OECD Symposium, fn 2, pp 19, 31.

47 Select Committee on Liaison, *Shifting the Balance: Select Committees and the Executive*, Session 1999–2000, HC 300, 2 March 2000.

48 Cabinet Office, *The Government's Response to the Liaison Select Committee*, Cm 4737, 2000, HMSO.

one commentator, was that 'for the first time since the 17th century, legislators would face down the executive'.[49]

Interestingly, too, the Government was unmoved by the call to establish new joint or cross-cutting committees which would reflect the Government's own priorities. Such committees would have the power of following spending and decisions through more than one department, which, in turn, could mean Treasury officials being called before Parliament too often. Joined up government, it appears, has its limits and only a particular kind of politics is to be allowed primacy in the foreseeable future. Unsurprisingly, 'the Government sees no reason to change the current arrangements for accountability of the intelligence and security services'.

The Liaison Committee was so disappointed with the Government response that it issued a Second Report, entitled *Independence or Control*, in which it regretted that the Government had 'rejected virtually every recommendation we had made':

> The Reply was both disappointing and surprising. We found it disappointing because our proposals were modest. We did not suggest line-by-line scrutiny of the Estimates as a condition for their approval; we did not suggest any change in the powers of Select Committees; for example, to allow them to require papers from Government Departments or to summon Ministers[50] – for all of which there are strong cases. And we found it surprising that a Government which has made so much of its policy of modernising Parliament[51] should apparently take so different a view when its own accountability and freedom of action are at issue.[52]

NPM and its offshoots have had extensive repercussions for the Civil Service and yet there is still no sign of its role, nature and future being given root-and-branch reconsideration – not least through a long-overdue Civil Service Act. The problems have been well rehearsed, especially through a series of Select Committee Reports during the 1990s, and they include the now well documented accountability hinterland occupied by Agency Chief Executives (CEs). As has frequently been said, current arrangements tend to allow the minister to take the credit when things go well, but to blame the CE when things go wrong. The separation of policy and management is advantageous to those on the policy side and disadvantageous to managers. Parliament has clearly failed, thus far, to seize the opportunities created by Next Steps to improve its scrutiny of government departments.[53] In fact, NS has simply

49 Walker, D, 'Executive powers' (2000) *The Guardian*, 29 June.

50 Though it appears to be the case that UK ministers may be summonable to the Scottish Parliament and the Welsh Assembly under the Scotland Act 1998, s 23 and the Government of Wales Act 1998, s 74.

51 It would have made more sense if they had substituted 'government' for 'parliament'.

52 Session 1999–2000, HC 748, 25 July 2000, para 3.

53 Rhodes, RAW, *Understanding Governance: Policy Networks etc*, 1997, OUP, pp 102–03.

heightened and exaggerated a problem that already existed before: viz, the barrenness of ministerial responsibility as a mechanism of effective accountability. Sadly, the FOI Act 2000 does very little to improve the position. Much of the concern has been brought to the fore again by the 16 volume report by Lord Phillips into the BSE affair.[54] At the end of Vol 1, a number of individuals are named as being, in varying degrees, culpable, including both ministers and civil servants. Sadly, it takes a national tragedy and an inquiry of this nature before responsibility can be anything like clearly identified in the British political system. Furthermore, Lord Phillips found that there 'was a clear policy of restricting the disclosure of information about BSE', a matter which no avid student of the British political system would be surprised by. As things currently stand, the FOI Act would be likely to ensure the continued restriction of much of the information which Lord Phillips' inquiry unearthed. Of course, promises of a more open culture followed the Scott Inquiry, but no Bill regulating arms exports had been produced four years later.

Things within the Civil Service have undoubtedly changed remarkably in recent years; it is just that the machinery of government has not changed overmuch as a result. The Treasury, for instance, has recently agreed more than 500 performance and efficiency targets with spending departments in return for extra money. This has resulted in Treasury officials being sent into public schools and hospitals, for example, so that they might be better equipped to agree appropriate spending and performance targets.[55] This follows a longer standing arrangement whereby civil servants have visited some of the larger private companies across the Kingdom in order to exchange world views. Private advisers have been moved in and out of Whitehall, ministers have increasingly used policy advisers from outside the Permanent Civil Service, new management initiatives have been encouraged and the whole ethos of the public service called into question. This is to say nothing of the inevitable problems for the Civil Service caused by the devolved administrations and the range of partnerships envisaged for the Government of the future.

The Government's response has been fitful. Sir Richard Wilson, Head of the Home Civil Service, recently set out his 'vision of a Civil Service for the next Millennium'. In a welter of generalities, he committed himself to 'top class performance, innovation and teamworking'. A key element in this programme of change is to be the new Centre for Management and Policy Studies, announced in the *Modernisation* White Paper. Although the new Centre will focus on training, it will also play a vital part in researching and evaluating policy making as well as identifying and spreading good practice.

---

54 Phillips (Lord), *Inquiry into BSE and Variant CJD in the UK*, HC, October 2000.

55 (2000) *Financial Times*, 4 January.

Sir Richard leaned heavily on the general aspirations of the White Paper with its emphasis on better policy making, better responsiveness to what people want and more effective public services. This will give 'a clear strategic sense of direction to a new phase in the development of the Civil Service'.[56] All this would be achieved while retaining faith in the 'core values' of the service. The most significant features of the report are the Departmental Action Plans, which are to explain how each Department's PSAs are to be delivered, and the statement on Vision and Values. As to the former, there was to be a tougher emphasis on results and outcomes, identifying the root causes of problems, especially for cross-cutting areas, and the need to give coherence to the many objectives being set. As to the latter, Sir Richard and his colleagues identified for each value a number of indicators of positive behaviour which will uphold it, together with negative behaviours which will work against it. It is difficult to improve on this exercise, for which the Cabinet Office should be congratulated.[57] Why it should not be included in a Civil Service Act, therefore, becomes the more baffling. As to the Departmental Action Plans, they are clearly a move in the right direction, but again, there is no indication of institutional change which would identify high performers and those who make culpable errors.

Sir Richard announced the most extensive staff consultation exercise ever in seeking out civil servants' own views as to the future. Thus far, however, there is little sign of genuine machinery-of-government reform – no new mechanisms of accountability and no Civil Service Act. What has been produced is a very substantial report produced after much debate between senior civil servants, the staff unions and others.[58] The reform programme was based around six key themes, including stronger leadership (largely in the form of the Civil Service Management Board), better business planning, and sharper performance management. No one can object to the reforms, but they are less than is required. One small point indicates the inadequacy of the report. Sharper performance management is to include tackling poor performance and incentivising high achievers. Fine, but no mention of the role of a reformed version of ministerial responsibility is in sight, so that the likelihood is that the public will continue to be kept in the dark as to who is responsible for what under what set of circumstances.

All of these issues have raised public concern. Lord Neill, Chairman of the Committee on Standards in Public Life, has been particularly vociferous. He was a leading critic of the Government's Freedom of Information Bill, not least for setting up formidable obstacles to prevent the disclosure of secret meetings between government ministers, civil servants and lobbying companies. He felt

56 CAB 100/99.

57 See Cabinet Office, *Vision and Values*, 1999, Cabinet Office, Annex B.

58 Wilson, R (Sir), *Report to the Prime Minister on Civil Service Reform*, CAB 99-5277/0001/D40, 1999.

it was vital to open up meetings with lobbyists trying to influence government policy. His Committee had already called on the UK to follow the US and Canada to keep public registers of meetings with lobbyists, and for the talks to be fully minuted. Two of the restrictions in what is now the FOI Act 2000 – the supply of information in confidence and discussions about public policy – created formidable obstacles to genuine reform. Among the many changes which Lord Neill had envisaged was a Civil Service Act. He argued that it would help to increase public confidence in the process of public sector reform if, like most other democracies, this country could have legislation to clarify the role and status of the Civil Service. The Committee recently produced a report making 41 recommendations covering Members of Parliament and disciplinary procedures, ministers, civil servants, including special advisers, lobbying of government by outside interests, sponsorship and government task forces.[59] The Wilson Report of December 1999 had proposed more short term contracts, more appointments of people from the private and voluntary sectors and more secondments for civil servants. In the light of this, Neill recommended measures to sustain the public service ethos of impartiality and objectivity. These included not only a timetable for a Civil Service Act to safeguard the core values of the service; he also called for a system of independent validation of the performance of Permanent Secretaries and heads of department since they are in the process of being given personal objectives to deliver the Government's key targets. Special advisers should be required to observe a code of conduct drafted to reflect their special position, sponsorship agreements should be publicly disclosed and task forces should be reviewed so that they would either be disbanded or reclassified as advisory non-departmental public bodies.

However, in many ways, it was the recommendation that ministers and civil servants should be required to keep a record of contacts with outside interests, alongside a code to improve the transparency of government consultation exercises, that contains the most radical potential. It clearly does not go far enough, and if a record exists simply to allow a judicial commission to investigate when things go wrong, then little will have been achieved. The US Government in the Sunshine legislation is what is needed.[60] This requires not only that records are maintained, but that they are publicly available and that any shielded information will be tested by a public official according to stringent requirements about the public's right to know. Anything less is unacceptable in a mature democracy. In the US, there is a long and admirable history of legislative commitment to outlawing *ex parte* dealings between governments and lobbyists which the UK would do well to follow. Naturally, such laws cannot be foolproof, but in the USA they are more honoured than

59 Committee on Conduct in Public Life, *Reinforcing Standards*, Vol 1 Report, Cm 455-7-1, 2000, HMSO.

60 And see the present author's contribution to these issues in Weir, S and Hall, W (eds), *EGO Trip, Democratic Audit of the UK*, 1994.

breached. It should also be added that the New Zealand Freedom of Information Commissioner regularly uses his office to expose *ex parted* meetings with government by a patient process of reconstructing the background to policy making. Gaps in the official record can be picked up by a diligent appreciation of how bureaucracy works.

The support for a Civil Service Act by Lord Neill is also to be welcomed. It is often forgotten that the last recommendation of Northcote-Trevelyan was to establish a Civil Service Commission on a statutory basis. The Treasury and Civil Service Select Committee in its 1994 Report[61] also recommended the introduction of a Civil Service Act, without going into specifics. This need has been recognised elsewhere. During the reforms of the 1980s, some countries, New Zealand for example, took the opportunity to legislate for certain aspects of the public service in order to raise the accountability standard above the reach of purely party politics in the belief that the service is a national asset and should be regarded as such. Each country regulates the public service in its own way, but most operate within at least a skeletal framework of law, sometimes expressed in the constitution itself, as in Germany. The TCSC's reasoning deserves to be repeated:

> ... it is better to have a culture with a strong sense of commitment to essential values than to have an Act without such a culture: we believe it is better still to have both. The passage of such an Act would reflect the interest of Parliament, as the representative of the electorate, in the preservation of the values of the Civil Service: it would set the terms of the custodial responsibility of the Government of the day for the Civil Service. Such an Act would require the Government to consult on a new Civil Service Code and lay such a Code before Parliament for approval by a resolution of both houses.[62]

The author has addressed this issue at greater length elsewhere.[63] The case for a Civil Service Act has been clearly made out and the dispute is largely about what it should contain. Apart from the basics, upon which there is probably much agreement, two issues must be attended to if old values are to inform new circumstances. They relate to the need for senior civil servants to give the best first hand evidence of major events to Committees of the House and much greater information about policy advice. Successive governments have refused to open up this area and there appears little likelihood of this changing in the near future. This refusal shames our democratic representatives and all pressure should be brought to bear to open up the policy process even if 'confidential information' remains cloaked. One way of doing this is to adopt the US system of building a 'record' of policy comments which would be available for inspection, following, to some extent, the model

61 Treasury and Civil Service Committee, 5th Report, Session 1993–94, HC 21-1.

62 *Ibid*, para 116.

63 Lewis, ND, 'A Civil Service Act for the United Kingdom' [1998] PL 463, pp 463–88.

already adopted by OFTEL in the UK. This raises again the role of publics in the consultation process.

The Cabinet Office now, encouragingly, has a 'consultation home page' on the internet. As was seen in Chapter 8, it has also now produced a draft Code of Practice about the way government carries out written consultations, following the Sixth Report of the Neill Committee on Standards in Public Life. Much of its content is to be applauded, although it would be stronger if all comments were made publicly available in a true record which could be inspected by all interested parties. Although this does not go quite as far as advanced practices in some other democratic countries, it is better than anything that has preceded it. In the past, of course, individual statutes have often required the minister to consult with interested parties and, from time to time, the courts have expressed a view on the adequacy of the consultation undertaken.[64] The record of the UK judiciary is mixed, if improving, but they have not had the legislative assistance of their American colleagues. It really is time that a mature UK Government introduced a wide ranging Administrative Procedure Act which includes, *inter alia*, provisions relating to the adequacy of consultation. If involving the courts seems too heady for the current generation of politicians, then at least the ombudsman could be substituted to enforce the public interest.

In this matter, as in others, UK governments believe that administrative discretion is almost always to be preferred to legal obligation. Such a view is becoming increasingly outdated in modern democracies and is beginning to call into question the reality of the commitment to democratic politics.

THE UK AND ADMINISTRATIVE LAW

One would think that in times of rapid, not to say dizzy change, the need to reassert basic principles in legislation which would act as a check on excesses in public life would be self-evident. In spite of genuinely important constitutional change since 1997, this is still not the case. We are left to wonder how long it will take our island nation to catch up with its neighbours and partners in this respect.

Throughout this extended essay, there have been extensive references to the US system of administrative law as a clear contrast to the distrust which the subject has historically held for the British. But the US is not alone in believing that party politicians should not be entirely trusted when it comes to the means and methods by which government operates. New Zealand, perhaps the world leader in NPM-style reforms, has relied on legislative

64 See, eg, Longley, D and James, R, *Administrative Justice*, 1999, Cavendish Publishing, pp 230–42.

support for the reform process much more than its former Mother Parliament. However, the trend does not stop there. Several OECD countries have established constitutional or legal rights for public consultation, including Finland, Portugal, Sweden and Switzerland.[65] In Australia, Germany and France, there has been legislation for a duty to state reasons for decisions, The Netherlands has extensively revised its system of administrative law, the Republic of Ireland is travelling down the same road, France has a 'strong legal tradition making it more likely that de jure reform programmes'[66] will be preferred, while since 1996, all Bills and draft decrees which go to the Conseil d'Etat inform legislators and the Government of the legal, economic, social and financial effects of proposals, and about the consequences for employment and for administrative simplification.[67] Germany has recently amended its Administrative Procedure Act, and so on.

Responsiveness in service delivery is one of the major concerns for governments and for citizens. Generally, initiatives to improve service quality involve user participation or consultation in the design and organisation of better services, information on the availability and functioning of the service, opportunities for complaint and compensation and so on. In the UK, striking improvements and successes have occurred in many of these areas with relatively little structural alteration in governing arrangements. Given the pace and scale of change, this is becoming increasingly difficult to justify. However, part of the problem is the failure to think through first principles; this is almost certainly as much to do with the absence of a developed system of administrative law as is the clinging to tradition.

It will be stressed in the final chapter that the Nation State is becoming less powerful as a basic unit of economic organisation as a result of the growth of the global economy, but it is equally clear to those who are used to thinking through from problem to solution that regions and cities are likely to become more powerful. We have seen that the UK has been much more half-hearted in recognising this than many of its allies and associates and does not even possess a machinery of government device which is capable of acting as a constitutional and administrative think tank for government. Some claims may appear simply fashionable, while others look a safer bet, and yet it is important for governments to have some means of separating the wheat from the chaff. The Centre for Management and Policy Studies is a promising innovation, while the Committee on Standards in Public Life is already showing its worth. Neither of them, however, is up to the task of overseeing the whole machinery of government set against changing patterns in a changing world. The Standing Administrative Conference which has been

65 *Consultation and Communications*, 1997, OECD.

66 *Op cit*, OECD, fn 42, p 16.

67 See Turc, A, 'Accountability in public organisations: responsiveness to political authorities, users and market forces', in OECD, *Democratic and Political Accountability*, 1997, Public Management Service, p 16.

argued for throughout this book is the very least which a modern government should insist upon, but there is no sign of its acceptance at this time.

UK governments up until 1997 were perhaps not expected to travel down this route, but a little more has been expected since that date. However, it still appears that paying attention to systems of governance means appeasing the chattering classes; that systems of governance are a bolt-on extra to the real business of politics. This is a mistake, as the OECD has been quick to point out:

> Systems of governance affect the performance of the State in executing its core functions and through this, the performance of countries in meeting their major economic and social goals:
>
> - Governments create the conditions for functioning of markets, operation of private firms, strength of civil society, and welfare of communities and individuals.
> - The quality of governance is recognised as fundamental to ensuring the quality of life of citizens.
> - In its own right, good governance is important as a determinant of the sustainability and strength of democracies.[68]

Modernising government is important and necessary, but modernising systems of government and governance is equally so, a fact which no British Government yet seems to have understood. It is a challenge which some day soon will have to be accepted.

CONCLUSION

The erosion of parliamentary oversight is likely to be a key issue in the democracy debate in the future. It is not just in the UK that institutional forms of democratic deficit are blatant. Nevertheless, parliamentary impotency in the UK is in urgent need of a sizeable dose of democratic Viagra. Currently there is little sign that the Executive is likely to castrate itself in order to make that possible. Parliament will simply have to assert itself in the way that successive generations of ancestors have done from the 13th century Barons through Simon de Montfort, the Peasants' Revolt to the emergence of the trade union movement. There is a tide in the affairs of men ... Rationally, we could predict a reformation through proportional representation, but that is itself largely in the hands of the Executive, and so will not emerge rationally. Parliamentary renewal will happen viscerally and probably in the not too distant future. However, given the thrust of the argument which has informed this essay, this alone will be insufficient to restore democratic politics.

68 'Promoting good governance' at the Emerging Market Economy Forum Workshop on Public Management in Support of Social and Economic Objectives, 10–11 December 1998, OECD, Summary of Session 1.

Ironically, politicians in the UK especially, though not uniquely, have been reaching out to the people increasingly in recent years. The Citizen's Charter was something of a landmark and its larger impetus continues, albeit not in the preferred form of a genuine marriage ceremony sworn before a priest; that is, in legal form. Even allowing for this, the reasons are not entirely philosophical, but largely born out of the need to discover the user's own thinking about service delivery in order to provide better value for money.

Interestingly, the move from NPM through user empowerment has caused successive governments to pay more attention to citizens as users than they have to their own parliaments, though not, for the most part, out of any obvious conviction that democratic politics needs new life breathed into it. However, taking this new-ish commitment to user empowerment and adding to it the revolution in information technology and the general globalisation of politics, it seems increasingly that traditional democratic mechanisms are being seriously weakened. What is really needed, of course, is the strengthening of national parliaments, both at the central and regional levels, accompanied by a genuine commitment to constructing a meaningful system of administrative law which allows everyone who wishes to make an input into public decision making. Strides are being made in that direction, but they are not considered enough. It is worth repeating that there is little fashionable enthusiasm for a coherent Administrative Procedure Act which takes in 'access' laws, 'Sunshine' legislation, the building of a public record with a legal obligation to consult effectively, and embracing everything from the contract culture to the new accountability problems which the commitment to partnerships produces.

All of this is, of course, compounded by the politics of globalisation.

As we have seen, individual government institutions – in particular, the sectoral specialists who work in them – are themselves adapting to a globalised environment by developing their own transnational linkages. Line ministries and finance ministries now routinely manage international contacts and the international dimensions of their policies.

The situation is more problematic when sub-national governments or their institutions also assume a role on the international stage, as they increasingly do. Some sub-national governments are directly represented in international decision making fora. The OECD cites the example of Spain, where some self-governing communities set up direct representation in Brussels, an initiative contested by central government, but supported by a ruling of the Constitutional Court.[69]

69 'The need for structural and institutional change', in OECD, *Strategic Management and Policy-Making*, 1997, PUMA, p 2.

These matters are not only of the utmost importance, but remind us of how UK governments tend to smuggle what they regard as solutions to managerial problems (when they are frequently political and constitutional problems) in through administrative means when others recognise that there should be publicly announced rules of the game to guide us through these changing times.

The OECD goes on to ask about the problems of co-ordination with a designated co-ordinator and traces the responsibility for such tasks in the OECD countries and places the responsibility, unsurprisingly in the Cabinet Office, historically not the most open of UK public institutions, for all its greater transparency in recent times. The OECD is clear that governments need to improve their capacities to set strategic goals and priorities in order to define the basis for participation in international fora and to help define the national interest in relation to international events. They concluded at the time that this capacity was largely lacking in most OECD countries, but that governments must have the ability to justify their position or actions on the basis of some set of principles or goals which could strengthen their legitimacy. They then outline a necessary framework for securing these objectives, which are worth quoting in full:

- the objectives of international action and policy making in each forum;
- competences and limitations of the instances and processes involved;
- the means by which a national government will participate and will influence international decision making;
- management of the continuing relationships among key parties, particularly the free flow of information and dispute resolution procedures (especially between ministries and the centre);
- consistency with related national goals and practices; and
- legal and constitutional compatibility.[70]

Progress towards establishing such a framework in the intervening period has been slow, and too little attention has been paid not only in the UK, but across the global community, to the distinctly legal, aspirational or constitutional components of this desideratum. In fact, there is both a lack of transparency and of coherence which are essential features of delivering on a regime of human rights, or what has been called 'cosmopolitan democracy'.[71] These issues form the background to the final chapter, which addresses issues which unquestionably require consistent and exclusive treatment. Even so, since they are issues which are linked to what has been discussed so far in regard to

---

70 *Op cit*, OECD, fn 69, p 4.

71 See, eg, Beetham, D, 'Human rights as a model for cosmopolitan democracy', in Archibuigi, D, Held, D, and Kohler, M (eds), *Re-Imagining Political Community: Studies in Cosmopolitan Democracy*, 1998, Polity, p 58.

changing patterns of governance on the more local levels, they will be outlined as a kind of postscript to concerns with governance and human values. The problematics of globalising law/governance should be occupying our serious attention for the next two decades.

CHAPTER 10

GOVERNANCE AND GLOBALISATION: THE NEXT FRONTIER

INTRODUCTION

Over 40 years ago, the British Foreign Secretary, Selwyn Lloyd, speaking about the European Convention on Human Rights, said:

> The position which Her Majesty's Government have continuously taken up is that they do not recognise the right of individual petition, *because they take the view that States are the proper subjects of international law* and if individuals are given rights under international treaties effect should be given to those rights through the national law of the States concerned.[1] (Emphasis added.)

As is well known, the UK later resiled from that position, but what is important is the view expressed about the nature of international law. Whatever definitions of that subject can be put forward today, it is becoming increasingly clear that there is now a different creature out there stalking the land. That creature is the law of the New World Order (NWO), or the law of globalisation. This latter concept may or may not absorb part of the former, but is clearly very different. What is going on in the new global order is that there is a bewildering array of actors striding the international stage whose individual and several actions can have crucial repercussions beyond national boundaries. Immense questions of legitimacy arise because of this phenomenon, which we are nowhere near resolving. Indeed, we are only just at the frontiers of recognising them. The influence of national governments is altering before our eyes; sometimes diminishing, sometimes growing through its participation in regional and global partnerships, while in some areas its relative autonomy can still be spotted as gaps appearing in the overall configuration. There is so much richness in all this, just a little of which has been hinted at. What is beyond dispute, however, is that globalisation poses enormous challenges for governance projects, national, regional and international. In some instances, governments are simply impotent to press their preferred policies in the face of the new global order; in others they can only do so through extensive partnerships with a wide variety of other players, and in yet others they are tasked to trace the outline shape of developments and seek ways of influencing them, either directly or through membership of a considerable number of organisations, some competing, at least on individual issues.

1 HC Deb, Vol 574, Cols 867–68, 29 July 1957.

This is the phenomenon which this chapter addresses. It argues that we must learn to understand and to master the emerging law of globalisation and its effects on patterns of governance. Furthermore, we are individually and collectively tasked with injecting concepts of justice into the new order; in particular, with injecting all three generations of human rights into projects whose legitimacy is often not subject to sufficient constraint. The old is meeting the new head on across this new frontier.

There will be those who will insist that the Byzantine complex of players, influences, arrangements and agreements unfolding is really not the business of lawyers. That view is rejected in its entirety. It is the next frontier for the public or constitutional lawyer, and this one has only resisted the temptation to title this last chapter 'the Global Constitution' after some considerable deliberation; but that is undoubtedly what we should be seeking. Only those with a very narrow and outmoded concept of the legal project[2] will fail to grasp the argument and to participate in the now and in the tomorrow.

THE BACKGROUND

Constitutionalising or re-constitutionalising the world order is beginning to sound, even to political pragmatists, like an idea whose time has come. There are many reasons for this, not least the growth in the power and influence of global corporations and the technological revolution of the last 20 years. In fact, there is more to be concerned with and about than just the enormous power of the multinational corporations (MNCs) in the information age. There are also governmental-political networks and *ersatz* governments to be brought into the account. Taken together, these phenomena are beginning to sideline traditional politics and to suggest a democratic deficit of major proportions. For these reasons, it is clear that revised institutional arrangements are now necessary in order to ensure that the big players in the global marketplace become accountable to governments and citizens alike, whether through reform of international organisations, reassertion of influence by national and regional governments, or by other means. It is time, in short, to start thinking about the concept of the global constitution: to set out at least a menu of institutional and substantive responses to the NWO.

Historically, global governance has occurred without global constitutions. A degree of governance through empires has been replaced with self-regulating, but unstable markets, and unilateral action by powerful nations.

2 The one adopted by the author is largely that proffered by Karl Llewellyn in his 'law jobs' theory. See Lewis, ND, 'Towards a sociology of lawyering in public administration' (1981) 32 NILQ 89, pp 89–105.

This is no longer acceptable, and the belief is emerging that rules and a sense of order are necessary for assuring 'public goods'. This is why the concept of governance has been on board corporate agendas increasingly in recent years.[3] However, accountable international institutions with an effective jurisdiction are barely perceptible, although the pace and quality of change are incontestable phenomena:

> The scale of our predicament is entirely new in human history. None of our experiences or existing models of society can cope with the complexity of managing our crowded, divided, planet. Few communities, companies or countries can say they have resolved the conundrums that confront them. Western Europe took over 40 years to create a single market, with many economic and political problems still unresolved. Yet the World Trade Organisation will take us towards a single global market even more diverse and unequal than Europe in just 10 years.[4]

First, the power of international capital. MNCs have been a bogy for the left since Karl Marx first chewed the end off his pencil. Yet, never have they offered more cause for concern than 10 years after the collapse of the socialist bloc, and five after the establishment of the World Trade Organisation (WTO). According to Corporate Watch, 51 of the world's largest economies are corporations and the combined revenues of just two of them – General Motors and Ford – exceed the combined GDP for all of south Saharan Africa.[5] General Motors, for instance, packs more punch than some European Member States. The decisions of international capital have enormous significance for communities across the world; strangling some and breathing (unequal) life into others. A social partnership Europe has the potential to help infuse some version of democratic politics into the balance. Many would feel this is long overdue, given the warning of Polyani that the profit maximising dictates of the self-regulating market were incompatible with social protection at least as long ago as 1944.[6] Things have accelerated considerably since then. A single example. In May 2000, the London Stock Exchange announced its intention to merge with the German Bourse. Although the initiative was later frustrated, the move would almost certainly have advanced the Anglo-Saxon pursuit of shareholder value at the expense of other stakeholders. Business remakes the world in its own image, but the issue which must be addressed is whether regulators and public authorities together with the business community will be able to keep pace with these developments.

---

3 See Chapter 8, and for a broader theoretical approach to global issues, see de Santos, B, *Toward a New Common Sense: Law, Science and Politics in Paradigmatic Transition*, 1995, Routledge and Held, D, *Global Transformations: Politics, Economics and Culture*, 1999, Polity.

4 Alexander, T, *Unravelling Global Apartheid*, 1996, Polity, p 4.

5 According to the UNDP Development Report, in 1999 the assets of the world's three richest men are worth the combined GDP of all the 48 least developed countries (LDCs).

6 Polyani, K, *The Great Transformation*, 1944, Beacon.

In terms of public consciousness, things have hopefully been brought to a head by the convocation of the United Nations Millennium Assembly and Summit on the future of the world which took place in New York in September 2000. The Assembly was the catalyst for the launch of Charter '99, which is a Charter for Global Democracy dedicated to international accountability, justice, sustainable development and democracy. However, these occurrences need to be seen as a culmination of developments and concerns expressed throughout most of the 1990s.

Charter '99 lists some of the salient moments of the period. They include:

- the Commission on Global Governance, which made an unprecedented international effort to draw up a framework for global politics;[7]
- the Earth Summit in Rio, Agenda 21, the Earth Charter and other declarations of support for global democracy and sustainable development which have had a very considerable and continuing impact;
- the adoption by the Inter-Parliamentary Union of the Universal Declaration of Democracy, since endorsed by most parliaments in the world;
- the promotion by the International Chamber of Commerce, World Business for Sustainable Development and others of higher standards in international business;
- the Human Development Report 1999, which recommended an agenda for action including a more coherent and democratic architecture for global governance in the 21st century.

Charter '99 is clear that the United Nations has been largely sidelined under the NWO. The real business of government is done elsewhere:

> Global policies are discussed and decided behind closed doors by exclusive groups such as the G8, OECD, the Bank of International Settlements, the World Bank, the International Monetary Fund, the World Trade Organisation and others. These agencies are reinforced by informal networks of high officials and powerful alliances. Together they have created what can be seen as dominant and exclusive institutions of world government. All too often they are influenced by transnational corporations which pursue their own world strategies.

In the public mind, perhaps the IMF and the World Bank are the central planks of the NWO. The IMF, in particular, rarely gets a good press from those who advocate social justice.[8] In particular, it has been berated for encouraging capital flows which have been occasioned by speculation rather

---

7 See Commission on Global Governance, *Our Global Neighbourhood*, 1995, UN, which was a seminal document. More recently it has responded with *The Millennium Year and the Reform Process*, 2000, UN.

8 Though see Tanzi, V, *Globalisation and the Future of Social Protection*, IMF Working Paper WP/00/12.

than long term investment.[9] The feeling has grown that it exists for the benefit of Wall Street and the American multinationals rather than the Third World. The Fund has conducted external evaluations of its performance, but resists the establishment of an independent evaluation department.

This is not the place to conduct a detailed analysis of the IMF or the World Bank, but certain general lessons stand out to be learned. First, there is a general lack of transparency – something that is common to public organisations around the world, although it has to be said that the World Bank now claims to pursue a policy of openness. *The World Bank Policy on Disclosure of Information*, January 1994, establishes a Public Information Center through which much of the material covered by its revised policies is publicly available. The exemptions, or 'constraints', as the document has it, are the usual ones, although, in this instance, the exemption of working documents and matters of commercial confidentiality make a considerable dent in the claims for transparency.

Secondly, there is no satisfactory regulatory regime (an opinion shared by such luminaries as George Soros and Joseph Stiglitz). In particular, the relationship between lenders and borrowers needs to be more egalitarian.[10]

It would be exhausting to list all the other major players – even if, in this state of our knowledge, we knew who they were. However, on the European level, three stand out for special comment. They are the Council of Europe, the OECD and the European Union itself. Of the EU, more later.

The Council of Europe, however, has been remarkably successful. Its primary role its to strengthen democracy, human rights and the rule of law. It is best known for the European Convention on Human Rights, but it has been responsible for much more besides. It is also a forum for examining issues such as social exclusion, intolerance, the integration of migrants, the threat to private life posed by new technology, bioethical issues, terrorism, drug trafficking and criminal activities. It has also given birth to the Congress of Local and Regional Authorities of Europe, whose function is to strengthen democratic institutions at the local level, and, in particular, to assist the new democracies. The main organisations which the Council is required to work with are the EU and the Organisation for Security and Co-operation in Europe (OSCE). The recent reform of the Council's monitoring machinery for implementation of the European Social Charter has also been a major achievement in the field of human rights. It is a remarkably open and consultative organisation with few parallels in the rest of the world.

The OECD groups 29 countries in an organisation that provides governments with a setting in which to discuss and develop economic and

9 And see the criticism of the Fund's handling of the South Korean economy: Wolf, M, (1997) *Financial Times*, 9 December.

10 The so called 'Tobin tax' is also an issue which refuses to go away.

social policy. They compare experiences, seek answers to common problems and work to co-ordinate domestic and international policies intended to form a web of practice across nations. Their exchanges may lead to agreements to act in a formal way – for example, by establishing legally binding codes for the free flow of capital services. More often, their deliberations make for better informed work within their own governments on the spectrum of public policy and clarify the impact of national policies on the international community. Its most significant recent output has been the *Guidelines for Multinational Enterprises* agreed by the governments of the 29 member countries of the OECD and of Argentina, Brazil, Chile and Slovakia at the OECD Ministerial Meeting of 27 June 2000. The exercise was conducted with the utmost openness. The guidelines are, of course, voluntary and heavily circumscribed, but nevertheless call upon TNCs to observe basic civil and political rights as well as to respect the environment and to communicate essential information on the plans of the organisation to employees and other stakeholders.

The OECD is an important player and clearly regards itself as such. At the Ministerial Council held on 26–27 June 2000, its growing importance was underlined:

> Ministers endorsed OECD's continuing programme of *co-operation with non-Member economies*. They welcomed the Special Dialogue conducted at high levels, and recognised the important contribution that such meetings make to the enrichment of policy dialogue, and to mutual understanding on global issues, between the OECD countries and non-Members. The global reach of the OECD programme of co-operation with non-Members reflects the growing interdependence of the world economy. The Organisation must deepen and extend its relations with non-OECD economies, in the fields where it has comparative advantage, toward the development of a rules-and-values based world economy. Furthermore, Ministers reiterated that OECD must remain open, on the basis of mutual interest, to membership by countries sharing the same values, while being selective and pursuing the Organisation's tradition of high standards for membership as well as efficiency and relevance to its Members.[11]

As we shall see, the dazzling complexity of the NWO needs to be unravelled as a first step to building a global constitution, a theme which will run through the whole of this chapter. However one, perhaps less obvious, issue should be exposed, viz, the power and influence of the media. Given the dominance of the media by a few Western interests, it is even more significant than might appear at first sight. This is because a Western, and particularly US, culture threatens to drown out other varieties.

Most media are, in fact, an extension of commerce rather than a vehicle for citizenship. As television, newspapers and magazines depend more and more

11 Official Communiqué, para 41.

on advertising for income, they become agents for global companies and 'consumer religion':

> Advertising accounts for over four-fifths of media revenues, making the advertiser the client paying for readers' attention. The main function of most media is not to inform, but to foster a climate of consumption ...
>
> Spending on advertising has risen dramatically since 1950, three times faster than world population and one-third faster than economic growth.[12]

The world's media are controlled by a relatively few giant firms. For example, in 1945, 80% of US daily newspapers were independently owned. By 1989, only 20% were. In 1981, 46 companies controlled most US newspapers, magazines, book publishers, television and films. In the UK, the position is such that, in 1995, Britain's prospective Prime Minister flew to seek support for his political portfolio to News International's global executives in Australia. And so on. On the other hand, new technologies present considerable opportunities for civil society which perhaps could be encouraged to provide a measure of global public-service broadcasting not linked to commercial interests.[13] As is the case with so many aspects of the NWO, windows of opportunity appear in the crowded spaces occupied by the big hitters.

Globalisation undoubtedly creates opportunities for increased growth and wealth and will not be put into reverse. The problem for the public lawyer, among others, is first to understand it and then to seek to control it. We are at the edge of understanding, but it is likely that calling globalisation to account will involve action by a combination of national governments, regional groupings, citizens and global institutions. These will be discussed in turn, but it is encouraging to note how the British government has shown itself aware of the challenges. The most serious is that an open and rule-based trading system has critical implications for the environment, conditions at work and on human and animal welfare. To this end, the Government is committed to take a long term look at how best to maintain the momentum for an open trading system while achieving improvements in social, health, environmental and animal welfare standards. The acronym for these concerns is SHE.[14] The Report describes the task which falls to the UK Government to influence the international arena. The conclusions, which do credit to the Government, are drawn up in the clear understanding that they are only achievable for the most part within the framework of active membership of the European Union.

This approach closely followed that adopted by the Commission on Global Governance:

---

12 *Op cit*, Alexander, fn 4, p 249.

13 See *op cit*, Commission on Global Governance, fn 7, p 14.

14 Cabinet Office, *Rights of Exchange: Social, Health, Environmental and Trade Objectives on the Global Stage*, 2000, HMSO.

> Both the dynamism and the instability of the process of global economic integration are linked to the fact that it largely originates in the private sector. Future stability requires that a carefully crafted balance be struck, nationally and internationally, between the freedom of markets and the provision of public goods. The pace of globalization of financial and other markets is currently outstripping the capacity of governments to provide the necessary framework of rules and co-operative arrangements to ensure stability and prevent abuses of monopoly and other market failures. National solutions to such failures within a global economy are severely limited.[15]

Governments have learned that command and control systems of economic management do not work. But they have yet to develop, especially at a global level, effective, alternative tools of governance, although some see the WTO, which is nothing if not rule-based, as a sound beginning. Others are less sanguine. The problems are truly formidable:

> At a global level, what model of decision making should an emerging system of economic governance adopt? It will have to draw on lessons from regional and national levels and from business organizations where inflexible, centralized command-and-control structures have been shown to be unsustainable. Multilayered decision making systems are emerging that depend on consultation, consensus and flexible 'rules of the game'. Intergovernmental organizations, however, still face basic questions as to who should set the rules and according to what principles.[16]

This theme will be pursued shortly, but the Commission was clearly right in stating that without strong international rules, the most powerful countries will act unilaterally or, equally worryingly, the market will pursue its own relentless logic, regardless of the fall-out. After all, the complex of activities variously described as telecommunications, information or multimedia, automobile production, banking and other financial services are being developed on a multinational basis. Their concerns are necessarily with the totality of their business operations rather than with any one country. This is one of the reasons why the United Nations has called for tougher rules on global governance, including principles of performance for multinationals on labour standards, fair trade and environmental protection. It has demanded a global forum to bring together multinational corporations, trade unions, NGOs and governments to reinforce the trend towards ethical codes of conduct. It states that multinationals are too dominant in the world economy for voluntary codes to be enough. International codes of conduct should also be developed for banks and other financial institutions.[17]

---

15 *Op cit*, Commission on Global Governance, fn 7.

16 *Op cit*, Commission on Global Governance, fn 7.

17 UNDP, *The Human Development Report*, 1999, OUP.

What is manifestly clear – and this will be pursued at greater length shortly – is that there is a deficit in multilateral policy coherence; there is a plethora of players, but a paucity of recipes for global governance. Even on SHE issues, it is plain that there is no lead organisation which is capable of carrying the banner. Elsewhere, although, for example, the World Bank and the IMF have struck accords on matters of common interest, as has the World Bank and the WTO, linkages between even the big international organisations are at a formative stage. There is also, sadly, the usual evidence of turf wars between them. Perhaps the most important development so far in terms of co-operation and linkage is the Integrated Framework for Trade-related Technical Assistance to the Least Developed Countries (LDCs). This involves the World Bank, WTO, IMF, the ITC, UNCTAD and UNDP. It seeks to make assistance to LDCs more effective and efficient by laying down a mechanism for closer co-ordination of trade-related technical assistance activities. This agreement was adopted in 1997 and reviewed in 2000. There is now, also, a clear determination to make the agreement fit into a broad development context. It is intended to operate through a country-led process of defining national poverty reduction strategies. The review resulted in the creation of a steering committee comprising not only the six donors, but LDCs as well. This is aimed at ensuring 'greater transparency, more accountability and ownership'. The Bank is to lead the 'mainstreaming process' – that is, to funnel it into the development architecture – while UNDP manages the trust fund and the WTO acts as secretariat. This is a relatively isolated, though encouraging, development of the kind which is sorely needed if coherence and legitimacy are to be lent to the NWO. Other linkages are for the future. For example, it has been suggested that the Bank could link with the WTO by assisting developing countries in the preparation of WTO-consistent laws and regulations, providing technical expertise and training, the organisation of seminars and so on. However, at the moment, such initiatives are merely on the horizon.

Presently, the lack of coherence and legitimacy in the NWO is stark. Just a few of the problematics have been outlined by the UK Government. They are:

- the need for arrangements to ensure that developing countries are sufficiently involved in decisions on trade rounds;
- the need for processes for engaging wider civil society into WTO discussions and in the trade debate more broadly;
- the need for a more rational relationship between the WTO and other international organisations;
- the need to reform the WTO dispute settlement process, including its fairness and transparency;
- the need for mechanisms to enable governments and international institutions to be sufficiently joined-up at both the strategic and the tactical

levels to achieve good integration between trade and SHE issues in decisions.[18]

The main reason for the UK Government embarking on the *Rights of Exchange* project was the concern that the present global trading arrangements fail to give sufficient weight to improving labour standards, the environment and human health and animal welfare. Added to this is the suspicion that Whitehall departments and European Commission directorates general are insufficiently integrated on trade issues, on the environment and on health. Indeed, the same question can be usefully posed in relation to Whitehall itself, not least regarding initiatives by the voluntary sector.

The Report was clear that mechanisms for resolving conflicts between multilateral regimes and for settling disputes are needed, although no clear lines of advance have so far been offered. In suggesting that, in the short term, the development of WTO case law is the main mechanism available to improve coherence between trade and SHE objectives, it is probably rowing against the tide. On the other hand, its prescription for the longer term is mere tokenism: 'In the medium to long term, efforts to achieve SHE objectives should be negotiated in legitimate fora outside the WTO.'

However, there is much to be said for the suggestion that enhanced co-operation between the IMF, World Bank and the WTO needs to be extended to relations between the WTO and intergovernmental bodies with expertise in social, development, health and environmental issues. In encouraging international agreements relevant to SHE standards as examples of 'soft law' or non-binding international legal instruments, the Government is endorsing a Llewellyn-esque view of law, for which it should be congratulated. There is currently controversy and 'potential conflict' between the international trade regime and the international environmental policy regime which is littered with Multilateral Environmental Agreements. These conflicts can potentially extend to other areas of international policy making involving, for example, the International Labour Organisation (ILO) and the World Health Organisation. At the moment, the WTO rules appear to trump all other hands, as witness the celebrated 'banana' dispute between the EU and Latin-American importers.[19]

The Report goes on to say that, when two systems of law come into conflict, there are three potential ways of dealing with the situation:

- to determine that one legal system is superior to others (wholly or in part); which is very much where the WTO seems to be at the moment;
- to modify either or both legal systems to bring them into harmony; or
- to create a superior referral body.

18 *Op cit*, Cabinet Office, fn 14, pp 8–9.

19 *Op cit*, Cabinet Office, fn 14, p 147.

The second option has been rigorously pursued by the EU as part of its key objectives for the Millennium round of negotiations between WTO rules and MEAs. For the most part, this involves suggesting modifications of the WTO regime which, whatever its merits, appears to accept the *de facto* superiority of the WTO.

The Government's preferred option, at least in the long term, is for the creation of a superior mechanism for dispute settlement between multilateral agreements – *prima facie* of equal status. It would benefit both the multilateral trading system and international policy making in the SHE areas. Two options were suggested: joint dispute panels or extending the role of the International Court of Justice. The latter would have a grander legitimacy, although the Government does not envisage it as acting as a final appeal court, but rather in the capacity of an advisory body. This would be to adopt a suggestion that is over 50 years old. The 1948 Charter for the International Trade Organisation[20] provided that a member country prejudiced by a decision of the WTO could seek an advisory opinion from the ICJ, whose opinion would then bind the ITO. The creation of such a system now would be much more difficult than it would have been at the time, but nevertheless seems the right way forward.

A number of proposals for improving co-operation between International Governmental Organisations (IGOs) are on the table. Concern about improving coherence between environmental and trade policy led to the 1995 Marrakesh WTO ministerial decision to set up the Committee on Trade and the Environment within the WTO. There has, however, been a lack of progress by the Committee which, in any event, is under fire for the very fact of being a WTO body with its assumed preferences and prejudices. It is for this reason that there is strong support for a World Environment Organisation with comparable status to the WTO.[21] Were such a body to emerge, it is assumed that joint working arrangements with the WTO would be created. Environmental law is one of the world's fastest growth areas, with around 200 international agreements, but with no supreme body to oversee and resolve disputes, commitments can be broken.[22] However, it remains unlikely that such a body would receive support from a trade-minded US.

There is also potential conflict between the provisions governing the WTO and the World Health Organisation, but as yet there is no formal machinery to govern their relationships. However, the Directors General meet on a six-

20 The ITO was the intended third leg of the Bretton Woods agreement that was never adopted because of US opposition.

21 See, eg, Biermann, F, 'The case for a World Environment Organization' (2000) 42 Environment 23, pp 23–31, but see Juma, C, 'The perils of centralizing global environmental governance' (2000) 42 Environment 23, pp 44–45.

22 The United Nations Environmental Programme (UNEP), based in Nairobi, has existed only since 1974 and is the overall co-ordinating environmental organisation of the UN. Its mission is to provide leadership and encourage partnerships in caring for the environment. It has no enforcement powers.

monthly basis and there is currently a proposal for a joint working group on access to medicines.

The conflict of interests between trade and labour standards regularly makes the headlines but there is, as yet, little prospect of immediate institutional reform in this area. The EU has proposed a joint ILO/WTO working party on trade and labour while the International Confederation of Free Trade Unions has suggested improving coherence between trade and labour policy, including a joint WTO/ILO advisory body, social impact assessments of trade policy, and the inclusion of reports on labour standards in the WTO's trade policy reviews. The ILO already has a working party on the Social Dimension of Globalisation which includes the WTO, IMF, World Bank and UNCTAD.

There is little doubt that producing greater policy and dispute-settling coherence among the various IGOs would enhance the concept of a global rule of law considerably, and this is one of the clear entry points into any system for globalised justice. As *Rules of Exchange* argues forcefully, analysing and building upon the strengths of the various systems the IGOs have developed would improve decision making and would help build civil society confidence in the global governance system. The UK Government's recommendations, as follows, should be warmly embraced: the UK should:

> ... encourage greater collaboration and joint working between the WTO and IGOs responsible for SHE issues. This should include:
>
> - better links between the staff of the IGOs on a day-to-day basis for better awareness of each other's work and to be able to identify their wider impacts at an early stage;
> - co-operation between IGOs in new analytical work so that future policies are more likely to be based on an agreed diagnosis of the problems, and optimal solutions;
> - explicit work within IGOs before introducing substantial new policies to evaluate the bearing that they would have on the policies of other IGOs; and
> - consideration of the enforcement mechanisms employed by each organisation and their wider effects.

There is a clear need to encourage a greater commitment to transparency and the improved participation of developing countries and NGOs in the work of IGOs. The UK Government is committed to building support for increased co-operation between existing international environmental institutions in the short term, and in the light of that to keep under review the case for establishing a World Environmental Organisation in the long term.[23]

There are other initiatives aimed at breaking 'constitutional deadlock'. For example, the World Social Summit at Geneva in 2000 was the first ever session

23 *Op cit*, Cabinet Office, fn 14, p 128.

of the UN General Assembly outside New York, following on from an earlier social summit at Copenhagen five years earlier. Its primary purpose was to encourage development not just in terms of growth, but also of equity and to ensure that people, their cultures, societies and organisations are all taken into account in the process of development. Copenhagen had set out 10 commitments aimed at eradicating poverty, improving health and education and working towards full employment. The Swiss are actively seeking to promote the idea of international co-operation to develop agreed rules of the game. The ILO, the Bretton Woods institutions, the WTO, UNCTAD, together with other organisations and society in general should be encouraged to launch a multilateral initiative aimed at mounting investigations into development, poverty, trade and labour and developing an analytical framework for their policies.

Not only is there difficulty in co-ordinating the primary players into action, but there are genuine political differences among the several constituencies. Most notable amongst the antagonists are the WTO and many of the leading NGOs, as was clearly demonstrated at Seattle. The terms of world trade are clearly stacked against the third world. For example, the rich countries spend about $350 bn on agricultural support; enough, it is said, to fly their 41 million dairy cows around the world one and a half times. However, the first world countries claim that agriculture is 'multifunctional'; that is, there are non-trade concerns such as food safety, environmental protection and the livelihood of agrarian populations to be taken into account. According to the UN, the poor also stand to lose about $700 bn a year as a result of protectionist measures which penalise third world exporters. If these figures are correct, then the cost of protectionism to developing countries is 14 times as high as total aid flows to those countries, which amount to just $50 bn. Agriculture and textiles, for example, have not traditionally been covered by GATT rules, although there is now some movement on these issues.

The issue of environmental and labour standards has been touched on and will be returned to, but it is worth remarking that Art XX of GATT 1994 permits restrictions relating to the environment in appropriate conditions. Labour standards are, of course, not covered by GATT and the third world argues, for the most part, that the best way to ensure compliance with labour standards is to promote free trade and, hence, the welfare of developing countries.

The Bretton Woods institutions, for their part, have accused the NGOs of trying to save the poor from the process of development. There are core differences of opinion over a number of issues from agriculture through anti-dumping, labour standards and market access. Each of these differences involve different constituencies, making reaching a consensus quite daunting. The world is made up of interest blocs and altruism is a rare commodity – even in the case of the donor communities. For example, there is a strong suspicion that the US, for example, calculates quite carefully how far World Bank lending will benefit the UK economy. On the other hand, middle income countries, such as India, China, Brazil, and Argentina, sometimes join hands with countries such as Australia and New Zealand, but they are largely uninterested in the problems of G77 countries. In other words, there is a need to calculate in any particular case whether the parties to negotiations want them to succeed, given the interplay of different interests. There is also the suspicion that if one of the participants dislikes the particular forum in which they are operating, then they jump ship and join another one. The only way to overcome such problems is by a far greater degree of transparency than is usually apparent in global negotiations.

It will be necessary to return to the subject of NGOs shortly, but they are seen by some as the great white hope of cosmopolitan democracy, while for others their legitimacy is, at the least, called into question. Yet others regard them (and, of course, it is not helpful to throw a blanket over the wide range of organisations and interests flying under the NGO banner) as positively inimical to the interests of the LDCs. The Millennium Summit in New York in September 2000 looked to NGOs as a way of injecting much-needed civil society concerns into the deliberations of the MNCs and the leading industrial nations, and to this end there emerged a number of potentially important suggestions for institutional reform – not least of the UN itself. There is little doubt that single-issue organisations, in particular, can collect information and move forward debate and propaganda with considerable rapidity given the current state of modern technological developments. On the other hand, there are continuing problems in determining just who such organisations represent and how representative they in fact are.

Be all that as it may, their influence on the NWO can be charted by examining their relationships with the World Bank. The Bank has been subject to enormous criticism by some of the cutting edge NGOs, but the history of the Bank in recent times can be seen very much as the history of the development of global networks of NGOs. They have even been called in some quarters 'the third arm of government'. It is worth repeating that between 1973 and 1988, only 6% of Bank-financed projects involved NGOs. In 1993, the figures were over one-third and by 1994, over one-half. The Bank defines them as 'private organisations that pursue activities to relieve suffering, promote the interests of the poor, protect the environment, provide basic social services, or undertake community development'.[24] The Bank tends to interact with two main categories of NGO. The first group consists of operational NGOs whose primary purpose is the design and implementation of development-related projects; the second consists of those whose primary function is advocacy. These latter generally seek to promote or defend a

24 Operational Directive 14.70, World Bank, Washington DC.

specific cause and then seek to influence the practices and policies of the Bank. There is, of course, a great difference between international organisations and community-based groups. The latter are becoming the ones whose co-operation is most often sought by international organisations such as the World Bank. Institutionally, it may be added that the NGOs/Civil Society Thematic Forum is in the Social Development Family of the World Bank. The Bank's civil society team works in co-operation with its NGO Working Group whose 26 NGO members meet twice a year with senior Bank management as part of the NGO-World Bank Committee. The Working Group has instituted a more decentralised structure than formerly and it now operates through six regional groupings that seek to broaden effective participation by NGOs in dialogue with the Bank. During 2000, the Working Group helped to establish the International Forum on Capacity Building, which brings together NGOs, donors, and other agencies to share experience and develop more effective capacity-building strategies and approaches.

It will be important to examine the work of the Bretton Woods institutions more closely as the years go by, but there is some evidence that the Bank, in particular, is sloughing off some of the old ways in favour of 'customer-led' development. However, many of the criticisms levelled at it are trenchant, to say the least. Furthermore, some have taken the view that freeing up trade is infinitely more important than funding individual projects (especially on terms which the LDCs cannot afford). Others have objected to the conditions which have historically been attached to loans. Zambia is often cited as an example where loan conditions have insisted on cuts in State spending and the privatisation of services, the cumulative effects of which were said to have contributed to a 25% increase in infant mortality since the 1980s. The World Development Movement has been particularly critical and its documentation of assistance given to the developing countries protests that they can request whatever they like so long as it is neo-liberalism.[25] Two more items should be added to this side of the account. The first is that 63.7% of the votes of the Bank belong to the West. The second is that the Bank will not lend to a country which has fallen foul of the IMF, whose prescriptions for the developing world have, over the years, tended to produce, according to some, a one-size-fits-all approach to economic policy and development, based to a considerable extent on the free market economics prevalent in the 1980s and 1990s.

One of the 'constitutional' difficulties with the current stage of globalised development is the plethora of players and the inability of the outsider to observe clear institutional, transparent, linkages between leading partners. This will be stressed continuously. Co-operation agreements between the leading actors is therefore, in principle, to be welcomed. Clearly, the Bank and

---

25 See, eg, Monbiot, G (2000) *The Guardian*, 21 September.

the IMF have inevitably close links, but in 1997, the Bank reached a Co-operation Arrangement with the WTO. Co-operation between the Bretton Woods institutions is critical in order to reach the common objective of the three institutions for greater coherence in policy making. The agreement provides for consultation and exchange of views between the Bank and the WTO on all matters of common interest, improved communications between the two institutions through exchange and sharing of information, and the provision of observer status to the Bank and the WTO to attend meetings of each other's policy making bodies. Naturally, the Bank must be careful to observe the WTO's rules, particularly on subsidies when seeking to support, in particular, the LDCs.[26]

Some of the criticism of the Bank is justified, especially historically, and many of the problems for effective cosmopolitan democracy relate to the absence of the essential public law virtues, viz, transparency, freedom of information (FOI), natural justice, consultation and a general regime of accountability. However, to pursue the example of the World Bank for a moment, it is clear that much globalised activity is a movable feast. There is a mood in the organisation which indicates that its role is currently going through a sea change. Naturally, it is about development, but that has meant different things in different periods of its history. At first, it helped to rebuild Europe and its first loan of $250 m was to France in 1947 for postwar reconstruction. Reconstruction remained its central role for many years, but it is now a very different institution from that which shaped post-war Europe.

During the 1980s, the Bank was brought face to face with macro-economic and debt rescheduling issues; later in the decade, social and environmental issues came to the fore in the popular imagination, and an increasingly vocal civil society accused the Bank of not observing its own policies in some high profile cases. As a result, the Bank instituted several reforms, including the creation of an Inspection Panel to investigate claims of impropriety or maladministration against the Bank. Since then, it has moved into civil society, social development and institutional reform. The current position being adopted is that economic growth remains crucial to the developing world, but is not sufficient to create conditions in which the poorest can improve their lives. The Annual Report for 2000 recommends that developing country government at all levels, donor countries, international agencies, NGOs, civil society and local communities all mobilise behind three priority areas:

26 Historically, there have been few formal linkages between UNEP and the WTO, although issues of trade and environment are clearly closely interrelated. More recently, constructive meetings have taken place between the two organisations. See, eg, WTO Committee on Trade and Environment, UNEP Statement at the Informational Session with MEAs, 7 July 2000, WT/CTE/W/155. For the necessary connections between trade and the environment, see UNEP and IISA, *Environment and Trade: A Handbook*, 2000, IISD.

opportunity, empowerment and security. Global action needs to complement national and local initiatives to achieve maximum benefit for the poor ...:

> It (the Bank) ... has deepened still further over the last decade its commitment to fighting poverty. It has shifted the structure of what it does. The balance has shifted towards health and education, for example, and it has changed the way it does things.[27]

The Bank has travelled across a development spectrum over the years; after the initial years of reconstruction, the journey went from privatisation/environment/anti-corruption/judicial and legal reform. At the moment, their emphasis is very much on the last-mentioned, recognising that money without stable institutions and a facilitative legal order will prove inadequate. Indeed, matters like competition and banking law are high on their list of concerns. Even more significant, perhaps, is the move to customer ownership of projects.

The Bank's present dilemmas sum up many of the problems which illustrate the difficulties of tracing the outlines of a Global Constitution. For instance, it can be asked whether the Bank should even try to operate everywhere, or whether it should find out who is doing what, where, and seek to support them. It needs to work more closely with the UN agencies, but the larger problem, perhaps, is how different institutional cultures work together, which is why the Bank is actively seeking out partnerships – not least with NGOs at the regional level. What is needed at this time is more empirical work in the form of observing global activities at a number of different levels, and to study the dynamics of governments, the private sector and so on, since events these days can proceed very swiftly. There are invariably turf battles and personality clashes, while individual governments will push hard on certain issues and suppress others, and will, therefore, look for partnership audiences. At present, we know too little about how these things work on the ground and how far problem solving mechanisms can be improved, although there is no doubt that the Bank's Inspection Panel is a move in the right direction.

One more reference to the World Bank before making a change of direction. There has been a feeling within the Bank over the years that supported projects were too short term and have been insufficiently co-ordinated. The result has been to introduce the *Comprehensive Development Framework*, which adopts a holistic approach to development.[28] The documents made available so far indicate that the new arrangements are reasonably comprehensive and interlocking in so far as they highlight the interdependence of all aspects of development: – social, structural, human,

27 N Stern (Chief Economist, World Bank) at press conference in Washington DC, 12 September 2000 and World Bank, *Attacking Poverty*, Stern, World Development Report 2000/2001.

28 Eg, such a framework document has recently been introduced between the Bank and the Government of Bolivia.

governance, environmental, financial and economic. They also emphasise partnerships among governments, donors and third parties (note that the donor community is frequently multilateral). For example, in the former Soviet Union, other donors have, from time to time, included USAID, CIDE, GTZ, the European Development Bank and the Asian Development Bank. The World Bank has, however, frequently expressed the view that resources were not being adequately integrated or co-ordinated.[29]

Under the new arrangements, the borrowing country is now supposed to be in the lead in both owning and directing the development agenda, with the Bank and other partners each defining their support for the respective plans. Of course, things do not always run that smoothly; some countries, for example, are relatively supine and are content to be led by the nose, while others may play one donor off against another, thus making integration extremely difficult. However, the CDF remains a promising initiative, which needs to be closely monitored, not least by public lawyers. The arrangements now being put in place are increasingly long term and recognise the importance of macro-economic fundamentals, but seek to give equal weight to the other issues mentioned above. A range of countries – largely, but not entirely, South American and African – have been offered CDFs. They have, thus far, been self-selecting governments who were made clearly aware of the terms on which a CDF was offered.

One more initiative may be mentioned at this point. It is the Development Committee, a joint ministerial committee of the Bank and the IMF, and at its September 1999 meeting it endorsed proposals that Poverty Reduction Strategies be prepared by national authorities, in close collaboration with Bank and Fund staff, in all low income countries receiving support from the IDA and ESAF.

The Bretton Woods organisations are clear about the need to change their organisational and, indeed, ideological habits. However, it is vital that their activities are monitored by bodies with the authority and legitimacy necessary for any independent auditor. This suggests the United Nations, of which more later.

So far, we have barely scratched the surface of the NWO. It is now time to move in a different direction.

THE NEW FACE OF CAPITAL CONFIGURATIONS AND PUBLIC/PRIVATE PARTNERSHIPS

A little has been said about MNCs, and there is more to say. However, as noted in earlier chapters, there are even more significant developments afoot

29 See, eg, World Bank, *Initiatives in Legal and Judicial Reform*, 2000, World Bank.

these days than the raw power of MNCs. The 'trillion dollar enterprise' is here and now and possesses enormous potential for good and for ill.

Let us start with oil. The network of alliances and relationships which take on the development and exploration of oil around the world are truly trillion dollar enterprises. A number of independent companies act increasingly as a unit, or a single enterprise, as they undertake huge, multiyear 'bet the ranch' projects. Frequently, the venture will continue for years:

> These new enterprises are becoming the rule, rather than the exception, as customers, suppliers, unregulated companies, and even competitors join together to accomplish big, expensive and risky jobs in the oil industry as well as in telecommunications, aerospace, and elsewhere.
>
> ... companies were struggling to deal with a business world that was irreversibly globalizing, just as nations were forming blocs and protecting their borders. The development of huge enterprises linking independent countries together was the solution developed by business – in the main unwittingly – to deal with these two incompatible forces.[30]

Freidheim is in do doubt about the potentially Frankensteinian nature of the creatures which are being brought into being:

> The potential power of a trillion dollar enterprise to sidestep laws, create cartels, dominate industries, and overrun sovereign nations is great. Its size and economic power could easily translate into political power, but could also spur massive economic development. The possibility of a new form of cultural imperialism is clear, as consumers across the world buy and adapt to products, media, and entertainment from these global giants.[31]

These giants will be the product of acquisitions, joint ventures and alliances of all kinds. They are not the conglomerates of the 1970s and 1980s that attempted to gain stability by diversifying risk and spreading their investments over separate businesses. Rather, these enterprises focus all their resources on dominating one, or a few, fields. They will restructure whole industries, and turn the basis of competition upside down.

In preceding decades, mergers and acquisitions have been the primary vehicles for this kind of consolidation. Today, alliances will play a major role in the consolidation of industries, in part because of the global corporation:

> Consolidation on a global scale is very expensive, and often the global corporation must make major compromises in the selection of acquisition partners because of cost or national restrictions (for example, on making purchases in the airlines, defense and oil industries). Hence, many of the best prizes are simply unavailable. The relationship enterprise slides by these limitations and goes directly to the best in any country with an offer to form an alliance with its crown jewel; no size problems, nor national restrictions, no

30 Freidheim, C, *The Trillion Dollar Enterprise*, 1998, Perseus, p x.

31 *Ibid*, p xiii.

> anti-trust, no funding limitations, just a strong relationship with the prime cut of the best company.
>
> The relationship enterprise is a network of such alliances that operates as a single company in selected key areas. It is consolidation without huge investment, battles over ownership, post-merger headaches, and regrets. The investment dollars can go into building market positions, new products, capacity, and capabilities for the enterprise rather than for shares of an acquired company. The relationship enterprise is a natural evolution, a consequence of the political and economic forces of our time.[32]

This evolution is a natural product of industrial globalisation and political polarisation. It stems from the need to capture the economies of scale and the scope of consolidation without the baggage and limitations of acquisitions and mergers. It stems from the historic drive of corporate leaders to overcome whatever obstacles lay in the way of their growth and progress. Of course, the major US car makers began co-operating in the 1970s and early 1980s by co-funding research to solve environmental problems – first, with catalytic converters and later, with the development of the electric car, but since that time, relational enterprises have grown exponentially and tend to operate more like a political federation than a business alliance.[33]

A principal advantage of the relationship enterprise is that it is on home turf almost everywhere, which dramatically reduces the impact of regulation and trade barriers. To the extent that an industry has restrictive and varying regulations and significant trade barriers, the relationship enterprise is likely to be built around those restrictions. Regulatory changes in areas such as telecommunications and utilities, changes in competition or anti-trust laws and a major new technology are all other sparks that may lead to the final stage of the relationship enterprise, in which networks of companies begin to act as a single entity in important areas.

All this raises significant accountability concerns. It is well known that, in Anglo-Saxon law at least, shareholder power has been heavily circumscribed in recent years, but when boards of directors go multinational to reflect the new arrangements, accountability seems to be even further out of the loop. To meet these concerns, Freidheim has suggested either International Advisory Boards, and/or Enterprise Boards.[34] Furthermore, he has canvassed the notion of further international organisations along the lines of the WTO, such as a world currency board or world aviation authority. Even more important, and a suggestion which is by no means new, is an International Competition Authority. Again, there is no other single body with the moral authority of the United Nations which could legitimately be charged with taking some of these ideas forward. As will be argued, those who see an effective democratic

32 *Op cit*, Freidheim, fn 30, p 2.

33 And see the Japanese Keiretsu in *op cit*, Freidheim, fn 30, pp 69–73.

34 *Op cit*, Freidheim, fn 30, pp 187–98.

response to the problems of globalisation being solely the preserve of the UN are almost certainly wrong; but its authority has undoubtedly to be reinforced. Part of the problem, however, is that at this time we have yet to conduct a successful mapping of the labyrinthine decision making processes of the NWO. Partnerships are now beginning to be critically examined in a national setting, but they are equally fashionable and equally important in the global arena. However, by no means all of them rise frequently above the observational parapet.

The first aim, according to Charter '99, is to make the already existing processes of world administration and governance accountable. There is a need to know what decisions are being taken by whom and why. On top of this, any decision making processes need to be informed by basic principles of respect for the principles of equality, human rights and justice, including social and economic justice. The task is clear:

> We therefore call on you to create effective mechanisms to hold every agency of actual world government to account. These include international economic alliances, military alliances, the central banking system and agencies for environmental, financial ... or other activity. All should have to answer regularly for what they have done and what they intend to do, for their impact on the world community and for their adherence to the UN Charter and international law.[35]

Correctly, they ask where we should start. The view taken here is that this a complex question with no clear answers and that institutional and substantive reform will need to take place at various interlocking levels: the UN, regional groupings (and, in particular, the EU), international labour organisations, industry – especially at the sectoral level – national governments, NGOs and a range of international organisations, both formal and informal. There is no straightforward recipe at this stage, but there is the possibility of working across a range of reinforcing positions. Charter '99 adopts a more hierarchical approach, with the UN very much at the heart of the needed reform process. While accepting a central position for the UN, it is nevertheless doubtful that all energies should be concentrated there. However, its crucial position will be reconsidered shortly.

It is not currently easy to determine lines of accountability in the NWO. The boundaries are blurred, and it is not clear where the process of international networking is leading. However, even though it is unclear where the new boundaries between nations, global business and international institutions are to be drawn, it is becoming ever more obvious that these latter bodies – so often cast as the enemy of national sovereignty – have become the vehicle by which States will seek to reclaim their sovereignty. Taxation is a case in point. The mobility of capital and labour undermines the ability of

35 Charter '99, *A Charter for Global Democracy*, 1999, Charter '99. The military aspects of globalisation are deliberately excluded here.

individual nations to set their own tax levels. The internet is further eroding that autonomy. Correspondingly, in order to preserve national freedom of action, governments will increasingly have to set multilateral rules.

Let us now return to the issue of partnerships. Nation States and regional and international organisations all feel the need to enter into partnerships directed at re-asserting political control over the global agenda. It is to be hoped that the UN will assume greater influence in terms of regulating the practices of corporations and assisting Member States to reassert control. At the same time, both the UN, national and local communities and regional and international organisations need to encourage the promulgation of voluntary codes, agreements and compacts. In particular, strong partnerships should be developed with the private sector at national and international level to combat poverty in all its aspects. These partnerships should also include consumers themselves. The lead organisation will vary as, for example, the WHO in relation to the Roll Back Malaria campaign or the UN itself in the case of the Global Compact with the private sector. As Kofi Annan, the Secretary General of the UN has indicated, the UN's involvement with global policy networks has been extensive, but largely unplanned. What is needed is a more focused and systematic approach. It is necessary to determine how best to help governments, civil society and the private sector to work together to ensure that policy networks succeed in achieving desired social, economic and environmental objectives. The position of NGOs as such will be reserved for a later section.

It has already been noted how dependent the World Bank is becoming on partnerships at the local level, and it should perhaps be stressed that, just as the Bank will seek out or respond to potential partners, so the host government will also frequently be in the best position to suggest partners on the ground which can add value to the Bank's efforts. The UK Government, too, has determined on a more concerted strategy to explain its position on SHE issues, in particular, to other countries, and to ensure that sympathetic groups within those countries have an opportunity to have their voice heard. This could be planned as a medium term strategy, taking particular account of major multilateral negotiations expected to come up over the next few years.[36] This observation reinforces the claims already made about the need to operate upon a number of reinforcing fronts and at a number of levels to deliver on expectations of a cosmopolitan democratic nature, to say nothing of pursuing international obligations in the field of human rights.

Kofi Annan's Special Report for the Millennium Assembly and Summit in 2000 was thought by some to be short on concrete proposals for democratic revival. Instead, there is a plea for 'healthy and balanced economic development, combined with human rights, minority rights and political

36 *Op cit*, Cabinet Office, fn 14, p 83.

arrangements in which all groups are fairly represented'. One of the more interesting proposals, however, was that for the UN to develop 'networking for change'. This would involve supplementing formal institutions with informal policy networks, bringing together international institutions, civil society and private sector organisations and national governments in pursuit of common goals. However, the proposal is short on detail; perhaps inevitably so at this point in time.[37] Perhaps a better place to start would be to trace the networks which currently exist, and to seek to indicate the more obvious gaps, as well as to highlight best practices.

Elsewhere, *Rights of Exchange* makes clear that one of the actions necessary to be taken by the UK Government for influencing the international arena is to develop partnerships with other stakeholders in developing countries to ensure shared ownership of SHE standards.[38] This is almost certainly unexceptionable, as is some broader attempt to incorporate genuinely representative NGOs into the international decision process. What is more insidious, perhaps, is that there are interest groups already penetrating the NWO whose activities are less open than one would hope from major players.

We are not yet in a position to unravel globalised activity sufficiently well to identify all the strands, and yet there are more players than will be singled out here. However, a few appear particularly influential while insufficiently exposed either at national, regional or international levels to be seen to be operating in a way which genuinely reflects the international commonweal, if such a creature can be imagined. Let us start with the planned acceleration of the EU's free market agenda eastwards and its implications for the environmental and social conditions of the continent.

A key driver has, of course, been the corporate sector, and in particular the little-known European Round Table of Industrialists (ERT). This consists of up to 45 'captains of industry' from large European MNCs. Virtually unnoticed, the ERT has played a central role in the shaping of the single market, the Maastricht Treaty, and, more recently, the single currency. For them, enlargement offers an enormous market, as well as a reservoir of cheap skilled labour. It has also to be said that market enlargement across the world has often been at the cost of environmental and social conditions, not least in central and eastern Europe. Caroline Lucas, a Green MEP, has taken Slovak Railways as a case in point. In 1998, the Slovak government announced a halving of the 50,000 staff in the rail sector, the country's biggest employer. The next year it signed a loan agreement with the European Investment Bank which resulted in a massive cut in State subsidies, a 30% rise in fares, and scaling back the railway network (all to the advantage of the global automobile industry, one would imagine). The EIB has since announced that

37 Annan, K, *We the Peoples: The Role of the UN in the 21st Century*, 11 April 2000, UN.

38 *Ibid*, p 207.

the agreement mirrors those agreed between the Bank and virtually every other railway company in eastern Europe and other applicant countries. This may or may not be desirable, but it is the influence of the 'inside trackers' that is worrying, as is the lack of general debate and transparency in such proceedings.

The drive towards expansion of the EU to the East, and the terms on which the expansion has occurred, means that Western MNCs have been gobbling up not just railways, but banking, motor manufacturing and brewing businesses. General Electric, too, has globalised its operations by shifting production to low wage countries, including Eastern Europe. One company director, according to Lucas, has remarked that 'ideally you'd have every plant on a barge' – ready to be towed away elsewhere if national governments attempt to impose constraints or if workers demand better wages and conditions.

This is why, no doubt, there were so many protesters at the EU summit in Nice in December 2000 who opposed the EU's present emphasis of restructuring and enlarging in pursuit of further globalisation. Others, including Lucas, have called for the protection and rebuilding of local communities and economies in a way that encourages maximum social and environmental sustainability. As Lucas remarks:

> The choice facing decision makers in Nice is to pursue ever more deregulated trade and investment in an EU which sees itself as nothing other than a giant supermarket of 500 m consumers or to adopt a more ambitious vision of a Europe of genuine stability and cooperation, based on rebuilding sustainable local economies.[39]

Now, these are grand arguments which require delicate analysis and appropriate outcomes which would challenge the wisdom of Solomon, but it is clear that the EU does not yet satisfy the tests of true democratic sentiments, especially in terms of its lack of transparency and consultation procedures on important issues. The preceding arguments in this essay, directed largely at the domestic level, which plead for subsidiarity and the further enfranchisement of local communities, apply equally across the rest of the world. Sadly, the NWO currently appears to be moving in the opposite direction, in spite of the best recent efforts of the World Bank.

There are other informal networks which appear to wield extraordinary influence, if not power. Gregory Palast, writing in *The Observer*,[40] stated:

> ... the next meeting of the New World Order will be held next Tuesday at the Swiss Hotel in Brussels at 9 am. This is the mid-year meeting of the Transatlantic Business Dialogue – and you aren't invited.

39 Lucas, C, From Seattle to Nice, 2001, website: carolinelucas@greenmeps.org.uk.

40 21 May 2000.

Palast was able to access information under the US Freedom of Information Act which described how the US Trade Secretary briefed the new British Government Trade and Industry Minister after the 1997 election (none of which information would be disclosed under the UK FOI Act 2000). He was alleged to have dictated a list of four changes in UK law and policy required to smooth the path of American corporations in Britain. Further guidance was to be provided by the most influential business group 'advising' government on US–EU relations – the Transatlantic Business Dialogue (TABD). This is a working group of the West's 100 most powerful chief executives. When presidents and prime ministers meet at the WTO, this more permanent grouping provides the agenda, at least according to Palast.

The TABD procedures pair one major US industrialist with his counterpart in Europe for each sector grouping. For example, Monsanto's Robert Harness and Unilever's Huib Vigeveno are in charge of agri-biotech. The US and the EU then assign an official/public servant to each industry pair. TABD enjoys privileged access to such figures as Pascal Lamy, European Commissioner for Trade, and Erkki Liikanen, Commissioner for Enterprise and the Information Society. At their May 2000 meeting, the officials were reported to be about to brief the corporate duos on the headway they made on the 33 items on the current TABD implementation table. This lists 33 environment, consumer and worker protection laws in selected nations which TABD wishes to defeat or water down. The agenda which emerges – including agenda items for the WTO – would then have been put to Presidents Clinton and Prodi at the summit meeting in Portugal a month later.

The so called 'implementation table', one of the first documents grudgingly conceded under the EU access to information rules, describes the need to expand the Mutual Recognition Agreement (MRA) which TABD describes as 'approved once, accepted everywhere'. Take, for example, GM products. The MRA rules for these are extraordinarily complex and disingenuous. They apply, in effect, only to the developing nations. If Brazil, for example, has objections to Monsanto's growth hormones, it will be to no avail, since the relevant WTO committee's approval means acceptance of the product or facing WTO trade sanctions. Even the US is a target for TABD's disregard for consumer protection.

Since then, *Rights of Exchange* tells a somewhat different story; this is, of course, post-Seattle 1999. Under its discussion of 'Civil society dialogue on trade issues', the UK Government lists the 'Trans-Atlantic Economic Partnership' (TAEP), which appears to encompass TABD. The Government's own description is very different.

The TAEP is described as a forum for the US Administration and the EU to discuss trans-atlantic trade issues and has four civil society 'dialogues' attached to it. These are the business dialogue (TABD), the consumer dialogue (TACD), the environment dialogue (TAED) and the labour dialogue (TALD).

Each dialogue brings together organisations on both side of the Atlantic to discuss and agree positions on issues of common concern. Meetings (or parts of meetings) are attended by representatives of the US and EU administrations so that there is direct feed in and exchange of views between the dialogues and officials.

According to the Report, the Directorate General for Trade has developed a range of mechanisms for consulting civil society groups which include open meetings, Commissioner Lamy's Contact Group and issue groups. The open meetings with the Commissioner take place twice a year and are open to all European civil society groups. The Contact Group has 12 members representing civil society interests – industry, agriculture, environment, labour and development – and meets with the Commissioner twice a year. The issue groups are forums for detailed discussions of trade-related topics. Currently, there are four groups – agriculture, services, trade and health, and trade, environment and sustainable development. They are chaired by Commission officials and bring together representatives of civil society groups for detailed discussions of specific issues such as the precautionary principle, TRIPs and food security and multifunctionality.[41]

The feeling, however, is that TABD is the dominant player and yet once more there is no clear 'access' to it in administrative law terms. It boasts a website and makes public a number of working documents and seeks out public opinion on a range of matters. However, it describes itself thus:

> The Trans-atlantic Business Dialogue (TABD) offers an effective framework for enhanced cooperation between the trans-atlantic business community and the governments of the European Union (EU) and the United States (US).
>
> It is an *informal* process whereby European and American companies and business associations *develop* joint EU–US trade policy recommendations, working together with the European Commission and the US Administration.[42] (Emphasis added.)

It is precisely the 'emphases' that need further airing. The author's instinct is that TABD is a genuinely big hitter in the NWO which needs further exposure.

There are other global elites which are too numerous to mention here, although a flavour might indicate the complexity of the global order. See, for example, Alexander:

> Considerable credit for the consistency of policies across the West is due to think-tanks such as the Council on Foreign Relations, the Bilderburg Group and the Trilateral Commission. Members of these groups influenced critical moments in Western development, helping to create the League of Nations,

41 TAFP has now ceased to function through lack of funding.

42 www.tabd.com/tabd.html.

> British Commonwealth, the United Nations, Treaty of Rome, NATO and G7 summits. Funding for these groups was almost entirely from charitable bodies set up by corporations such as Carnegie ... Chase Manhattan Bank, Ford and Rockefeller. In 1976 more than half of the world's 115 largest corporations and banks were represented on the Trilateral Commission.[43]

And so on. There are many more elite networks whose influence has been barely charted.

THE ROLE OF NATIONAL GOVERNMENTS

Where does globalisation leave national governments? The answer is not easy to give, but it is clear that an enormous amount can be done by governments both jointly and severally. In April 2000, Kofi Annan released his report in preparation for the Millennium Assembly and Summit. His emphasis was somewhat different from that of Charter '99 which expects, according to many, too much from the UN as presently constituted, dominated as it is by the larger countries, and especially the US. Annan stressed the need for the powers of Nation States to be strengthened. They can, he argued, draw strength from each other by acting within common institutions based on shared rules and values. Bowing to the practical – and avoiding the ideal – he warned against neglecting the realities of the distribution of existing power. The existing institutions should serve as an arena for States to co-operate with non-State actors, including global companies. In many cases, they need to be complemented by less formal policy networks which can respond quickly to the changing social agenda. In other words, quite apart from the effects of their own autonomous actions (for example, in the field of human rights), Nation States can and should combine with others to affect desired outcomes.

There is little doubt that the pace of globalisation means that the Nation State is increasingly constrained in its freedom of action, although the US remains very much *primus inter pares*. However, it is premature to write it off. Although the future will necessitate greater co-operation if democratic ideals are to be vindicated, there is a great deal that the Nation State can contribute to the larger ideal of global enfranchisement.

In early 2000, Barclays Bank announced the closure of large numbers of UK outlets, particularly in rural communities. It is evident that this network is an essential building block of many local communities, so that closure is not simply an issue for shareholders. Indeed, the newly established Welsh Assembly in Cardiff immediately announced its intention to move its bank account elsewhere. Too many countries, the UK included, have failed to reform national company law to embrace the concerns of a wide variety of

43 *Op cit*, Alexander, fn 4, pp 206 *et seq*.

stakeholders. The annual publication of a social audit stating policies towards the workforce, community, customers, and the environment could be a legal requirement for a company being listed on the stock exchange. Although the EU has notably failed so far to introduce a Community-wide company law statute, Germany has shown what can be done to protect the interests of the social partners. So also, oddly it may seem, has the US. There, the Community Reinvestment Act bars closing a bank branch unless the bank can prove to the satisfaction of the Federal Reserve or the courts that it will continue to look after the community's banking needs. Indeed, in October 1999, President Clinton refused to sign a financial deregulation Bill until the Senate removed provisions intended to weaken the Act. Over the years, banks have been forced to commit over four trillion dollars to not-for-profit loan funds when seeking merger approvals or branch relocations. Added to this, the US Security and Exchange Commission makes a greater demand for information disclosure from publicly listed companies than is the case in most countries. This information includes information on environmental impact. The Swedish Government has recently produced guidelines for environmental performance reporting for Swedish companies quoted on the Stockholm stock exchange. Similar disclosure requirements are being discussed in most countries of the EU. The necessity to please MNCs at all costs can be resisted. The leading industrial States remain major players whose genuine interests will be ignored at their peril.

Although environmental regulation for a sustainable future needs action on the international front, individual governments can also have a vital influence. As well as strengthening conventional regulation, they can also create a regime where many environmental costs are internalised. Companies can receive a mix of positive incentives and tough penalties to achieve environmental performance. The World Business Council for Sustainable Development (WBCSD), in its 1998 *Challenge Brief*, recommended improved research to improve the efficiency with which energy is used. Government was encouraged to support and accelerate this process since inadequate market incentives and the long payback of such research seldom provides sufficient attraction for business. Governments should build policies on properly designed market-based approaches, eliminate counterproductive subsidies and establish incentives for exploring and promoting highly efficient techniques.

Governments such as those of the UK have been less than bold in encouraging social and environmental initiatives by the business community. The Blair government has failed to address social finance issues or to look actively at tax regimes which support environmentally sound policies. The odd socially conscious business seems to survive in spite of (the lack of) government support. For example, the Triodos Bank, founded in The Netherlands in 1980, and which came to the UK in 1995, is a prime example of a 'social' bank. Its borrowers must be socially, ethically and environmentally sound. The Bank does important business with organic farmers and food companies, wind farms and other renewable energy businesses, social and community organisations. It is, of course, very small in comparison to the Barclays of this world, but the big banks could usefully be cajoled, encouraged and even bullied into more responsible behaviour.

The beginnings of concern by the UK Government are, however, capable of being detected, granted that this has come about largely as a result of its wish to address relative economic and industrial failure. For example, the Chancellor of the Exchequer, Gordon Brown, has expressed concern about the City of London's failure to invest in Britain's manufacturing sector. This has led to a review of institutional investment which will identify accounting, regulatory and legal issues. In his view, too little funding has been invested in venture capital, with inevitable effects on the progress of manufacturing industry. Mr Brown expressed the view that: 'We believe that the City should serve the interests of the wider economy and those are not being served.'[44] The Government-backed review of the pension fund industry was put to a breakfast meeting of 25 major investors from the US and Europe by Mr Brown. He remarked that, although the Government had no intention of second-guessing investment decisions, it foresaw a role in removing any distortions created by structural or regulatory factors.

Governments must increasingly formulate domestic policy in a global context, but they retain a considerable degree of autonomy. Although governments need to act to attract investment – not least in the new technologies – through transport and infrastructure, regulatory reform and trade liberalisation – the reverse side of the deal should be responsive and responsible behaviour from business. Indeed, government/industry partnerships are actively encouraged by the OECD, especially in the area of corporate governance.[45] The OECD's *Guidelines for Multinational Enterprises* has been mentioned in Chapter 8, but it is accompanied by a document on the *Implementation of National Contact Points* which stresses that, although the enterprises are themselves responsible for observing the Guidelines in their day to day behaviour, the responsibility lies on national governments in furthering the Guidelines' goals by offering guidance for the conduct and activities of National Contact Points and by encouraging more follow up of their activities and opening them up to peer review through annual meetings and better oversight by CIME.[46]

44 (2000) *The Guardian*, 8 May.

45 See, eg, OECD, *Corporate Governance: Improving Competitiveness and Access to Capital in Global Markets*, 1998, OECD.

46 This is the OECD's Committee on International Investment and Multinational Enterprises, which provides a forum for consultation, clarification and review of the role and functioning of the Guidelines.

There are genuine difficulties in regulating in the public interest when global capital is so footloose and when, for example, industry headquarters are situated outside the boundaries of the regulating State. To return to the issue of the failed proposal to merge the London Stock Exchange and the German Bourse. Although the combination would have traded more than half of Europe's stocks, its turnover would still fall below the European Union competition threshold. Protecting the public interest, then, would fall to the Financial Services Authority in London and the Federal Securities Supervisory Office in Frankfurt. While it is perfectly possible to expect some degree of co-operation between the two agencies, things would become more difficult with the joining, say, of the Spanish and Italian exchanges, to say nothing of the anticipated European appearance of Nasdaq. At that point, the European Union would need to offer a regional response. That, in turn, would require the Union to adopt more transparent and accountable processes than have characterised its conduct so far.[47]

All this produces a seeming paradox. As national autonomy wanes, so international action at the level of politics becomes significant. Even so, national governments can often give a lead as soon as they recognise the nature of their dilemma. Even when they are to some extent disempowered, it is still important for them to relate more directly and forcefully to their electorates.

Similarly, *The Challenge Brief* had reported that at the national and local level there are growing demands for governance that satisfies some basic standards. Increasingly, they believed, frustration with governance on the national and international level will raise the expectations at the local level. There is near unanimity here, for the Commission on Global Governance had called for reform of governance within societies, for decentralisation, for new forms of participation, and for the wider involvement of people than traditional democratic systems have allowed.[48]

Rights of Exchange represents a running commentary on responsibilities and opportunities on and for national governments to influence the growing globalisation process. One of the simplest inputs is to ensure that mechanisms exist to enable governments and international institutions to be sufficiently joined up at both the strategic and tactical levels to achieve good integration between trade and SHE issues. The Government also recognises that national governments can do much to raise domestic SHE standards without coming into conflict with international trade rules and can encourage voluntary action by business in addressing those standards. It also accepts that, to the extent that voluntary initiatives are demonstrably effective in achieving better SHE

47 Currently, the UK is isolated in opposing a pan-European financial services regulator; see, eg, (2000) *The Guardian*, 17 July.

48 *Ibid*, p 17.

outcomes, it makes sense to support them through its own procurement practices. Current guidance to departments, and where relevant to the wider public sector, should therefore be reviewed taking into account current developments in EU and broader international obligations:

> The UK Government should adopt a more integrated approach to CSR[49] across departments including on international issues. This should be based on a review of the level of Government support needed to enable voluntary initiatives to work effectively to achieve desirable SHE outcomes and to create wider incentives for participation. It should also be informed by further research into the impact of voluntary initiatives on SHE outcomes.[50]

It should also be remembered that WTO rules allow national governments sufficient discretion to regulate many SHE issues, not least in the field of protection of human health and safety. Furthermore, the Government takes the view that when there are trans-boundary SHE spillover effects, multilateral agreements are the best option and should be vigorously sought. A decision then has to be made about whether trade or non-trade instruments, or a combined package, are most appropriate. If multilateral instruments cannot be negotiated or are ineffective, then voluntary initiatives and national level (externally focused) instruments are the second-best options.

The UK should, of course, be pressing the EU to take action over SHE issues and, in any event, should adopt a more concerted strategy to explain its concerns to other countries and to ensure that sympathetic groups, including NGOs, within those countries have an opportunity to have their voice heard:

> This could be planned as a medium-term strategy, taking particular account of major multilateral negotiations expected to come up over the next few years.[51]

At this point, mention must be made of the work of the Department for International Development. In December 2000, it produced its second report on globalisation.[52] The controversial Report underlined the arguments being made here quite strikingly:

> ... developing countries need an efficient private sector and effective government, alongside strong international institutions, focused on the systematic reduction of poverty. And we need to work together to reduce conflict and corruption, boost investment in education and health, spread the benefits of modern technology and reduce barriers to trade.

It went on to make a number of specific announcements, indicating just how much there is left for national governments to do in a global world. The main ones are as follows:

---

49 Corporate Social Responsibility.

50 *Op cit*, Cabinet Office, fn 14, p 13.

51 *Op cit*, Cabinet Office, fn 14, p 83.

52 DFID, *Eliminating World Poverty: Making Globalisation Work for the Poor*, WP 2/01.

- All aid from the UK will be spent on goods and services which provide the best quality and service at the best price. The practice of using aid on condition that a proportion of the goods and services are from the UK will end with effect from 1 April 2001.
- A new Africa Trade and Poverty Programme is to be launched to provide technical support for national governments and regional organisations in Sub Saharan Africa. This could include advice and assistance on complying with WTO rules.
- Also to be launched is a new Infrastructure Financing Facility for Africa to complement the DFID initiated World Bank facility to encourage Public-Private investment in infrastructure.
- It will importantly establish a Commission to examine ways in which intellectual property rules need to develop to take greater account of the interests of developing countries.
- It is to support a 50% increase to the Global Environmental Facility – the mechanism which helps developing countries to address global environmental objectives – and encourage others to do the same.

The UK Government has also sought to ensure that development policy is integrated into areas of UK policy through the establishment of an interdepartmental working group on development. All this has been greatly assisted by the higher profile which the DFID has gained through Cabinet status. Examples of joint government action include:

- debt relief with the Treasury;
- core labour standards with the DfEE;
- security sector reform with MoD and FCO;
- joint work with the DTI on a 'development round' for the WTO ministerial meetings;
- the export credit guarantee review.

The Government's commitments to co-ordinating trade and SHE standards are already well known. The new Report strikes a positive and innovative note:

> DTI, in consultation with other relevant departments, should produce an integrated strategy for promoting domestic and international corporate social responsibility and consider appropriate cross-cutting objectives and targets for departments. This should include action to promote best practice in relation to global supply chains and operations in developing countries ...[53]

There are numerous ways, therefore, that individual nations can affect the global commons for good or ill. At the one extreme is US intransigence,

53 *Op cit*, Cabinet Office, fn 14, p 167.

whether it be refusal to pay its appropriate UN membership contributions or its unwillingness to reform the Bretton Woods institutions in any material fashion. The UK, too, can be a force for either good or ill. On the debit side is its present unwillingness to enact anti-corruption laws in line with OECD agreements while on the credit side is the recent launch by the PM of the Sustainable Development Commission.[54] More generally, organisations like the World Bank are incapable of being a genuine force for good without the active assistance of the host nation.

What is even more evident is that individual Nation States are capable of producing genuine advances in co-operation with other actors, both public and private. This is a suitable time to return to the influence of the MNCs.

THE PRIVATE FIEFDOMS

The democratisation of the globalisation phenomenon is not just about business. But, it is very decidedly about the role and function of the largest corporations. To this extent, the theme of corporate governance must be seen as a central preoccupation. And, corporate governance must be viewed broadly. It embraces more than just the constitutional frameworks which States impose through company law. As described in Chapter 7, it includes regulation of various sorts – competition law, consumer and unfair business practice law, and the regime adopted by individual companies and sectors for promoting their several purposes. Increasingly, it has an international and global dimension and embraces accords of various sorts struck between regional and international agencies and the corporate sector. The experiments have only just begun. They have much further to go. However, just to take one example, Rights of Exchange was able to report that 60% of the UK's top 500 companies had signed up to voluntary codes of conduct on labour standards.

One of the reasons why governance has become a hot topic globally is that the big investment funds have gone global and are pressing for consistent standards across the world's main stock markets. The WBCSD has, as noted earlier, graphically spoken of the wider issues involved in globalisation. However, perhaps the prime mover in this great debate was the UN Commission of Environment and Development, headed by the Norwegian Prime Minister Gro Harlem Brundtland as far back as 1987 (the Brundtland Commission). It suggested reviving growth in a context of sustainable development that must address the issue of poverty because poverty increases pressure in the environment. But it talked, too, about changing the quality of growth – that is to say, making growth less materialistic, less energy intensive and more equitable, so that it can meet essential human needs for food,

54 See DETR, News Release 665, 24 October 2000.

energy, basic housing, fresh water and health. The Commission made it clear that business has a central role to play in all this. What was being urged was a partnership between government (broadly conceived) and business, since we are part of a complex system that is not limitless, but interconnected. Since then, of course, we have seen the Earth Summit in Rio in 1992, where 135 countries signed a Framework Convention on Climate Change, a Framework Convention on Biodiversity, and Agenda 21, a commitment to implement the objectives of the Earth Summit. The latter, in particular, stressed the necessity for partnerships, transparency and broad-based consultation around both environmental and social issues.

The Challenge Brief had argued that the concept of governance was appearing on an increasing number of board agendas, in part because of a growing feeling that international, national and local systems of government are increasingly out of step with emerging challenges. The debate also raised the concern that capitalism was, in a very real sense, 'beyond control'. In conformity with the position being adopted here, it also took the view that governance was not solely a matter of State intervention. Rather, it is a function that is necessarily performed by a wide variety of public and private, State and non-State, national and international institutions and practices. The institutions of global society are being reinvented as technology redefines relationships between individuals and organisations. Despite the existence of the United Nations and its many agencies, it seemed to the authors that there was no overall body with the legitimacy and authority to ensure that sustainable development happens around the world. UNEP has made it quite clear that it believes it has the authority and experience to become that body, should the political will exist. The resistance of some national governments to develop more federal regional structures along the lines of the European Union seemed to indicate that it was likely to be many decades before strong international government systems are in place.[55] In the meantime, the business world must deal with a raft of partners. Nevertheless, the challenge for national governments and international government agencies was to evolve corporate governance systems that help business to deliver sustainable growth and social justice rather than hindering them in this task. The roots of the current crisis, they continued, are political and social issues that exceed the mandate and capabilities of any corporation. Yet, at the same time, corporations are the only organisations with the resources, the technology, the global reach and, ultimately, motivation to achieve sustainability. The following were singled out as issues which need to be addressed:

- economic/environment issues which include eco-efficiency, ecological tax reform and environmental accounting;

55 This appears to be changing, as witness the emergence of the East African Community.

- environmental/social issues which include environmental justice and intergenerational equity;
- social/economic issues which include business ethics, human and minority rights.

In addition, a number of MNCs have been heavily criticised for steamrollering local concerns across many parts of the world. BP, for example, has recently been caught in a crossfire over Tibet and its participation with Chinese firms in an oil and gas pipeline. The Tibetan Government in exile believes that the project would have a devastating impact on the region's remaining Tibetans, and their prospects. It, along with numerous NGOs, had already caused the World Bank to resile from its proposal to grant a loan to resettle Chinese farmers.[56] BAT has also been the subject of considerable pressure about allegations of cigarette smuggling which has upset not only the World Health Organisation, which is sponsoring a Treaty on Tobacco Control, but also the UK DTI, which recently announced a departmental investigation into the company's affairs.[57]

Not only do these examples indicate the potential power and influence of MNCs, they also indicate that acceptable global action can probably only come about as a result of networking with MNCs by governments, civil society and other interests. It is clear that many MNCs recognise the potential of NGOs and, to that extent, occasionally engage in defensive alliances against them. Thus, Sony, the electronics giant, is reported to have advocated spying on eco-friendly groups who criticise the fact that many of Sony's profits contain toxins and are difficult to dispose of. Environmentalists will certainly take heed of these warnings:

> Its [Sony's] strategy is outlined in a leaked paper currently doing the rounds of the alternative internet community. Titled 'NGO Strategy', it bears all the Cold War histrionics of J Edgar Hoover's G-men ... The document discloses the names, contacts and internet addresses of leading environmental groups that pose a public relations threat to the company – the Northern Alliance for Sustainability, Greenpeace, the European Environment Bureau, the Silicon Valley Toxics Coalition and Friends of the Earth.[58]

The range of actors playing the global drama is further exhibited when we add the fact that the EU has recently produced a Directive on Waste from Electrical and Electronic Equipment, which would have devastating effects on many of the MNCs, since they would take responsibility for the whole life of their products – including disposal. Fighting the EU head-on in this trade war

56 See, eg, (2000) *The Guardian*, 2 October.

57 (2000) *The Guardian*, 1 November.

58 The Big Brother of internet investigation agencies, America's E-Watch, helps more than 800 of the world's largest corporations keep track of their reputations across Cyberspace. See Wazir, B, 'Eating the greens' (2000) *The Observer*, 1 October.

is the American Electronic Association, an umbrella body for more than 3,000 companies. Unsurprisingly, the Association is claiming that EU action would offend WTO rules. Examples are legion and could be multiplied, but just one more will be used to indicate how the world's poor can be seriously disadvantaged (as well as benefited) by the behaviour of MNCs. Just as this book was going to press, the UK International Development Secretary was warning that an effort by the EU Commission to allow in goods from the world's poorest countries is in danger of being killed off by powerful multinational sugar firms. Interestingly, not all the EU's agencies are pulling in the same direction, with the Agricultural Directorate reportedly more sympathetic to the MNCs than is the Trade Directorate, which wishes to remove tariffs into the EU for the 48 LDCs.[59]

Now these are hugely complicated matters, and there are so many forces tugging in opposite directions. On the one hand, it is almost consensual that some of the best MNCs are innovative and more socially advanced than many of the international organisations. It was also noted in Chapter 8 that there exist many industry codes, especially at the sectoral level, which have made considerable progress in terms of both environmental and social impact reports. The UK Government's own view is that multinational agreements on specific SHE issues with international dimensions are desirable and that international trade rules can and should accommodate these agreements.[60] Even allowing for this, a degree of scepticism may still be called for. So, for example, the New Economics Foundation, which has developed modern methods of social auditing, has described social reports produced by companies such as Barclays and Ford as 'corporate spin' and which have been taken over by marketing departments. They concluded by arguing for legal obligations to produce such reports which would then be subject to more stringent and enforceable requirements.[61]

It should already be clear that traditional ways of looking at the international community are inadequate if what concerns us is a global rule of law, informed by all three generations of human rights. A huge mapping exercise needs to be undertaken and reform to a range of institutions – national, regional and international – undertaken.

59 (2000) *The Guardian*, 27 November.

60 *Op cit*, Cabinet Office, fn 14, p 7. And for some of the best UK examples, encouraged by Government see *ibid*, pp 154–55. For international voluntary initiatives, see pp 162–63.

61 New Economics Foundation, *Corporate Spin: The Troubled Teenage Years of Social Reporting*, November 2000, NEF.

THE INTERNATIONAL INSTITUTIONS

Charter '99 has asked where we should start in the process of legitimating the NWO. The view taken here is that this is a complex question with no clear answers and that institutional and substantive reform will need to take place at various interlocking levels: the UN, regional groupings (and, in particular, the EU), international labour organisations, industry – especially at the sectoral level, national governments, NGOs and a range of international institutions, both formal and informal. There is no straightforward recipe at this stage, but there is the possibility of working across a range of reinforcing positions. Charter '99 adopts a more hierarchical approach.

The line adopted by them is that, for all its weaknesses, the UN retains an unmatched legitimacy in world affairs and that the work should begin there. Article 1 of the UN Charter mandates the UN to achieve international co-operation in solving international problems of an economic, social, cultural or humanitarian character and to be a centre for harmonising the action of nations. Correspondingly, this is where the search for the global constitution should begin. This is an attractive proposition, but the UN does not at this time have the ability to counter-punch the major power players and this is unlikely to change in the near future. Of course, the argument for its hegemony should be made constantly and persuasively, but it is probably necessary to begin the task of democratic reconstruction elsewhere. However, it is important at the outset to make reference to the 12 areas which Charter '99 singles out for urgent action. This chapter will avoid any reference to military issues and the maintenance of international peace and security, and will concentrate on institutional suggestions for bridging the accountability gap – and on human rights. On this basis, the following issues and areas are the ones highlighted here:

- the UN General Assembly to be given powers to scrutinise the work of UN agencies and other agencies of global governance; the creation of an annual Forum of Civil Society, opening international organisations to increased participation by civil society and elected representatives from member countries; bringing the WTO into the UN system and strengthened co-operation between all international groupings under the UN system;
- to create within the UN system an accountable, equitable and effective mechanism to monitor, supervise and regulate transnational corporations and financial institutions; and require transnational companies to adhere to an international code of conduct covering agreed principles concerning human rights, the environment and core labour standards;
- to give UN institutions an additional independent source of income such as taxation of foreign exchange transactions, aircraft and shipping fuels, arms sales and licensing use of the global commons;

- reform the UN Security Council and to open up all decision making to public scrutiny;
- to strengthen world citizenship based on compliance with and respect for the Universal Declaration of Human Rights, including the six core treaties on economic, social and cultural rights; civil and political rights; racial discrimination; discrimination against women, children's rights, torture and the convention on genocide, refugees and labour standards;
- to establish a strong UN institution for economic and environmental security, to promote international prosperity, protect the global commons and secure sustainable development;
- to establish an International Environmental Court to enforce international treaties on the environment and protect the global commons.

One promising UN initiative has already been mentioned. It is the 'Global Compact'. This is a coalition of the worlds of business, labour and civil society in order to forge a new coalition in support of universal values, launched by Kofi Annan in July 2000. The Compact is based on nine key principles of the Universal Declaration of Human Rights, the ILO's fundamental principles on rights at work, and the Rio Principles on environment and development. The initiative is primarily directed at the business community which has agreed on three items:

- they will become public advocates for the Compact in their corporate mission statements, annual reports and similar venues;
- at least once a year they will post on their websites specific examples of progress they have made, or lessons they have learned, in putting the principles into practice in their own corporate domains;
- they will join the UN in partnership projects, either at the policy level – for instance, a dialogue on the role of corporations in zones of conflict – or at the operational level, such as helping African or South Asian villagers link up to the internet, or strengthening SMCs in developing countries.

The record of business in general suggests they rarely live up to their mission statements in these matters, but the fact of the UN monitoring their progress can only be an advance.

More generally, there is no doubt that the UN can be improved and that heavy concentration on ways of doing so is one of the directions in which we should all be moving. But there are other international organisations which may have seized the initiative from the UN at this point in time, especially the WTO.

Some of the other big players in the chart of international organisations have been mentioned, but it is worth returning at this point to the lack of general co-ordination of SHE issues before we turn directly to the WTO.

WHICH ORGANISATIONS ARE RESPONSIBLE FOR SHE ISSUES?

As we have noted, the WTO is essentially trade-based with environmental, labour and other social issues left to a raft of other organisations. In such a loose-based set of arrangements, especially when WTO rules are the most legally solid, there are bound to be tensions between different sets of interests. As noted, the UK Government has suggested that international trade rules could learn to accommodate specific SHE issues after multilateral agreements have been struck, though how exactly this is to be achieved is not made clear:

> International agreements on SHE issues should wherever possible be reached in multilateral fora with specific responsibility for the issue, rather than in trade rounds. Where necessary, existing multilateral institutions should be strengthened to allow for this, including establishing their own dispute resolution and enforcement mechanisms.[62]

The difficulty with this proposal is that we could be faced with jurisdictional conflict, unresolvable by any institution with superior authority. Elsewhere, the Government appears to recognise this dilemma and simply calls for greater co-operation between the various world bodies and sets of arrangements.

As a further illustration of how progress on the democratisation of the NWO is multilayered, it is worth noting that *Rules of Exchange* recommended that the interactions between trade and SHE issues should be given more prominence in development assistance programmes, including in UK country strategies. Such progress also depends on clarifying certain WTO rules as they might be thought to apply to the LDCs. It is clear that WTO rules do set limits on the action that national governments can take as part of the balance to be struck between protection and protectionism. It is true that the WTO dispute settlement rules have been interpreted to protect environmental concerns under Article XX, but this was mainly pre-Uruguay. There has also been pressure for updating Article XX to include specific reference to environment and animal welfare issues and even to include a social clause. However, as usual, the problem may be political will, in which case there is little alternative for scholars and members of civil society to provide more accurate research findings outlining the shortcomings of the system and to press for improvements outside the scope of particular national governments.

Although the EU can and should be a key player in resolving many of these issues, it is clear that we can expect a certain number of stand-offs between it and the US. However, it should be mentioned that pressure is emerging from the European Commission to persuade members to redefine

62 *Op cit*, Cabinet Office, fn 14, p 11.

its agenda for the next trade round. Up to now, only Japan has supported the EU in seeking to add to the trade round new issues such as the environment, investment, competition, and labour standards as well as agricultural services. Up until now it has faced opposition from the US and the Cairns Group of agricultural exporting countries, as well as from a number of developing countries. It remains to be seen what progress, if any, can be made at this time. However, what does appear to be the case is that NGOs are beginning to win the battle of public opinion, if research findings are anything to go by. Thus, recent research has found that the general public trust NGOs (some more than others) infinitely more than they trust national governments or business. Interestingly, the WTO and Monsanto received extremely low scores in the research findings, which were based on surveys of opinion leaders in the US, Europe and Australia.[63]

Perhaps no single-issue group has affected the global order in recent years like Jubilee 2000, established to eradicate debts owed by the third world to the first. Almost at the death (Jubilee 2000 is a sunset organisation which dissolved at the end of 2000),[64] it saw the World Bank and the IMF working to remove $34 bn of the debt burden owed by 22 of the world's poorest countries. Jubilee 2000 was, itself, a coalition of extremely broad-based constituencies which brought considerable pressure on the Group of 7 countries to exert leverage on the Bretton Woods institutions. Although, therefore, we see once more a broad network influencing the World Order, there is little doubt that Jubilee 2000 was the lead player in seeking some measure of accountability as well as justice in the global community. Apart from the substantive change achieved in debt reduction, an impetus has developed for altering the architecture of globalisation. First, the UK Government is to host a conference in February 2001 which will bring the World Bank, IMF, UNICEF, the UN Development Programme, governments from the developing and the developed world, the business community and civil society together to discuss how to meet international targets for poverty reduction by 2015. Secondly, Kofi Annan has kick-started the debate on reform of the international organisations by proposing an independent panel of experts to mediate between creditors and debtors, thereby lessening the influence of the IMF. All this goes with the grain of changes at the World Bank, which now urges institutional and social change amongst the poorest countries through their working with international agencies, NGOs and local communities. However, there is little doubt that responsibility for SHE issues needs to be made much more coherent than is currently the case.

As indicated, part of the problem is that the WTO is generally regarded as the lead organisation in terms of the rules of the game at least, so that altering

63 See (2000) *Financial Times*, 6 December.

64 It is expected to continue in some form as Drop the Debt.

its articles to include respect for SHE issues may be the best solution on offer. However, the culture of the WTO seems signally unsuited for this role and the creation of some kind of Court of Jurisdictional Conflict may ultimately be thought to be necessary. At this point, the centrality of the WTO needs to be stressed, not least since it appears to have as many detractors as it does supporters.

The orthodox view is that by establishing clear rules, the WTO raises economic growth through trade liberalisation which benefits developing countries by encouraging them to grow and raise their own welfare. It was established by the Marrakesh Declaration signed by the majority of GATT members in April 1994. Its essential functions were to administer the Uruguay Round, provide a forum for multilateral trade negotiations, administer the trade dispute settlement procedures, review national trade policies and co-operate with other international institutions, in particular the World Bank, to achieve greater coherence in global economic policy making. It has had its successes and failures, but most criticism has centred on the dispute settlement system, not least in the light of the long running disputes between the US and the EU in recent years over bananas, Cuba and beef. The new Director General, Mike Moore, has recently expressed the wish that the WTO and the UN work more closely together; however, it is by no means certain that the agendas of the two agencies are compatible. For example, it is unlikely that the US auto or oil industry (highly influential in settling the agenda of the WTO) would allow the US government to sign up to a world environmental organisation, much favoured by leading officials within the UN secretariat. Furthermore, although there have been calls to establish a WTO/ILO permanent working group, progress has been halting. Although such a body could work on mechanisms to integrate labour rights into WTO rules, agreement has proved difficult to reach.

On the other hand, whatever the genuine legitimacy of the WTO, it has developed a strong juridical authority, having replaced, according to leading scholars in the field, a 'power-oriented approach' with a 'rule-oriented approach'.[65] Indeed, its success in this respect caused President Clinton to suggest that it assumes responsibility for global anti-trust and competition policy. Such a development would not enjoy universal support as long as it was seen as a community without a Parliament, and is currently served by 'self-appointing officials answerable only to leaders of the world's richest States'.[66] A global monetary authority, publicly accountable to democratic governments, would be another matter. In such a case, there may be

65 See, eg, Merrills, JG, *International Dispute Settlement*, 3rd edn, 1998, Sweet & Maxwell, p 218.

66 *Op cit*, Alexander, fn 4, p 136.

something to be said for it assuming responsibility for curbing the excesses of the international financial system.[67]

Many of the leading NGOs, however, view the WTO in a different light. It has been described as a secretive organisation with enormous power that effectively upholds a Bill of rights for transnational corporations. Recent decisions, according to this view, on bananas and beef allow the WTO to challenge standards adopted to protect the environment, public health, animal welfare and the interests of poor farmers. Even the UK Government has recommended WTO institutional reform to allow for greater transparency, including earlier derestriction of documents and the development of practical proposals for the involvement of NGOs.[68] Currently, the rules require that dispute panels meet in closed session, and the parties to the dispute (and other WTO member countries who have expressed an interest in the case) can only attend when invited. All documents are confidential, except that parties to the dispute can release their own statements and can request a non-confidential summary from the other party to release to the public. Panel deliberations are confidential and it is up to the panels themselves to decide whether to seek information from third parties. NGOs would like to be able to intervene through, for example, amicus curiae briefs. Unlike many other IGOs, the WTO has no formal accreditation system or working arrangements for NGOs.

Other concerns expressed are the following:

- developing country participation: most of the smaller developing countries find it difficult to participate in the WTO's negotiation processes and, as a result, do not trust the organisation;
- it is insufficiently transparent to civil society which does not trust national governments to negotiate agreements that reflect their interests;
- there is insufficient involvement of civil society organisations;
- there is a lack of coherence/insufficient involvement of other NGOs;
- there are extensive provisions for developing and least developing countries, although the distinctions between these countries are rather unclear and the legal enforceability of the provisions is doubtful.

The UK Government has come out strongly in favour of greater transparency in international fora. Given that an increasing number of policy decisions are negotiated internationally, this is perhaps the most urgent reform to be pressed for.[69]

---

67 And see Cavanagh, J, Wysham, D and Arruda, M, *Beyond Bretton Woods: Alternatives to the Global Economic Order*, 1994, Pluto.

68 *Op cit*, Cabinet Office, fn 14, p 87.

69 *Op cit*, Cabinet Office, fn 14, p 104.

Several more items are a cause for concern. First, agriculture has never been fully covered by GATT arrangements and even the provisions on agriculture in the Uruguay round are thought to be discriminatory against developing countries. Secondly, the so called TRIPs agreement on intellectual property rights which establishes minimum standards of protection are generally considered to be detrimental to the least developed countries. Being part of the Uruguay Round, the agreement establishes strong ground rules which are enforced by the disputes panels. Thus, there is a kind of rule of law, but no obvious fairness in the arrangements by which the rules are established. Thirdly, there is the GATS agreement on trade in services which opens up public services to the market. Its aim is to remove all internal government controls over service delivery that are barriers to trade. In effect, the rules make government actions to keep local control over these services illegal. The motor for this development has been large US corporations such as American Express and Citicorp. Although these are early days, there is a strong suggestion that the interests of the third world will not be uppermost.

Having a rule-based system is, in general terms, desirable. However, when the bargaining chips are held by just a few players, there has to be doubt about the overall legitimacy of the system. Again, the UK Government, with diplomatic understatement, makes the case:

> International agreements on SHE issues should wherever possible be reached in multilateral fora with specific responsibility for the issue, rather than in trade rounds. Where necessary, existing multilateral institutions should be strengthened to allow for this, including establishing their own dispute resolution and enforcement mechanisms.[70]

In 1996, the WTO established a Committee on Trade and the Environment which, thus far, has produced little which environmentalists would applaud. Although the celebrated Article XX provides consolation for environmentalists, the whole culture of the WTO is trade dominated and has assumed a centrality in the twilight constitution of the global order which has no popular support. In the UK, the royal prerogative survives intact from the 17th century settlement and the Executive, harried by the TNCs, is scarcely troubled by the Mother of Parliaments when negotiating away many of the rules which Parliament itself has passed. At the end of the day, what the WTO says, goes; this is the real and true face of the NWO and its system of law and governance. When the WTO was established, the UK, along with other governments, signed up to the agreement when belief in the virtues of free trade exceeded concerns about food safety, health, animal welfare and environmental damage. In retrospect, there must be serious doubt that the balance was wisely struck.

70 *Op cit*, Cabinet Office, fn 14, p 11.

The WTO has assumed a particular significance in the World Order, but of course it does not have the field to itself. There are many other powerful players, such as the Group of 7/8 (and, since 1999, the Financial Stability Forum),[71] the OECD, the Council of Europe, etc. A problem, however, is that things are moving at such a pace it is difficult to piece together the whole picture, let alone to invest it with a democratic core. Regulation is a case in point; from the perspective of a regulator in a large, developed market, one prime need seems to be to upgrade the quality of supervision in countries where it has been shown to be wanting. There are agreed international codes of practice setting out the principles of banking, securities and insurance supervision, and most countries are nominally signed up to them. But, there is no effective means of enforcing those standards, or of policing their implementation. The Financial Stability Forum was, to some extent, a response to these concerns:

> Similarly, all the groupings of regulators have been wrestling with the problem of how to spread best regulatory practice to offshore financial centres. But that requires political support, and a better constructed portfolio of carrots and sticks than we now have available.[72]

At this time, it would be unprofitable to nominate other salient bodies which clearly have some influence on the global stage, because the research and hard data are not yet there, even though some commentators have provided a service by producing a checklist of many of the bodies which undoubtedly play an influential role.[73]

REGIONAL POLITICS

The European Union, given its unique juristic nature and its social aspirations, is very clearly one of the major players on the global stage, and has the opportunity to become ever more significant, not least given the social and cultural traditions of its main memberships. Naturally, its relations with the US/NAFTA[74] are central and any effective mapping exercise and/or research programmes into the NWO must regard this phenomenon as pretty much core. One of the first governance issues to be addressed, however, is the notorious secrecy of the EU, and its failure to satisfy the highest standards of accountability, although both these issues have been more seriously

71 This brings together finance ministries, central banks and regulators from the G7, together with international financial institutions and regulatory organisations.

72 Davies, H, 'A forum for stability' (1999) *Financial Times*, 14 April.

73 See, esp, *op cit*, Alexander, fn 4.

74 Although NAFTA is a rule-bound organisation, it would be foolish to expect anything other than US hegemony for some time to come. The EU is clearly much more heterogeneous and multicentred.

addressed in recent times. A full blown constitution, including arrangements for relationships with other international actors, is clearly the way forward. To some extent, it is a model of social and economic growth; a unique model of national reconciliation and a reservoir of pluralism and diversity. Its supporters have urged it to understand that a united Europe is not merely a means to an end, but an end in itself.[75]

The UK Government has recently expressed the view that the EU's competence in external trade policy is of fundamental importance to the trade policy debate. For members of the EU, this means that all external trade issues have first to be agreed in the EU, with negotiations with the wider international community being conducted at EU rather than at national level; in practice, by the Commission acting on instructions from the Council of Ministers. Competence in SHE issues is vested partly in the EU and partly in Member States, depending on the issue, but many standards are set by the EU as part of the completion of the single market. This means that, for the time being at least, the EU's role is more significant in relation to environmental standards than to health and labour standards.

Even so, the EU has proposed a joint ILO/WTO working party on trade and labour and has given tacit support to the ICFTU proposal for improving coherence between trade and labour policy. The ILO already has a working party on the Social Dimension of Globalisation which includes the WTO, IMF, World Bank and UNCTAD. This is an initiative that could be built on, and if anyone is capable of acting as honest broker, it is probably the EU itself.[76]

Perhaps the issue of poverty has been underplayed in what has gone before. It is clearly the most urgent problem facing the international community and a number of initiatives have emerged partly from the EU and partly from its member constituents, in alliance with others, regarding poverty reduction. It is now broadly accepted, for example, that high priority should be given to widening access to EU markets for the least developed countries and that the interactions between trade and SHE issues should be given more prominence in development assistance programmes, partly at the EU level and partly through country strategies.[77]

It needs to be added here that other regional organisations, though less developed than the EU, are important. The other major players are NAFTA and MERCOSUR (the South American States). The East African Community has been mentioned, while the OAU itself has often been active, especially on the environmental front. Other import fora include the Association of South-East Asian Nations, the Asia-Pacific Economic Co-operation Forum and the

---

75 See, eg, Moisi, M, (1997) *Financial Times*, 9 December.

76 *Op cit*, Cabinet Office, fn 14, Chapter 7.

77 Proposals have recently been laid on the table by the Commission to redefine the US stance on the agenda for a world trade round: (2000) *Financial Times*, 6 December.

Association of Caribbean States. There are other straws in the wind, of which just two will be mentioned. The first is the Millennium Africa Recovery Plan being prepared by South Africa, Nigeria and Algeria, three of the continent's biggest economies. The Plan, supported in principle by the US, the EU and Japan, aims to link hitherto uncoordinated efforts to promote foreign investment, trade concessions and further debt relief.[78] The second has been moved by Mexico's new President, Vincente Fox, who has called for a radical change with Latin American neighbours, based on free trade and regional co-operation in human rights and the treatment of migrants. Mexico, with its special status with both the US and the EU, may be well placed to relaunch the idea for a hemispheric free trade area. Señor Fox has offered free trade arrangements with MERCOSUR, a trade group made up of Brazil, Argentina, Uruguay and Paraguay.[79]

It appears increasingly likely that a tranche of regional organisations will emerge, of varying degrees of coherence and settled will, which have a clear role to play in conjunction with civil society to help provide a division of labour and to prevent overburdening the UN. Again, it should be stressed that the developing global order has shifted seismically from that understood by Mr Selwyn Lloyd in 1957.

THE NGO PHENOMENON

The role of civil society under new systems of governance, national, local, regional and international, has been touched on from time to time, as has the question of methodologies to calibrate their legitimacy. But the role of NGOs, in particular, in the global order, has become such a striking feature of recent years that a little more needs to be said about them.

There are, of course, all manner of NGOs; some long standing, some transient, some single-issue, others dealing with issues of interlinked complexity, etc. One criticism has been levelled at single-issue groups as creating 'the potential for unproductive competition' among, for example, environmental and development goals.[80] Achieving a sustainable world will almost certainly require improved institutional arrangements, involving governments, the private sector, non-profits and so on at the national, regional and global levels. Important progress can be made through the formation of new partnerships among key actors.[81] This may necessitate reshaping and

78 (2000) *Financial Times*, 27 November.

79 (2000) *Financial Times*, 15 September.

80 See, eg, UNEP, USNASA and World Bank, *Protecting our Planet; Securing our Future*, 1998, UNEP, p x.

81 *Ibid*, p xvii.

refocusing certain organisations if maximum effectiveness is to be achieved.[82] The World Bank, through its integrated development programme, is increasingly linking up with NGOs through its director-based missions so that the country directors will be *in situ* with local staff. There will be a civil society/social development specialist recruited locally by advert. As noted, the Bank, in particular, has made increasing use of NGOs over the past decade when their local knowledge can be crucial.

UNEP has especially strong links with NGOs and, again, has formal structures for incorporating them into policy proposals. Oddly, UNEP is, in certain ways, dependent on the NGOs pressing their case to national governments who are indirectly their paymasters. The global world is truly one of interdependence.

Be that as it may, what we see is an increasing reliance on NGOs by the IGOs, while at the same time finding themselves in conflict with some of the more militant. Thus, there is little doubt that some of the more vociferous have impeded both the OECD and the WTO in terms of plans for new trade rounds. As well as the celebrated shambles in Seattle, a number of lead NGOs will perhaps claim as the greatest scalp the Multilateral Agreement on Investments. On the other hand, we have noted the constructive success of Jubilee 2000. Yet, even in the new climate when NGOs are increasingly being sought as partners, influential bodies such as the International Chamber of Commerce appear to reject the idea of consultation with leading NGOs.

There is probably a need for IGOs, in particular, to draw up agreements with NGOs and their representative groups for the purposes of ensuring that they comply with certain uniform standards about their own accountability and competence. When such standards are satisfied, such representative groups should be consulted as a matter of course.

LABOUR AND ENVIRONMENTAL ISSUES

Labour and environmental issues have been touched on from time to time, but aside from the basic issue of poverty, there are few other more sensitive issues on the global agenda.

Although there has been little progress in recent years, the main emphasis in the social sphere has been placed on labour standards. In spite of that, there have been institutional links between trade and labour standards and no trade

82 Particularly useful has been FIELD, a group of international lawyers coming together since 1989 to protect the global environment through recruiting and training young lawyers from around the world and providing legal assistance to non-governmental organisations. For developing countries, much of this legal support is free. In November 2000, its lawyers provided back-up for 42 countries from the Alliance of Small Island States (Aosis) at the Hague summit on climate change: (2000) *The Guardian*, 4 December.

disputes (in a rule-based sense) that have yet covered their interactions. The EU has, however, through its Generalised System of Preferences, incorporated some labour standards (forced labour and prison labour) and, following agreement on a Commission proposal, there are now special incentives for countries to adhere to additional labour standards (collective bargaining, freedom of association). The rationale for the scheme is that intolerable forms of labour deserve sanctions, while the other core labour standards warrant incentives. Since this agreement was established in 1998, it has not been conspicuously successful, especially since the LDCs are unhappy about linking labour standards to trade issues. Products made from forced labour are, alone among the ILO standards, subject to the possibility of unilateral trade measures as allowed for in WTO rules.

The ILO has produced very important work over the years, but the feeling is that its influence has been on the wane, particularly since 1994 and the ascendance of the WTO. It has been responsible for encouraging labour standards and labelling initiatives, but most of these are in the 'soft law' form of private codes. It has its own, somewhat outdated, code for TNCs, and it collects and monitors information on best and worst practice and does a certain amount of 'naming and shaming'. However, it has to be remembered that the ILO is a tripartite organisation and, at this point in time, employers in general are unenthusiastic about labour standards. In reality, the business world is part of an informal alliance with the developing world, so that the opposition to the ILO is truly formidable.

It is clear that the world simply must address labour and indeed other social standards if the second generation of human rights is to have any meaning. How this is to be achieved is less clear, but interlocking alliances at various levels will have to be formed in order to put pressure on the IGOs to produce some form of policy coherence or superior body dealing with jurisdictional conflict as touched upon already. It should be added that domestic trade union strength has been weakening in recent years, but globalised developments may be about to change that situation too. Pan-European unions, operating with the co-operation and assistance of the EU, might be a powerful presence in the future.[83] The ICFTU proposal for a workers' rights clause based on the seven core ILO labour standards would see them included in WTO rules. Again, it is doubtful if this would be presently found acceptable and would have to be pressed for through a range of networks, strategically co-ordinated.

Environmental matters are even more complex. It has already been noted that the role of the EU is more significant here than in relation to, say, labour standards. *Rights of Exchange* posed the question as to whether Whitehall

83 See the proposal for a merger between the AEEU in the UK and Germany's giant IG Metall: (2000) *The Observer*, 10 December.

departments and EU directorates general were sufficiently integrated on issues such as trade and the environment. It has also called for a closer study of the potential effects of Sustainability Impact Assessments (SIAs). These are defined as frameworks to facilitate the assessment of the environmental, social and economic impact of trade policies within the overall framework of promoting sustainable development. A number of stakeholders have called for SIAs to be incorporated into the trade negotiation process as part of the commitment to sustainable development. For its own part, the Government believes that it needs a more concerted strategy to explain its position to other countries, and to ensure that sympathetic groups within those countries (that is, NGOs) to have their voice heard and taken into account. This could be planned as a medium term strategy, taking particular account of major multilateral negotiations expected to come up over the next few years.[84]

There are some Multilateral Environment Agreements linked with trade measures. International co-operation in the field of environmental protection has led to 200 or so agreements for the protection of the global environment and conservation of natural resources. Many of these agreements do not have an impact on trade, but around 20 of them contain trade provisions for the achievement of environmental goals. Although this is a small number, many of them are exceedingly important; for example, CITES, the Montreal and Basel Conventions and the Kyoto Protocol. The UK Government takes the view that these MEAs with trade measures have been largely successful in achieving their aims.[85]

Marrakesh did, however, produce some movement on the environmental front. A Committee on Trade and the Environment (CTE) was established within the WTO, although to date it has little to show for its deliberations. The establishment of a World Environment Organisation with equal status to the WTO would naturally change matters dramatically, but we are back to the question of whether US business would allow its government to accede to such an arrangement. Environmental law is growing apace; that is undeniable, but with no supreme body to oversee and resolve disputes, commitments can be broken. We have seen that there are numerous voluntary initiatives, including at the sectoral level, which seek to protect the environment, but valuable though they are, they will not of themselves compensate for market failure.

The World Bank is once more seeking to encourage sustainable development, even though it has been condemned for supporting certain projects which might be thought to have the opposite effect.[86] The Bank's loan agreements are now tending to included environmental and social goals as

84 *Op cit*, Cabinet Office, fn 14, Chapter 5.

85 *Op cit*, Cabinet Office, fn 14, Chapter 7.

86 Most recently, in particular, the Chad/Cameroon oil-pipeline project and the Western China Project (Tibet), from the latter of which the Bank eventually withdrew.

part of the small print, and they will undoubtedly be a major player in terms of sustainable development over the years to come. They are right to argue, however, that there is a dysfunctional global governance structure – certainly as far as environmental matters are concerned. The four global conventions, for example, have separate, non-linked secretariats. This means that there are scientific and policy connections which are not made. Furthermore, different governments have different agendas and favour different agencies and conventions. It is difficult to believe real progress can be made without a change in environmental watchdogs. They certainly exist at the national levels and, to a lesser extent, at the regional levels.

Environmental matters cannot be entirely satisfactorily resolved at the national level, although, even here, much can be done. For instance, the UK Government recently established a Sustainable Development Commission whose main remit is to advocate sustainable development across all sectors in the UK, review progress towards it, and build consensus on the actions needed if further progress is to be achieved. However, the Commission is merely to be an advisory NDPB reporting to the Prime Minister, while the DETR will handle day to day issues. Considerably more robust, and one which might be replicated in a broader setting, regional perhaps at first, is the New Zealand Parliamentary Commissioner for the Environment. The Commissioner is a genuine Ombudsman and an Officer of Parliament appointed under the Environment Act 1986. He enjoys power to investigate and report on any matter where the environment may be, or has been, adversely affected. Investigations can include the effectiveness of New Zealand legislation, and planning and management by public agencies. He is both environmental systems guardian, environmental investigator, environmental management auditor and provider of advice and assistance to Parliamentary Select Committees. In his strategic plan, Future Directions 1997–2001, he placed particular stress and attention on public participation and the provision of information. Again, old values in a new setting of the sort which would repay close study by a number of IGOs with interest in the field.

CONCLUSIONS

Having a rule-based global system, rather than one based on economic power or the silk skills of an Iago, has to be one of the aims of cosmopolitan democracy. However, first, the power brokers have to be identified. We know a good deal about some of the major players in the new international order, but we know nothing like enough, and we are certainly, as a global public, insufficiently informed about the quotidian interaction between vital pulses of a series of influential networks. It goes without saying that transparency is a desideratum in the global sphere as much as in the domestic parlour, but we know a good deal more about the latter than the former. The problem with the NWO is its incredible complexity. Occasionally, we find that larger-than-domestic-life rules exist which bring us municipally to heel. For example, the FOI Act 2000 had to be favourably amended in terms of environmental information as a result both of EU directives and a UN convention on the environment. This combination of EU directives and the Aarhus Convention, signed by 39 European countries, including the UK, oblige the government to 'guarantee the rights of access to information, public participation in decision making, and access to justice in environmental matters'.[87] Given the weakness of the Act in general, it says a great deal about the danger of seeking to reduce the NWO either to alliances of national governments or to the dominance of TNCs. The NWO is certainly infected by vested interests, but it is also subject to unexpected bouts of rule-of-law contingencies. To return to the environment: occasionally command and control is the only way forward (assuming agreement can be brokered). International conventions have been negotiated in four key areas; climate change, ozone depletion, biodiversity and desertification. However, money, as ever, is always the key. The World Bank spends about $50 bn per year and, naturally, some of this is spent on furthering environmental objectives mandated by the various conventions. However, private industry will spend infinitely more in the developing world so that quasi-contractual arrangements with large corporations will have to be struck against the background of the conventions. Thus, we have relatively hard law and then soft law to bring into the equation. This is as it is bound to be, but few would claim that the process, taken as a whole, is as open and participative as it might be. Once we have a clearer idea of the partners and the processes of negotiation, then the traditional public and constitutional law values can be openly reasserted as global entitlements.

As it stands, even the IGOs are more secretive than one might expect. This, perhaps surprisingly, includes the UN as witnessed by the unedifying processes of appointing the High Commissioner for Refugees in late 2000. The International Council of Voluntary Organisations, which represents most of the non-governmental aid organisations, was extremely critical of the secrecy against which the appointment was conducted. The head of programmes for *Médecins sans Frontières* was particularly scathing about the lack of transparency in the appointment process which did not even inform interested publics about who was being considered for the post.[88] By now, it should go without saying that all decision making processes in the global order, especially those involving national governments and IGOs, should be informed by respect for basic principles of equality, human rights and justice,

87 See, now, FOI Act 2000, s 74. The Aarhus Convention is the Convention on Access to Information, Public Participation in Decision-making and Access to Justice in Environmental Matters. It was signed at Aarhus on 25 June 1998.

88 (2000) *The Guardian*, 5 October.

including social and economic justice. Without wishing to dwell on the issue overlong, both the IMF and the World Bank need to be further opened up to scrutiny. Apart from general problems of transparency, there is no obvious attempt to re-balance the inequality between lenders and borrowers.[89] All necessary reforms need to be reconsidered in the full light of day, with input received from the widest possible range of sources.

Transparency is the goal which we should aim for. The NWO is simply too complex for grand schemes to be paraded. Mapping and openness are the primary needs. From there, we can propose. We have a new ball game and we shall have to make up the rules as we go along. However, there are some aims which a rule of law world would find inescapable:

> The creation of a superior independent referral body or mechanisms for disputes arising between multilateral agreements – *prima facie* of equal status – represents the most legitimate option; but it can only be considered as a long-term goal. It would benefit both the multilateral trading system and international policy making in the SHE areas. Two possible options have been suggested:
>
> - joint dispute panels; and
> - extending the role of the International Court of Justice ...

This is not a new idea. The 1948 Charter for the International Trade Organisation provided that a member country prejudiced by an ITO decision could seek an advisory opinion from the ICJ, whose opinion would then bind the ITO.[90]

Rights of Exchange is, perhaps, the most forward looking document produced by any government in the world on the problematics of the global order. Who could dispute that the UK should:

> ... encourage greater collaboration and joint working between the WTO and IGOs responsible for SHE issues. This should include:
>
> - better links between the staff of the IGOs on a day-to-day basis for better awareness of each other's work and to be able to identify their wider impacts at an early stage;
> - co-operation between IGOs in new analytical work so that future policies are more likely to be based on an agreed diagnosis of the problems, and optimal solutions;
> - explicit work within IGOs before introducing substantial new policies to evaluate the bearing that they would have on the policies of other IGOs; and

89 See, eg, the criticism of the IMF's handling of the South Korean Economy: Wolf, M, (1997) *Financial Times*, 9 December.

90 *Op cit*, Cabinet Office, fn 14, pp 124–25. The ITO was the intended third leg of the Bretton Woods system, which was never adopted because of US opposition.

- consideration of the enforcement mechanisms employed by each organisation and their wider effects.[91]

In fact, the proposals for action by the UK government to influence the international arena are almost flawless. They include the following:

- pressing for more co-ordinated strategic stock takes between the EU Commission and Member States on the interaction between trade and SHE objectives;
- the use of sustainability impact assessments;
- research on the impact of the TRIPs agreement on SHE objectives;
- the need for the EU collectively to produce a regularly updated medium term strategy to explain its position to other countries on the links between trade and SHE issues;
- using the agricultural negotiations to provide greater equity in general and consistently to liberalise trade and advance SHE objectives;
- to press for the TRIPs agreement to be examined for its impact on SHE issues. The review should take place in collaboration with the relevant IGOs;
- to encourage the use of a dispute settlement mechanism in multilateral SHE agreements where necessary; to seek amendments to WTO rules to ensure that properly targeted trade measures in MEAs are regarded as legitimate, and to consider the longer term option for resolving conflicts between multilateral agreements involving trade and SHE issues, including a referral mechanism to decide the choice of a determining forum;
- to encourage the WTO and the other IGOs to produce better links between the staff of IGOs in relation to each other's work and to co-operate in new analytical work so that an agreed diagnosis of problems and optimal solutions could emerge;
- to encourage commitment to greater transparency and improved participation of developing countries and NGOs in the work of IGOs;
- to build support for increased co-operation between environmental institutions in the short term and to press for the establishment of a WEO in the longer term;
- to enhance development assistance to build capacity in developing countries for trade liberalisation and SHE issues. The Government's country strategies for development assistance should give prominence to trade and SHE issues consistent with the country's development priorities;
- to develop a strategy for a systematic dialogue with civil society groups on the interactions between trade, SHE and development issues;

91 *Op cit*, Cabinet Office, fn 14, p 128.

- that the DTI should produce an integrated strategy for promoting domestic and international corporate social responsibility.

An overdue word needs also to be added on development issues. The need to alleviate the poverty of the third world is self-evident; the disputes centre around the mechanisms to achieve this end. The expansion of world trade alone is as unlikely to produce an international trickle-down effect as untargeted expansion has produced it in national economies. Long term development partnerships are almost certainly desirable, although the UK has also identified other measures which need to be adopted.[92] There is clearly a need for the next round of trade talks to have a development dimension, which once again brings us back to the WTO and the need for reform of international institutions. The UN and the WTO need to be on better terms than they currently appear to be. Furthermore, the UN, in conjunction with lead national governments, needs to ensure that aid and development policies are co-ordinated with local actors rather than imposed from above.[93]

This is an agenda which more or less dovetails with the proposals of Kofi Annan in April 2000 in his report which preceded the Millennium Assembly and Summit. He stressed the need for the powers of Nation States to be reinforced and to draw strength from each other by acting with common institutions based on shared rules and values. The existing institutions should serve as an arena for States to co-operate with non-State actors including global companies. In many cases, they need to be complemented by less formal policy networks which can respond quickly to the changing global agenda. There are other general propositions which urgently need to be addressed:

> Better governance means greater participation, coupled with accountability. Therefore, the international public domain – including the United Nations – must be opened up further to the participation of the many actors whose contributions are essential to managing the path of globalization. Depending on the issues at hand, this may include civil society organizations, the private sector, parliamentarians, local authorities, scientific associations, educational institutions and many others.[94]

It is, of course, easier to state this proposition than to flesh it out. A great deal more work needs to be done at this time – not least in finding out how each of the players on the global stage acts and interacts with each other. Only then will it be possible to work comprehensively towards substantive and institutional change.

92 *Op cit*, Cabinet Office, fn 14, p 132.

93 And see 'Foreign aid itself in need of aid' (2000) *Evening Post* (Wellington), 10 November.

94 *Op cit*, Alexander, fn 4, p 249.

Some formal institutional arrangements will need to be revisited, although it must be accepted that they often lack the scope, speed and informational capacity to keep up with the rapidly changing global agenda. Mobilising the skills and other resources of diverse global actors, therefore, may increasingly involve forming loose and temporary global policy networks that cut across national, institutional, and disciplinary lines. Kofi Annan argues that the UN is well situated to nurture such informal coalitions for change across various areas of responsibility. The essential role that formal governance structures must continue to play is normative: defining objectives, setting standards and monitoring compliance. It may well be, therefore, that the UN has more chance of promoting accountability in the global village by acting as facilitator, rather than by pursuing internal, structural, reform. Realistically, it will probably need to move forward on both fronts.

In the present state of the World Order, networks are clearly crucial and action to pursue desired social and economic objectives will need to be taken at a number of levels and within a number of frameworks. The role of national government will be ignored at our peril. Only strong governments will be able to cope with the problems of tomorrow, and they will have to do so in a changing context. That context is about co-ordinating, integrating and facilitating as much as in undertaking specific tasks itself, although a transcendent commitment to human rights should shine through all its actions. Kofi Annan again underlines this point of view, stating that weak States are one of the main impediments to effective governance today, at national and international levels alike. The UN must do all in its power to help to strengthen the capacity of those States to govern. Each State now acts in a dual capacity; in addition to the responsibility each owes to its own citizens, States are collectively the custodians of the common life of the planet. Some international organisations – the Council of Europe, for example – labour consistently to assist States in these endeavours, although it is arguable that the major international economic institutions are capable of pulling in the opposite direction.

States, in other words, should act to implement their international obligations and to follow best practices directly. Their progress, however, needs to be monitored by the most appropriate international organisation so that twin reliance will be placed both on national and international action. Furthermore, in order to preserve national freedom of action, governments will increasingly have to set multilateral rules. The EU is a major player in this respect, but so, also, are the WTO, IMF and a handful of other IGOs. What is absolutely vital, therefore, is that each of these agencies be reformed to guarantee the maximum degree of transparency and accountability.

It is not easy, currently, to determine the lines of accountability in the NWO. The boundaries are blurred and it is not clear where the process of international networking is leading. However, even though it is unclear where the new boundaries between nations, global business and international institutions are to be drawn, it is becoming ever more obvious that these latter bodies – so often cast as the enemy of national sovereignty – have become the vehicle by which States reclaim their sovereignty. Taxation is a case in point. The mobility of capital and labour undermines the ability of individual nations to set their own tax levels. The internet is further eroding that autonomy. Correspondingly, in order to preserve national freedom of action, governments will increasingly have to set multilateral rules.

One element, nevertheless, is constituted by partnerships. Nation States and regional and international organisations all need to enter into partnerships directed at reasserting political control over the global agenda. It is to be hoped that the UN will assume greater influence in terms of regulating the practices of corporations and assisting Member States to reassert control. At the same time, the UN, national and local communities, and regional and international organisations should all encourage the promulgation of voluntary codes, agreements and compacts. In particular, strong partnerships should be developed with the private sector at national and international level to combat poverty in all its aspects. These partnerships should also include consumers themselves. The lead organisation will vary, as, for example, the WHO in relation to the Roll Back Malaria campaign or the UN itself in the case of the Global Compact with the private sector. Again, as Annan has indicated, the UN's involvement with global policy networks has been extensive, but largely unplanned. What is needed is a more focused and systematic approach. It is necessary to determine how best to help governments, civil society and the private sector to work together to ensure that policy networks succeed in achieving desired, social, economic and environmental objectives.

In recent years, NGOs have played a vital, if uneven, part in advancing the cause of global accountability. The internet has undoubtedly strengthened their position, even if there are sometimes problems with affirming the legitimacy and representativeness of particular organisations. The good and the bad were equally in evidence at Seattle in late 1999. In the former category, mention should be made of the *Public Citizen Global Trade Watch* which was particularly active and particularly informative. Most notably, many significant documents were produced by NGOs during the processes of the great UN conferences of the 1990s. The most important were drawn together in the *Millennium Forum Declaration*.[95] They were also hugely influential in drafting the global action plans produced by UN Member States at these conferences and also UN-based studies by, for example, UNESCO, UNRISD and UNDP. Perhaps most famously, the Earth Charter was produced over a period of eight years after consultation with thousands of individuals and

95 An agenda of Annan, in *op cit*, fn 37, esp pp 3, 18.

organisations when the governments of the world were unable to reach agreement.

Because of this history, there has come the call to give NGOs a stronger institutional presence in the NWO:

> In keeping with this overall vision of global inclusion, we urge the United Nations to forge a stronger partnership with the organizations of civil society at all levels. In particular, we ask that NGOs be granted increased access to United Nations bodies and meetings so that civil society can both offer its expertise and make its views known. More specifically, we wish to propose that the United Nations grant observer status to a new entity, which we shall call here the 'Global Civil Society Forum'. This entity ... would function to channel the expertise and experience of global civil society to the United Nations by allowing appropriate representatives to comment directly on any ... items before the General Assembly.[96]

In addition, the Declaration calls for the extension of consultative rights to civil society at the regional and national levels of the UN. Governments should complete the process of extending NGOs' rights of access and participation to the General Assembly and its main committees and subsidiary bodies based on the arrangements agreed to in Resolution 1996/31. In his Millennium address, Kofi Annan called on the General Assembly to convene an expert group, including representatives of civil society organisations, to prepare a study of innovative best practices in how those organisations can contribute to the work of the UN in all its aspects. Nor should it be overlooked that private organisations are often asked by the UN secretariat or by national delegations to convene groups of Member State representatives, international officials and outside experts to consider issues too controversial or forward looking for official gatherings. All these activities need to be brought into the net of the international rule of law.

On a different level, it is crucial that regional and international organisations network as between themselves. Naturally, many of them will do so in the ordinary course of events. For example, the OECD countries claim to share a vision of societies based on market economics, democratic political systems, and respect for human rights and social values. They have decided to fulfil this vision through encouraging broad cultural, social and economic interaction with the rest of the world. Even so, there is clearly a role here, too, for the UN in highlighting best practices and offering the opportunities for hosting joint meetings and fora.

96 *Op cit*, Annan, fn 37, p 16.

Human rights

The record of the Council of Europe in advancing the case of human rights – both civil and political and social and economic – has already been touched upon. On the level of environmental rights, progress has been uneven and the European Union is probably rightly seen as the lead organisation in this respect. It is shameful that the UK has hindered the potential of the original draft of the European Charter of Fundamental Rights.

There is no doubt that individual member countries could do more to advance the social and economic rights in particular, but the revised procedures recently adopted by the Council of Europe for monitoring progress may yet force improvements in this area.

The Universal Declaration of Human Rights, adopted by the UN General Assembly in 1948, together with the International Covenant on Civil and Political Rights and the International Covenant on Economic, Social and Cultural Rights, form what is commonly known as the International Bill of Rights. Together with subsequent instruments, this represents a significant body of human rights standards and law. There is no lack of internationally agreed standards; only a failure of implementation and of procedures for raising the profile of their neglect.

NGOs are among the prime supporters of the international human rights regime. They help to monitor and to call attention to human rights violations, work on the national level for the ratification of various human rights treaties and the establishment of national implementing machinery, and engage actively in human rights education and public awareness throughout the world. Their status could be affirmed by an International Administrative Procedure Act, referred to later.

The issue of social and economic rights across the world is bound to be a delicate matter, especially in the case of the developing nations, and is intimately bound up with the actions of the IMF, World Bank and other international institutions. A review of this whole area would be timely,[97] as would the current status and aspirations of refugees. The role of the ILO also calls for re-examination – not least in its relations with the WTO. The adoption of the Earth Charter in the UN General Assembly has also been called for by the Millennium Forum Declaration.

97 Note that a legally binding Convention for Overcoming Human Poverty has been advocated by the ILO Director General and the Chair of the World Summit for Social Development. The UN-sponsored Education for All Conference early in 2000 announced a new Global Initiative for Education, with the World Bank also expected to play a leading role.

A review of the role of the United Nations

The view has already been adopted that the UN cannot, at this time, constitute the hub of a new Global Constitution, but it does enjoy a unique authority and legitimacy which has allowed it to conduct work of enormous importance. Even so, a number of reforms have been called for which deserve close attention. It should be added that no view is taken here on the reform of the Security Council, although there is significant pressure to bring this about.

The Millennium Forum's Working Group on 'Strengthening and democratising the United Nations and other international organisations' will repay close study and attention, and is bound to figure prominently in future discussions on the NWO. This is as it should be, especially when it is recalled that the UN Conferences of the 1990s have played a central role in forging normative consensus and spelling out practical solutions on the great issues of the day.

The Working Group also makes recommendations on the reform of the General Assembly. One proposal is the creation of a Parliamentary Assembly, whose memberships would be based on proportional representation by population. In a process that resembles the evolution of the European Parliament, the members of this UN body might be appointed at first by their respective governments – drawing, perhaps, from both the diplomatic corps and the respective national parliaments. Then, at an appropriate time, they could be directly elected by the populations that they represent. The initial role of this body would be to advise the Secretary General and the other main organisations of the UN and could perhaps grow to including the drafting of binding legislation. This body would, eventually, assume the responsibilities of the General Assembly, but with an increased mandate. This is a far reaching proposal, but given time and the evolutionary nature of the idea, it may be found acceptable in time.

A suggestion to deal with a particularly pressing issue is the convening of a conference similar to that of Bretton Woods to discuss what sort of new financial architecture is needed for the New World Order. Allied to this is the suggestion for an ombudsman mechanism within the WTO, World Bank and IMF to investigate cases of alleged bias and corruption, a task which the Ombudsmen of India (the Lokayukta) have undertaken with some success.

Another most useful suggestion is that the General Assembly mandate the Secretary General to set up an independent panel of eminent 'Friends of the Secretary General', with expert support to undertake a technical review of progress made on multilateral treaties, international commitments, Art 1 of the Charter, and the development targets. It would report to the General Assembly, which could conduct hearings through the UN Economic and

Social Council.[98] A related idea is the establishment of a Humanitarian Commission composed of independent experts proposed by Member States and elected by the General Assembly. The mandate of this Commission would be to count victims, assess humanitarian needs, and recommend protective measures for civil populations in times of armed conflict. This is related to the suggestion of producing 'Global legal rankings' proposed by William Twining.[99]

Kofi Annan, while accepting the need for change within the UN itself, nevertheless takes the view that it must be sensitive to the need not to usurp the role of other actors on the world stage, but rather to become a more effective catalyst for change and co-ordination among them. Its most vital role will be to stimulate collective action at the global level.

New legal architecture

In addressing the issue of global legal architecture, it is important to interpret the legal in a very broad sense, given the relative unimportance of courts in international and transnational relations. Law, in these terms, is concerned with relations between agents or persons – human, legal unincorporated and otherwise – at a wide variety of levels, not just relations within a single nation or society. For example, William Twining suggests that we are witnessing the emergence of a new *lex mercatoria*, being a system of largely private regulation within the capitalist world economy with institutions such as international arbitration playing an increasingly significant role.[100]

When businesses enter into transnational relationships, the contract typically calls for private arbitration in the event of any dispute arising out of the contractual agreement. This allows each party to avoid being forced to submit to the courts of the other. It is also essentially a secret process. International arbitration can be institutional or *ad hoc*. If the former, it will follow the rules of one of a half dozen of the leading associations, although the world leader is still the International Chamber of Commerce in Paris.[101] A number of countries have changed their domestic laws to satisfy the business users of international arbitration, thereby engaging in a process of 'regulatory competition'. This is an attempt to gain the business of arbitration and, along the way, has helped promote a form of arbitration detached from the scrutiny and regulation of the national court systems. Thus, what emerges is a system of internationalised private justice lacking the legitimacy of the State court

98 See, eg, *Global Citizen*, being the International Newsletter of Charter '99.

99 See Twining, W, *Globalisation and Legal Theory*, 2000, Butterworths, p 158.

100 *Ibid*, p 51.

101 The ICC has been known to boast of having become a United Nations of commerce and international arbitration.

system. Furthermore, some of the celebrated oil arbitrations have involved contracts between Sovereign States and TNCs, thereby posing conflicts between the public rights of a developing country set against the private interests of a foreign corporation. Arbitration can allow companies and their governments to slip away from laws and regulations unfavourable to Western interests. The nature of international arbitration is such that 'general principles of international commerce' have developed which, unsurprisingly, generally reflect Anglo-American views of the world. The leading commentators on this phenomenon have described these developments as producing a 'homology between the field of arbitration and that of international relations'.[102]

Where the parties to those relations enjoy monopolistic or oligopolistic powers, then it assumes significance for citizens of the world. What an adequate response to such developments would be remains to be worked on. However, international arbitration, like other aspects of the NWO, are changing, posing exactly the same set of questions that this chapter has been consistently posing. The following illustrates the problems and the opportunities:

> We now ask if the construction of large regional markets – the European Community, NAFTA – or detailed mechanisms for regulating international commerce – the World Trade Organization under GATT – could also disrupt the landscape and introduce new stakes and even 'an international new deal'. The restructuring of the international market of disputes would build on emerging institutions such as the European Court of Justice, NAFTA, GATT, and even revived and transformed antitrust regulations. These institutions and approaches offer new opportunities for business. Even if it is not at first apparent, these institutions compete with the International Chamber of Commerce and private arbitration. At the same time, new approaches and institutions may facilitate the recomposition of this field of practice closer to the pole of the State.[103]

While in the area of dispute settlement, it should be added that there is wide agreement that all countries be urged to sign and ratify the Rome Statute of the International Criminal Court, to consolidate and extend the gains achieved in bringing to justice those responsible for crimes against humanity. So, too, there is considerable pressure building up for the establishment of an International Environmental Court or Commission to assure measured progress to genuine sustainability. Even if a court able to issue binding judgments is thought presently to be unattainable, the establishment of an International Environmental Commission with powers of investigation, monitoring and report might be found acceptable.

In the light of what has been said earlier, it is perhaps time to give some thought to the notion of an International Administrative Procedure Act

102 Dezaly, Y and Garth, BG, *Dealing in Virtue*, 1996, Chicago UP, p 89.

103 *Ibid*, p 312.

embodying at least some of the principles adopted by the domestic administrative law jurisdiction in the US. These are usually referred to as 'access laws', and embody as well as administrative requirements of fairness, freedom of information, open meetings in the 'Sunshine', and restrictions on ex parte proceedings where a government body hears information from one interested party in the absence of others. A special status could be accorded to designated NGOs in any provisions relating to obligations to consult interested and affected parties. Naturally, there are problems in projecting national legal requirements into the international arena, but US administrative law is a world leader in these matters and its experience could prove particularly valuable.

The problems confronting citizens and groups in the face of the globalisation phenomenon are, to a considerable extent, the same as those confronted when dealing with national or local administrations. As the *Millennium Forum Declaration*, for example, states clearly:

> Consumers must have access to information about the health and environmental impacts of products and production processes, and citizens must participate in related areas of decision making. Local communities must have the right to participate in decision making where global trade and investment patterns affect their livelihoods. Effective mechanisms must be put in place to ensure that abuse of corporate power is countered, and decision making within corporations needs to be democratized.[104]

This nicely makes the point that individual States and sub-national governments should attend to accountability concerns at the domestic level in the first place, even if the effect is to expose the fact that decisions are taken at a higher level – or, in any event, elsewhere. That recognition is the more likely to result in pressure for change in the legal architecture at higher – including global – levels.

This is a matter again recognised by the *Millennium Forum Declaration* which argues for:

> ... the highest possible standard of transparency and democracy in all regulatory, administrative and information-gathering meetings of all its bodies. This applied to the United Nations and all of its agencies in the widest definition, including the World Bank, the International Monetary Fund, as well as the World Trade Organisation.[105]

A serious examination of the case for international access laws should now be undertaken. The content of such laws can be debated, although the underlying principles are now generally recognised across the world as being central tenets of claims to operate democratically. So, also, enforcement should not be a vitiating issue. A spectrum of mechanisms ranging from

104 *Op cit*, Annan, fn 37, p 10.
105 *Op cit*, Annan, fn 37, p 20.

monitoring and reporting through ombudsmen to courts all merit serious consideration. One thing, however, has to be faced. Decision making in the world economy is concentrated in relatively few hands. The G7/8 members, with 12% of the world's population, possess over half the votes in the major trade and business arenas. Reform of the world's financial system is long overdue.

These are early days for blueprinting a Global Constitution and a democratic system of global governance. However, a juristic agenda needs to be worked out which embraces a number of different levels: the domestic – directed to ensuring maximum openness, and the connections and linkages to other 'levels of law'; the regional level; the new *lex mercatoria*; the international and global levels (with the UN at the pinnacle of the latter). There is some similarity between what is being urged here and the research agenda of Boaventura de Santos. In particular, there is common ground with three of his categories: viz, transnationalisation of Nation State law – for example, movement to harmonise or unify branches of municipal law and programmes of structural adjustment, spearheaded by the World Bank, IMF and others; the development of legal regimes of regional integration – most notably the EU; and (to some extent) the *ius humanitatis* or the somewhat aspirational idea of a common heritage of man.[106] There are also differences, but they are unimportant when set against the common ground.

Where do we go from here? The work to be undertaken seems to me to be threefold. First, there is the theoretical case to be made for a philosophic underpinning of the interrelated set of institutions which constitute or might constitute the NWO based on shared democratic understandings. Secondly, there is a great need to map out – to construct some kind of anatomy of – the actual relationships between the salient actors in the drama. The third stage would be to identify the problematics and move to a concrete set of proposals for the establishment of a genuinely consensual global constitution.

On the global stage, it may perhaps be perverse to talk of governance. What exists is a largely unguided newness. A genuine sense of order is called for, informed by first principles.

106 *Op cit*, de Santos, fn 3, esp pp 313 *et seq*.

POSTSCRIPT

There has probably been more ambition than genuine coherence in what has preceded. However, it is worth one last attempt to seek to pull the agenda together and to turn what is essentially an essay into something slightly more programmatic than appears at first sight.

The first, perhaps central, theme is that 'dissipated' government undermines traditional constitutional/accountability mechanisms. Government has become ever more dissipated and less capable of organisational ownership from the centre for a host of reasons; to some extent, this process has been ongoing for over a hundred years. But there is little doubt that it has accelerated and become more diffused at a rapid rate in recent times.

Given the logic of the times in which we live, greater constitutional subsidiarity is called for; this has become the case for a host of reasons, some of which were celebratedly described by Osborne and Gaebler as 'steering rather than rowing'. Since value is added by farming out former State tasks to others nearer the point of action, or with more experience and/or expertise, not only have the functions of government been altering, but the older institutions of parliamentary accountability have become less relevant and less influential. This is not to say that they are, or need to be, powerless – merely that they need to alter and adjust and reassert authority which had been seeping away, even in periods of strong centralisation.

So far, subsidiarity has been used in a general sense, but it is occurring, too, in a distinctly governmental sense. The Europe of the Regions, Scottish and Welsh chambers, the move toward a regional system of government for England and so on. Added to this is the push for greater community involvement, which encourages local governments to seek out partners and to network for the delivery of public policies. This involves a raft of government levels operating with business and civil society; interacting with each other at a number of different points of entry. This clearly alters traditional conceptions of governance and its strengths could well prove its weaknesses too. Its strengths are that the new wholes should be greater than the parts, while the downside includes identifying the pulses of responsibility and building different kinds of accountability and consultation mechanisms away from the political centre. We have hardly begun to think this through in the UK, but doing so is an urgent need.

This means that we – political theorists, activists, public lawyers and others – should be thinking constructively and on a grand scale unless we find ourselves cobbling together solutions which will inevitably have built-in ambiguities, inconsistencies and contradictions. In the UK, at least, the one body which deserves credit for attempting this in both an institutional and intellectual setting is the Constitutional Unit of University College London. However, as especially Chapter 10 makes clear, we have to think more broadly than the confines of the UK; we must reach out to Europe and far beyond. We need a framework for thinking about this change, and we need it sooner rather than later.

To return to dissipated government. There has been a (continuing) revolution in the Civil Service; a managerial revolution which the early chapters of this essay outline as part of a move from governing to governance. That is to say that elected government(s) are less deliverers of services than formerly, but are forced to act more as facilitators of national policies and needs. Whether they are capable of orchestrating the new order is an open question, but there is clearly a duty owed to citizens and each other to try, as well as to understand the nature of the changes occurring in the public/private world of today's State.

The managerial revolution in the public service, and its challenges for government, has been most recently described in the 1999 White Paper, *Modernising Government*, and its continuing nature is being recognised by the establishment of the Centre for Management and Policy Studies at the heart of Whitehall. All these many changes – some pulling in the same direction, others not – necessitates transparency, the consultation of all parties, 'government in the sunshine', a public record of consultations and meetings and their influence on policy outcomes. There is a need for new institutional machinery for the monitoring and evaluation, not only of policies, but also of the value of networks in which a range of actors are seeking to deliver on public promises. Much more needs to be done in this direction than currently exists and I, for my part, have no doubt that we need a new constitutional and administrative law settlement. To this end, a number of suggestions have been made, but we need more information and considered study of the various strains of governance than we currently have. I remain totally convinced that all this needs changes in the machinery of government, the most important of which would be the establishment of a Standing Administrative Conference with powers considerably wider than those of the Australian Administrative Review Council.

The privatisation of former public bodies, the contracting out of government functions and the establishment of regulatory agencies are all part of the same stream of changing governance patterns and they have been touched upon against the background of a changing scene and against the need for transparency and new forms of accountability which underscore older, even ancient, values such as natural justice – albeit natural justice writ large. In this new order, new solutions to old dilemmas need to be sought out. Do we need a Regulatory Commission? A Contracts Commissioner? Can a Standing Administrative Conference be established with a broad-brush brief, or should it be composed of divisions or sections with expertise in regulation, government-business relations and so on? These things have all been considered in what has gone before, albeit without coming to many firm conclusions. It is as much a call for a new agenda for public lawyers and political scientists as it is anything else.

Our relations with the European Union (where our future increasingly lies) has perhaps been underplayed here, not least because its significance is not exactly a State secret, but there is clearly a need for the UK to be more proactive in its dealings with the Union for a host of reasons – some because of the pressures and processes of globalisation, some also because of the genuine problems of the Third World. These are connected, but not the same thing. We need to ask whether the present institutions of government are fitted for this role. Again, the SAC, with a broad intellectual remit, could almost certainly play a crucial role in this respect. The exceptionally thoughtful and coherent report by the Cabinet Office in 2000 (*Rights of Exchange*) is so scholarly, yet politically realistic, that it is a reminder of how rare such public documents are in a British setting. The machinery of government is distinctly lop-sided, although it is clear that there are people around capable of making important contributions to a changing world given the institutional opportunity and the time and reflection to think on a large scale.

Partnerships and/or networks are a core feature of modern governance systems. They apply at national, regional, local, semi-global and global levels. It is clearly impossible for any single actor – including governments – to deliver policies and goals sought by citizens (howsoever they might be identified) unaided. Thus the need to join hands and to collaborate over agreed ends, and to bargain and negotiate over differences. Leaving aside for the moment the difficulties inherent in these exercises at the global and intra-regional Community levels, there has been little coherent thought evident as yet about how to handle more localised partnerships.

The Local Government Act 2000 has made legislative changes to allow local authorities to enter into partnerships which are increasingly seen to be necessary both by local government itself and by central government. Even so, the legislation says next to nothing about the accountability problems which accompany the new networks working towards common goals and pulling away from parts of the programme which individual partners find uncongenial. The problems which partnerships throw up pose questions about audit, which are partly being addressed by the Public Audit Forum, but it is likely that some legislative reform will be needed even in this area. As to how different policy interests are accommodated, to which of the partners are exerting undue influence where there is insufficient transparency, to say nothing of problems of grievance redress and policy evaluation, we are very much in the dark.

Add to this heady mix the involvement of regional and national government, the influence of the EU and others, and it becomes apparent that policy networks and partnerships can stretch out like DNA. We are nowhere near up to scratch in tracking the progress and influence of these many partnerships, let alone in identifying the inevitable democratic deficits and seeking to remedy them. There is a great need for *independent* research among these clusters sooner rather than later, even if all that emerges at the beginning is the identification of a series of best practices which might be taken into account by other groupings struggling with similar problems. A properly funded Community Development Forum could clearly contribute a great deal to our understanding of the workings of the new arrangements, but there is a need for institutional change across the board.

All these issues and more need to be addressed especially, though not solely, by the public law community. If even the beginnings of an understanding of the new agenda which needs to be addressed could be achieved, then at the very least we might be able to launch a collective push for the greatest single needed reform in our system of administrative and political oversight – a Standing Administrative Conference. At the moment there are only isolated voices which can easily be sidelined. As ever, safety will be in numbers.

Finally, the essay has attempted to bring the phenomenon of globalised justice (or its absence) to a new audience. There is a law of globalisation going on out there which is different from traditional international law. It is rarely coherent, it is frequently unjust and it is largely uncharted. There is a clear need for a Global Constitution, but we are only on the threshold of knowing what it should look like and how it can be achieved. A huge programme of work needs to be carried out through a global research programme conducted by integrated teams with broad international support.

This, then, is the agenda thrown up by governance at all levels. It is time for public lawyers and others to play a more active role than is currently the case to put the old (in terms of values) in touch with the new.

Douglas Lewis

Centre for Socio-Legal Studies

April 2001

BIBLIOGRAPHY

Aaronson, R, *The Future of UK Competition Policy*, 1996, IPPR

Aberbach, J and Rockman, BA, 'Does governance matter – and if so, how? Process, performance and outcomes' (1992) 5(2) Governance: An International Journal of Policy and Administration

Administrative Conference of the United States, *Government Contract Bid Protests*, 1995

Alexander, T, *Unravelling Global Apartheid*, 1996, Polity

Alexander, Z, 'Public partners' (1998) Local Government Management 14

Annan, K, *We the Peoples: The Role of the UN in the 21st Century*, 2000, UN

Aucoin, P, 'Comment: assessing managerial reforms' (1990) 3 Governance 202

Audit Commission, *Realising the Benefits of Competition: The Client Role for Contractual Services*, 1993, HMSO

Audit Commission Deakin, N and Walsh, K, 'The enabling State: the role of markets and contracts' (1996) 74 Public Administration 33, p 44

Bailey, M and Sutcliffe, J, 'Exacting the most out of Best Value' (1999) 29 Local Government Management 8

Barker, T *et al*, *Ruling by Task Force, Democratic Audit of the United Kingdom*, 1999, Politico's

Beetham, D, 'Human rights as a model for cosmopolitan democracy', in Archibuigi, D, Held D and Kohler, M (eds), *Re-Imagining Political Community: Studies in Cosmopolitan Democracy*, 1998, Polity

Bercusson, B, *European Labour Law*, 1996, Butterworths

Biermann, F, 'The case for a World Environment Organization' (2000) 42 Environment 23

Birkinshaw, P, Harden, I and Lewis, ND, *Government by Moonlight*, 1990, Hyman Unwin

Bradley, AW and Ewing, KD, *Constitutional and Administrative Law*, 12th edn, 1997, Addison Wesley Longman

British Council, 'Civil society and civil society organisations: a review' (1998) Governance and Law

Brownsword, R, *Contract Law: Themes for the Twenty-First Century*, 2000, Butterworths

Business Information Publications, *Market Testing Bulletin*, Vol 2, 1995, Business Information Publications

Cabinet Office, *What We Want from our Public Services*, CAB 326/00

Cabinet Office, *The Government's Response to the Liaison Select Committee*, Cm 4737, 2000, HMSO

Cabinet Office, *Rights of Exchange: Social, Health, Environmental and Trade Objectives on the Global Stage*, 2000, HMSO

Cabinet Office, *Executive Agencies 1999 Report: Focus on Achievement*, 2000, HMSO

Cabinet Office, *Modernising Government: Action Plan*, 1999, HMSO

Cabinet Office, *Modernising Government*, Cm 4310, 1999, HMSO

Cabinet Office, *Self-Regulation: A Substitute for the State?*, Better Regulation Task Force, 1999, HMSO

Cabinet Office, *Vision and Values*, 1999, Cabinet Office

Cabinet Office, *Better Quality Services: Handbook on Creating Public/Private Partnerships through Market Testing and Contracting Out*, 1998, HMSO

Cabinet Office, *Involving Users: Improving the Delivery of Local Public Services*, Service First, June 1998, Consumer Congress and National Consumer Council

Cabinet Office, *Next Steps Report*, Cm 3889, 1998, HMSO

Cabinet Office, *Quangos: Opening Up Public Appointments*, 1998, HMSO

Cabinet Office, *Finding Your Way Round Whitehall and Beyond*, March 1997, Cabinet Office

Cabinet Office, *Government Response to the Second Report from the Public Service Committee (Session 1995–96) on Ministerial Accountability and Responsibility*, 1997, HMSO

Cabinet Office, *PFI Initiative: Report on the NIRS2 Project*, 1995, CCTA

Cabinet Office, *Taking Forward Continuity and Change*, Cm 2748, 1995, HMSO

Cabinet Office, 'Regional charter networks enter the 21st century', Press Notice No 90/97

Cabinet Office, *The Civil Service: Continuity and Change*, Cm 2627, 1994, HMSO

Campbell, D and Lewis, ND, *Promoting Participation: Law or Politics?*, 1999, Cavendish Publishing

Canadian Centre for Management Development, *Programme Review: Lessons Learned and Challenges Ahead*, 1997, Ottawa

Cavanagh, J, Wysham, D and Arruda, M, *Beyond Bretton Woods: Alternatives to the Global Economic Order*, 1994, Pluto

CEPR, *Trade Policy and Economic Growth: A Sceptic's Guide to the Cross-National Evidence*, 1999, CEPR

Charter '99, *A Charter for Global Democracy*, 1999, Charter '99

CIPFA, *Corporate Governance in the Public Services*, 1994, CIPFA

Commission on Global Governance, *Managing Economic Interdependence*, 1995, UN

Commission on Global Governance, *Our Global Neighbourhood*, 1995, UN

Commission on Global Governance, *Global Decision-Making*, 2000, UN

Commission on Global Governance, *The Millennium Year and the Reform Process*, 2000, UN

Committee on Conduct in Public Life, *Reinforcing Standards*, Vol 1, Cm 455-7-1, 2000, HMSO

Competition Commission, *Annual Review and Accounts 1999–2000*, HMSO

Comptroller and Auditor General, *The Market Testing of ED5*, Session 1995–96, HC 281

Cook, P, *Privatization and Regulation*, 1996, British Council Briefing on Law and Governance

Council of Europe, *Europe Through Its Associations*, 1999, Council of Europe

Davis, G, 'The great wheel: public sector futures in Canberra and Brisbane', 84 Canberra Bulletin of Public Administration 61

De Santos, B, *Toward a New Common Sense: Law, Science and Politics in Paradigmatic Transition*, 1995, Routledge

Deakin, N and Walsh, K, 'The enabling State: the role of markets and contracts' (1996) 74 Public Administration 33

DETR, *Modern Government in Touch with the People*, 1999, DETR

DETR, *New Deal for Communities*, 1999, DETR

Dezaly, Y and Garth, BG, *Dealing in Virtue*, 1996, Chicago UP

DFID, *Eliminating World Poverty: Making Globalisation Work for the Poor*, WP 2/01

Director General of Fair Trading, *Annual Report of the Director General of Fair Trading 1999*, 2000, HMSO

DTI, *A Fair Deal for Consumers: Modernising the Framework for Utility Regulation*, 1998

DTI, *Modernising the Framework for Utility Regulation*, 27 July 1998

DTI, *Modern Company Law for a Competitive Economy: Developing the Framework*, 2000, HMSO

Durkheim, E, *The Division of Labour in Society*, 1933, Free Press

Dyson, K, *The State Tradition in Western Europe*, 1980, Martin Robertson

Ernst and Young, *Program Review: Lessons Learned and Challenges Ahead (A Report for the Canadian Centre for Management Development)*, 1997, Government of Canada

Fox, CJ and Miller, HT, *Postmodern Public Administration: Towards Discourse*, 1995, Sage

Freidheim, C, *The Trillion Dollar Enterprise*, 1998, Perseus

Goh, J and Lewis, ND, *The Private World of Government (occasional papers)*, 1998, Centre for Socio-Legal Studies, University of Sheffield

Government of Canada, *Public Service 2000*, Taskforce Report, 1990, Ottawa

Green, DG, *Reinventing Civil Society*, 1993, Institute of Economic Affairs, Health and Welfare Unit

Harden, I, *The Contracting State*, 1992, OUP

Harden, I and Lewis, ND, *The Noble Lie: The British Constitution and the Rule of Law*, 1986, Century Hutchinson

Held, D, *Global Transformations: Politics, Economics and Culture*, 1999, Polity

Hennessy, P, 'The essence of public service' (1997) 85 Canberra Bulletin of Public Administration 3

Hirst, P, *Representative Democracy and Its Limits*, 1990, Polity

HM Treasury, *Using Private Enterprise in Government*, 1988, HMSO

HM Treasury, *The Government's Expenditure Plans 1999–2000 to 2001–2002*, Cm 4218, HMSO

HM Treasury, *Public Services for the Future: Modernisation, Reform and Accountability*, Cm 4315, 1999, HMSO

Holland, J, 'Self-regulation and the financial aspects of corporate governance' [1996] J Bus Law 127

Holmes, JW and Wileman, TA, *Reform in the Australian Public Service 1983–86*, 1997, Office of the Auditor-General of Canada

Home Office, *Review of Policy Core and Ancillary Tasks*, 1995, HMSO

House of Lords' Select Committee on the European Communities, *Compliance with Procurement Directives*, Session 1987–88, HL 72

Jackson, MW, 'The public interest, public service and democracy', 47 Aust J of Public Administration 13

James, R and Lewis, ND, 'Joined-up justice: the reform of the UK Ombudsman system', in *International Ombudsman Yearbook 2000*, 2001, Kluwer

Juma, C, 'The perils of centralizing global environmental governance' (2000) 42 Environment 23

Keating, M, *Public Management Reform and Economic and Social Development*, 1997, OECD

Keating, MS, 'Managing for results in the public interest' (1990) 49 Aust J of Public Administration 9

Knight, B, 'Community politics', in Campbell, D and Lewis, ND, *Promoting Participation: Law or Politics?*, 1999, Cavendish Publishing

Kroeger, A, *The Central Agencies and Program Review*, 1997, Ottawa

Leadbeater, C, *Living on Thin Air: The New Economy*, 1999, Viking

Leftwich, A, 'Governance, democracy and development in the Third World' (1993) 14 Third World Quarterly 610

Lewis, ND, 'The constitutional implications of participation' in Campbell, D and Lewis, ND (eds), *Promoting Participation: Law or Politics?*, 1999, Cavendish Publishing, pp 1–30

Lewis, ND, 'A Civil Service Act for the United Kingdom' [1998] PL 463

Lewis, ND, 'A standing administrative conference' (1998) 60 Political Quarterly 316

Lewis, ND, 'Good governance: the UK experience' (1998) XLIV (Special Number) Indian Journal of Public Administration 616

Lewis, ND, 'Governance, corporate governance and the public interest' (1998) 2 Corporate Governance International 13

Lewis, ND, *Choice and the Legal Order: Rising Above Politics*, 1996, Butterworths

Lewis, ND, 'Modernizing government: management theory or constitutional theory?' (1996) 6 EPL 201

Lewis, ND, *How to Reinvent British Government*, 1993, European Policy Forum

Lewis, ND, 'Markets, regulation and citizenship: a constitutional analysis', in Brownsword, R (ed), *Law and the Public Interest*, 1993, Franz Steiner Verlag

Lewis, ND, 'The Citizen's Charter and Next Steps: a new way of governing?' (1993) 64 Political Quarterly 316

Lewis, ND, *Evidence to the Treasury and Civil Service Committee on the Role of the Civil Service*, Session 1993–94, Vol 11, HMSO

Lewis, ND, 'Regulating non-governmental bodies: privatization, accountability and the public-private divide', in Jowell, J and Oliver, D (eds), *The Changing Constitution*, 2nd edn, 1989, OUP

Lewis, ND, 'Towards a sociology of lawyering in public administration' (1981) 32 NILQ 89

Lewis, ND and Longley, D, 'Ministerial responsibility: the next steps' [1996] PL 490

Longley, D and James, R, *Administrative Justice*, 1999, Cavendish Publishing

Lucas, C, *From Seattle to Nice*, 2001, www.carolinelucas@greenmeps.org.uk

Lundenburg, WV, 'Contracting out by the Federal Government for legal services: a legal and empirical analysis' (1988) 63 Notre Dame L Rev 399

Management Advisory Board and its Management Advisory Committee, *Building a Better Public Service*, June 1993, Canberra

Management Advisory Board and its Management Advisory Committee, *Contracting Out for the Provision of Services in Commonwealth Agencies*, 1992

Management Advisory Board, *The Australian Public Service Reformed*, 1992, Task Force on Management Improvement

Martin, J, *Changing Accountability Relations: Politics, Consumers and the Market*, 1997, Public Management Service, OECD

Matheson, A, *The Impact of Contracts on Public Service Management in New Zealand*, 1995, Wellington State Services Commission

McRae, H, *The World in 2000: Power, Culture and Prosperity: A Vision of the Future*, 1994, HarperCollins

Merrills, JG, *International Dispute Settlement*, 3rd edn, 1998, Sweet & Maxwell

Michael, DC, 'Federal agency use of audited self-regulation as a regulatory technique' (1995) 47 Administrative L Rev 171

Minogue, M, *Law and Governance*, 1996, British Council

National Council for Voluntary Organisations, *Meeting the Challenge of Change in Voluntary Action into the 21st Century*, 1996, Commission on the Future of the Voluntary Sector

New Economics Foundation, *Corporate Spin: The Troubled Teenage Years of Social Reporting*, November 2000, NEF

New Zealand Ombudsman, *Annual Report 1989* and *Annual Report 1992*, Wellington State Services Commission

OECD, *Contracting Out Government Services: Best Practice Guidelines and Case Studies*, Public Management Occasional Papers No 20, 1998, OECD

OECD, *Corporate Governance: Improving Competitiveness and Access to Capital in Global Markets*, 1998, OECD

OECD, *Managing Across Levels of Government*, PUMA on Multi-level Governance, 1998, OECD

OECD, *The New Zealand Approach to Strategic Management, Public Reform and Economic and Social Development*, 1998, PUMA

OECD, *Consultation and Communications*, 1997, OECD

OECD, *Improving Ethical Conduct in the Public Service: Recommendation of the OECD Council*, 1997, PUMA

OECD, *In Search of Results: Performance Management Practices*, 1997, PUMA

OECD, 'New directions in public policy', Policy Brief No 3, 1997

OECD, *Report on Regulatory Reform*, June 1997, OECD

OECD, 'Strategic management and policy-making', in *Building Policy Coherence*, 1997, OECD

OECD, *Issues and Developments in Public Management*, Survey 1996–97, PUMA

OECD, *Ethics in the Public Service: Current Issues and Practice*, 1996, PUMA

OECD, 'Globalisation: what challenges and opportunities for government? The need for structural and institutional change', in PUMA, *Strategic Management and Policy-Making*, 1996, PUMA, p 2

OECD, 'Globalisation – what implications for democratic decision-making?', in PUMA, *Strategic Management and Policy-Making*, 1996, PUMA

OECD, *Strategic Management and Policy-Making*, 1996, PUMA

Office of Electricity Regulation, *Response to the Green Paper on Regulation*, Offer Press Release R39/98

Office of Fair Trading, *Guidelines on the Calculation of Penalties*, 2000, OFT

Office of Fair Trading, *The Chapter 11 Prohibition*, 2000, OFT

Office of the Auditor General of Canada, *Toward Better Governance: Public Service Reform in New Zealand and its Relevance to Canada*, 1995, Government of Canada

OFWAT, *The Approval of Companies' Charging Schemes*, Consultation Paper, 2000, OFWAT

OMB, *Enhancing Government Productivity Through Competition*, 1988, OMB

Osborne, D and Gaebler, T, *Reinventing Government*, 1992, Addison Wesley Longman

Parkinson, J, 'In whose interest should the directors act?' (1998) 1 Corporate Governance International 44

Parkinson, JE, 'Participation and corporate governance', in Campbell, D and Lewis, ND (eds), *Promoting Participation: Law or Politics?*, 1999, Cavendish Publishing

Perri 6 *et al*, *Governing in the Round: Strategies for Holistic Government*, 1999, Demos

Phillips (Lord), *Inquiry into BSE and Variant CJD in the UK*, HC, October 2000

Political Action Committee, *Improving the Delivery of Government IT Projects*, 1st Report, Session 1999–2000, HC 65

Polyani, K, *The Great Transformation*, 1944, Beacon

Prosser, T, *Law and the Regulators*, 1997, Clarendon

Prosser, T and Graham, C, *Regulating the Privatised Industries*, 1991, OUP

Public Audit Forum, *Implications for Audit of the Modernising Government Agenda*, 22 April 1999

Republic of Ireland Government, *Delivering Better Government: A Programme of Change for the Irish Civil Service*, 2nd Report of the Co-ordinating Group of Secretaries: A Programme of Change for the Irish Civil Service, 1996, Government of Ireland

Rhodes, RAW, *Understanding Governance: Policy Networks etc*, 1997, OUP

Scott, R (Sir), *Report of the Inquiry into the Export of Defence Equipment to Iraq*, 1996, HC 115

Select Committee on Liaison, *Independence or Control?*, Second Report, Session 1999–2000, HC 748

Select Committee on Liaison, *Shifting the Balance: Select Committees and the Executive*, Session 1999–2000, HC 300

Select Committee on Public Administration, *Responses to the Sixth Report from the Select Committee on Public Administration*, Session 1998–99 on Quangos, 1st Special Report, Session 1999–2000, HC 317

Shick, A, *The Spirit of Reform: Managing the New Zealand State Sector in a Time of Change*, Report for the Treasury, 1996, Wellington State Services Commission

State Services Commission, *Briefing Papers for the Minister of State Services*, 1996, Wellington State Services Commission

State Services Commission, *Strategic Management in Government: Extending the Reform Model in New Zealand*, 1996, Wellington State Services Commission

Taggart, M, 'The impact of corporatisation and privatisation in administrative law' (1992) 51 Aust J of Public Administration

Tanzi, V, *Globalisation and the Future of Social Protection*, IMF Working Paper WP/00/12

The UN Commission of Environment and Development, *Our Common Future*, 1987, UN

Thurrow, L, *The Future of Capitalism*, 1996, Nicholas Brealey

Trade and Industry Select Committee, *Aspects of the Electricity Supply Industry*, Session 1994–95, HC 481

Trade and Industry Select Committee, *Government Observations on the Fifth Report of the Trade and Industry Committee*, Session 1994–95, HC 748

Treasury and Civil Service Select Committee, *The Role of the Civil Service*, 5th Report, 1994, HMSO

Treasury Select Committee, *The Private Finance Initiative*, 4th Report, HC 147, Session 1999–2000

Treasury Select Committee, *The Private Finance Initiative*, 6th Report, Session 1995–96, HC 146

TUC, *Your Stake at Work*, 1996, TUC

Turc, A, 'Accountability in public organisations: responsiveness to political authorities, users and market forces', in OECD, *Democratic and Political Accountability*, 1997, Public Management Service

Twining, W, *Globalisation and Legal Theory*, 2000, Butterworths

Uhr, J, 'Accountability without independent external review?' (1997) 84 Canberra J of Public Administration 11

UNDP, *The Human Development Report*, 1999, OUP

UNEP, USNASA and World Bank, *Protecting our Planet: Securing our Future*, 1998, UNEP

US President's Council on Management Improvement, *Study of OMB Circular A-76*, 1990, Inter-Agency Task Force

Veljanovski, C, *The Future of Industry Regulation in the UK*, 1993, European Policy Forum

Ward, G, 'Reforming the public sector' (1993) 64 Political Quarterly 301

WBCSD, *Corporate Leadership and Governance: Securing the Social License to Operate (The Challenge Brief)*, 1987, WBCSD

WBCSD, *A Challenge for Today's Business Leaders*, 1997, WBCSD

Weir, S and Hall, W (eds), *EGO Trip, Democratic Audit of the UK*, 1994

Wilenski, P, 'Administrative reform – general principles and the Australian experience' (1986) Public Administration 268

Williams, M, 'The political economy of privatization', in Holland, M and Boston, J (eds), *The Fourth Labour Government: Politics and Policy in New Zealand*, 2nd edn, 1992, OUP

Wilson, R (Sir), *Report to the Prime Minister on Civil Service Reform*, CAB 99-5277/0001/D40, 1999

Wilson, R (Sir), *Vision of a Civil Service for the Next Millennium*, 1999, Cabinet Office

World Bank and UN Development Programme, *Business as Partners in Development*, 1996, World Bank

World Bank, *Attacking Poverty*, World Development Report 2000/2001

World Bank, *Initiatives in Legal and Judicial Reform*, 2000, World Bank

Zimmeck, M, 'To boldly go – the voluntary sector and voluntary action in the new world of work' (1998) RSA Journal 19

INDEX

B

C

G

O

P

U

For Product Safety Concerns and Information please contact our EU representative GPSR@taylorandfrancis.com
Taylor & Francis Verlag GmbH, Kaufingerstraße 24, 80331 München, Germany

www.ingramcontent.com/pod-product-compliance
Lightning Source LLC
LaVergne TN
LVHW011113300926
849160LV00008B/368

9781859415474